This is volume 12!

When this comes out, the TV anime will be reaching its climax

and it will be very exciting!

I'm looking forward to seeing what it looks like!

Naoshi Komi

NAOSHI KOMI was born in Kochi Prefecture, Japan, on March 28, 1986. His first serialized work in *Weekly Shonen Jump* was the series *Double Arts*. His current series, *Nisekoi*, is serialized in *Weekly Shonen Jump*.

NISEKOI:
False Love
VOLUME 12
SHONEN JUMP Manga Edition

Story and Art by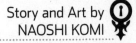
NAOSHI KOMI

Translation ✒ Camellia Nieh
Touch-Up Art & Lettering ✒ Stephen Dutro
Design ✒ Fawn Lau
Shonen Jump Series Editor ✒ John Bae
Graphic Novel Editor ✒ Amy Yu

NISEKOI © 2011 by Naoshi Komi
All rights reserved.
First published in Japan in 2011
by SHUEISHA Inc., Tokyo.
English translation rights arranged
by SHUEISHA Inc.

The stories, characters and incidents mentioned
in this publication are entirely fictional.

No portion of this book may be reproduced or
transmitted in any form or by any means without
written permission from the copyright holders.

Printed in the U.S.A.

Published by VIZ Media, LLC
P.O. Box 77010
San Francisco, CA 94107

10 9 8 7 6 5 4 3 2 1
First printing, November 2015

PARENTAL ADVISORY
NISEKOI: FALSE LOVE is rated T for Teen and is
recommended for ages 13 and up. This volume
contains realistic and fantasy violence.
ratings.viz.com

www.shonenjump.com   www.viz.com

NISEKOI

False Love

vol. 12: Festival

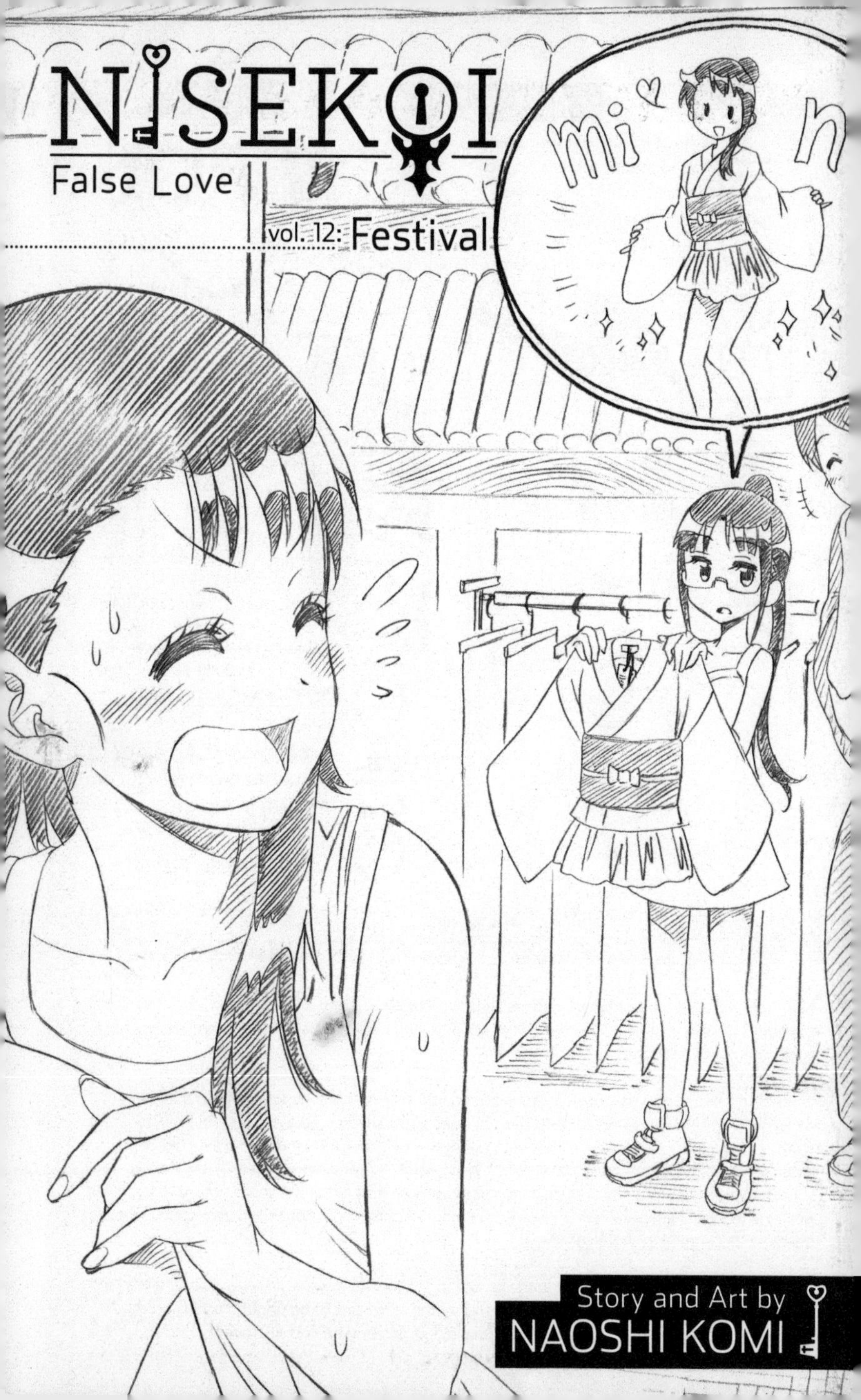

Story and Art by
NAOSHI KOMI

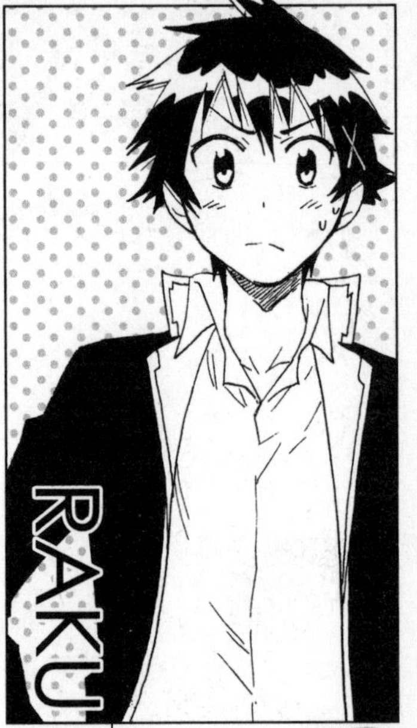

RAKU ICHIJO

A normal teen whose family happens to be yakuza. Cherishes a pendant given to him by a girl he met ten years ago. Has a crush on Kosaki.

CHITOGE KIRISAKI

A half-Japanese bombshell with stellar athletic abilities. Short-tempered and violent. Comes from a family of gangsters.

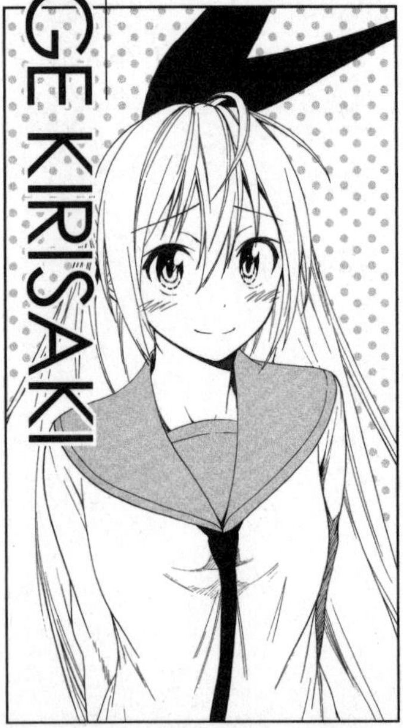

CHARACTERS & STORY

Raku Ichijo is an ordinary teen...who just happens to come from a family of yakuza! His most treasured item is a pendant he was given ten years ago by a girl whom he promised to meet again one day and marry.

Thanks to family circumstances, Raku is forced into a false relationship with Chitoge, the daughter of a rival gangster, to keep their families from shedding blood. Despite their constant spats, Raku and Chitoge manage to fool everyone. One day, Chitoge discovers an old key, jogging memories of her own first love ten years earlier. Meanwhile, Raku's crush, Kosaki, confesses that she also has a key and made a promise with a boy ten years ago. To complicate matters, Marika Tachibana has a key as well and remembers a promise ten years ago. The mystery keeps getting more complex!

Raku recovers from his bout with amnesia just in time for Chitoge's birthday. But when an old friend of Marika's named Mikage comes to visit, she turns out to be under the illusion that Raku and Marika are dating! Raku has to play along, causing no end of trouble...

KOSAKI ONODERA

A girl Raku has a crush on. Beautiful and sweet, Kosaki has no shortage of admirers. She's a terrible cook but makes food that *looks* amazing.

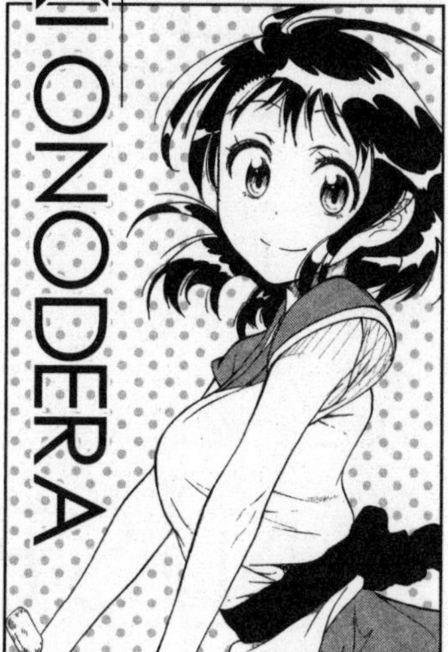

MARIKA TACHIBANA

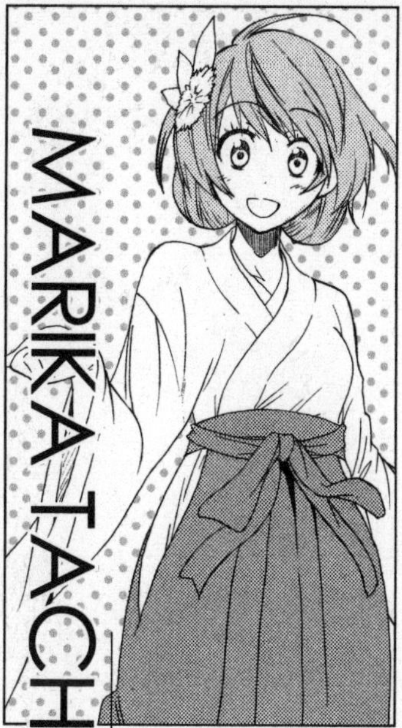

Daughter of the chief of police, Marika is Raku's fiancée, according to an agreement made by their fathers—an agreement Marika takes very seriously! Also has a key and remembers making a promise with Raku ten years ago.

SHU MAIKO

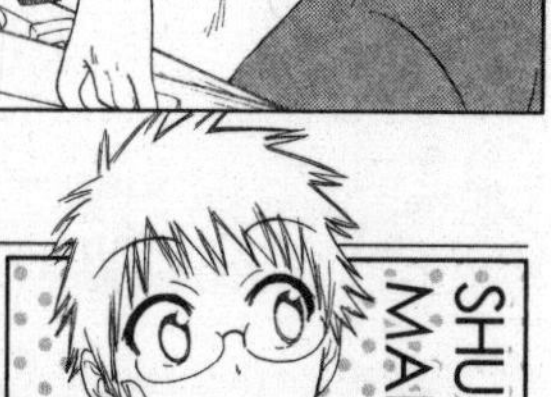

Raku's best friend is outgoing and girl-crazy.

SEISHIRO TSUGUMI

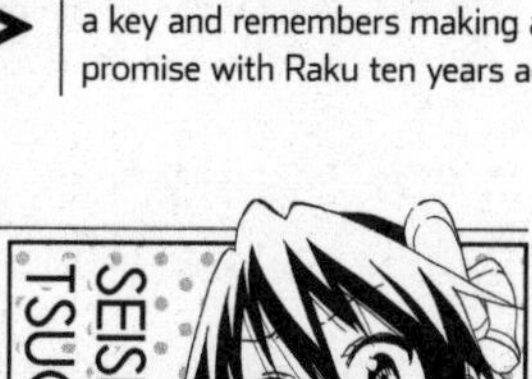

Trained as an assassin in order to protect Chitoge, Tsugumi is often mistaken for a boy.

RURI MIYAMOTO

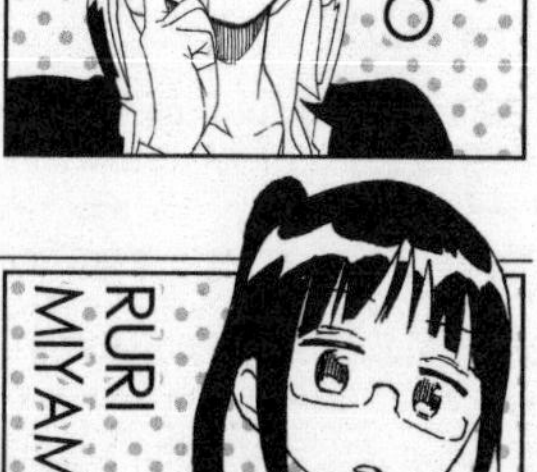

Kosaki's best gal pal. Comes off as aloof, but is actually a devoted and highly intuitive friend.

HARU ONODERA

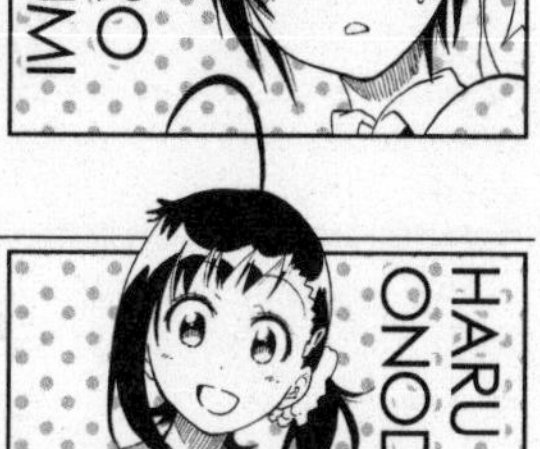

Kosaki's adoring younger sister. Has a low opinion of Raku.

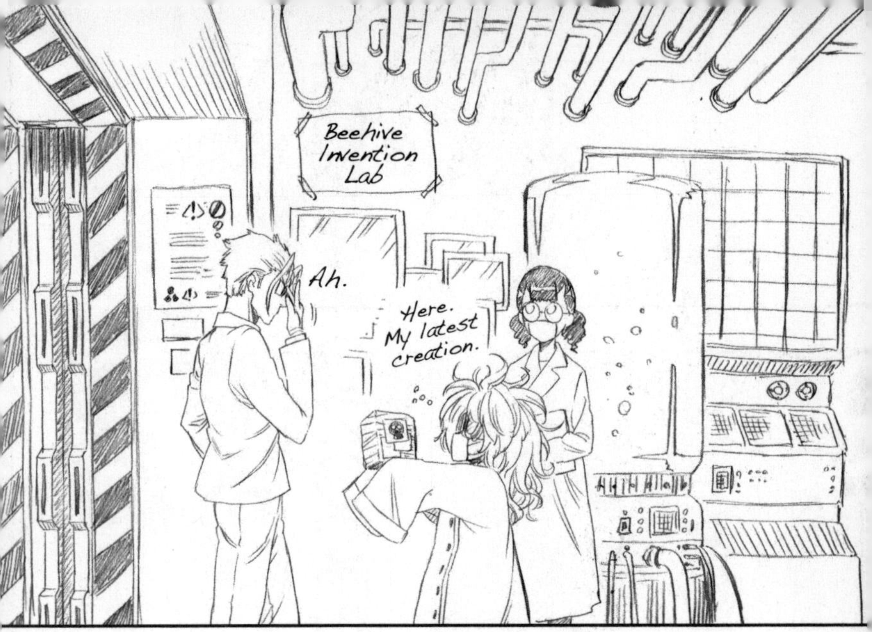
Beehive Invention Lab
Here. My latest creation.
Ah.

NISEKOI
False Love

vol. 12: Festival

TABLE OF CONTENTS

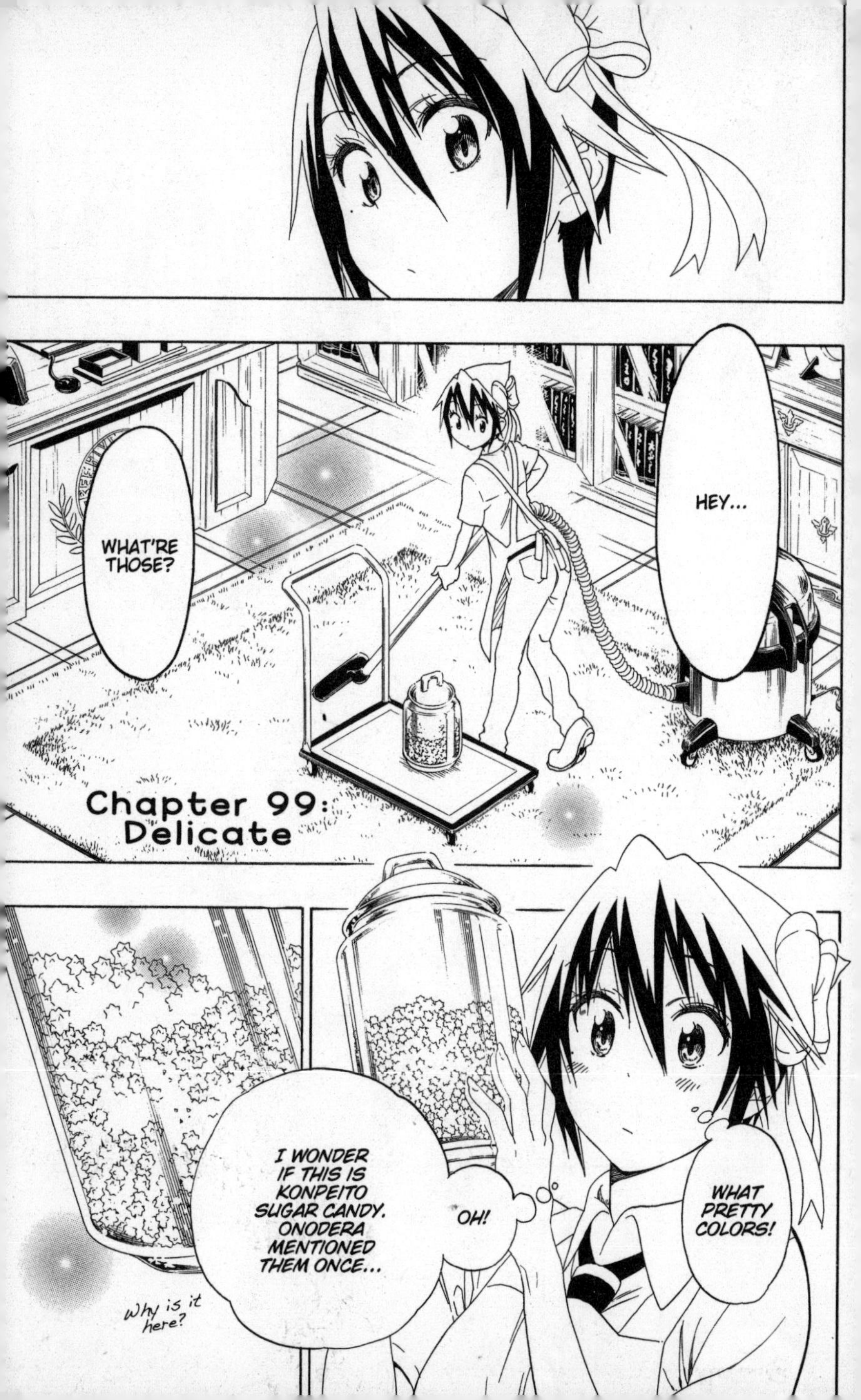
HEY...
WHAT'RE THOSE?
Chapter 99: Delicate
WHAT PRETTY COLORS!
OH!
I WONDER IF THIS IS KONPEITO SUGAR CANDY. ONODERA MENTIONED THEM ONCE...
Why is it here?

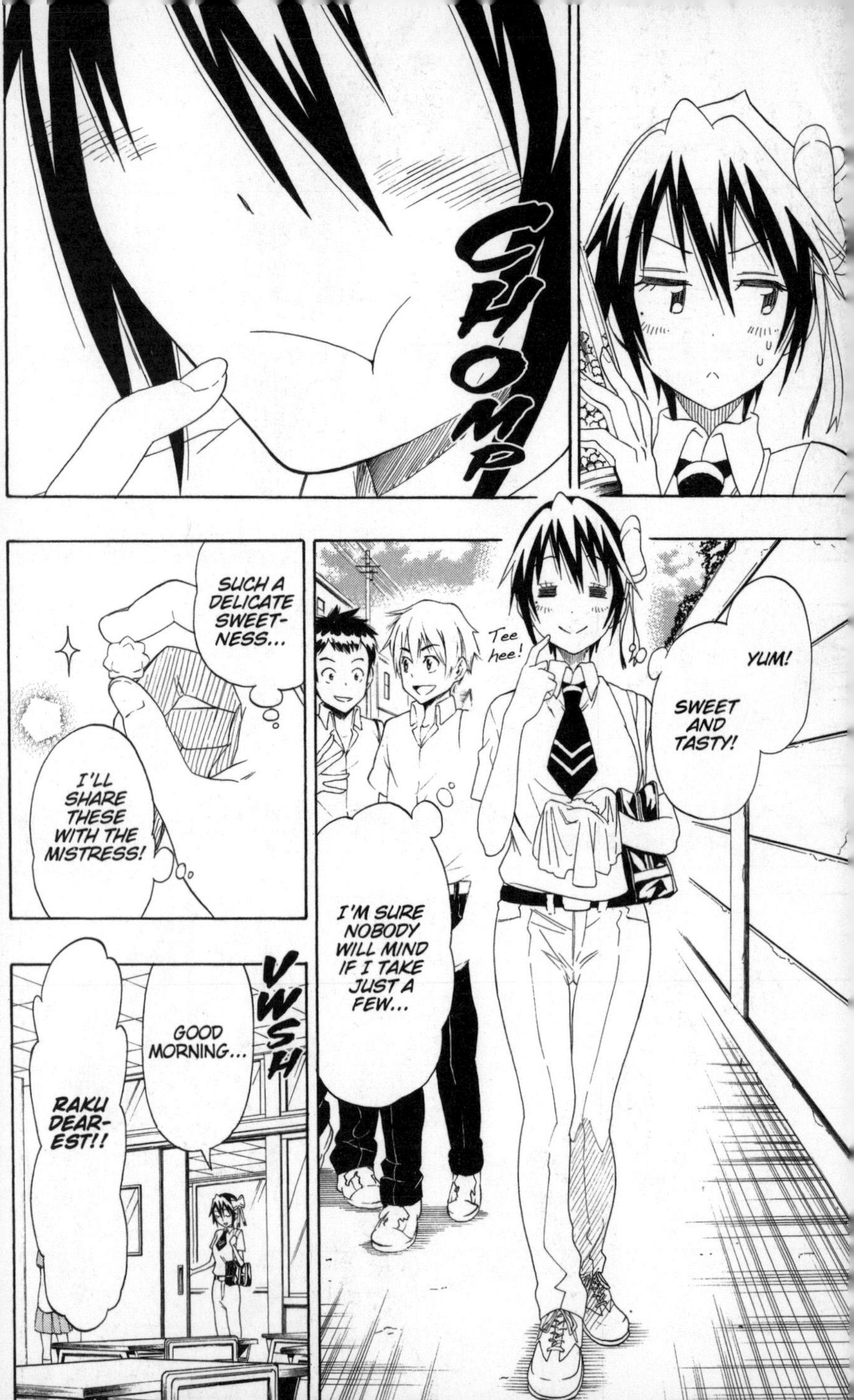
CHOMP
YUM!
SWEET AND TASTY!
Tee hee!
I'M SURE NOBODY WILL MIND IF I TAKE JUST A FEW...
SUCH A DELICATE SWEET-NESS...
I'LL SHARE THESE WITH THE MISTRESS!
VWSH
GOOD MORNING...
RAKU DEAR-EST!!

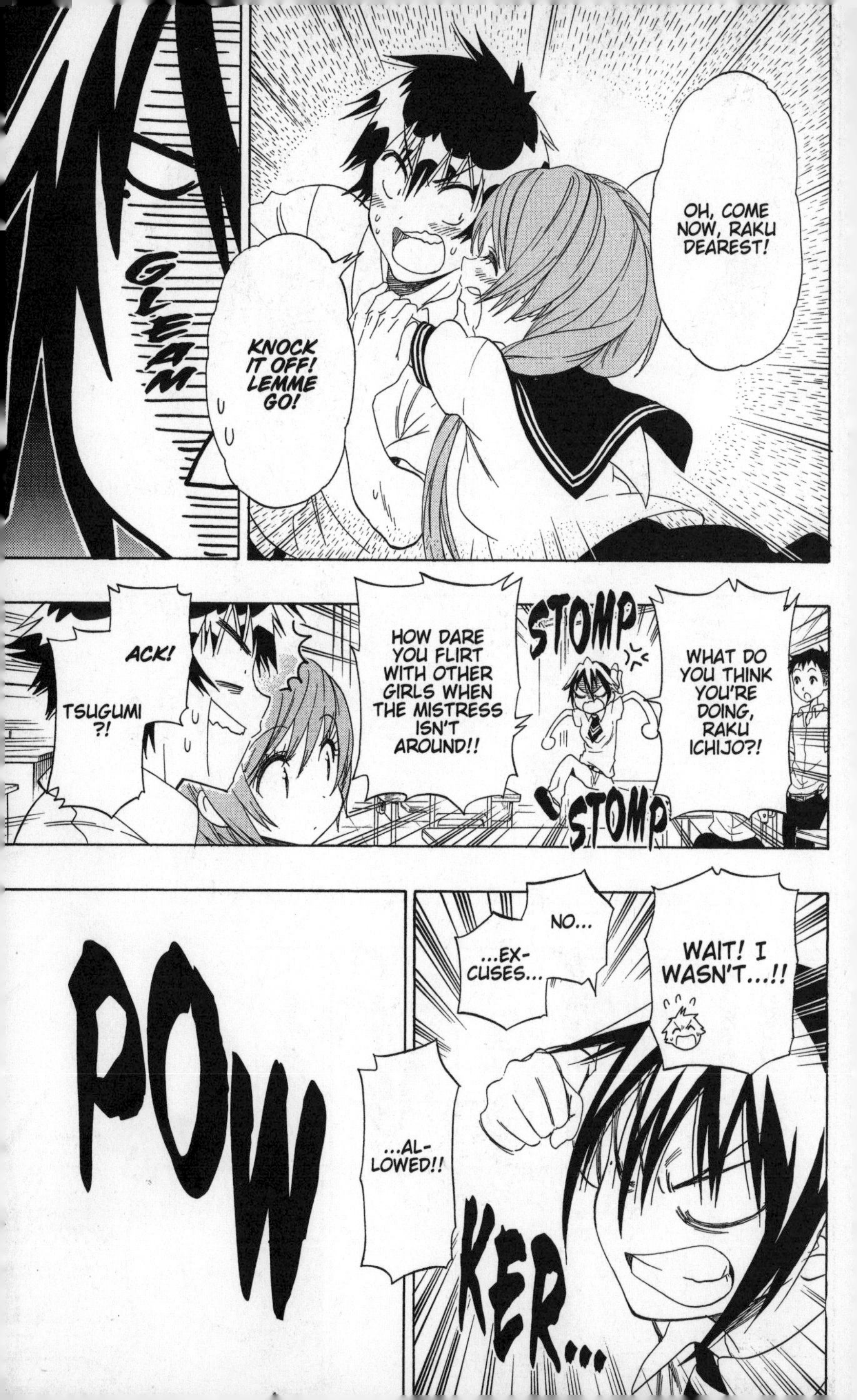
OH, COME NOW, RAKU DEAREST!
KNOCK IT OFF! LEMME GO!
GLEAM
WHAT DO YOU THINK YOU'RE DOING, RAKU ICHIJO?!
STOMP
STOMP
HOW DARE YOU FLIRT WITH OTHER GIRLS WHEN THE MISTRESS ISN'T AROUND!!
ACK!
TSUGUMI ?!
WAIT! I WASN'T...!!
NO...
...EX-CUSES...
...AL-LOWED!!
KER...
POW

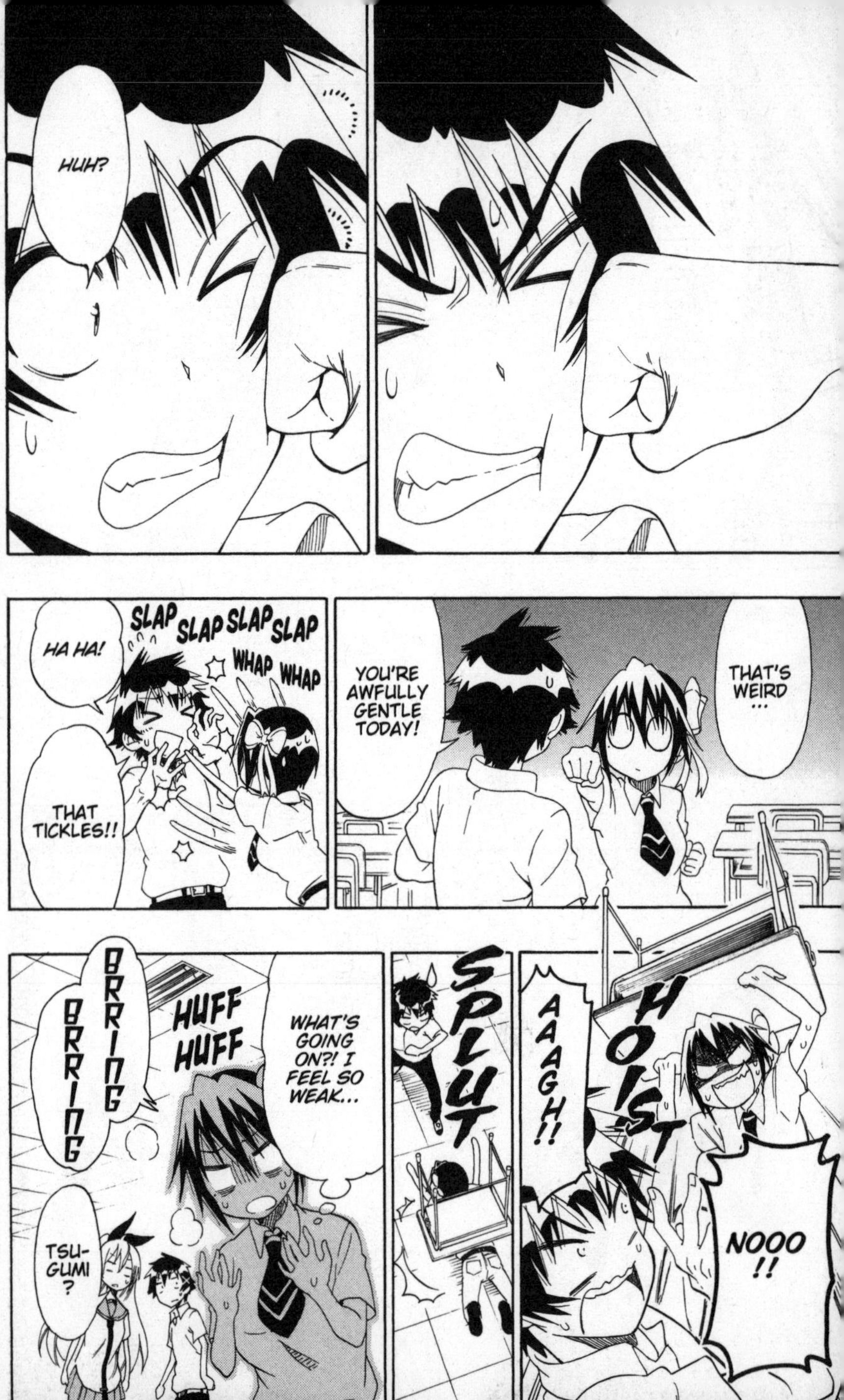
HUH?
THAT'S WEIRD...
YOU'RE AWFULLY GENTLE TODAY!
HA HA!
SLAP SLAP SLAP SLAP
WHAP WHAP
THAT TICKLES!!
HOIST
AAAGH!!
NOOO!!
SPLUT
WHAT'S GOING ON?! I FEEL SO WEAK...
HUFF HUFF
BRRING BRRING
TSU-GUMI?

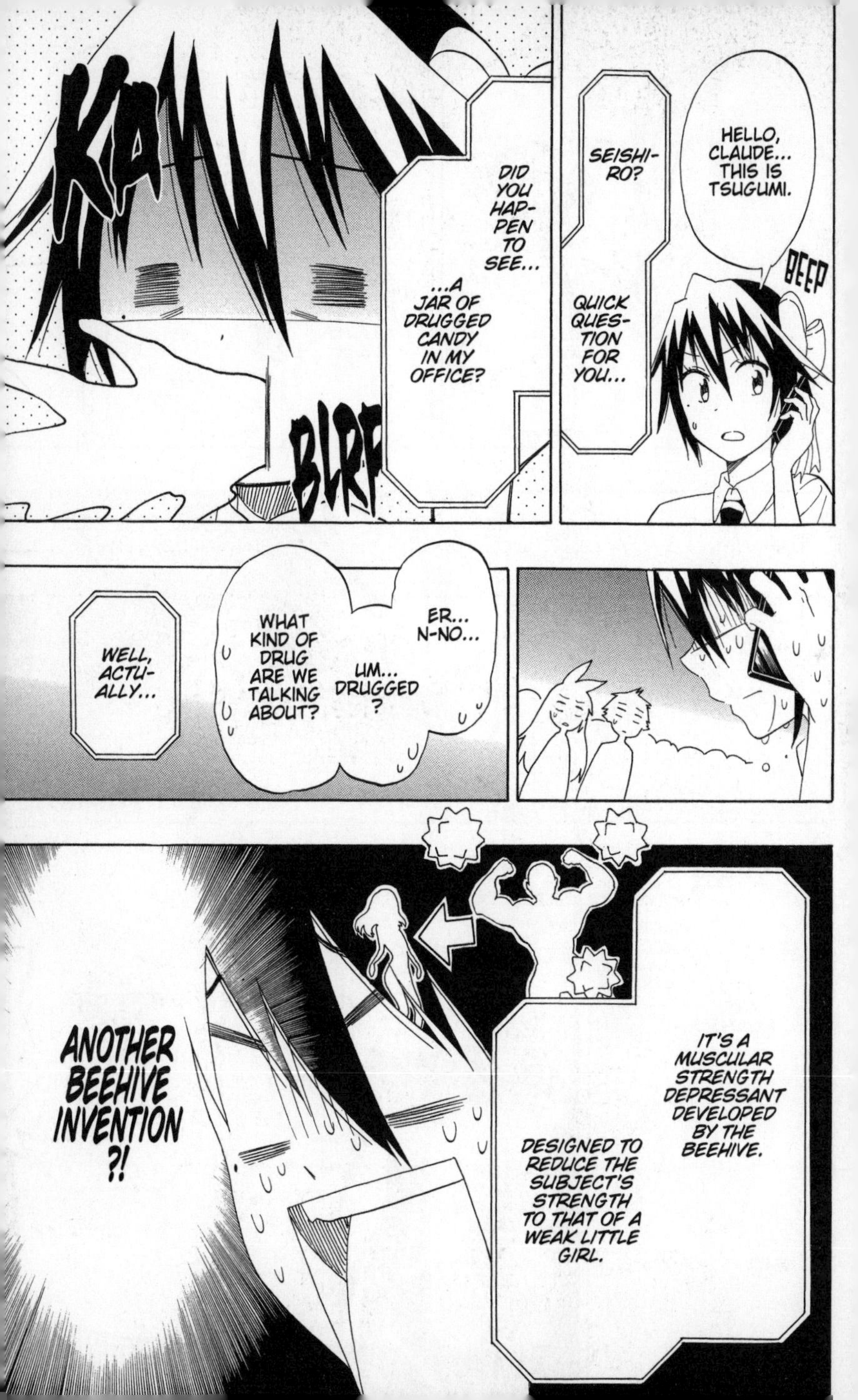
BEEP
HELLO, CLAUDE... THIS IS TSUGUMI.
SEISHIRO?
QUICK QUESTION FOR YOU...
DID YOU HAPPEN TO SEE...
...A JAR OF DRUGGED CANDY IN MY OFFICE?
BLRF
ER... N-NO...
UM... DRUGGED?
WHAT KIND OF DRUG ARE WE TALKING ABOUT?
WELL, ACTUALLY...
IT'S A MUSCULAR STRENGTH DEPRESSANT DEVELOPED BY THE BEEHIVE.
DESIGNED TO REDUCE THE SUBJECT'S STRENGTH TO THAT OF A WEAK LITTLE GIRL.
ANOTHER BEEHIVE INVENTION?!

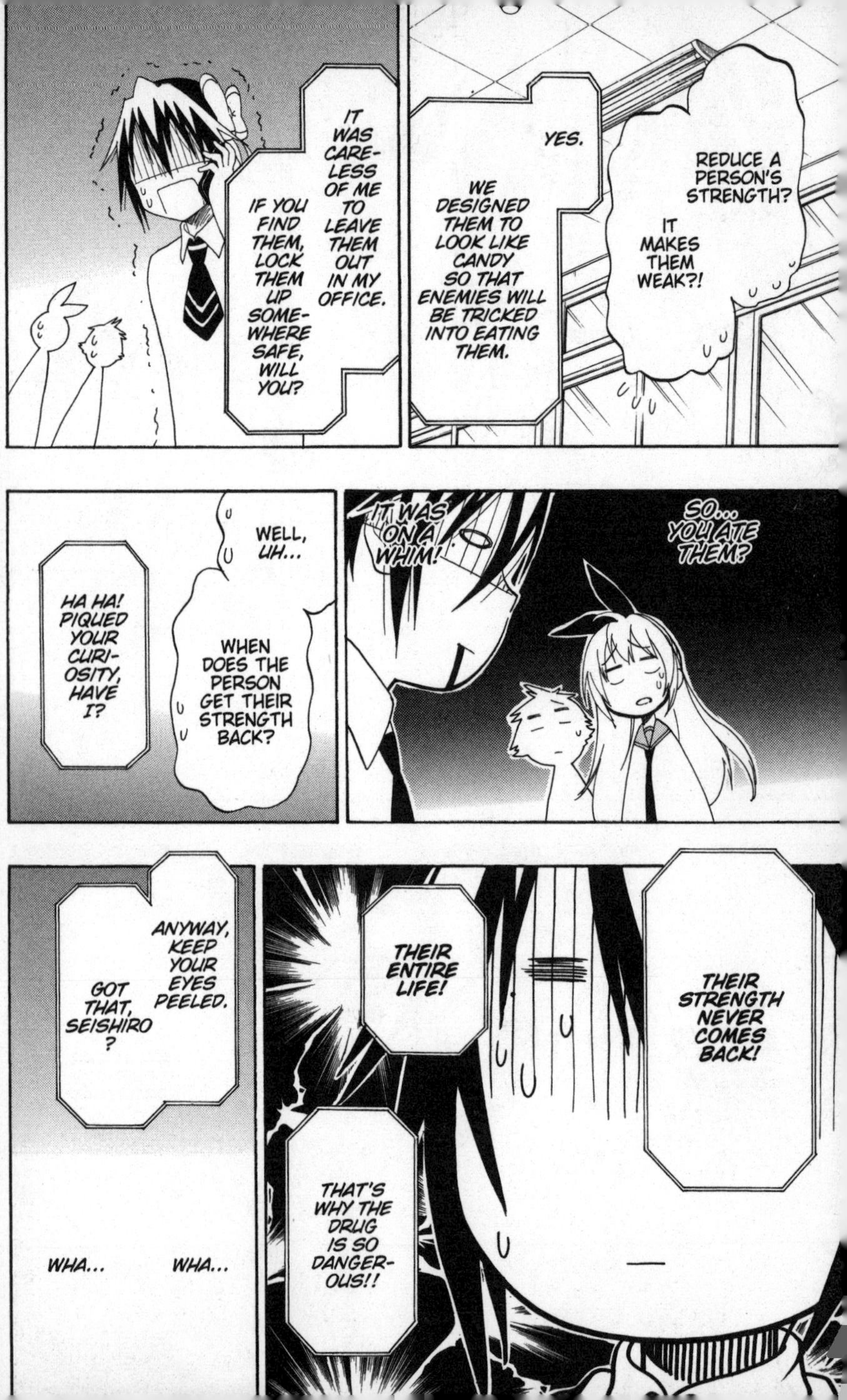
REDUCE A PERSON'S STRENGTH?
IT MAKES THEM WEAK?!
YES.
WE DESIGNED THEM TO LOOK LIKE CANDY SO THAT ENEMIES WILL BE TRICKED INTO EATING THEM.
IT WAS CARE-LESS OF ME TO LEAVE THEM OUT IN MY OFFICE.
IF YOU FIND THEM, LOCK THEM UP SOME-WHERE SAFE, WILL YOU?
SO... YOU ATE THEM?
IT WAS ON A WHIM!
WELL, UH...
WHEN DOES THE PERSON GET THEIR STRENGTH BACK?
HA HA! PIQUED YOUR CURI-OSITY, HAVE I?
THEIR STRENGTH NEVER COMES BACK!
THEIR ENTIRE LIFE!
THAT'S WHY THE DRUG IS SO DANGER-OUS!!
ANYWAY, KEEP YOUR EYES PEELED.
GOT THAT, SEISHIRO?
WHA...
WHA...

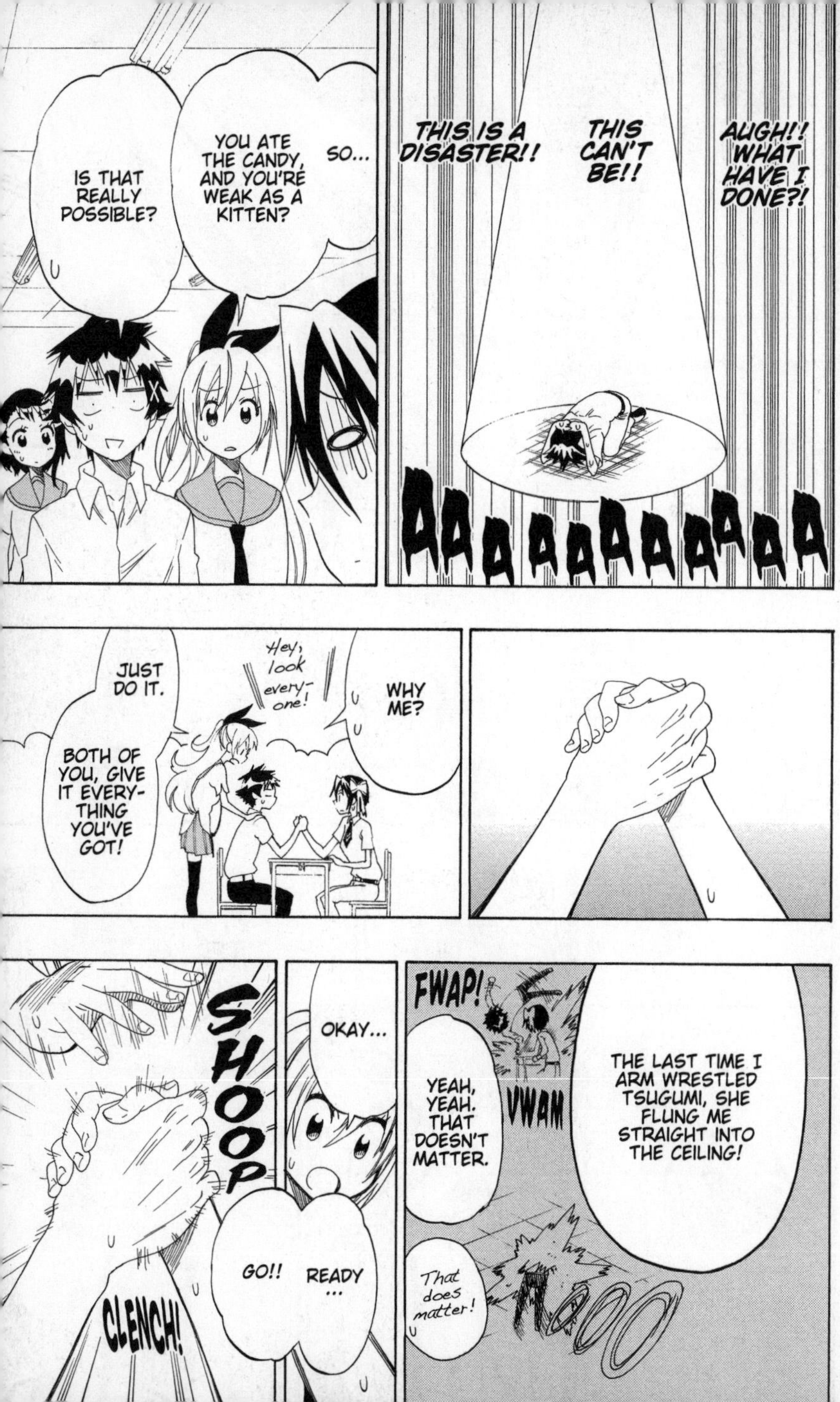
AUGH!! WHAT HAVE I DONE?!
THIS CAN'T BE!!
THIS IS A DISASTER!!
AAAAAAAAAAA
SO...
YOU ATE THE CANDY, AND YOU'RE WEAK AS A KITTEN?
IS THAT REALLY POSSIBLE?
WHY ME?
Hey, look every-one!
JUST DO IT.
BOTH OF YOU, GIVE IT EVERY-THING YOU'VE GOT!
THE LAST TIME I ARM WRESTLED TSUGUMI, SHE FLUNG ME STRAIGHT INTO THE CEILING!
FWAP!
VWAM
YEAH, YEAH. THAT DOESN'T MATTER.
That does matter!
OKAY...
READY ...
GO!!
SHOOP
CLENCH!

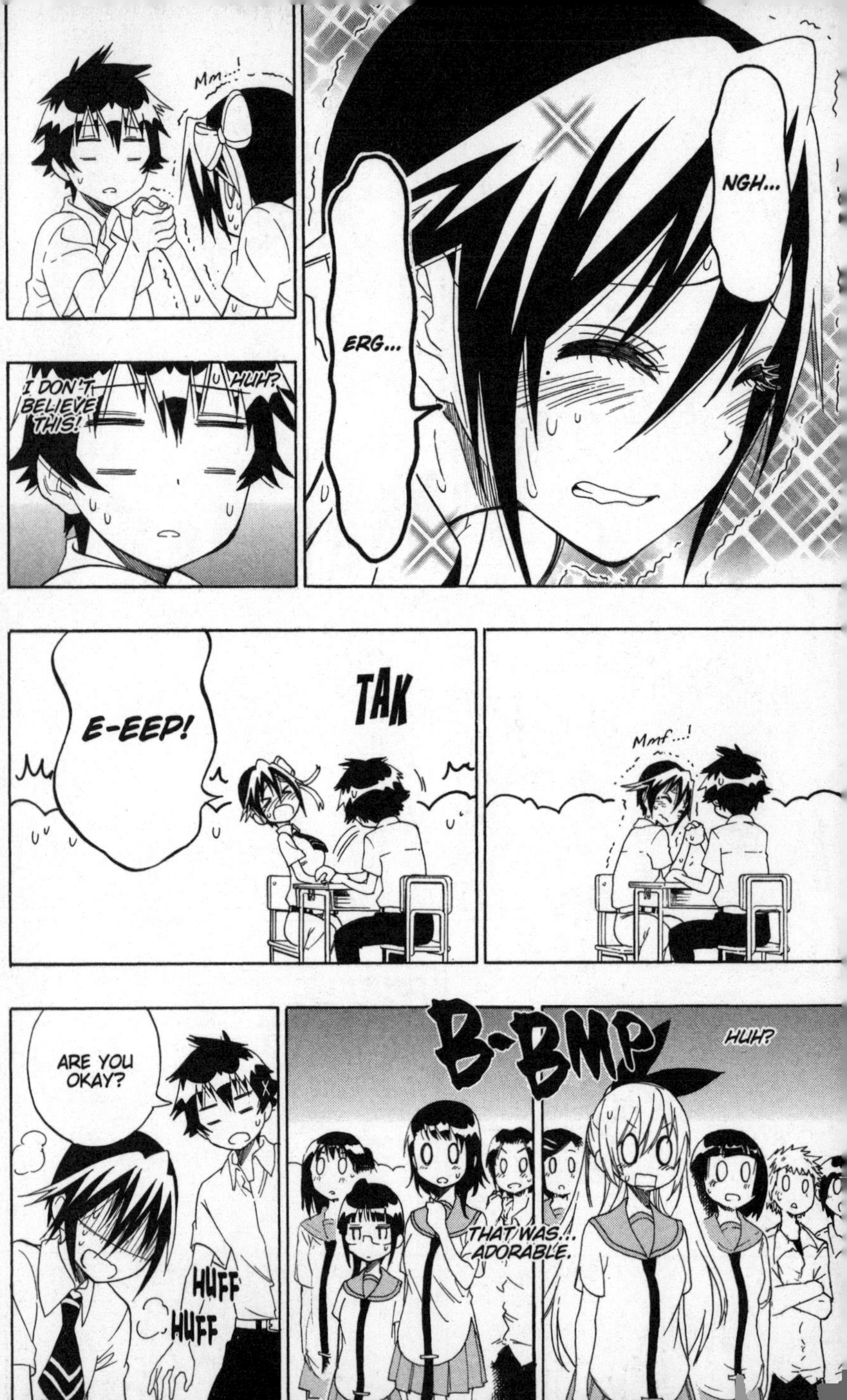
NGH...
ERG...
Mm...!
HUH?
I DON'T BELIEVE THIS!
Mmf...!
TAK
E-EEP!
B-BMP
HUH?
THAT WAS... ADORABLE.
ARE YOU OKAY?
HUFF
HUFF

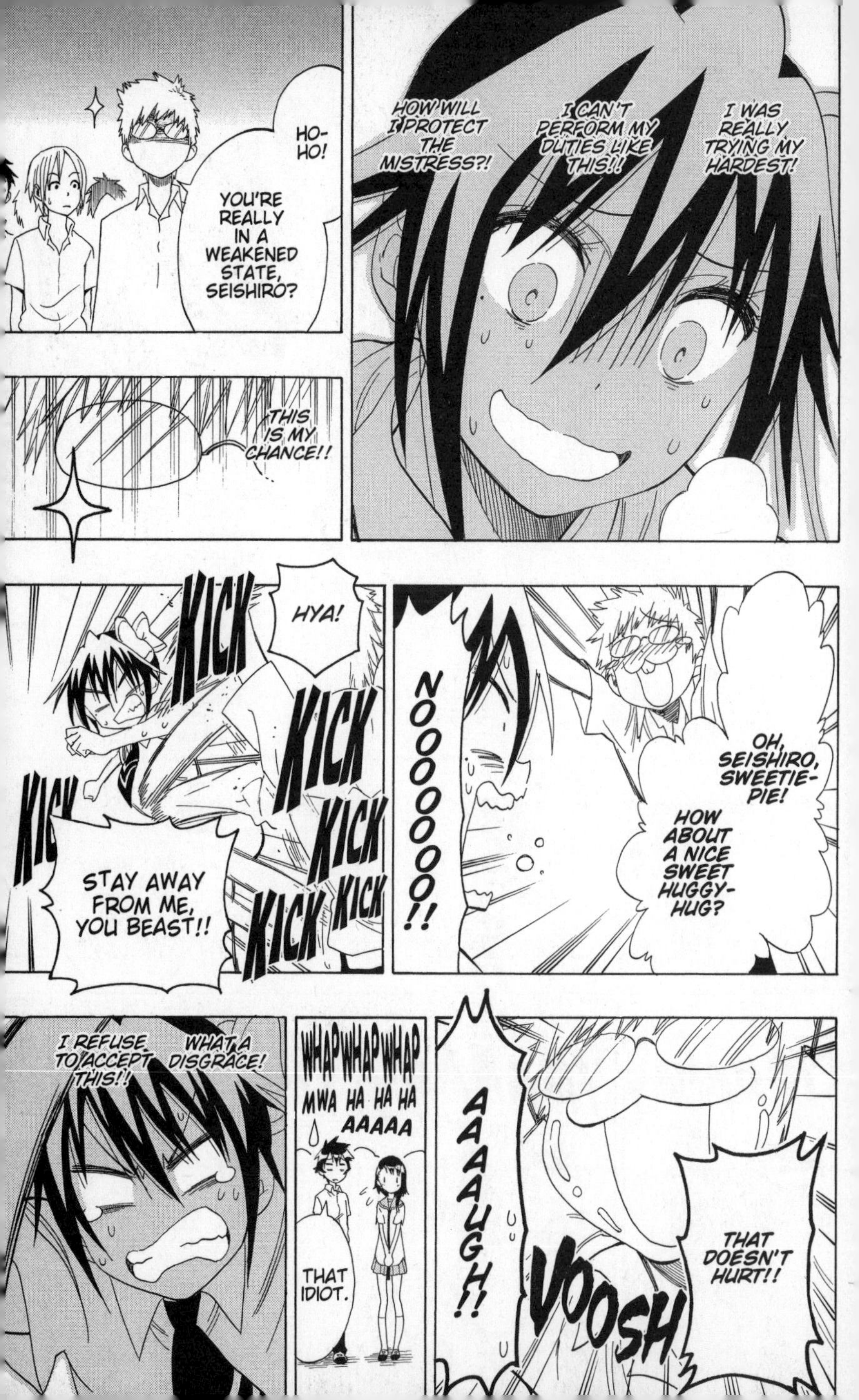
I WAS REALLY TRYING MY HARDEST!
I CAN'T PERFORM MY DUTIES LIKE THIS!!
HOW WILL I PROTECT THE MISTRESS?!
HO-HO!
YOU'RE REALLY IN A WEAKENED STATE, SEISHIRO?
THIS IS MY CHANCE!!
OH, SEISHIRO, SWEETIE-PIE!
HOW ABOUT A NICE SWEET HUGGY-HUG?
NOOOOOOOOO!!
HYA!
KICK
KICK
KICK
KICK
KICK
KICK
STAY AWAY FROM ME, YOU BEAST!!
THAT DOESN'T HURT!!
AAAAAUGH!!
VOOSH
WHAP WHAP WHAP
MWA HA HA HA
AAAAA
THAT IDIOT.
WHAT A DISGRACE!
I REFUSE TO ACCEPT THIS!!

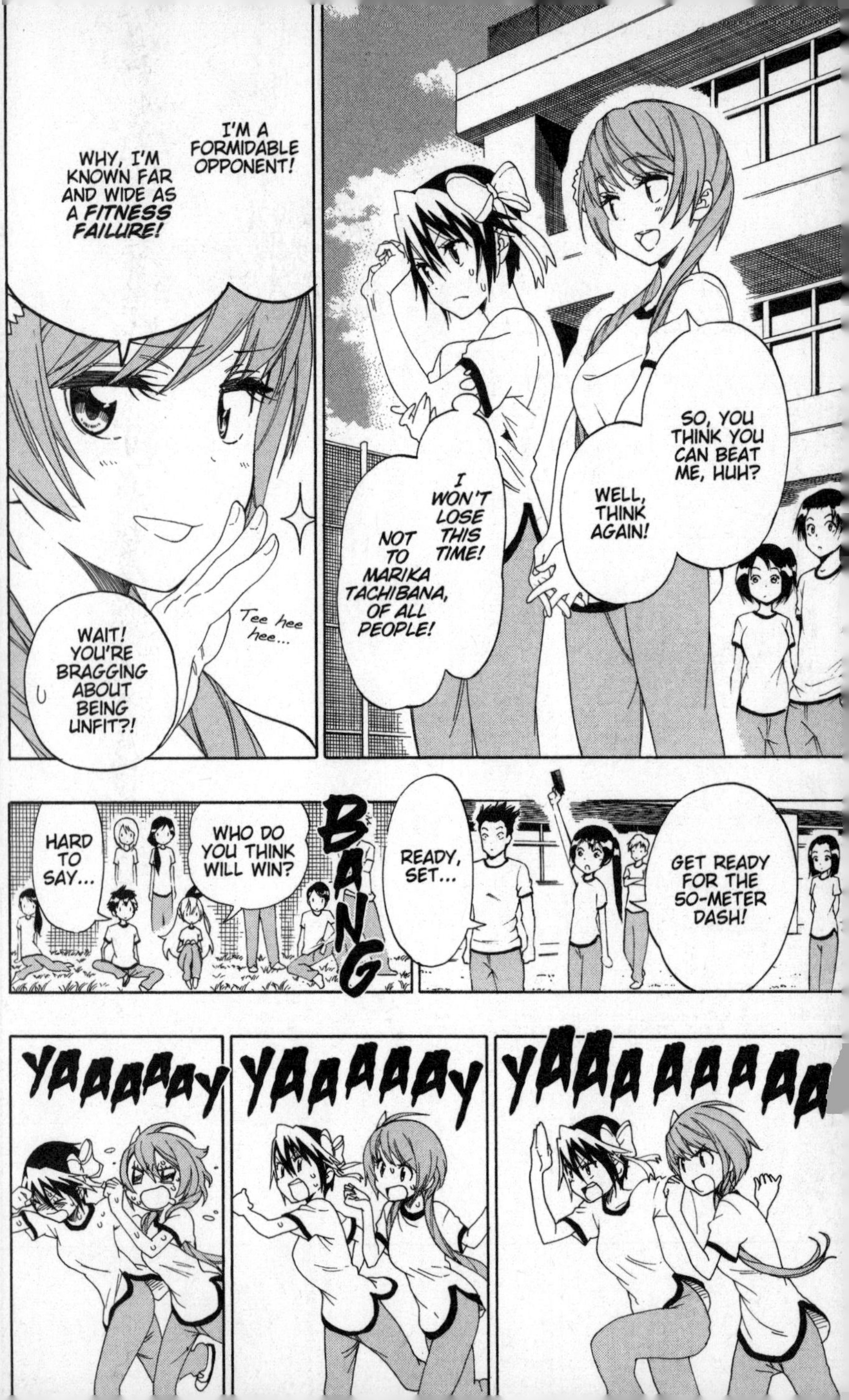
SO, YOU THINK YOU CAN BEAT ME, HUH?
WELL, THINK AGAIN!
I WON'T LOSE THIS TIME!
NOT TO MARIKA TACHIBANA, OF ALL PEOPLE!
I'M A FORMIDABLE OPPONENT!
WHY, I'M KNOWN FAR AND WIDE AS A *FITNESS FAILURE!*
Tee hee hee...
WAIT! YOU'RE BRAGGING ABOUT BEING UNFIT?!
GET READY FOR THE 50-METER DASH!
READY, SET...
BANG
WHO DO YOU THINK WILL WIN?
HARD TO SAY...
YAAAAAAAA
YAAAAAAY
YAAAAAY

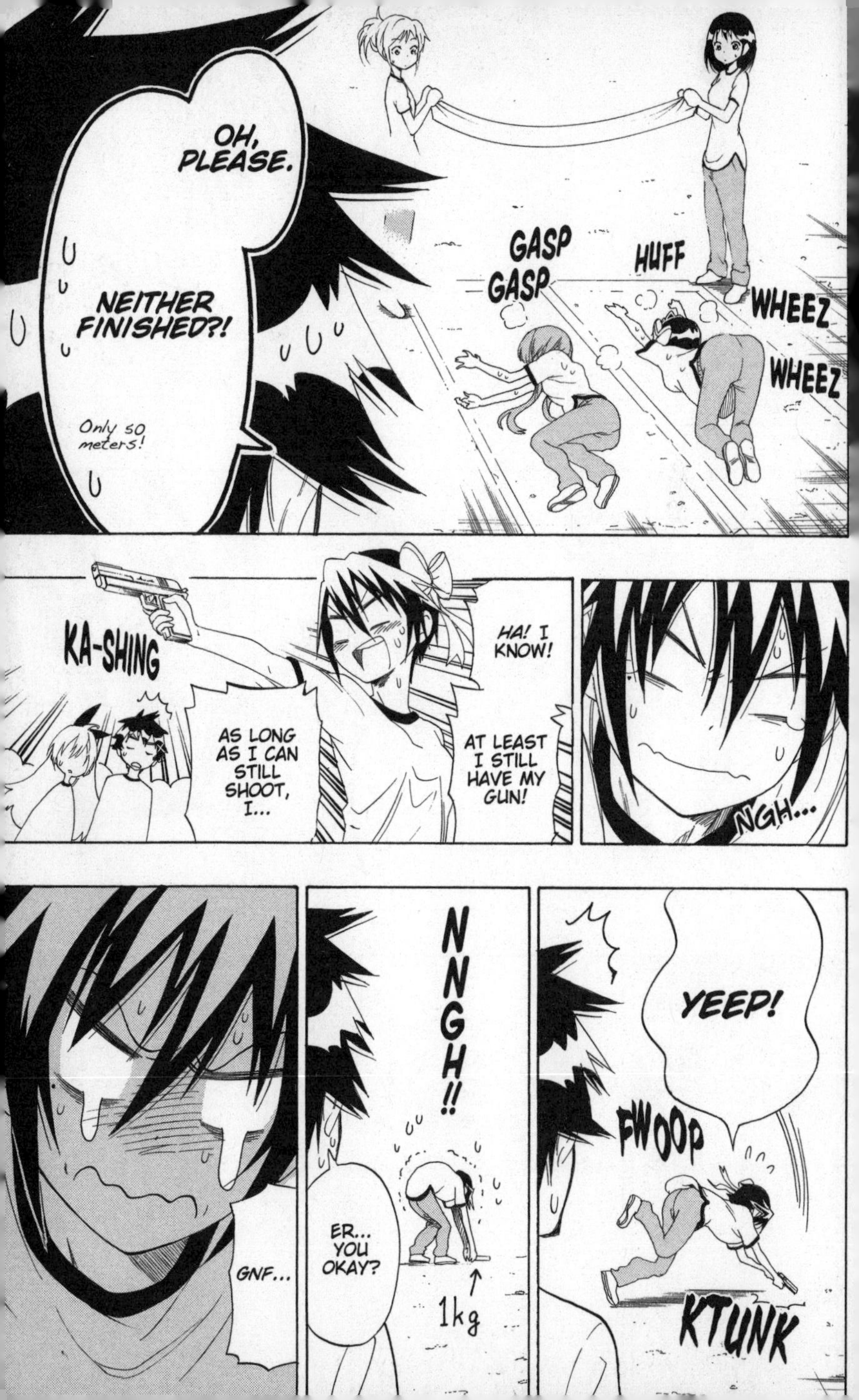
WHEEZ WHEEZ
HUFF
GASP GASP
OH, PLEASE.
NEITHER FINISHED?!
Only 50 meters!
NGH...
HA! I KNOW!
AT LEAST I STILL HAVE MY GUN!
KA-SHING
AS LONG AS I CAN STILL SHOOT, I...
YEEP!
FWOOP
KTUNK
NNGH!!
ER... YOU OKAY?
1kg
GNF...

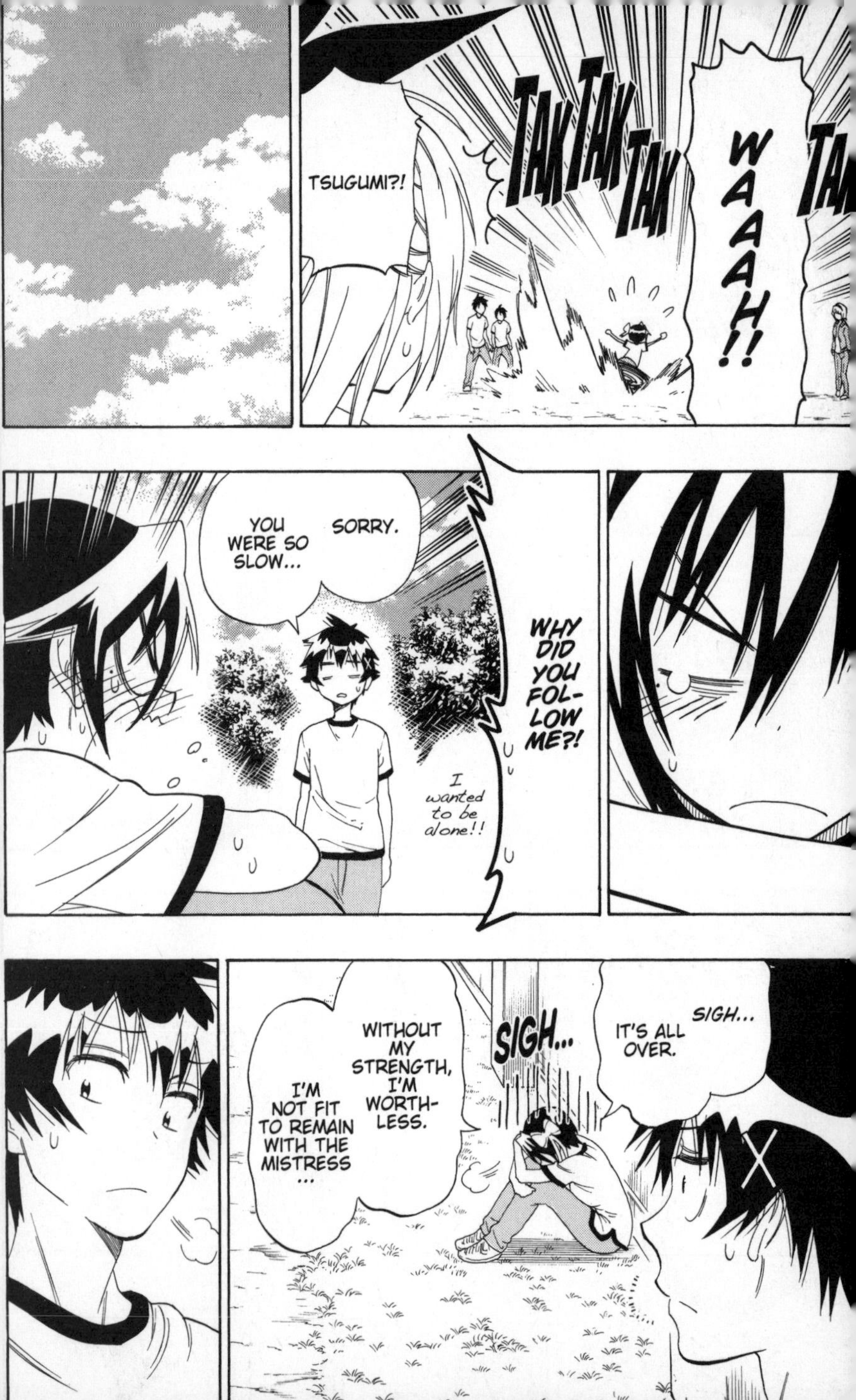
WAAAAH!!
TAK TAK TAK
TSUGUMI?!
WHY DID YOU FOL-LOW ME?!
I wanted to be alone!!
SORRY.
YOU WERE SO SLOW...
SIGH...
IT'S ALL OVER.
SIGH...
WITHOUT MY STRENGTH, I'M WORTH-LESS.
I'M NOT FIT TO REMAIN WITH THE MISTRESS...

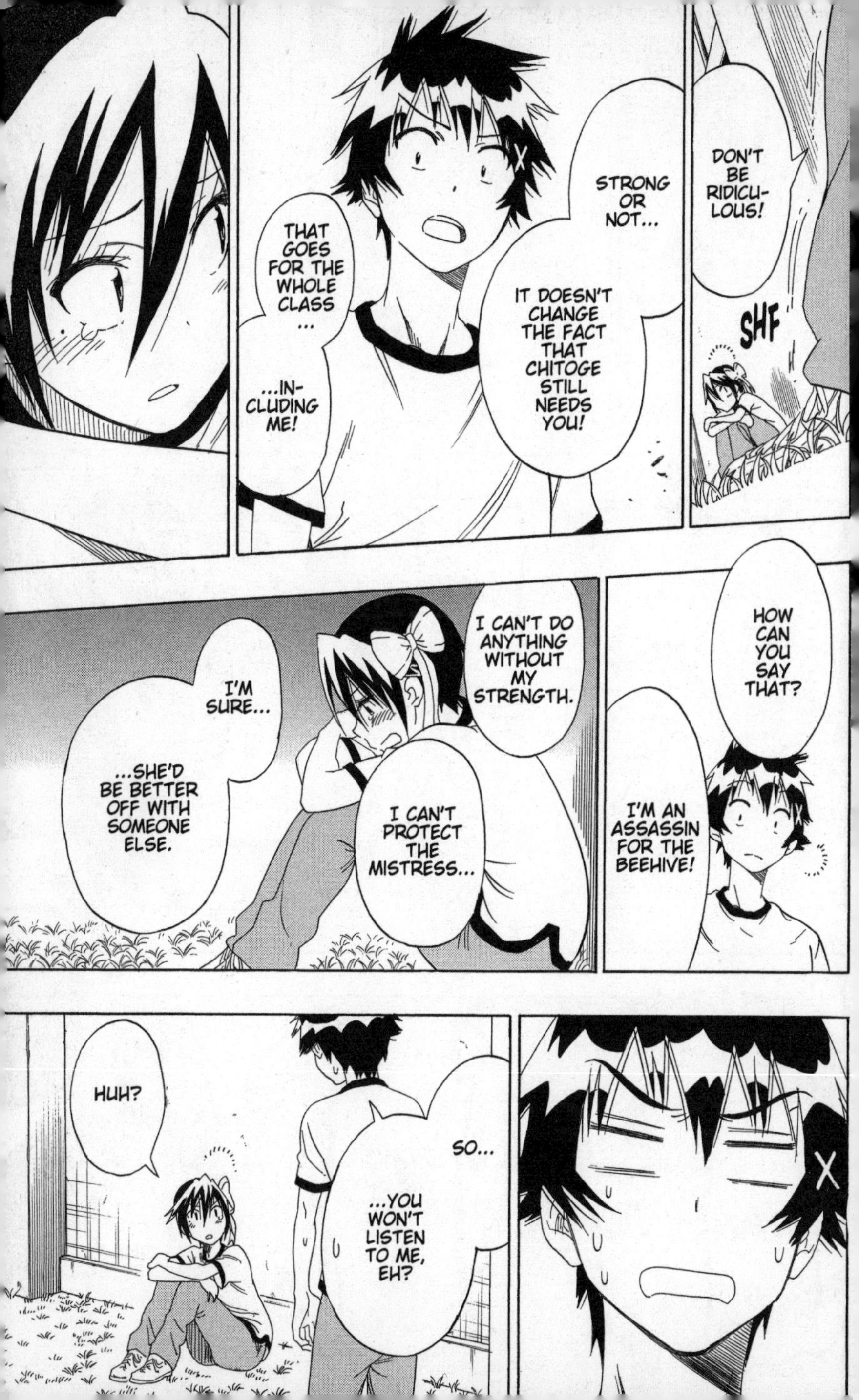
DON'T BE RIDICULOUS!
SHF
STRONG OR NOT...
IT DOESN'T CHANGE THE FACT THAT CHITOGE STILL NEEDS YOU!
THAT GOES FOR THE WHOLE CLASS...
...INCLUDING ME!
HOW CAN YOU SAY THAT?
I'M AN ASSASSIN FOR THE BEEHIVE!
I CAN'T DO ANYTHING WITHOUT MY STRENGTH.
I CAN'T PROTECT THE MISTRESS...
I'M SURE...
...SHE'D BE BETTER OFF WITH SOMEONE ELSE.
SO...
...YOU WON'T LISTEN TO ME, EH?
HUH?

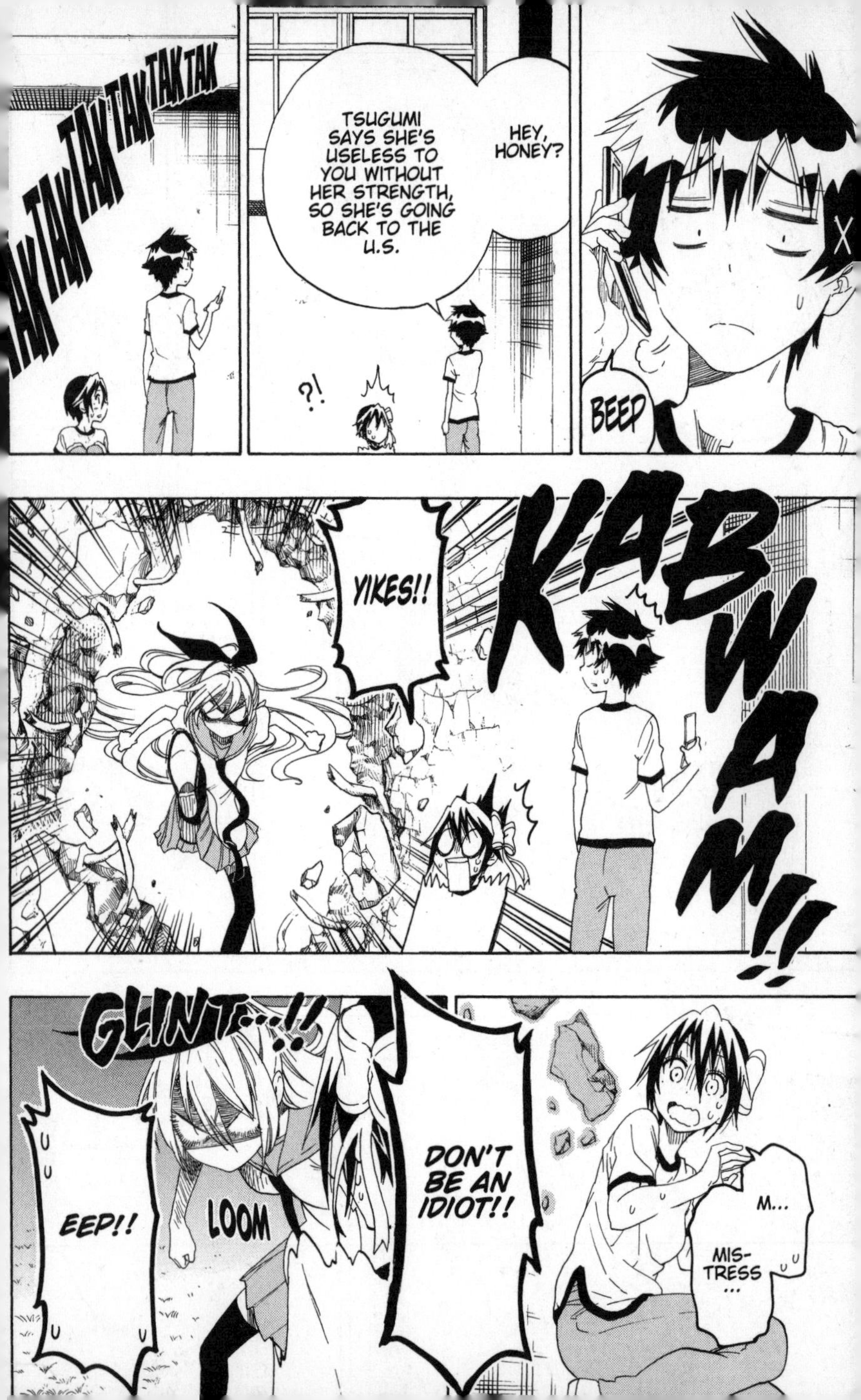
BEEP
HEY, HONEY?
TSUGUMI SAYS SHE'S USELESS TO YOU WITHOUT HER STRENGTH, SO SHE'S GOING BACK TO THE U.S.
?!
TAK TAK TAK TAK TAK TAK
KABWAMM!!
YIKES!!
M... MIS-TRESS...
DON'T BE AN IDIOT!!
GLINT...!!
LOOM
EEP!!

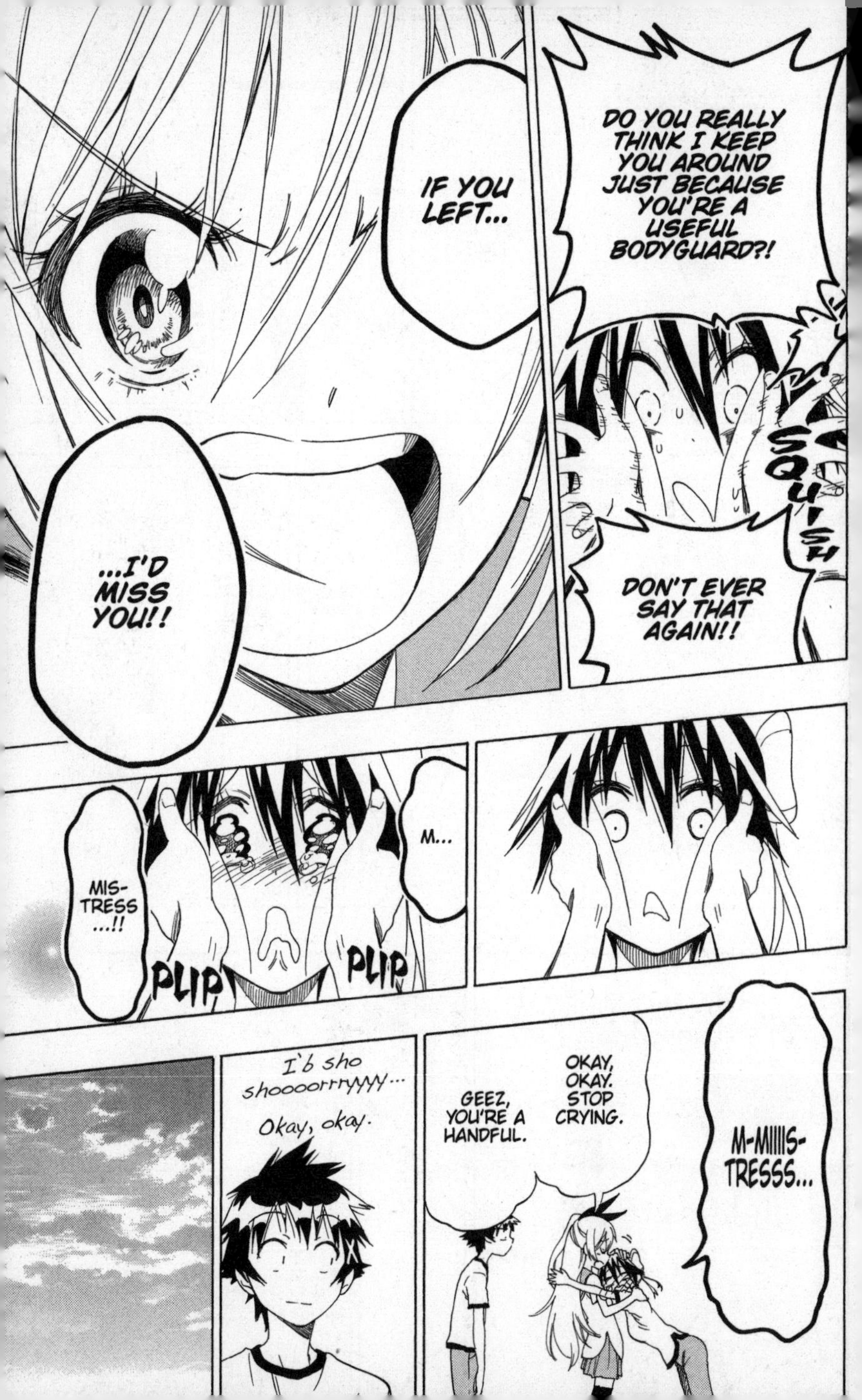
DO YOU REALLY THINK I KEEP YOU AROUND JUST BECAUSE YOU'RE A USEFUL BODYGUARD?!
SQUISH
DON'T EVER SAY THAT AGAIN!!
IF YOU LEFT...
...I'D MISS YOU!!
M...
MIS-TRESS ...!!
PLIP
PLIP
M-MIIIIS-TRESSS...
OKAY, OKAY. STOP CRYING.
GEEZ, YOU'RE A HANDFUL.
I'b sho shoooorrryyyy...
Okay, okay.

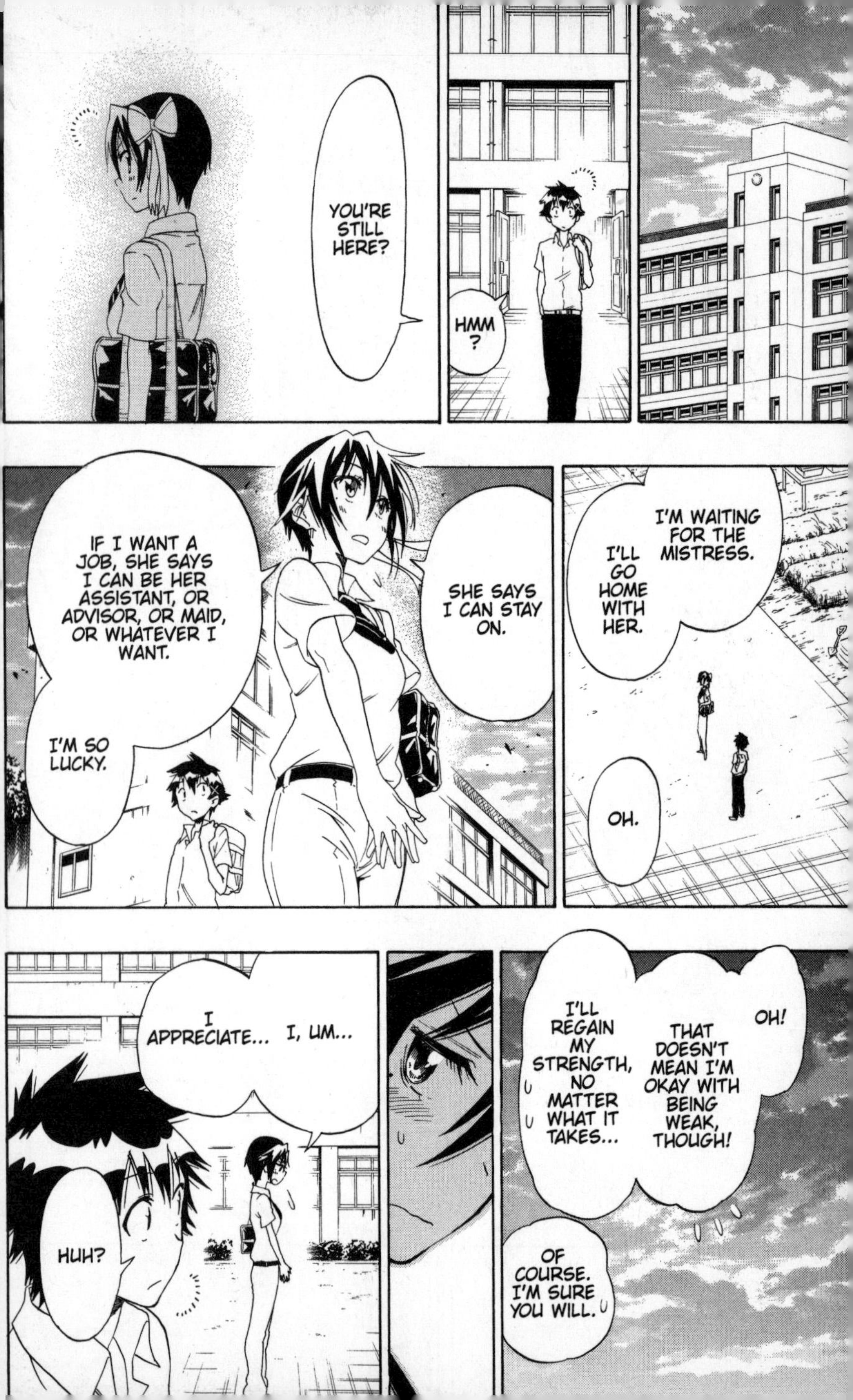
HMM ?
YOU'RE STILL HERE?
I'M WAITING FOR THE MISTRESS.
I'LL GO HOME WITH HER.
OH.
SHE SAYS I CAN STAY ON.
IF I WANT A JOB, SHE SAYS I CAN BE HER ASSISTANT, OR ADVISOR, OR MAID, OR WHATEVER I WANT.
I'M SO LUCKY.
OH!
THAT DOESN'T MEAN I'M OKAY WITH BEING WEAK, THOUGH!
I'LL REGAIN MY STRENGTH, NO MATTER WHAT IT TAKES...
OF COURSE. I'M SURE YOU WILL.
I, UM...
I APPRECIATE...
HUH?

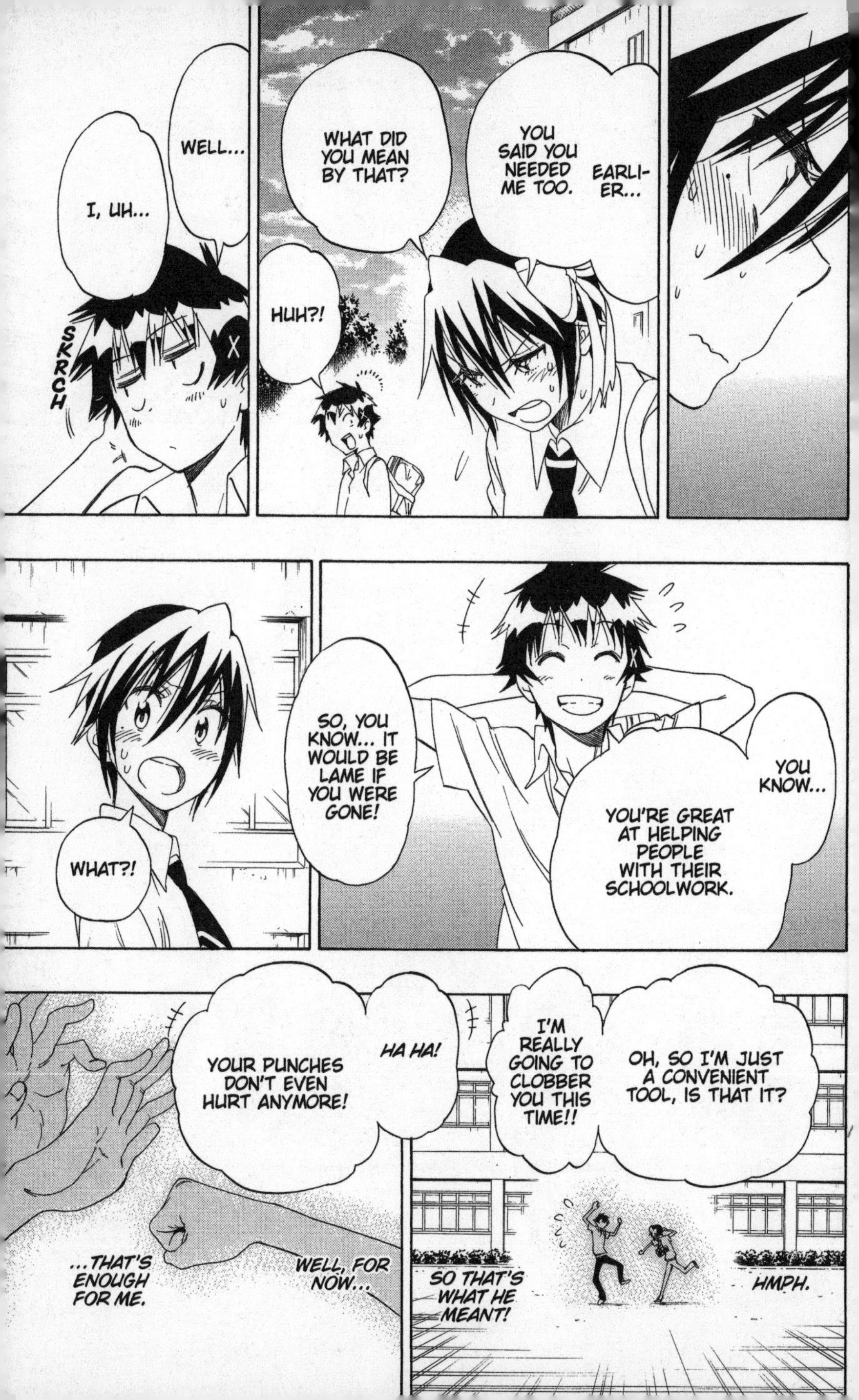
EARLI-ER...
YOU SAID YOU NEEDED ME TOO.
WHAT DID YOU MEAN BY THAT?
HUH?!
WELL...
I, UH...
SKRCH
YOU KNOW...
YOU'RE GREAT AT HELPING PEOPLE WITH THEIR SCHOOLWORK.
SO, YOU KNOW... IT WOULD BE LAME IF YOU WERE GONE!
WHAT?!
OH, SO I'M JUST A CONVENIENT TOOL, IS THAT IT?
I'M REALLY GOING TO CLOBBER YOU THIS TIME!!
HA HA!
YOUR PUNCHES DON'T EVEN HURT ANYMORE!
HMPH.
SO THAT'S WHAT HE MEANT!
WELL, FOR NOW...
...THAT'S ENOUGH FOR ME.

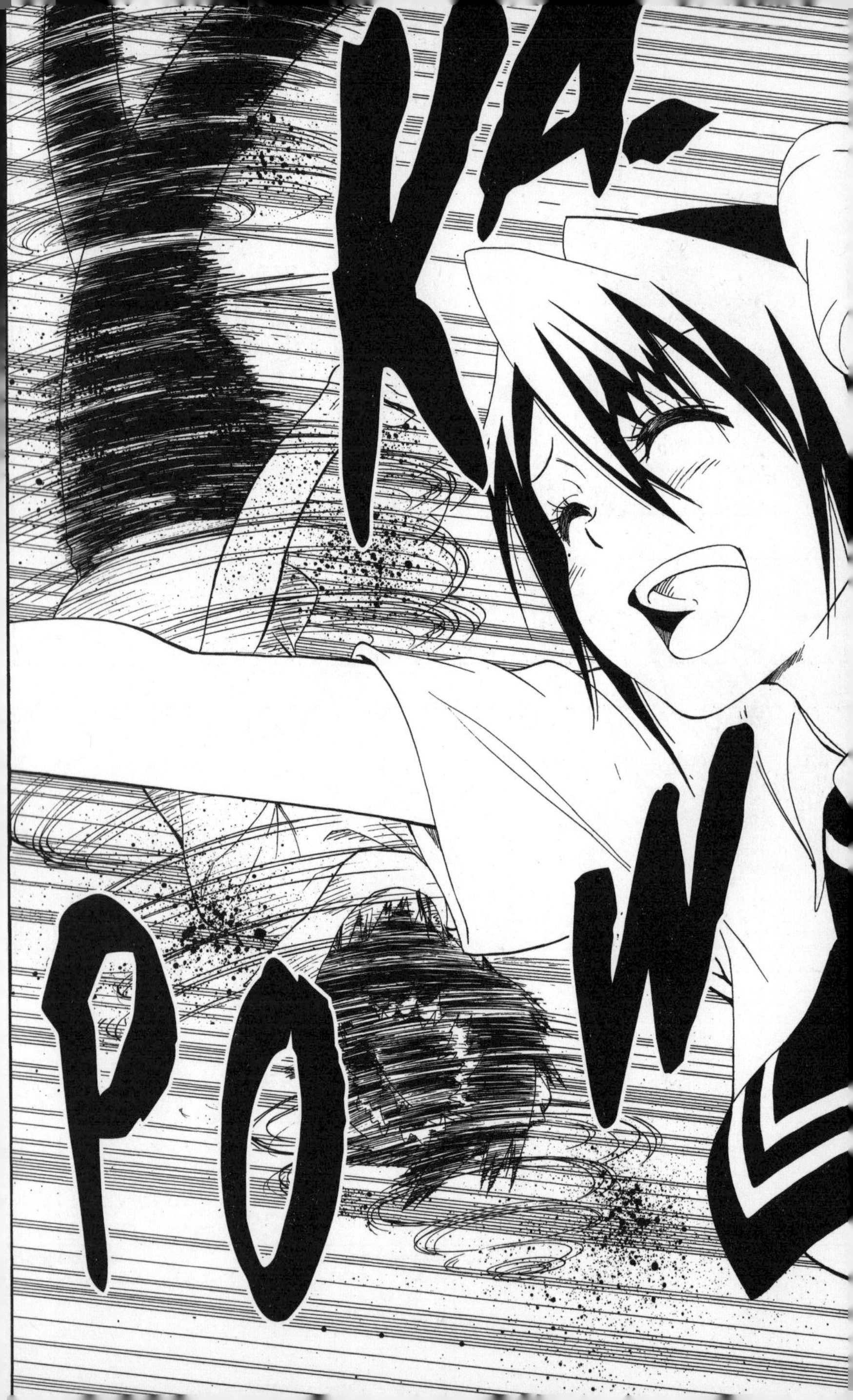
KYA-
POW

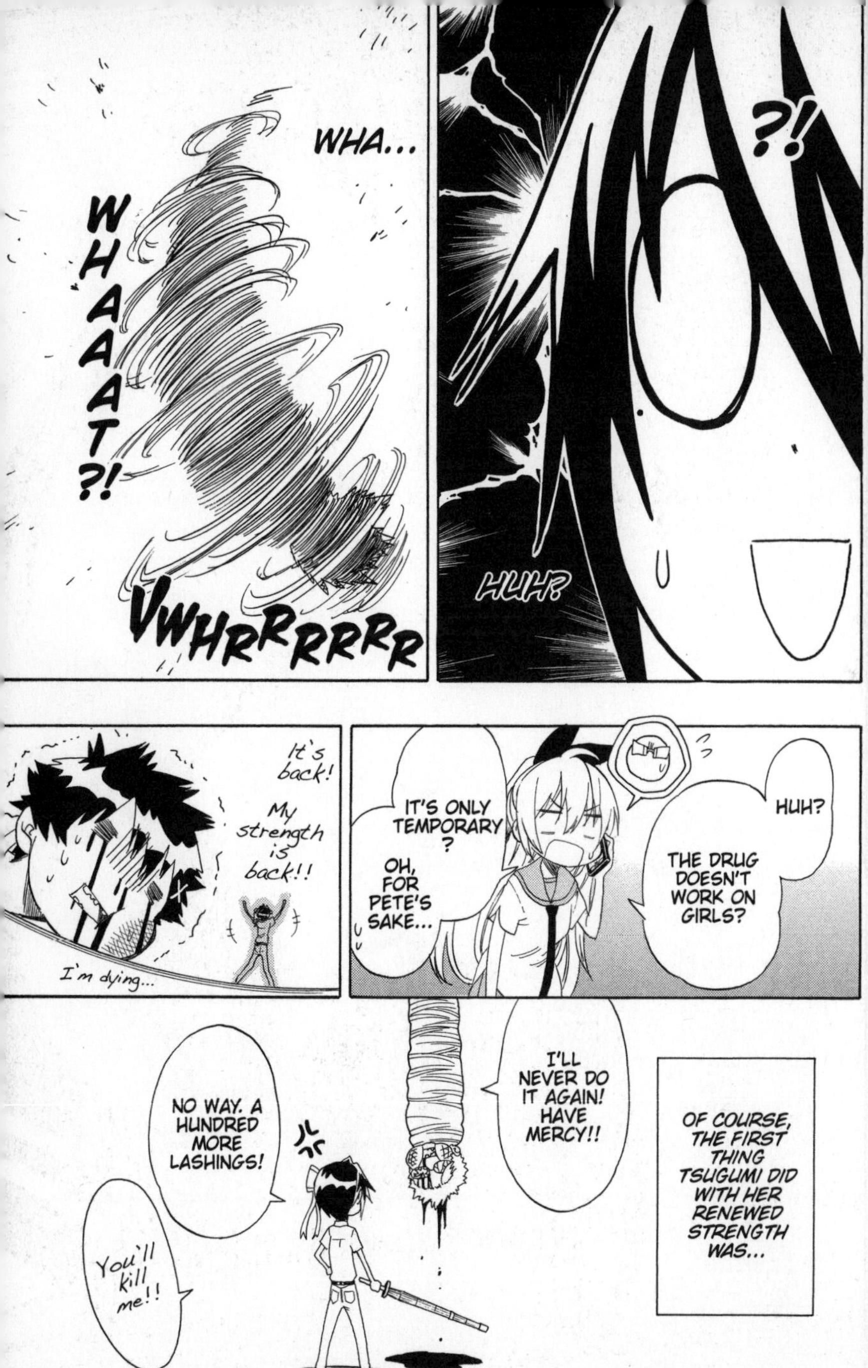

?!
HUH?
WHA...
WHAAAAT?!
VWHRRRRRR
HUH?
THE DRUG DOESN'T WORK ON GIRLS?
IT'S ONLY TEMPORARY?
OH, FOR PETE'S SAKE...
It's back!
My strength is back!!
I'm dying...
OF COURSE, THE FIRST THING TSUGUMI DID WITH HER RENEWED STRENGTH WAS...
I'LL NEVER DO IT AGAIN! HAVE MERCY!!
NO WAY. A HUNDRED MORE LASHINGS!
You'll kill me!!

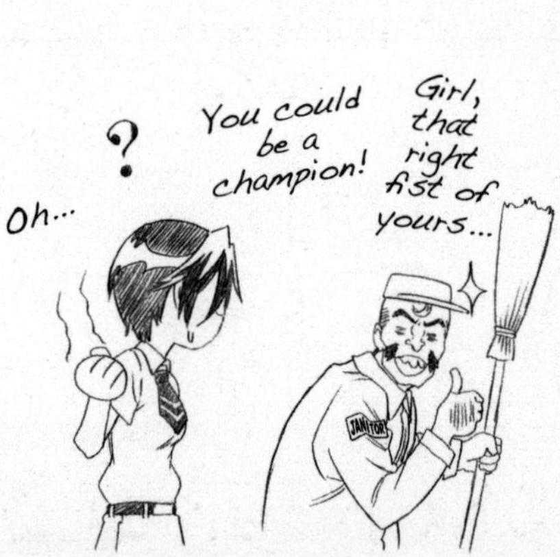
Girl, that right fist of yours...
You could be a champion!
?
Oh...
JANITOR

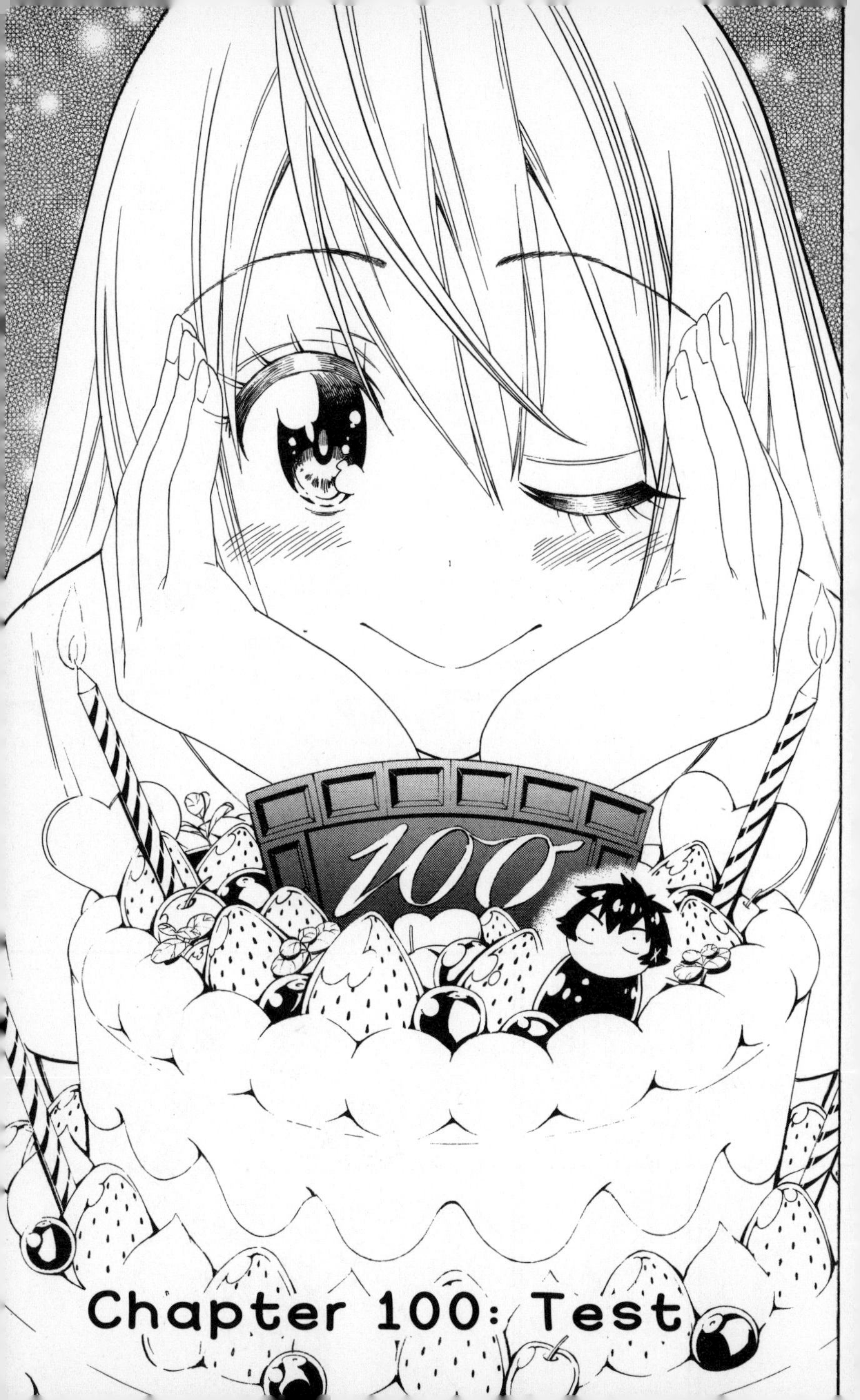
100

Chapter 100: Test

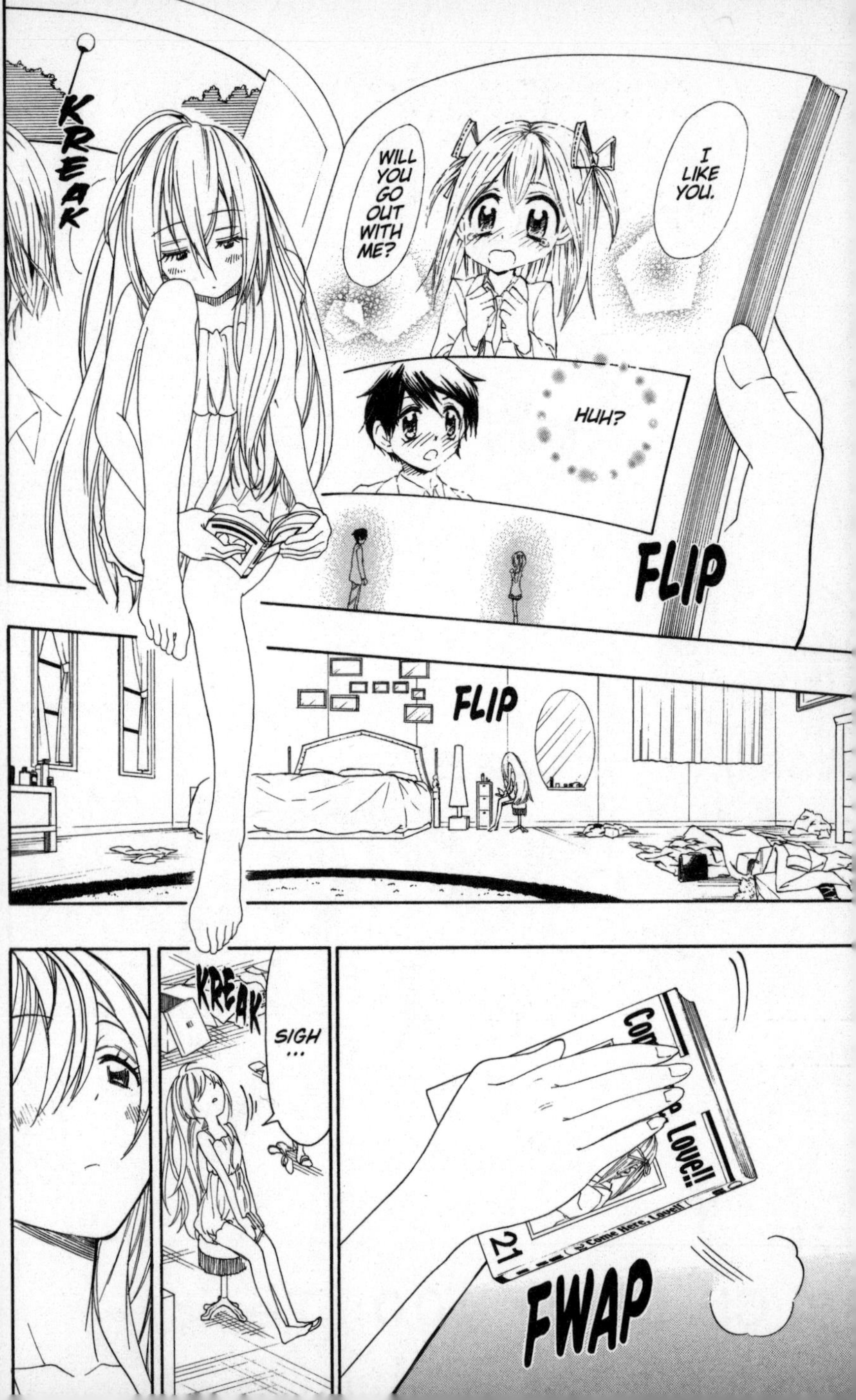
I LIKE YOU.
WILL YOU GO OUT WITH ME?
HUH?
FLIP
KREAK
FLIP
FWAP
21
Come Here, Love!!
KREAK
SIGH...

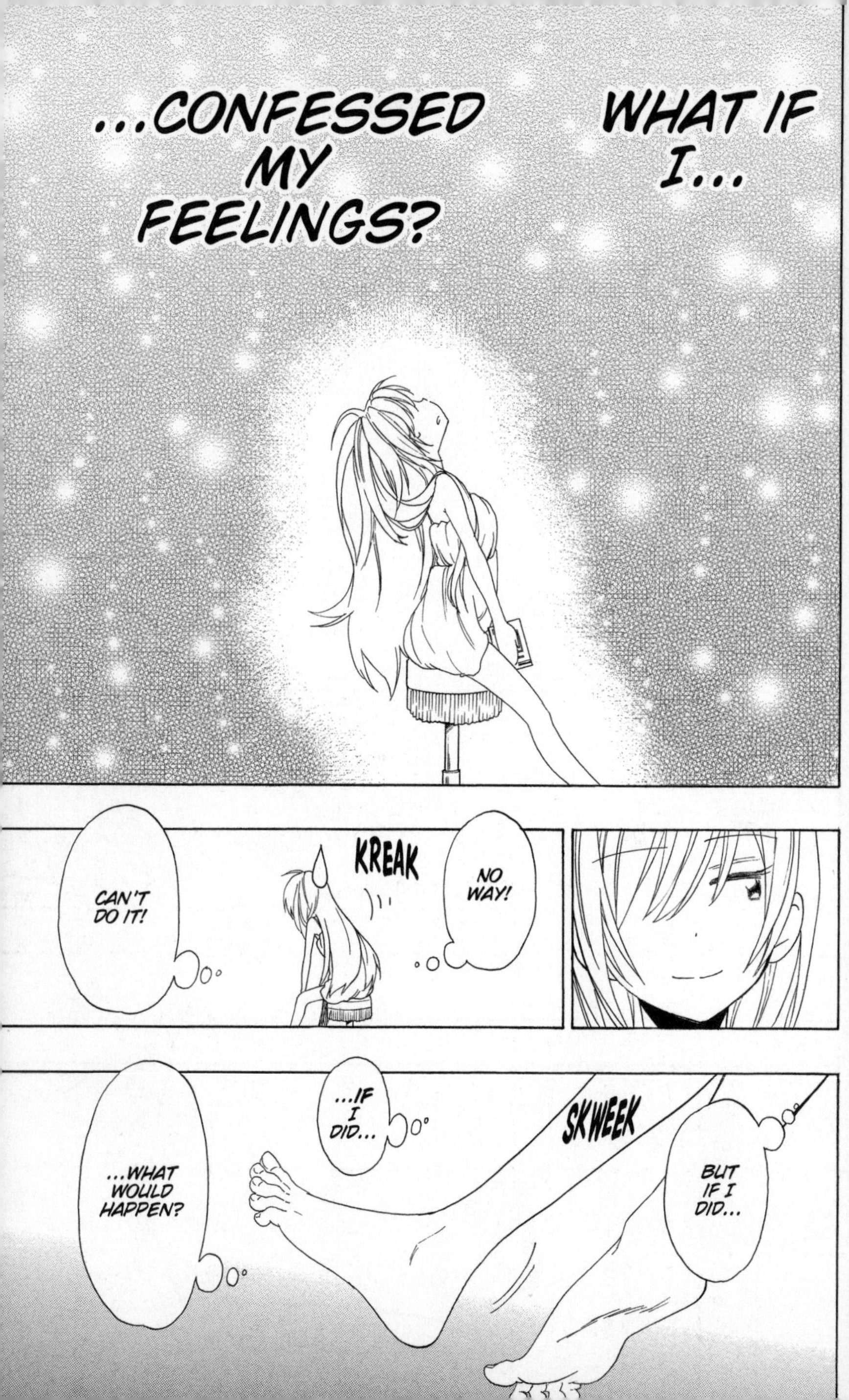
WHAT IF I...
...CONFESSED MY FEELINGS?
NO WAY!
KREAK
CAN'T DO IT!
BUT IF I DID...
SKWEEK
...IF I DID...
...WHAT WOULD HAPPEN?

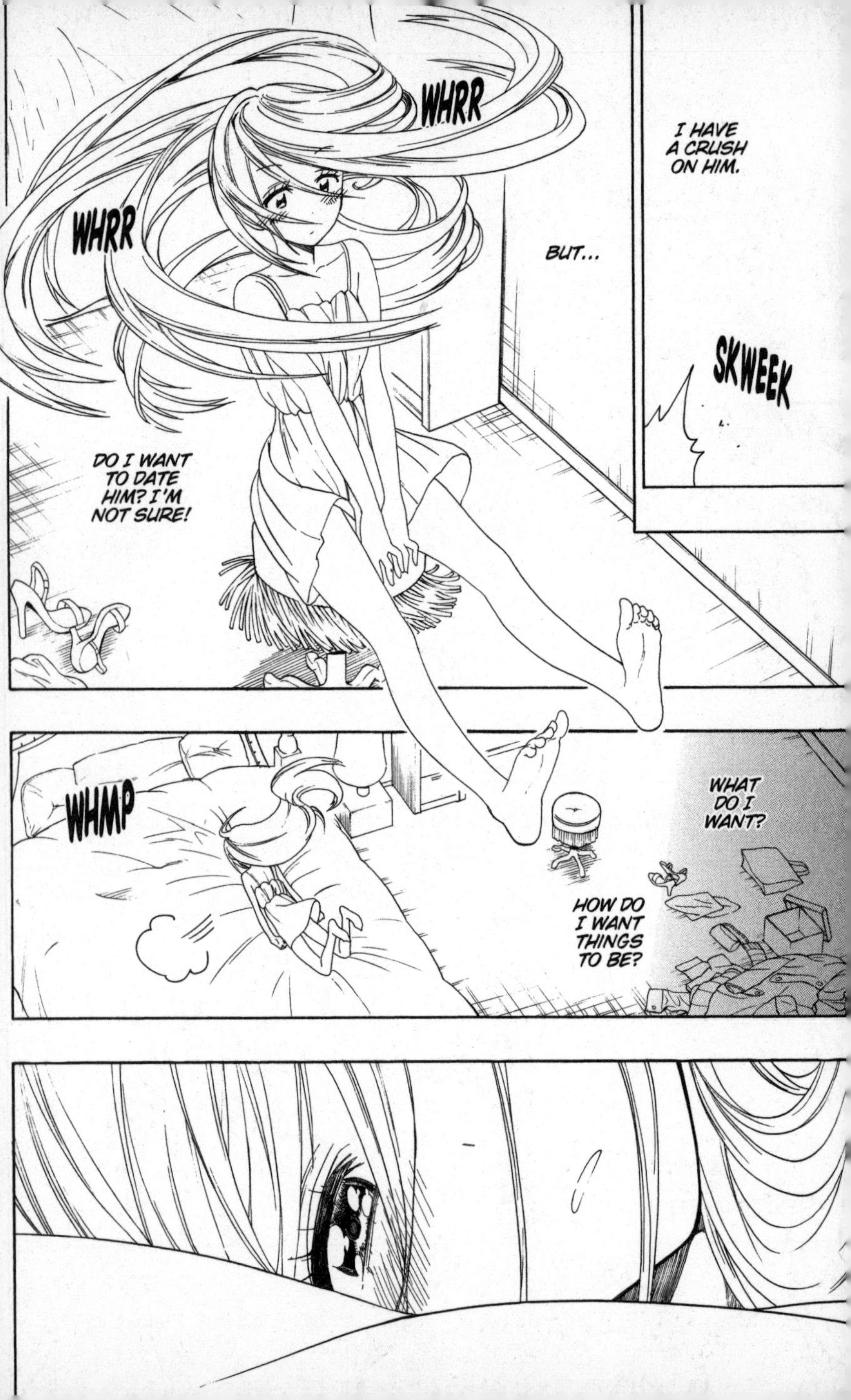
I HAVE A CRUSH ON HIM.
SKWEEK
BUT...
WHRR
WHRR
DO I WANT TO DATE HIM? I'M NOT SURE!
WHAT DO I WANT?
HOW DO I WANT THINGS TO BE?
WHMP

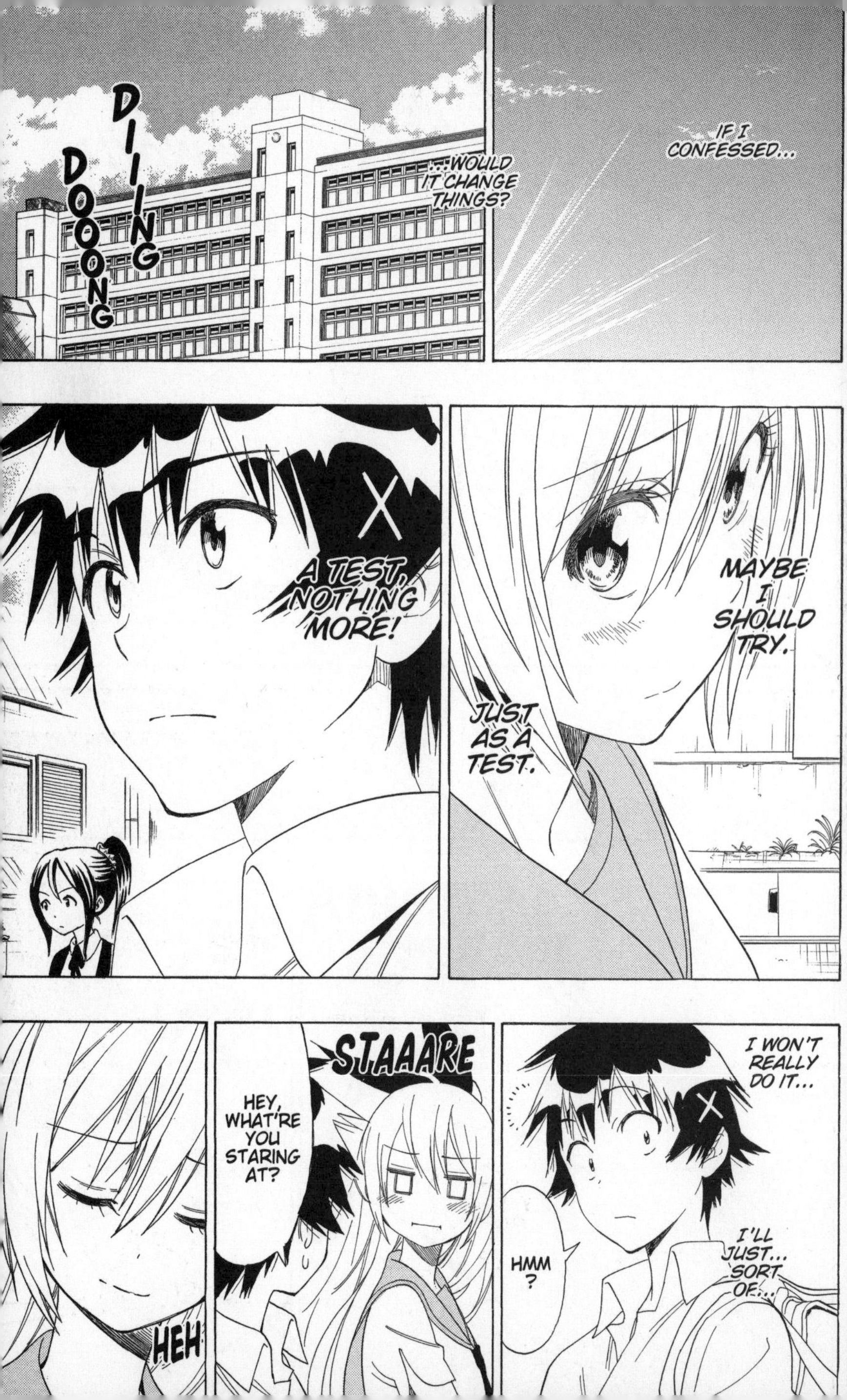
IF I CONFESSED...
...WOULD IT CHANGE THINGS?
DIIING
DOOONG
MAYBE I SHOULD TRY.
JUST AS A TEST.
A TEST, NOTHING MORE!
I WON'T REALLY DO IT...
HMM?
I'LL JUST... SORT OF...
STAAARE
HEY, WHAT'RE YOU STARING AT?
HEH

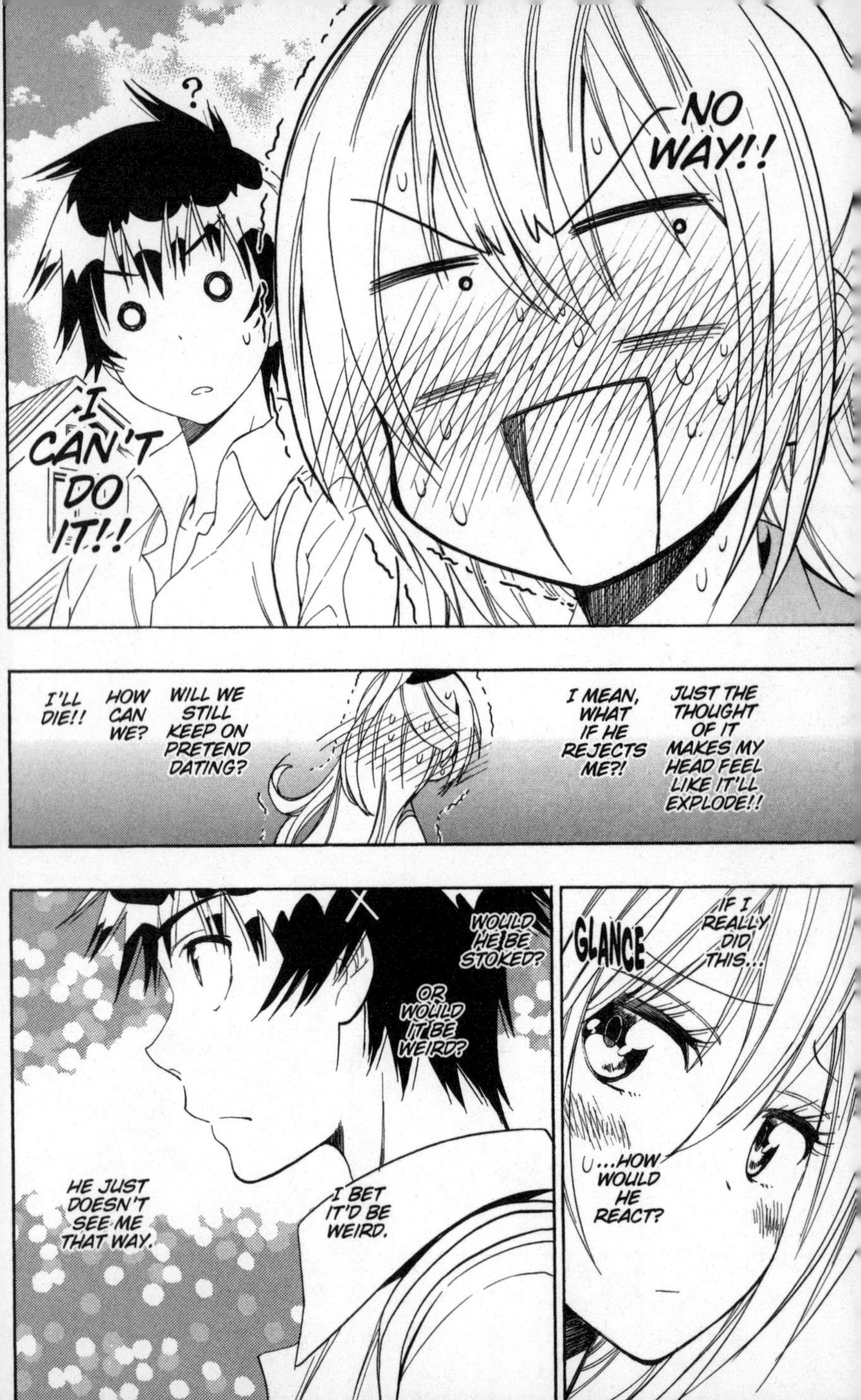
?
NO WAY!!
I CAN'T DO IT!!
JUST THE THOUGHT OF IT MAKES MY HEAD FEEL LIKE IT'LL EXPLODE!!
I MEAN, WHAT IF HE REJECTS ME?!
WILL WE STILL KEEP ON PRETEND DATING?
HOW CAN WE?
I'LL DIE!!
IF I REALLY DID THIS...
GLANCE
...HOW WOULD HE REACT?
WOULD HE BE STOKED?
OR WOULD IT BE WEIRD?
I BET IT'D BE WEIRD.
HE JUST DOESN'T SEE ME THAT WAY.

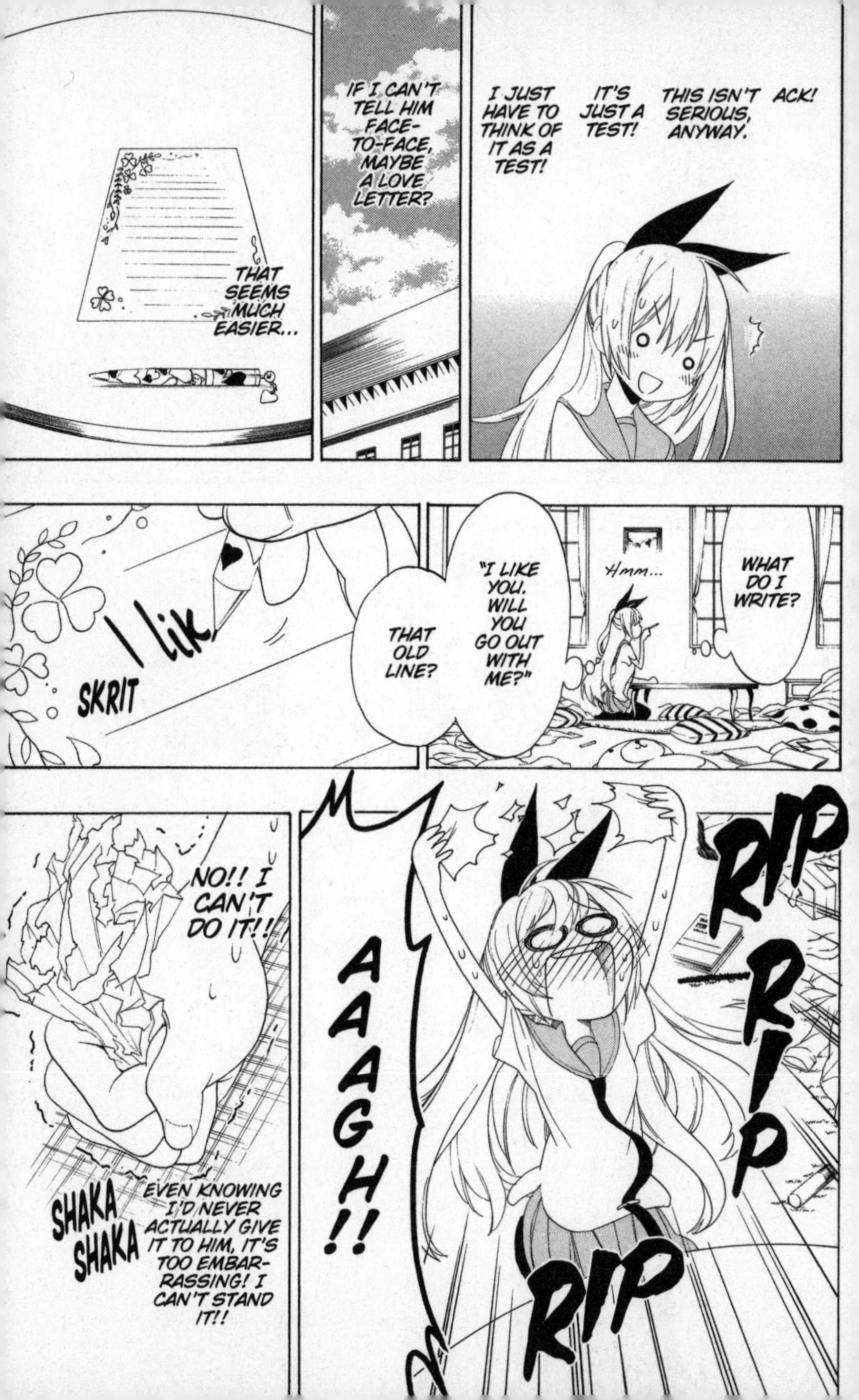
ACK!
THIS ISN'T SERIOUS, ANYWAY.
IT'S JUST A TEST!
I JUST HAVE TO THINK OF IT AS A TEST!
IF I CAN'T TELL HIM FACE-TO-FACE, MAYBE A LOVE LETTER?
THAT SEEMS MUCH EASIER...
WHAT DO I WRITE?
Hmm...
"I LIKE YOU. WILL YOU GO OUT WITH ME?"
THAT OLD LINE?
I lik
SKRIT
RIP
RIP
RIP
AAAAGH!!
NO!! I CAN'T DO IT!!
EVEN KNOWING I'D NEVER ACTUALLY GIVE IT TO HIM, IT'S TOO EMBARRASSING! I CAN'T STAND IT!!
SHAKA SHAKA

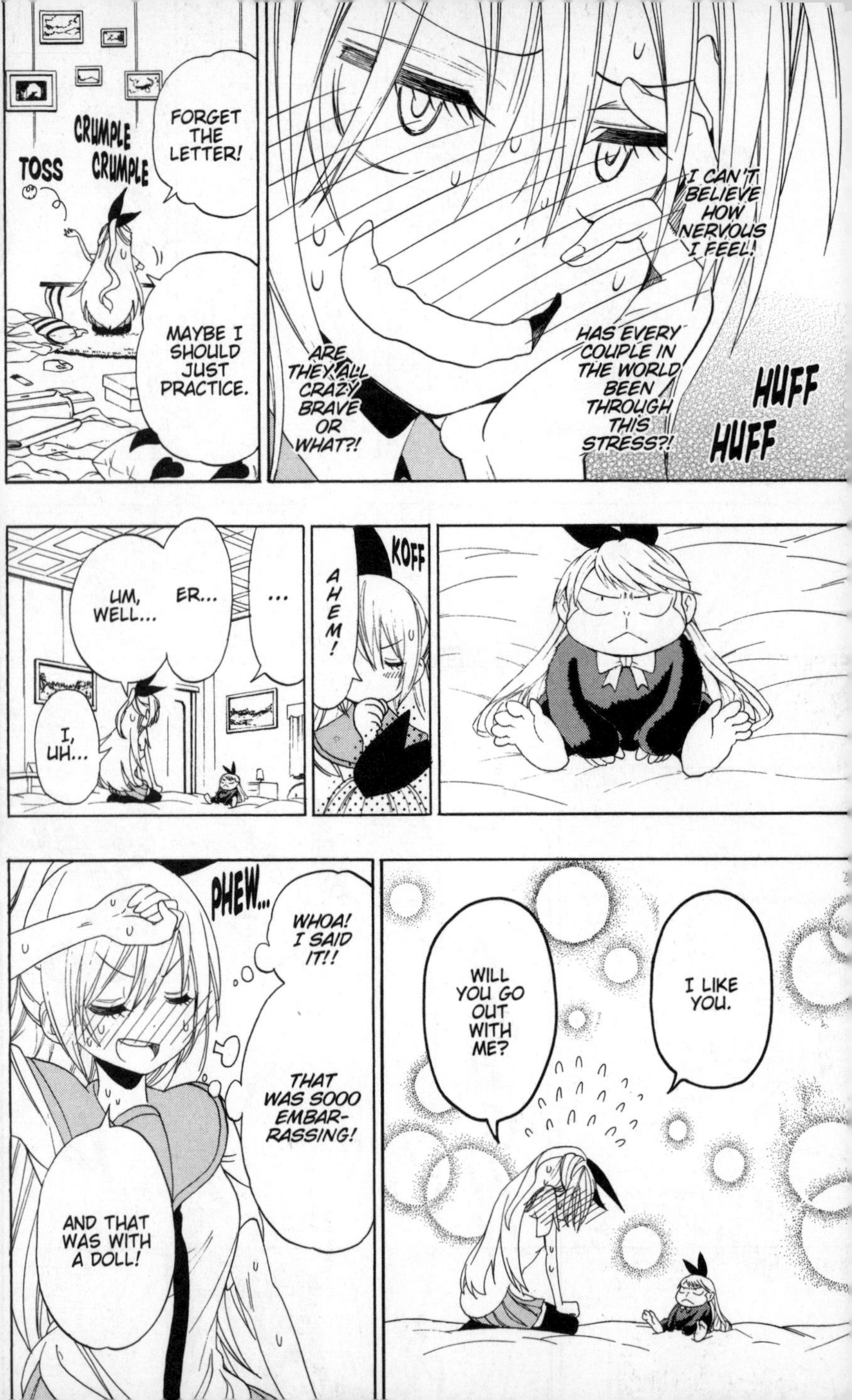
I CAN'T BELIEVE HOW NERVOUS I FEEL!
HAS EVERY COUPLE IN THE WORLD BEEN THROUGH THIS STRESS?!
HUFF HUFF
ARE THEY ALL CRAZY BRAVE OR WHAT?!
FORGET THE LETTER!
CRUMPLE CRUMPLE
TOSS
MAYBE I SHOULD JUST PRACTICE.
KOFF
AHEM!
...
ER...
UM, WELL...
I, UH...
I LIKE YOU.
WILL YOU GO OUT WITH ME?
WHOA! I SAID IT!!
PHEW...
THAT WAS SOOO EMBAR-RASSING!
AND THAT WAS WITH A DOLL!

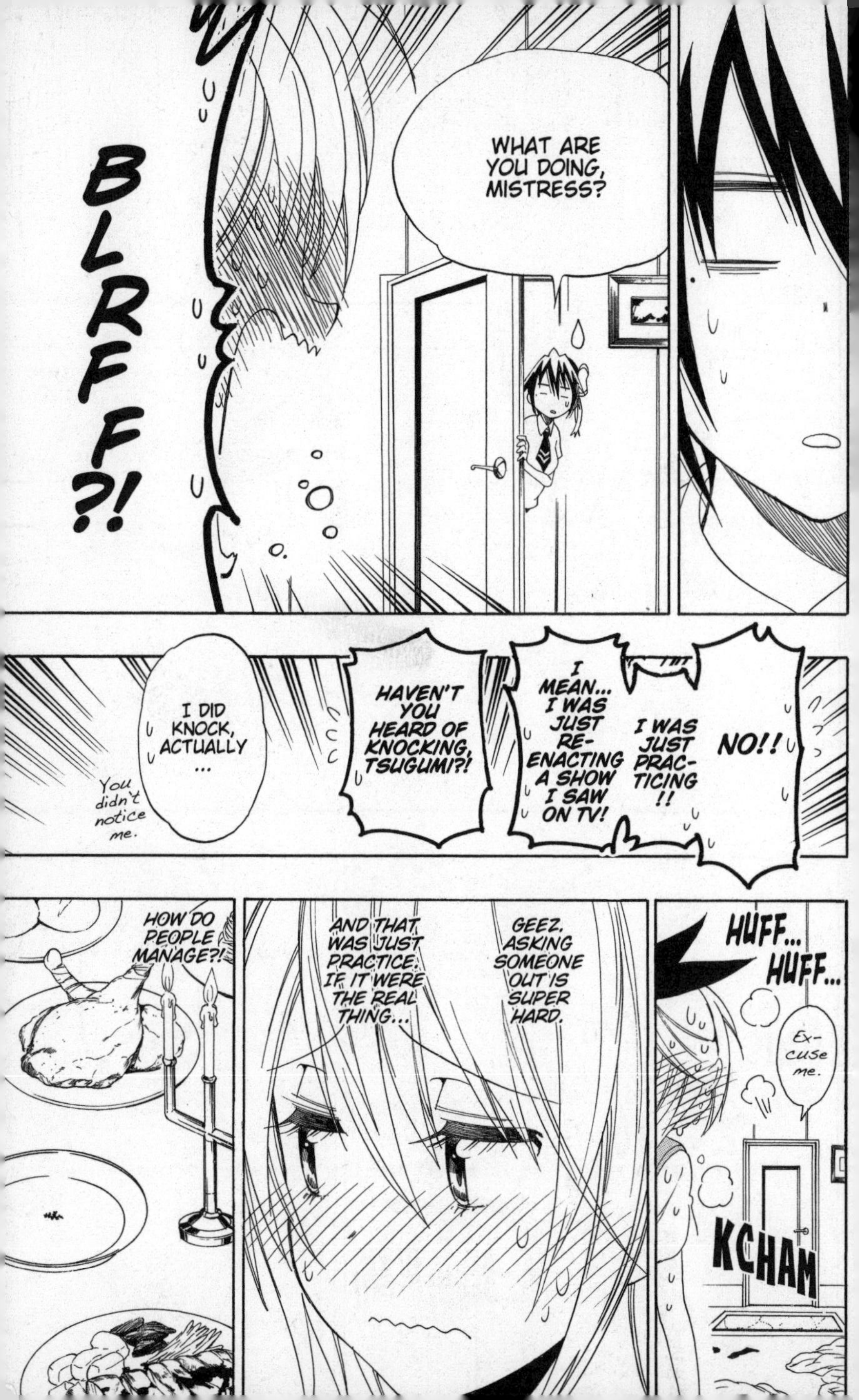
WHAT ARE YOU DOING, MISTRESS?
BLRFF?!
NO!!
I WAS JUST PRACTICING!!
I MEAN... I WAS JUST RE-ENACTING A SHOW I SAW ON TV!
HAVEN'T YOU HEARD OF KNOCKING, TSUGUMI?!
I DID KNOCK, ACTUALLY...
You didn't notice me.
HUFF... HUFF...
Excuse me.
KCHAM
GEEZ. ASKING SOMEONE OUT IS SUPER HARD.
AND THAT WAS JUST PRACTICE. IF IT WERE THE REAL THING...
HOW DO PEOPLE MANAGE?!

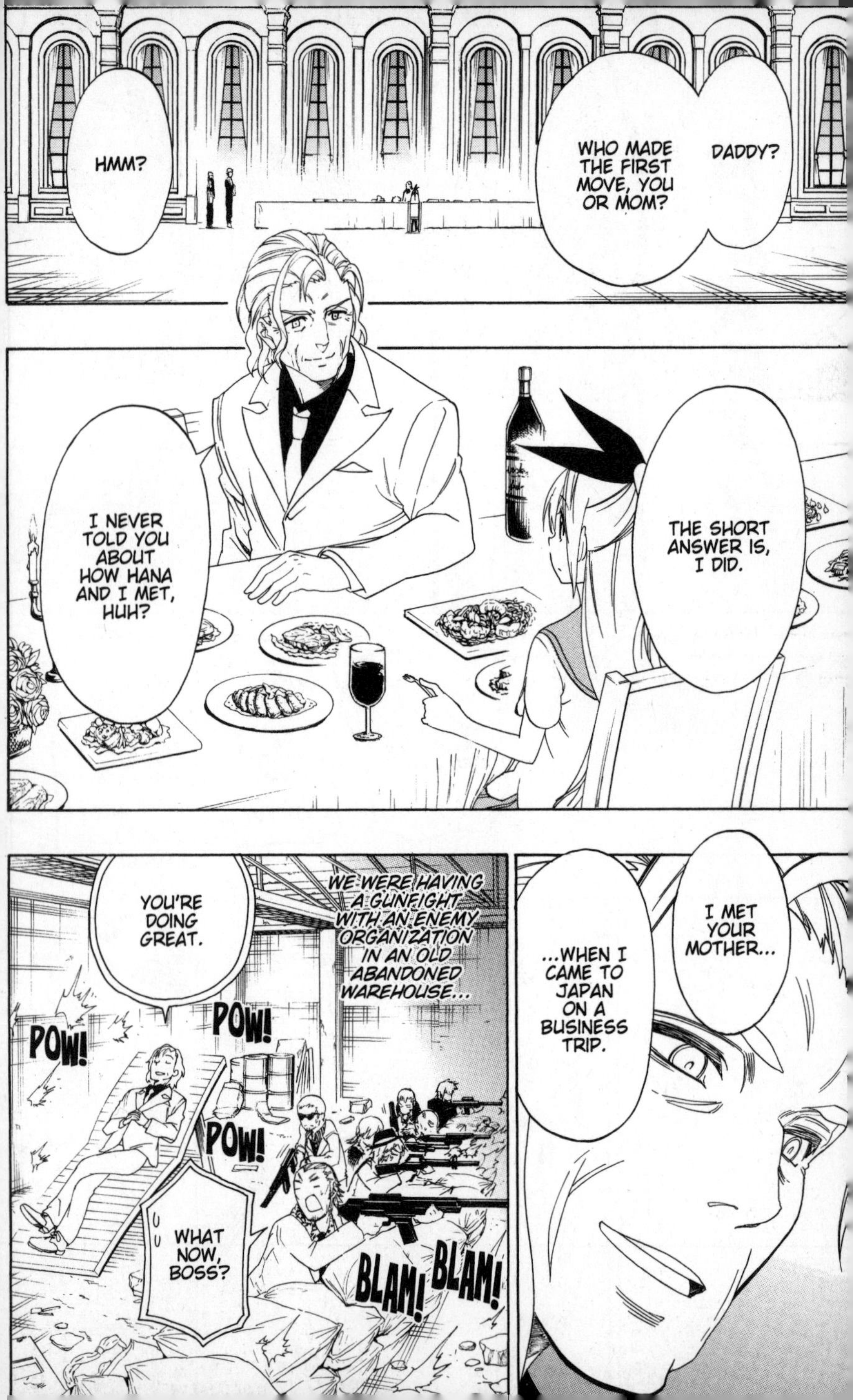
DADDY?
WHO MADE THE FIRST MOVE, YOU OR MOM?
HMM?
THE SHORT ANSWER IS, I DID.
I NEVER TOLD YOU ABOUT HOW HANA AND I MET, HUH?
I MET YOUR MOTHER...
...WHEN I CAME TO JAPAN ON A BUSINESS TRIP.
WE WERE HAVING A GUNFIGHT WITH AN ENEMY ORGANIZATION IN AN OLD ABANDONED WAREHOUSE...
YOU'RE DOING GREAT.
POW!
POW!
POW!
WHAT NOW, BOSS?
BLAM!
BLAM!

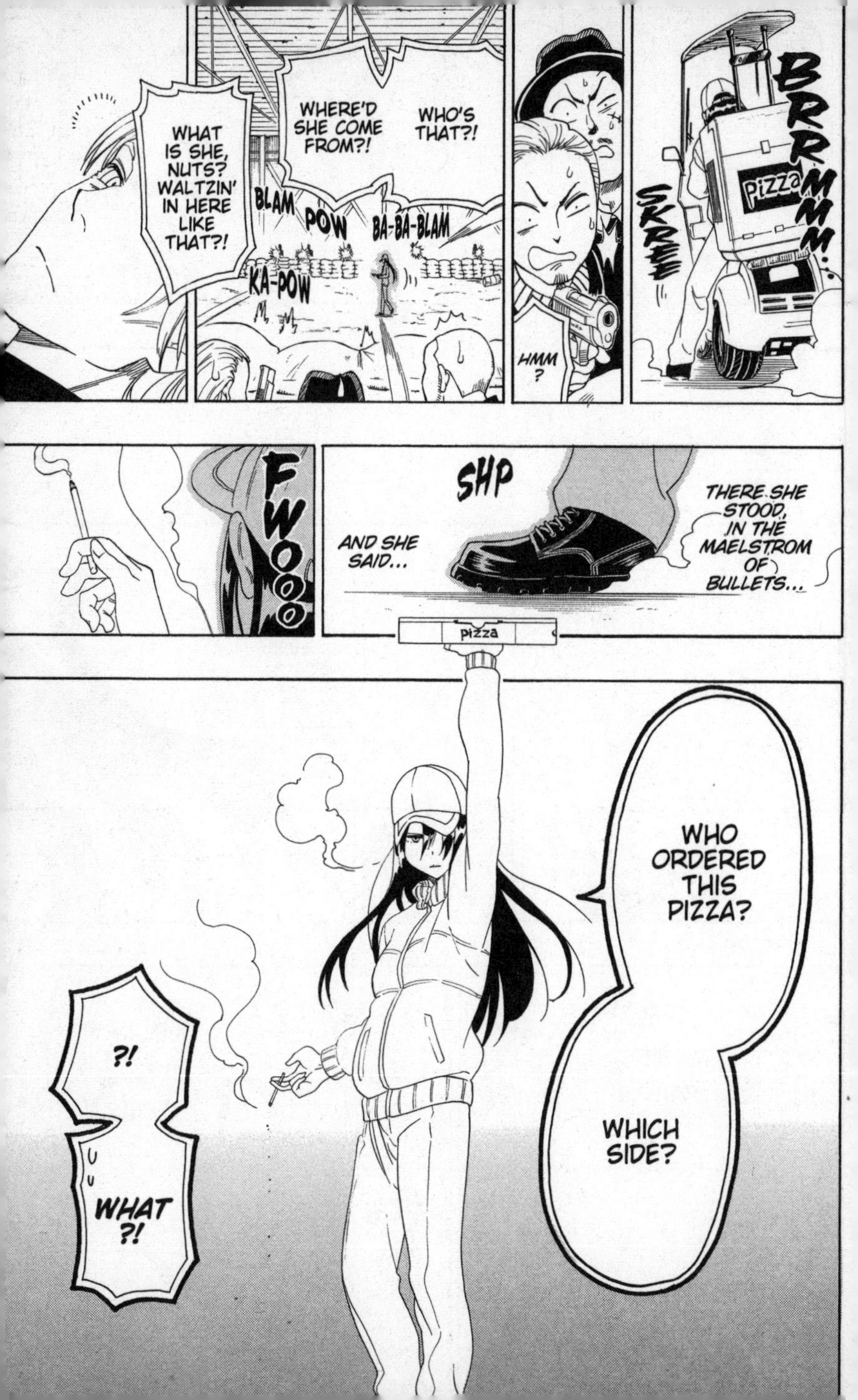
BRRMMMM!
pizza
SKREE
HMM?
WHO'S THAT?!
WHERE'D SHE COME FROM?!
BLAM
POW
BA-BA-BLAM
KA-POW
WHAT IS SHE, NUTS? WALTZIN' IN HERE LIKE THAT?!
THERE SHE STOOD, IN THE MAELSTROM OF BULLETS...
SHP
AND SHE SAID...
FWOOO
pizza
WHO ORDERED THIS PIZZA?
WHICH SIDE?
?!
WHAT?!

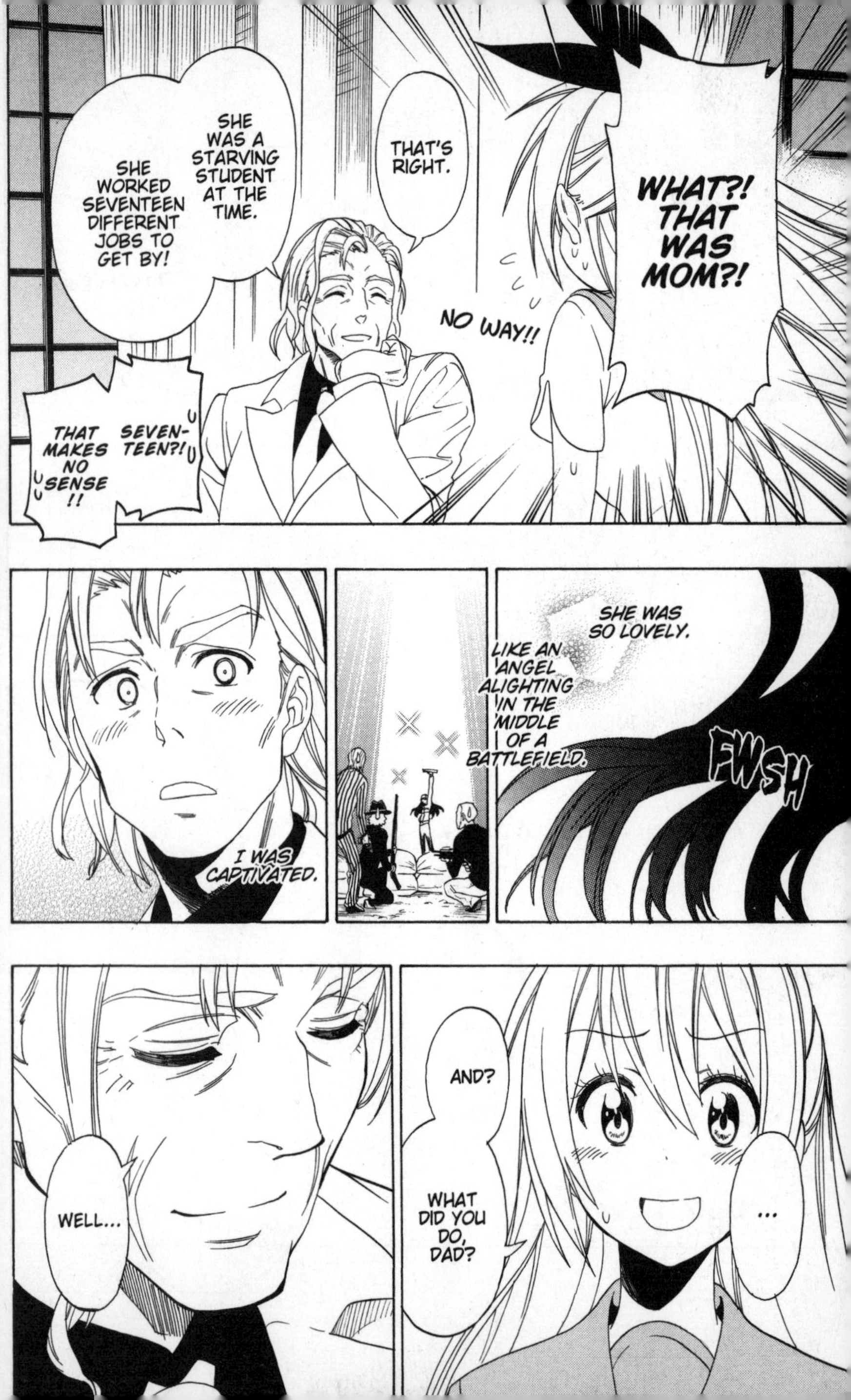
WHAT?! THAT WAS MOM?!
NO WAY!!
THAT'S RIGHT.
SHE WAS A STARVING STUDENT AT THE TIME.
SHE WORKED SEVENTEEN DIFFERENT JOBS TO GET BY!
SEVENTEEN?!
THAT MAKES NO SENSE!!
SHE WAS SO LOVELY.
LIKE AN ANGEL ALIGHTING IN THE MIDDLE OF A BATTLEFIELD.
FWSH
I WAS CAPTIVATED.
AND?
...
WHAT DID YOU DO, DAD?
WELL...

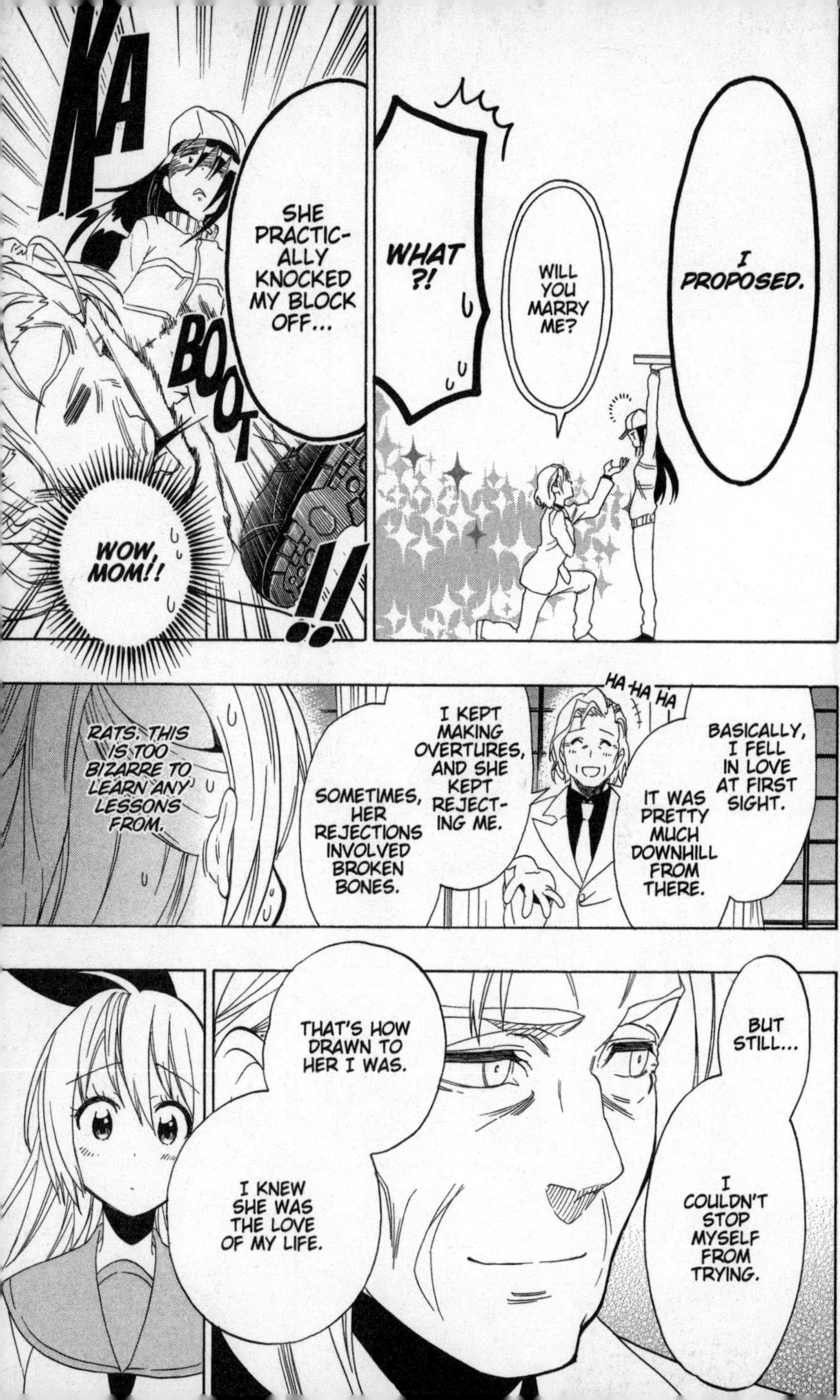
I PROPOSED.
WILL YOU MARRY ME?
WHAT ?!
SHE PRACTIC-ALLY KNOCKED MY BLOCK OFF...
KA
BOOT
WOW, MOM!!
BASICALLY, I FELL IN LOVE AT FIRST SIGHT.
IT WAS PRETTY MUCH DOWNHILL FROM THERE.
HA HA HA
I KEPT MAKING OVERTURES, AND SHE KEPT REJECT-ING ME.
SOMETIMES, HER REJECTIONS INVOLVED BROKEN BONES.
RATS. THIS IS TOO BIZARRE TO LEARN ANY LESSONS FROM.
BUT STILL...
I COULDN'T STOP MYSELF FROM TRYING.
THAT'S HOW DRAWN TO HER I WAS.
I KNEW SHE WAS THE LOVE OF MY LIFE.

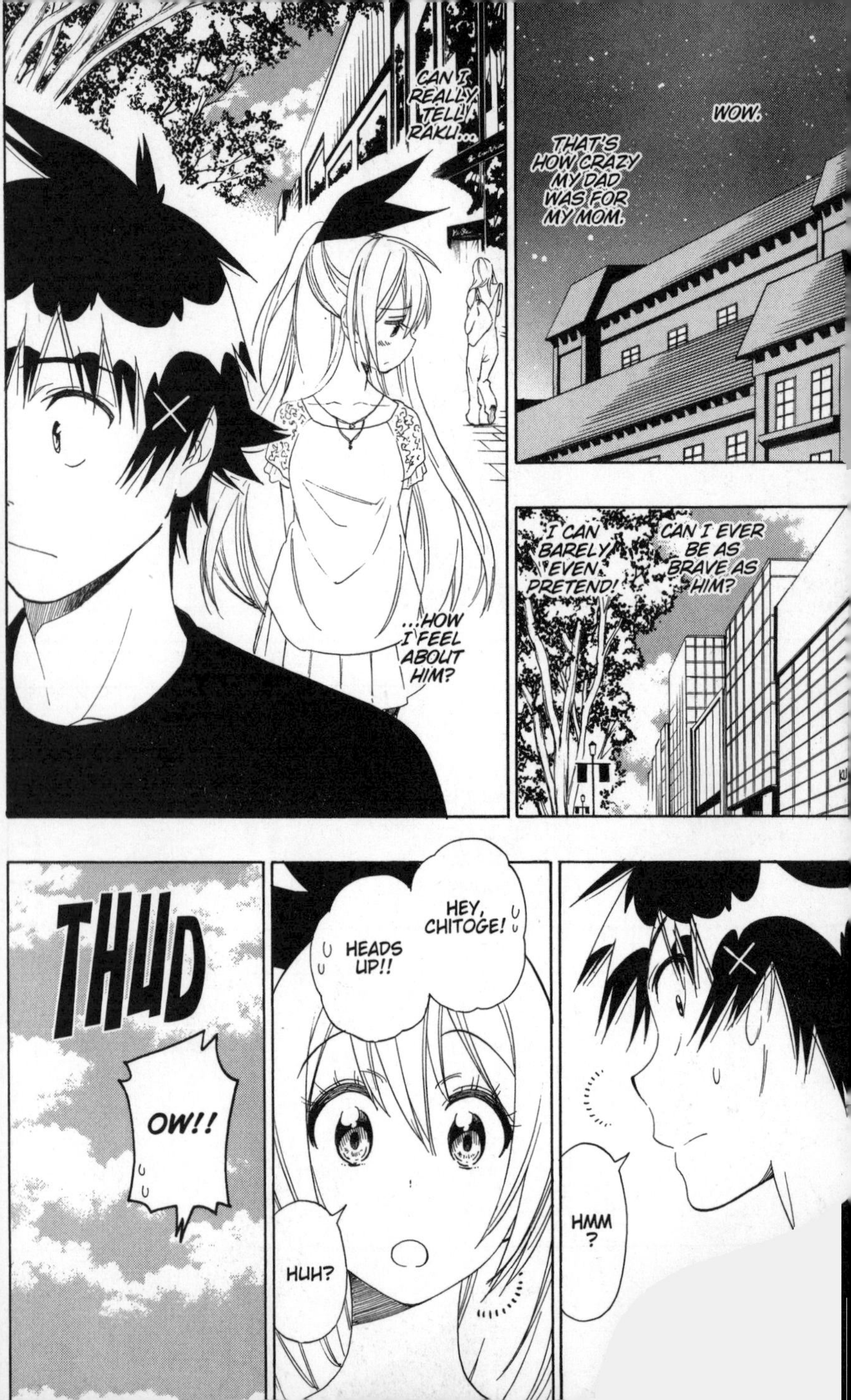
WOW.
THAT'S HOW CRAZY MY DAD WAS FOR MY MOM.
CAN I EVER BE AS BRAVE AS HIM?
I CAN BARELY EVEN PRETEND!
CAN I REALLY TELL RAKU...
...HOW I FEEL ABOUT HIM?
HMM?
HEY, CHITOGE!
HEADS UP!!
HUH?
THUD
OW!!

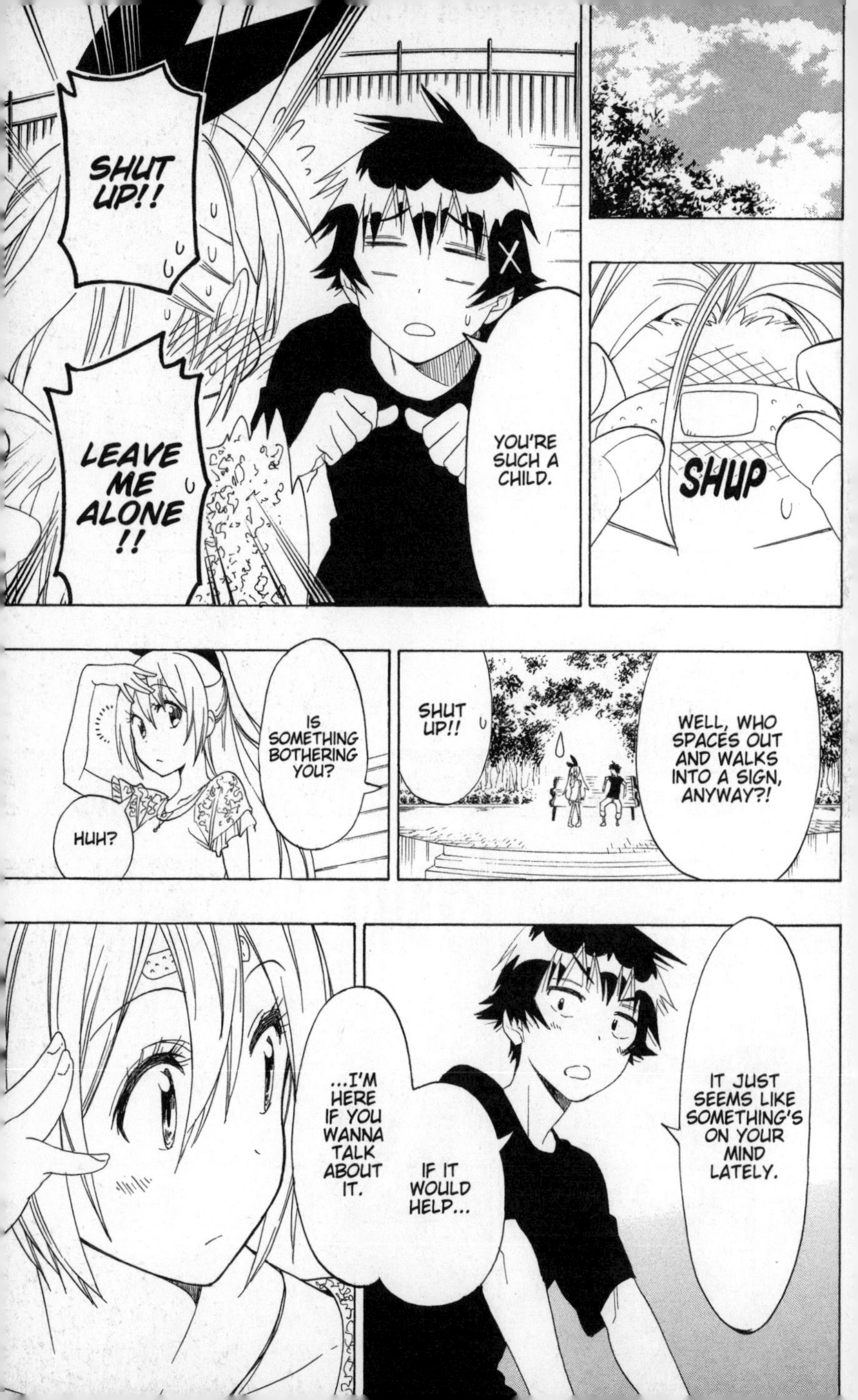
SHUP
YOU'RE SUCH A CHILD.
SHUT UP!!
LEAVE ME ALONE!!
WELL, WHO SPACES OUT AND WALKS INTO A SIGN, ANYWAY?!
SHUT UP!!
IS SOMETHING BOTHERING YOU?
HUH?
IT JUST SEEMS LIKE SOMETHING'S ON YOUR MIND LATELY.
IF IT WOULD HELP...
...I'M HERE IF YOU WANNA TALK ABOUT IT.

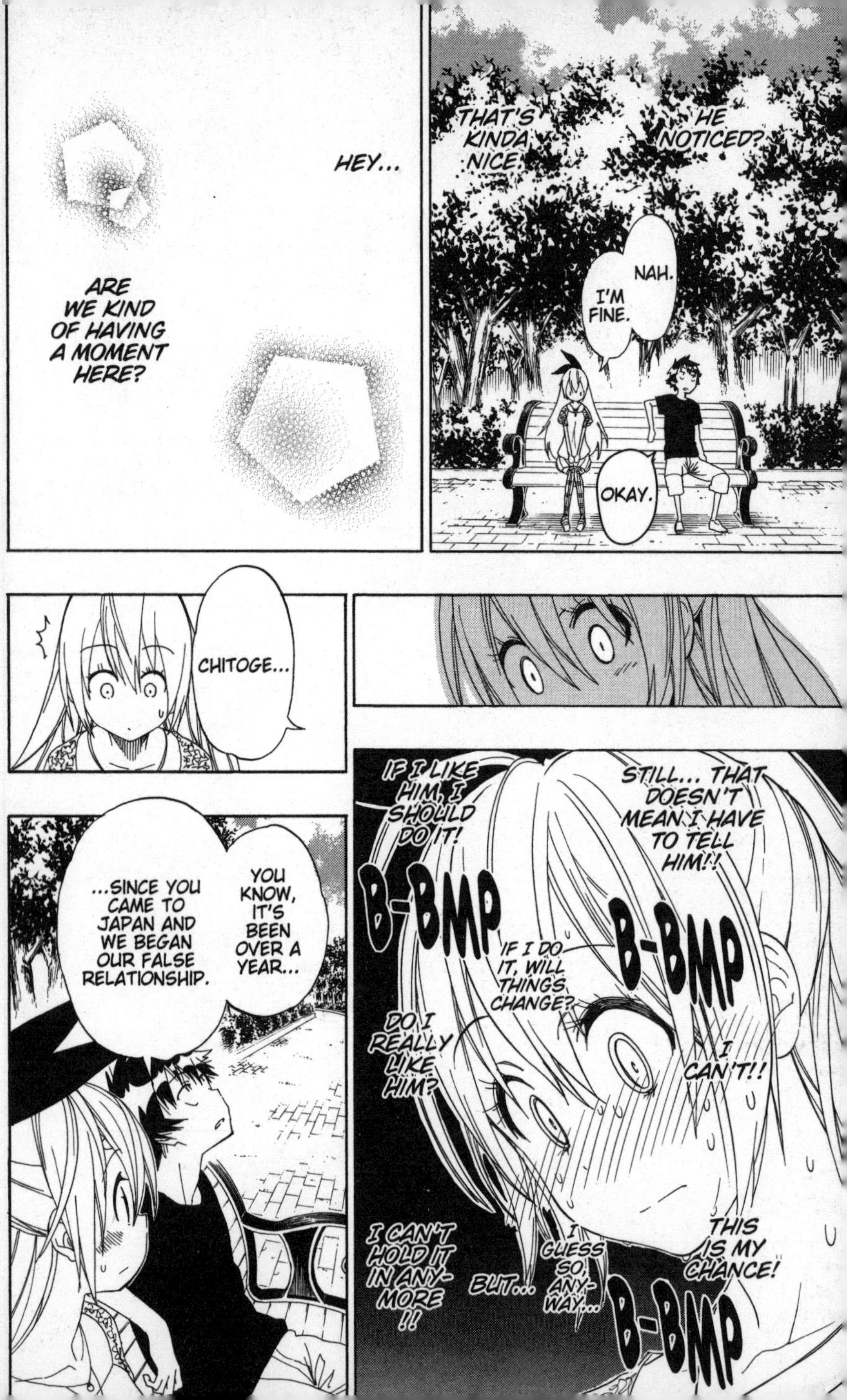
HE NOTICED?
THAT'S KINDA NICE.
NAH.
I'M FINE.
OKAY.
HEY...
ARE WE KIND OF HAVING A MOMENT HERE?
CHITOGE...
STILL... THAT DOESN'T MEAN I HAVE TO TELL HIM!!
IF I LIKE HIM, I SHOULD DO IT!
B-BMP
B-BMP
IF I DO IT, WILL THINGS CHANGE?
I CAN'T!!
DO I REALLY LIKE HIM?
THIS IS MY CHANCE!
I GUESS SO, ANYWAY...
BUT...
I CAN'T HOLD IT IN ANYMORE!!
B-BMP
YOU KNOW, IT'S BEEN OVER A YEAR...
...SINCE YOU CAME TO JAPAN AND WE BEGAN OUR FALSE RELATIONSHIP.

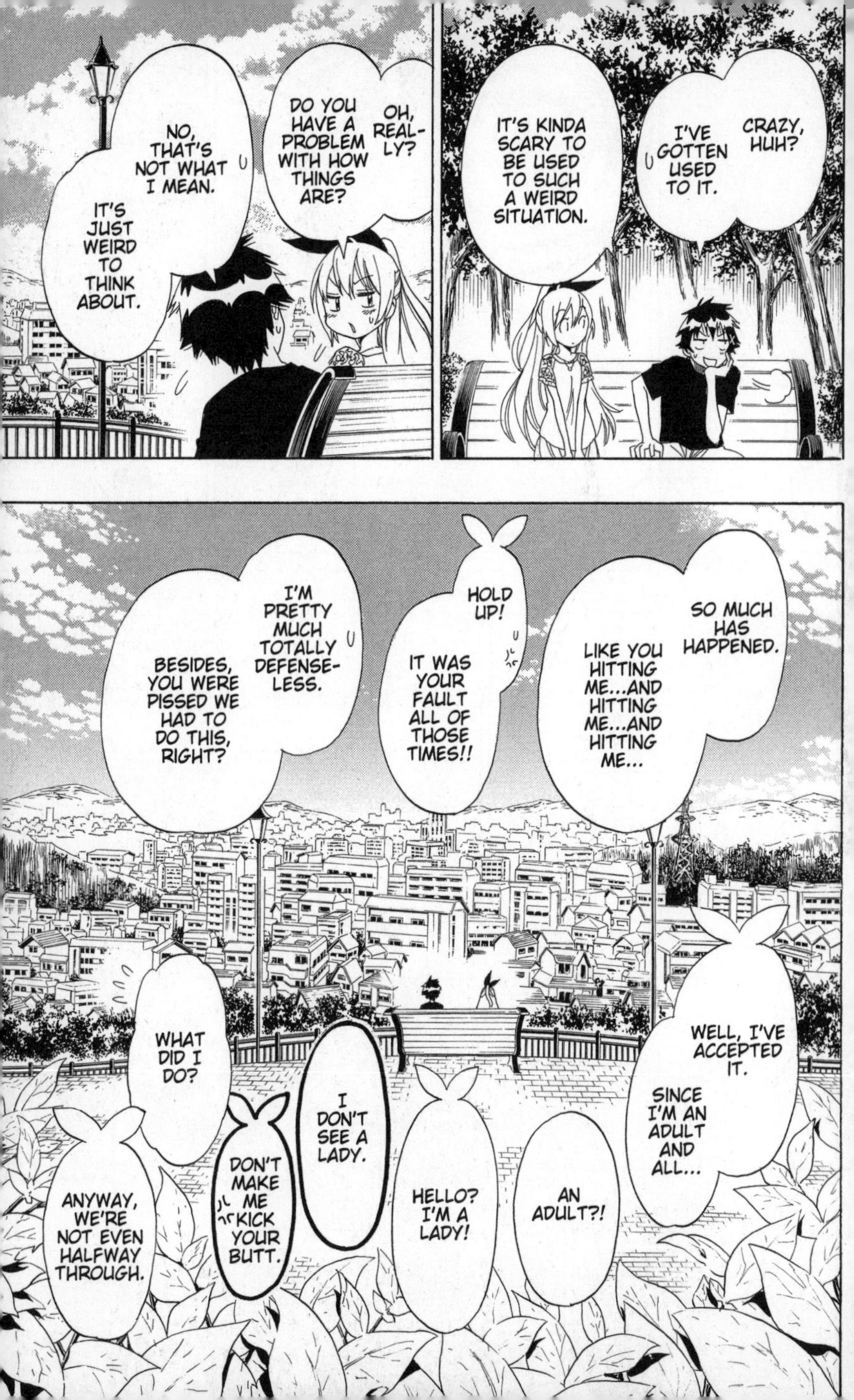
CRAZY, HUH?
I'VE GOTTEN USED TO IT.
IT'S KINDA SCARY TO BE USED TO SUCH A WEIRD SITUATION.
OH, REALLY?
DO YOU HAVE A PROBLEM WITH HOW THINGS ARE?
NO, THAT'S NOT WHAT I MEAN.
IT'S JUST WEIRD TO THINK ABOUT.
SO MUCH HAS HAPPENED.
LIKE YOU HITTING ME...AND HITTING ME...AND HITTING ME...
HOLD UP!
IT WAS YOUR FAULT ALL OF THOSE TIMES!!
I'M PRETTY MUCH TOTALLY DEFENSELESS.
BESIDES, YOU WERE PISSED WE HAD TO DO THIS, RIGHT?
WELL, I'VE ACCEPTED IT.
SINCE I'M AN ADULT AND ALL...
AN ADULT?!
HELLO? I'M A LADY!
I DON'T SEE A LADY.
DON'T MAKE ME KICK YOUR BUTT.
WHAT DID I DO?
ANYWAY, WE'RE NOT EVEN HALFWAY THROUGH.

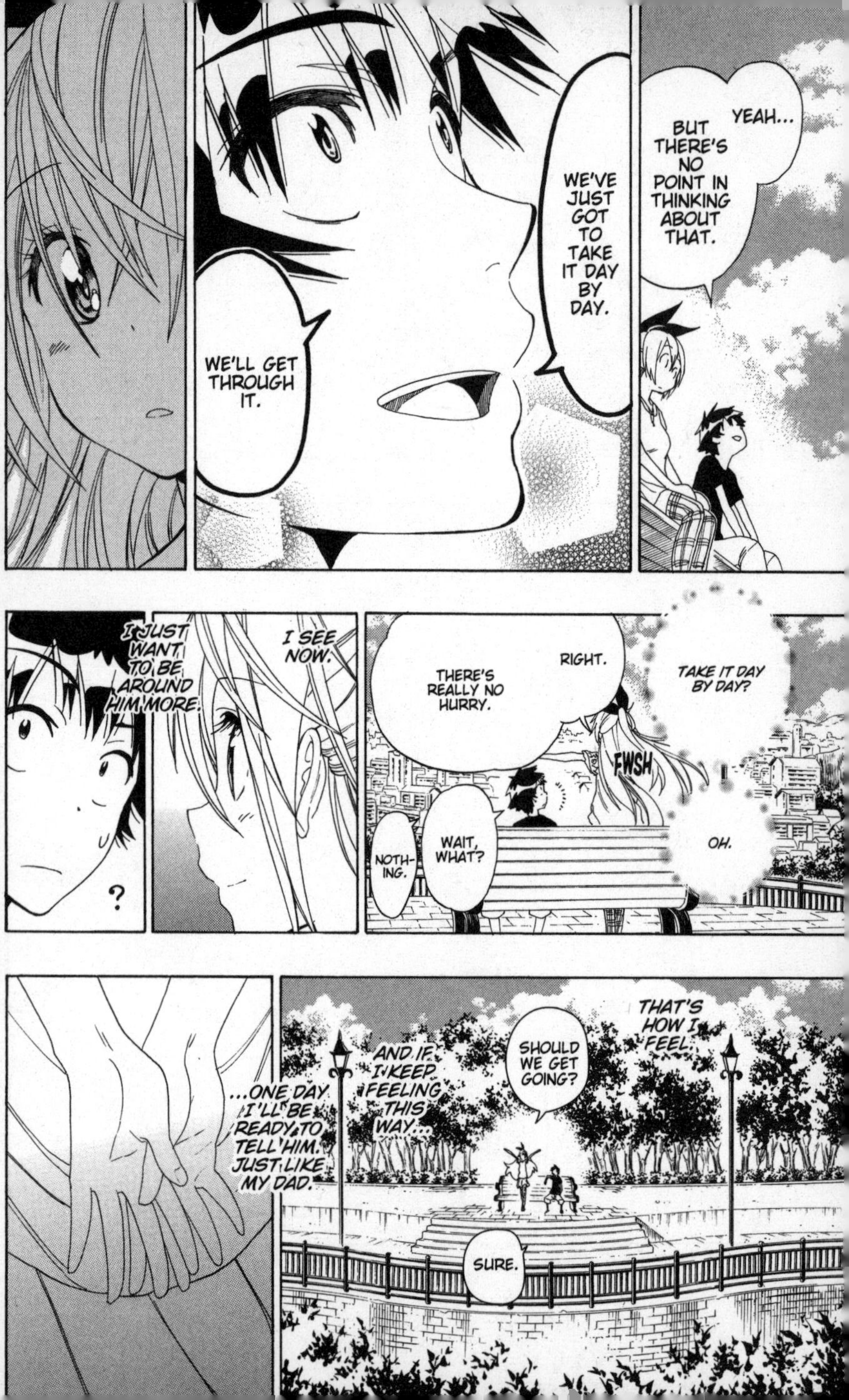
YEAH...
BUT THERE'S NO POINT IN THINKING ABOUT THAT.
WE'VE JUST GOT TO TAKE IT DAY BY DAY.
WE'LL GET THROUGH IT.
TAKE IT DAY BY DAY?
OH.
RIGHT.
THERE'S REALLY NO HURRY.
FWSH
WAIT, WHAT?
NOTH-ING.
I SEE NOW.
I JUST WANT TO BE AROUND HIM MORE.
?
THAT'S HOW I FEEL.
SHOULD WE GET GOING?
AND IF I KEEP FEELING THIS WAY...
SURE.
...ONE DAY I'LL BE READY TO TELL HIM. JUST LIKE MY DAD.

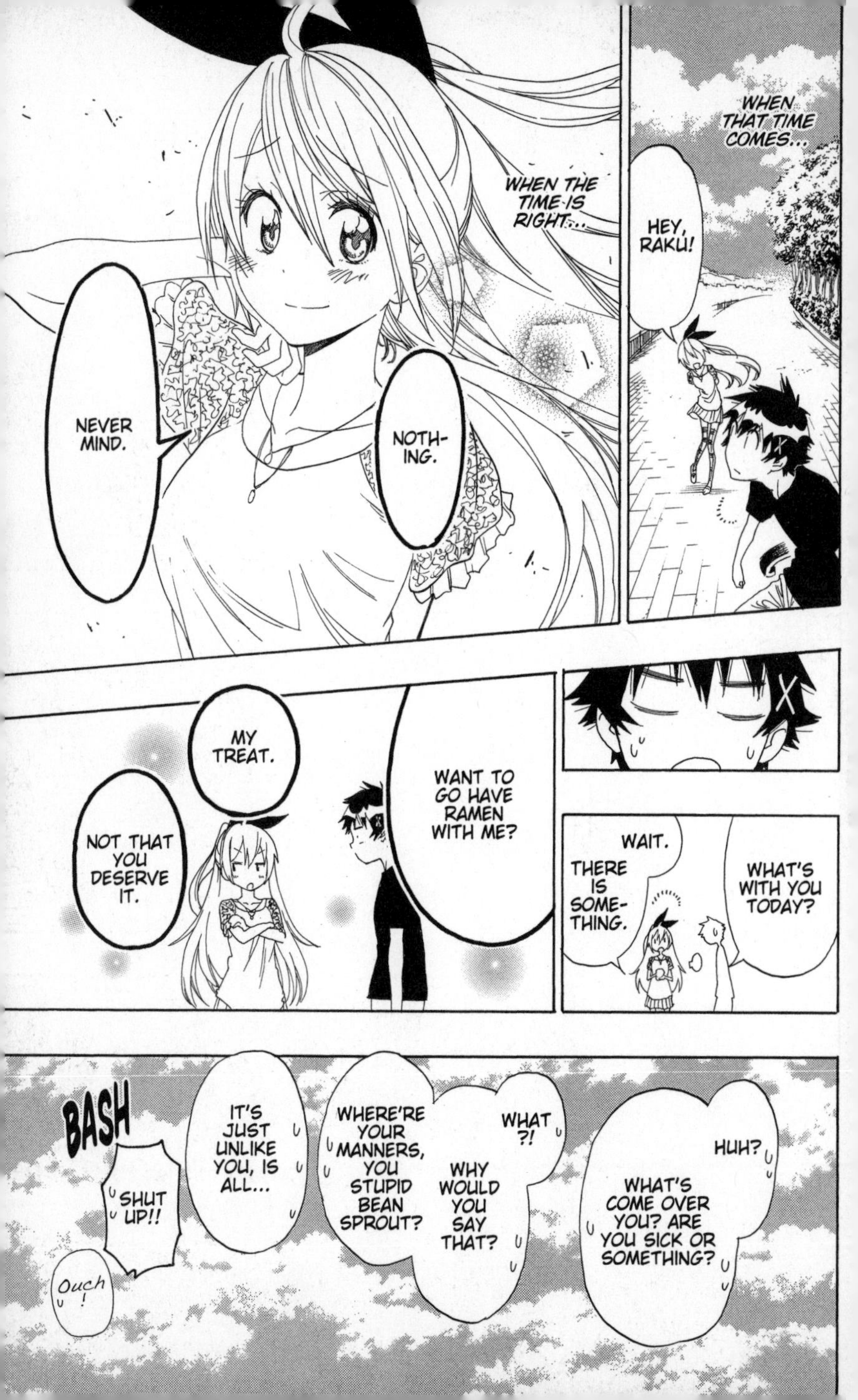
WHEN THAT TIME COMES...
HEY, RAKU!
WHEN THE TIME IS RIGHT...
NOTH-ING.
NEVER MIND.
WHAT'S WITH YOU TODAY?
WAIT.
THERE IS SOME-THING.
WANT TO GO HAVE RAMEN WITH ME?
MY TREAT.
NOT THAT YOU DESERVE IT.
HUH?
WHAT'S COME OVER YOU? ARE YOU SICK OR SOMETHING?
WHAT?!
WHY WOULD YOU SAY THAT?
WHERE'RE YOUR MANNERS, YOU STUPID BEAN SPROUT?
IT'S JUST UNLIKE YOU, IS ALL...
BASH
SHUT UP!!
Ouch!

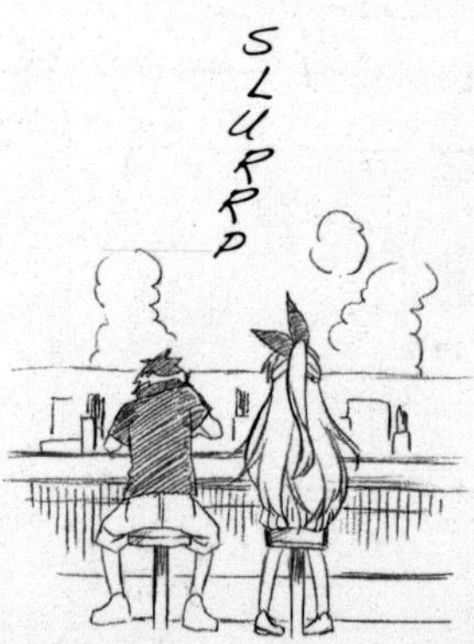
SLURRP

Chapter 101: Cake Shop

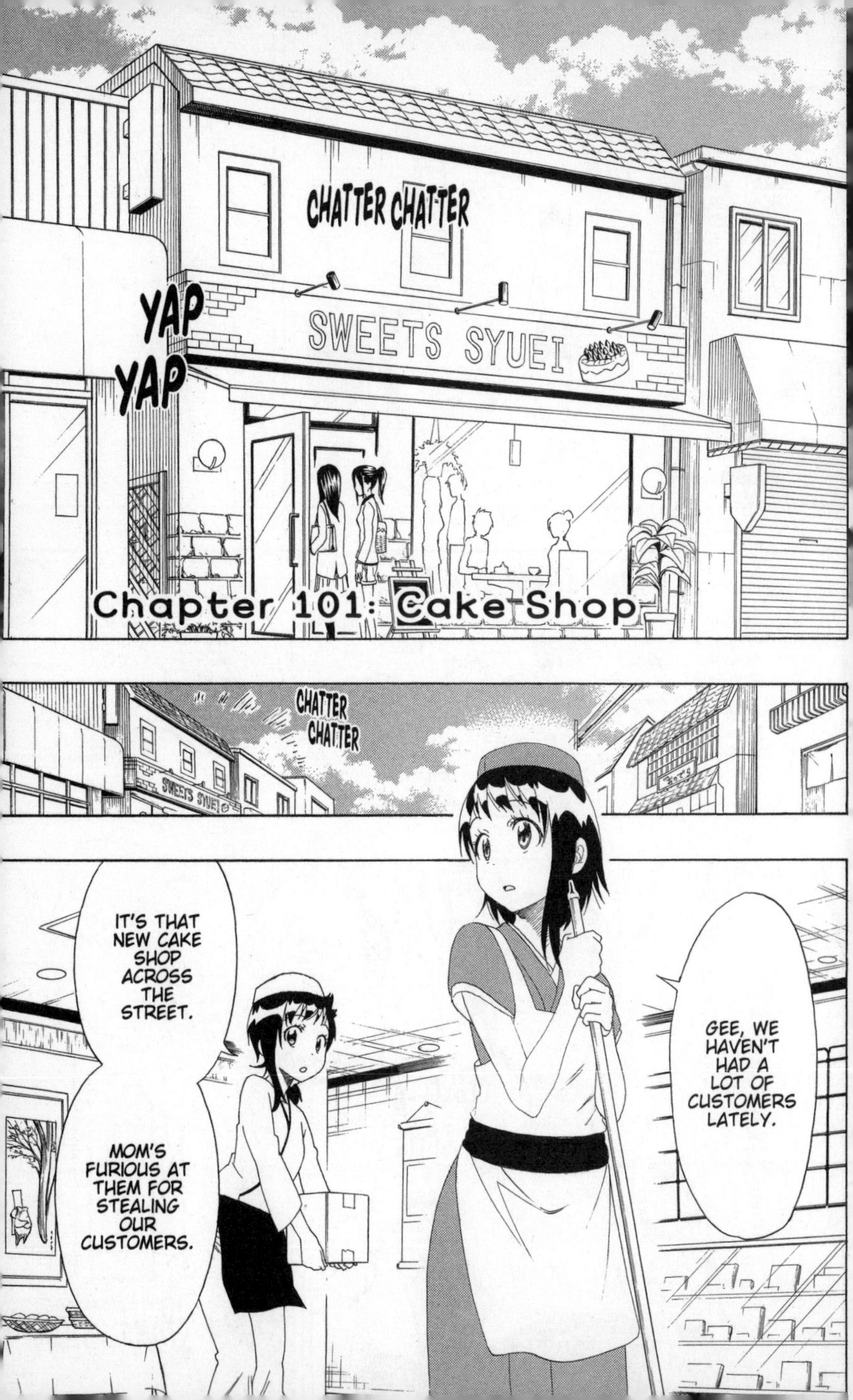
CHATTER CHATTER
SWEETS SYUEI
YAP YAP
CHATTER CHATTER
SWEETS SYUEI
GEE, WE HAVEN'T HAD A LOT OF CUSTOMERS LATELY.
IT'S THAT NEW CAKE SHOP ACROSS THE STREET.
MOM'S FURIOUS AT THEM FOR STEALING OUR CUSTOMERS.

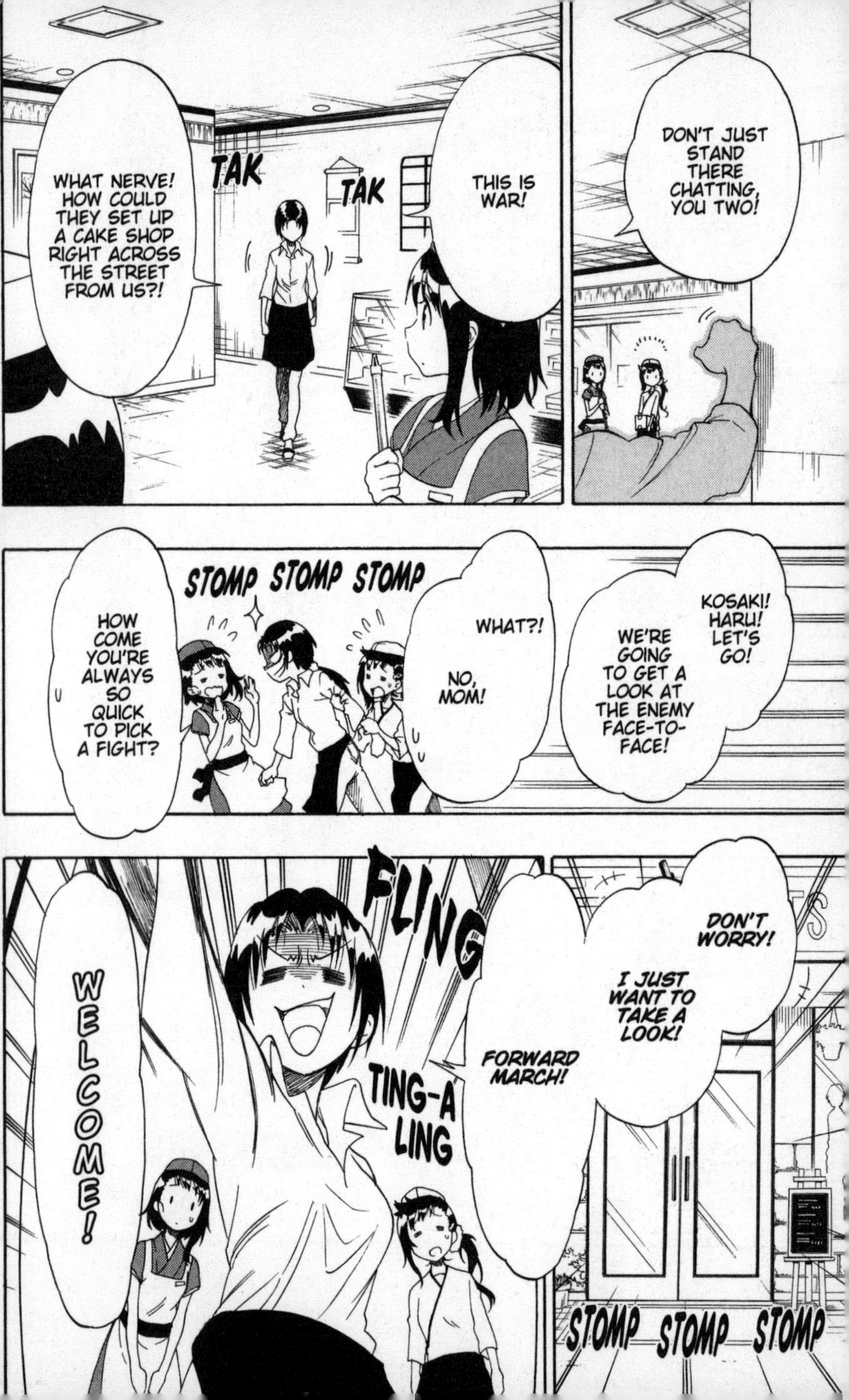
DON'T JUST STAND THERE CHATTING, YOU TWO!
THIS IS WAR!
TAK
TAK
WHAT NERVE! HOW COULD THEY SET UP A CAKE SHOP RIGHT ACROSS THE STREET FROM US?!
KOSAKI! HARU! LET'S GO!
WE'RE GOING TO GET A LOOK AT THE ENEMY FACE-TO-FACE!
WHAT?!
NO, MOM!
STOMP STOMP STOMP
HOW COME YOU'RE ALWAYS SO QUICK TO PICK A FIGHT?
DON'T WORRY!
I JUST WANT TO TAKE A LOOK!
FORWARD MARCH!
STOMP STOMP STOMP
FLING
TING-A LING
WELCOME!

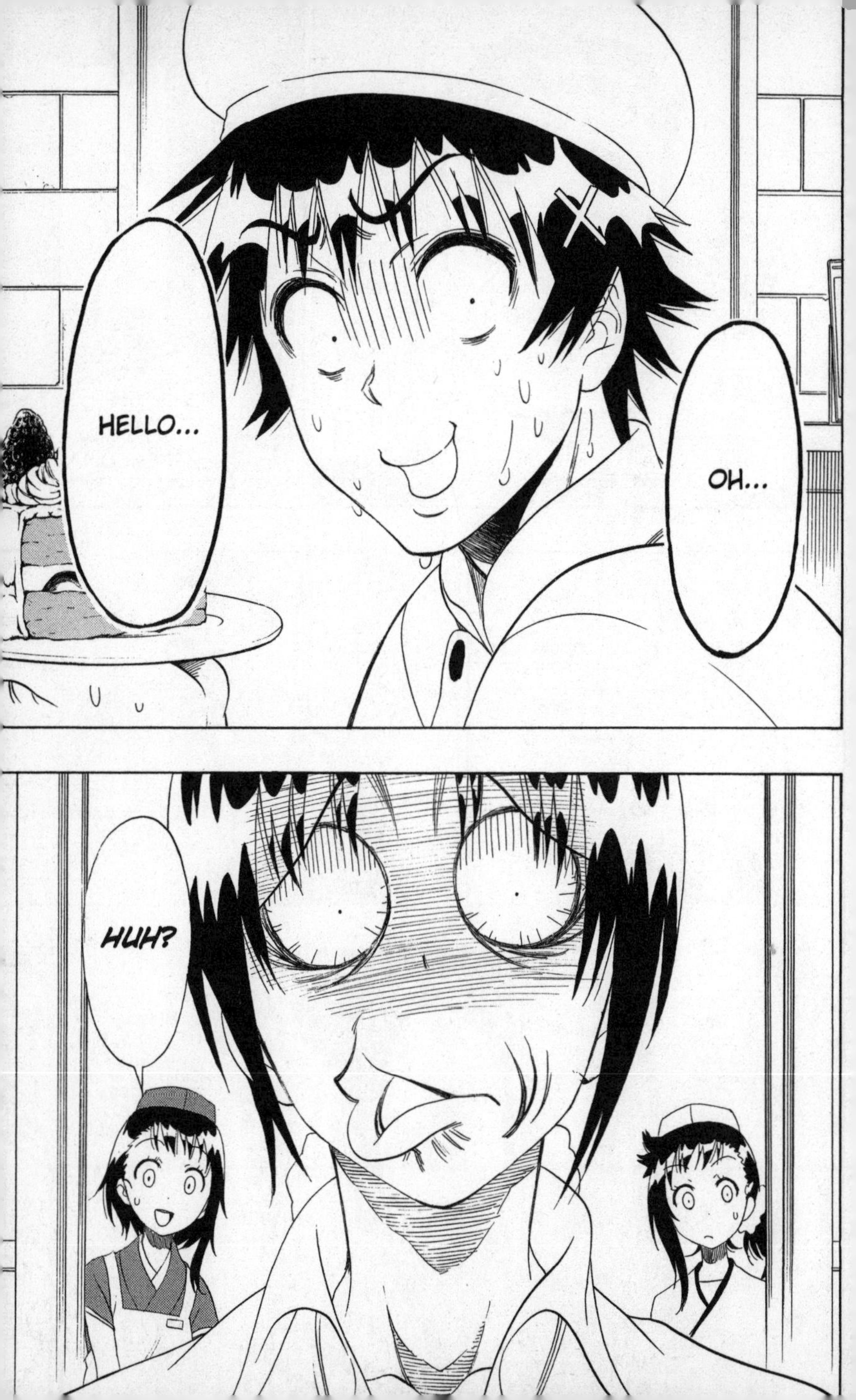
OH...
HELLO...
HUH?

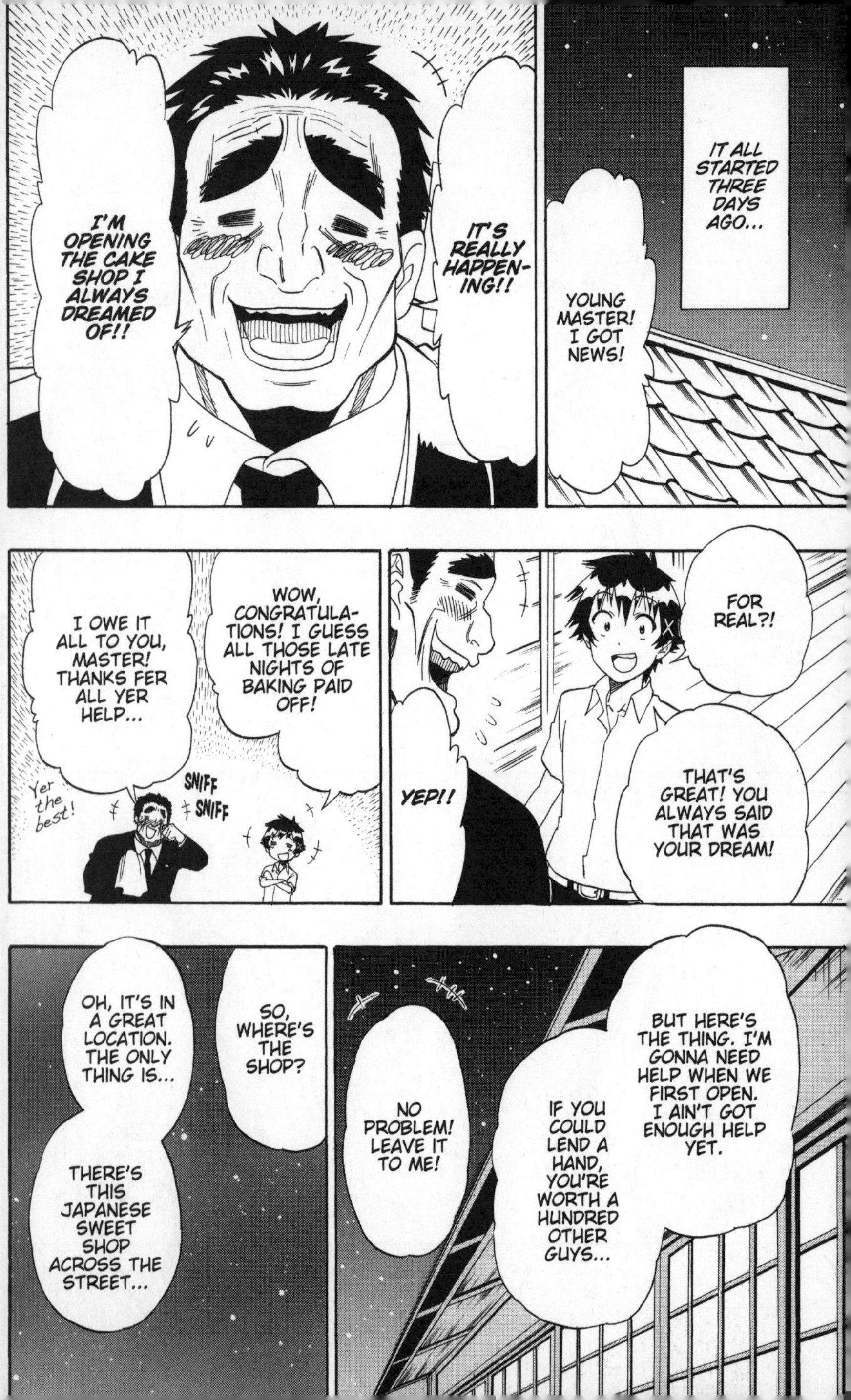
IT ALL STARTED THREE DAYS AGO...
YOUNG MASTER! I GOT NEWS!
IT'S REALLY HAPPENING!!
I'M OPENING THE CAKE SHOP I ALWAYS DREAMED OF!!
FOR REAL?!
THAT'S GREAT! YOU ALWAYS SAID THAT WAS YOUR DREAM!
YEP!!
WOW, CONGRATULATIONS! I GUESS ALL THOSE LATE NIGHTS OF BAKING PAID OFF!
I OWE IT ALL TO YOU, MASTER! THANKS FER ALL YER HELP...
SNIFF
SNIFF
Yer the best!
BUT HERE'S THE THING. I'M GONNA NEED HELP WHEN WE FIRST OPEN. I AIN'T GOT ENOUGH HELP YET.
IF YOU COULD LEND A HAND, YOU'RE WORTH A HUNDRED OTHER GUYS...
NO PROBLEM! LEAVE IT TO ME!
SO, WHERE'S THE SHOP?
OH, IT'S IN A GREAT LOCATION. THE ONLY THING IS...
THERE'S THIS JAPANESE SWEET SHOP ACROSS THE STREET...

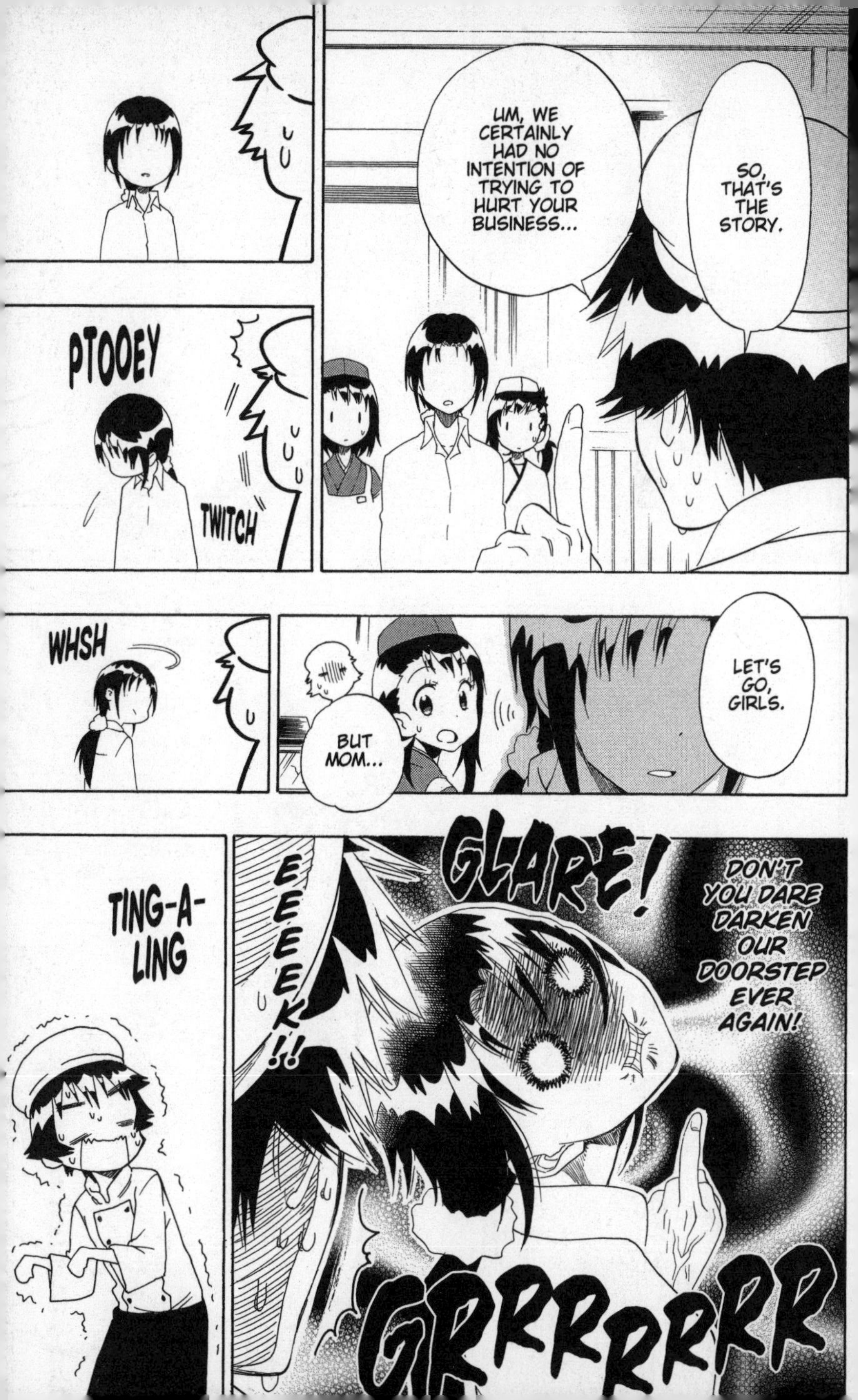
SO, THAT'S THE STORY.
UM, WE CERTAINLY HAD NO INTENTION OF TRYING TO HURT YOUR BUSINESS...
PTOOEY
TWITCH
LET'S GO, GIRLS.
BUT MOM...
WHSH
DON'T YOU DARE DARKEN OUR DOORSTEP EVER AGAIN!
GLARE!
EEEEEK!!
GRRRRRRR
TING-A-LING

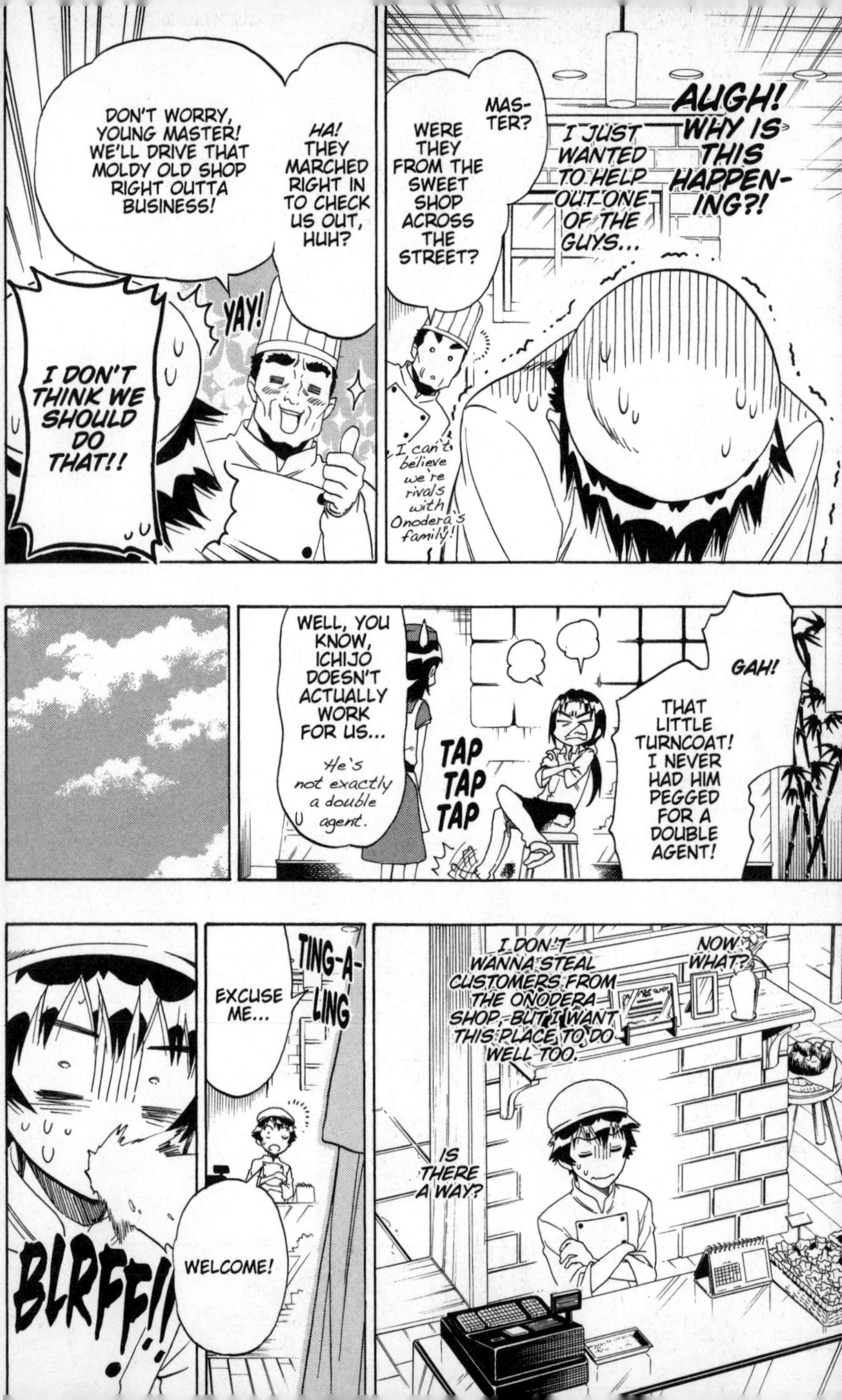
AUGH! WHY IS THIS HAPPEN-ING?!
I JUST WANTED TO HELP OUT ONE OF THE GUYS...
MAS-TER?
WERE THEY FROM THE SWEET SHOP ACROSS THE STREET?
I can't believe we're rivals with Onodera's family!
HA! THEY MARCHED RIGHT IN TO CHECK US OUT, HUH?
DON'T WORRY, YOUNG MASTER! WE'LL DRIVE THAT MOLDY OLD SHOP RIGHT OUTTA BUSINESS!
YAY!
I DON'T THINK WE SHOULD DO THAT!!
GAH!
THAT LITTLE TURNCOAT! I NEVER HAD HIM PEGGED FOR A DOUBLE AGENT!
TAP TAP TAP
WELL, YOU KNOW, ICHIJO DOESN'T ACTUALLY WORK FOR US...
He's not exactly a double agent.
NOW WHAT?
I DON'T WANNA STEAL CUSTOMERS FROM THE ONODERA SHOP, BUT I WANT THIS PLACE TO DO WELL TOO.
IS THERE A WAY?
TING-A-LING
EXCUSE ME...
WELCOME!
BLRFF!!

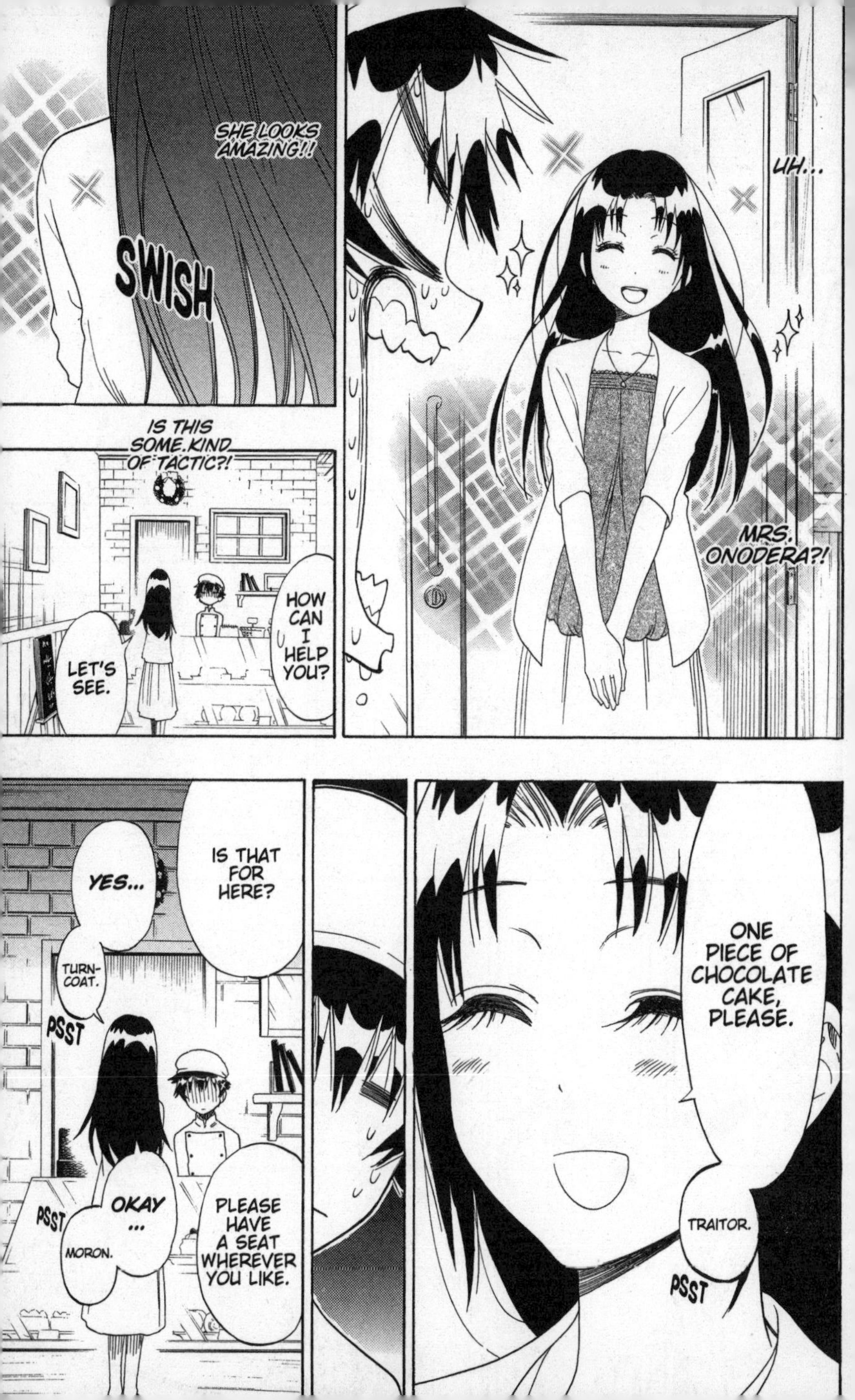
UH...
MRS. ONODERA?!
SHE LOOKS AMAZING!!
SWISH
IS THIS SOME KIND OF TACTIC?!
HOW CAN I HELP YOU?
LET'S SEE.
ONE PIECE OF CHOCOLATE CAKE, PLEASE.
TRAITOR.
PSST
IS THAT FOR HERE?
YES...
TURN-COAT.
PSST
PLEASE HAVE A SEAT WHEREVER YOU LIKE.
OKAY...
PSST
MORON.

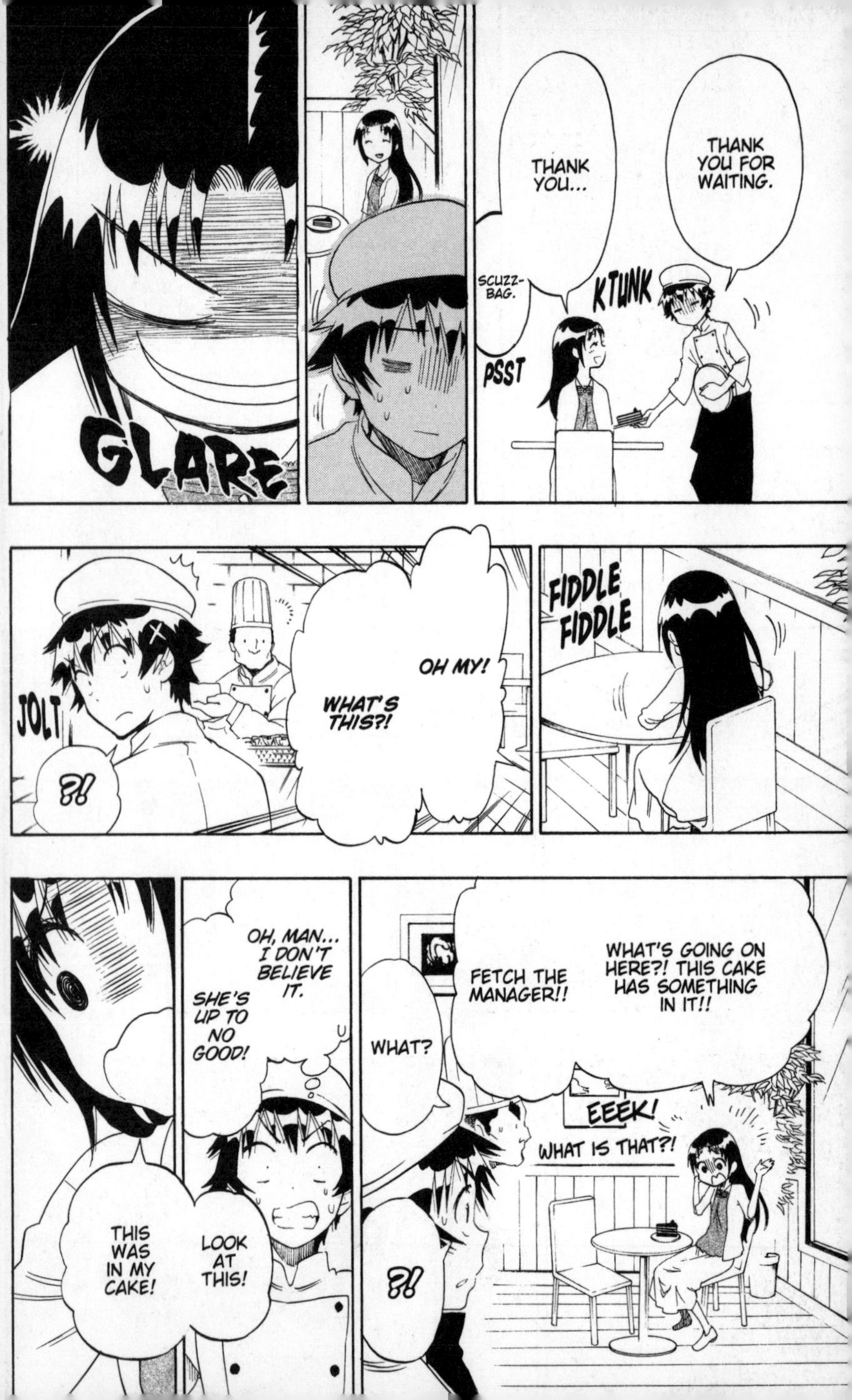
THANK YOU FOR WAITING.
KTUNK
THANK YOU...
SCUZZ-BAG.
PSST
GLARE
FIDDLE FIDDLE
OH MY!
WHAT'S THIS?!
JOLT
?!
WHAT'S GOING ON HERE?! THIS CAKE HAS SOMETHING IN IT!!
FETCH THE MANAGER!!
EEEK!
WHAT IS THAT?!
WHAT?
?!
OH, MAN... I DON'T BELIEVE IT.
SHE'S UP TO NO GOOD!
LOOK AT THIS!
THIS WAS IN MY CAKE!

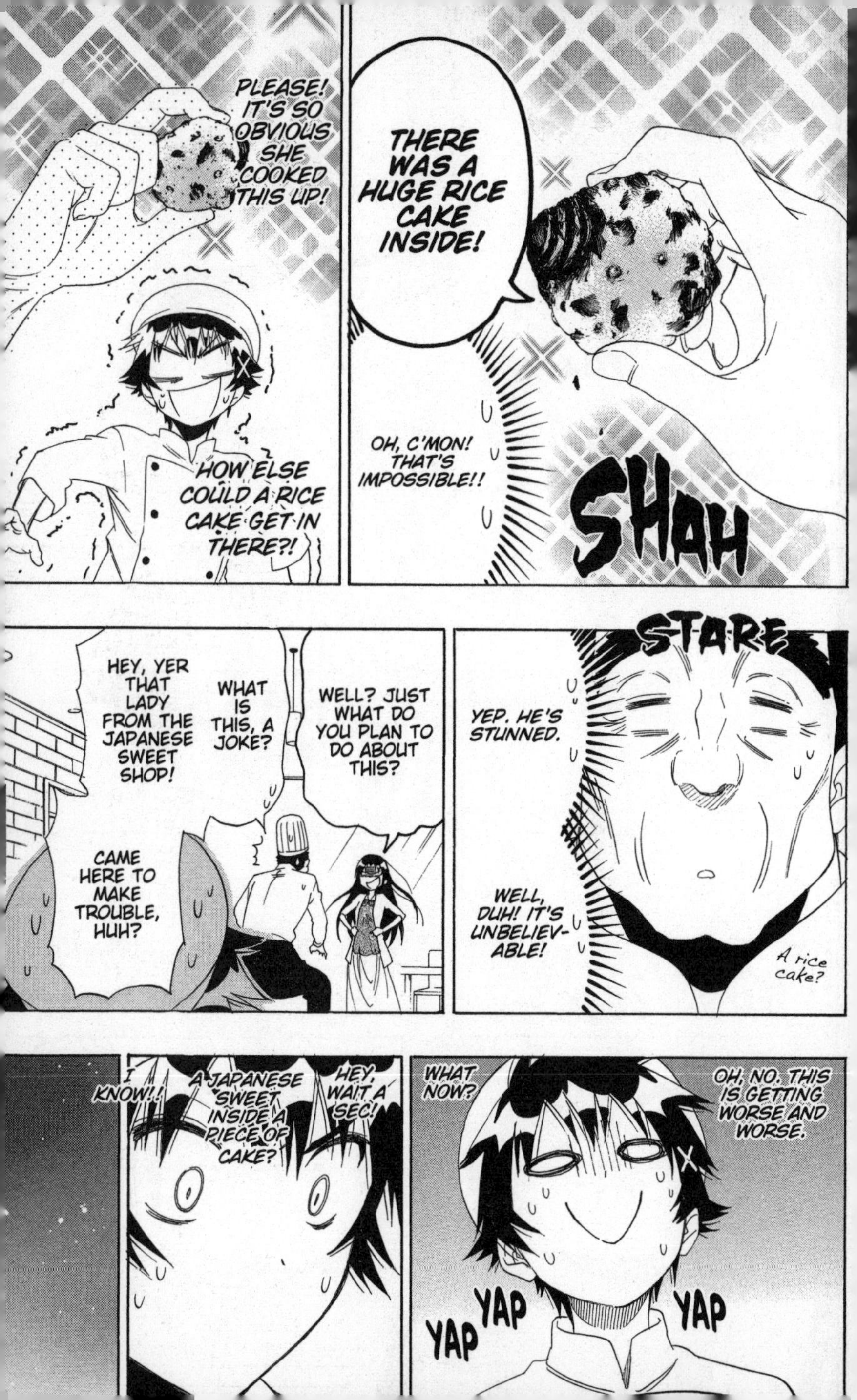
THERE WAS A HUGE RICE CAKE INSIDE!
OH, C'MON! THAT'S IMPOSSIBLE!!
SHAH
PLEASE! IT'S SO OBVIOUS SHE COOKED THIS UP!
HOW ELSE COULD A RICE CAKE GET IN THERE?!
STARE
YEP. HE'S STUNNED.
WELL, DUH! IT'S UNBELIEV-ABLE!
A rice cake?
WELL? JUST WHAT DO YOU PLAN TO DO ABOUT THIS?
WHAT IS THIS, A JOKE?
HEY, YER THAT LADY FROM THE JAPANESE SWEET SHOP!
CAME HERE TO MAKE TROUBLE, HUH?
OH, NO. THIS IS GETTING WORSE AND WORSE.
WHAT NOW?
YAP
YAP
YAP
HEY, WAIT A SEC!
A JAPANESE SWEET INSIDE A PIECE OF CAKE?
I KNOW!!

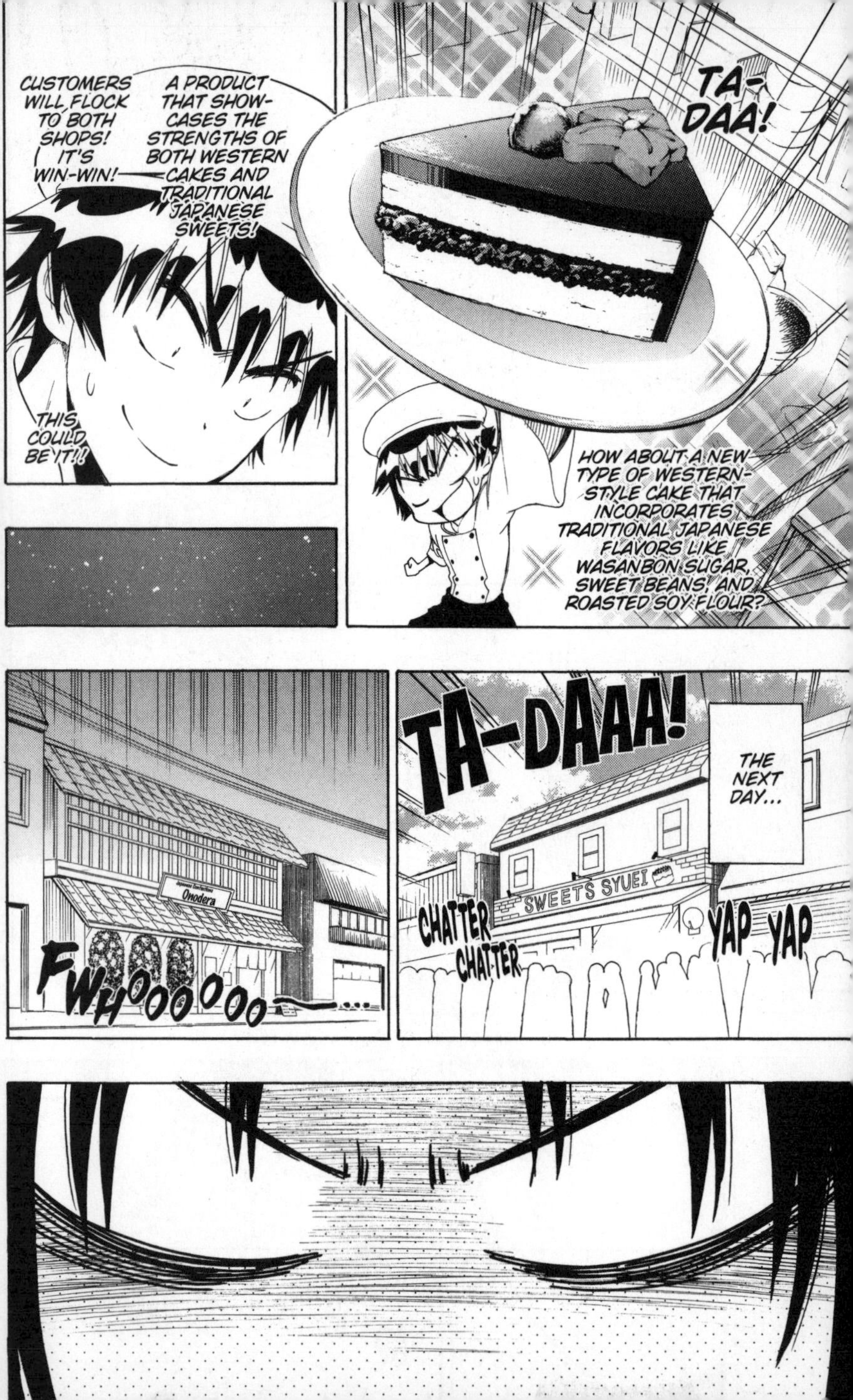
TA-DAA!
HOW ABOUT A NEW TYPE OF WESTERN-STYLE CAKE THAT INCORPORATES TRADITIONAL JAPANESE FLAVORS LIKE WASANBON SUGAR, SWEET BEANS, AND ROASTED SOY FLOUR?
A PRODUCT THAT SHOWCASES THE STRENGTHS OF BOTH WESTERN CAKES AND TRADITIONAL JAPANESE SWEETS!
CUSTOMERS WILL FLOCK TO BOTH SHOPS! IT'S WIN-WIN!
THIS COULD BE IT!!
TA-DAAA!
THE NEXT DAY...
YAP YAP
SWEETS SYUEI
CHATTER CHATTER
Onodera
FWHOOOOOO

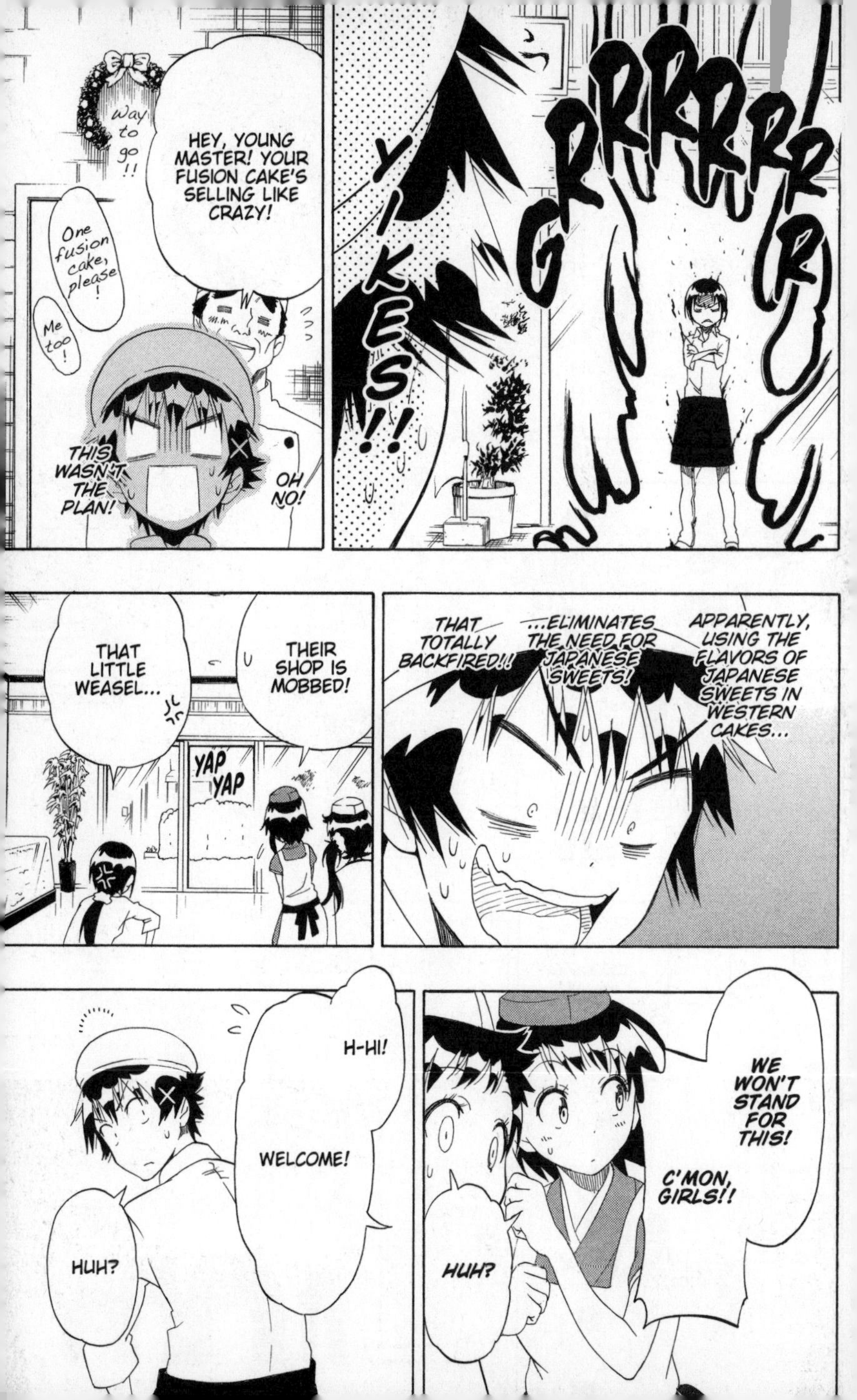
GRRRRRRRR
YI-KES!!
HEY, YOUNG MASTER! YOUR FUSION CAKE'S SELLING LIKE CRAZY!
Way to go!!
One fusion cake, please!
Me too!
OH NO!
THIS WASN'T THE PLAN!
APPARENTLY, USING THE FLAVORS OF JAPANESE SWEETS IN WESTERN CAKES...
...ELIMINATES THE NEED FOR JAPANESE SWEETS!
THAT TOTALLY BACKFIRED!!
THEIR SHOP IS MOBBED!
YAP YAP
THAT LITTLE WEASEL...
WE WON'T STAND FOR THIS!
C'MON, GIRLS!!
HUH?
H-HI!
WELCOME!
HUH?

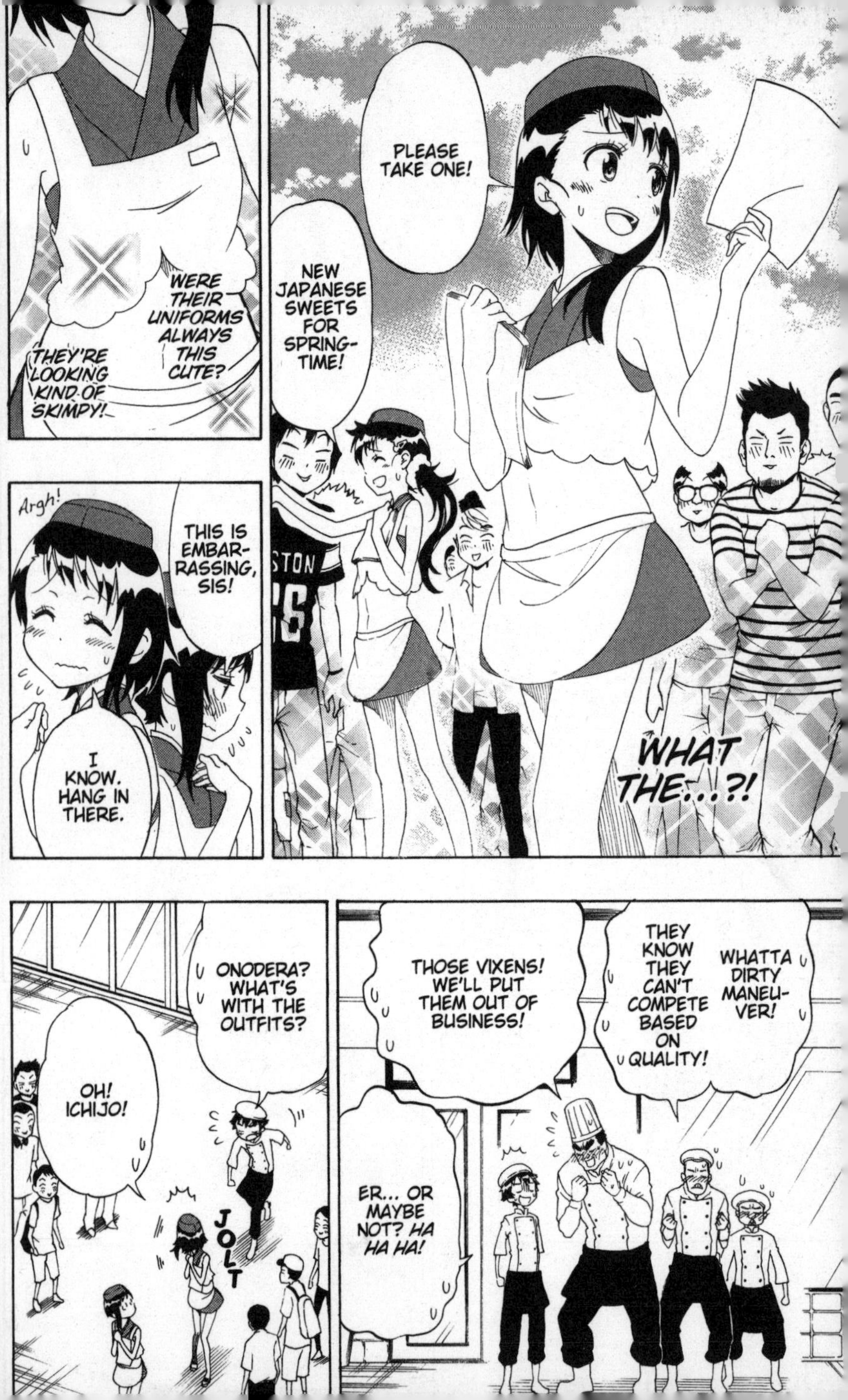
PLEASE TAKE ONE!
NEW JAPANESE SWEETS FOR SPRING-TIME!
WHAT THE...?!
WERE THEIR UNIFORMS ALWAYS THIS CUTE?
THEY'RE LOOKING KIND OF SKIMPY!
Argh!
THIS IS EMBARRASSING, SIS!
I KNOW. HANG IN THERE.
WHATTA DIRTY MANEUVER!
THEY KNOW THEY CAN'T COMPETE BASED ON QUALITY!
THOSE VIXENS! WE'LL PUT THEM OUT OF BUSINESS!
ER... OR MAYBE NOT? HA HA HA!
ONODERA? WHAT'S WITH THE OUTFITS?
OH! ICHIJO!
JOLT

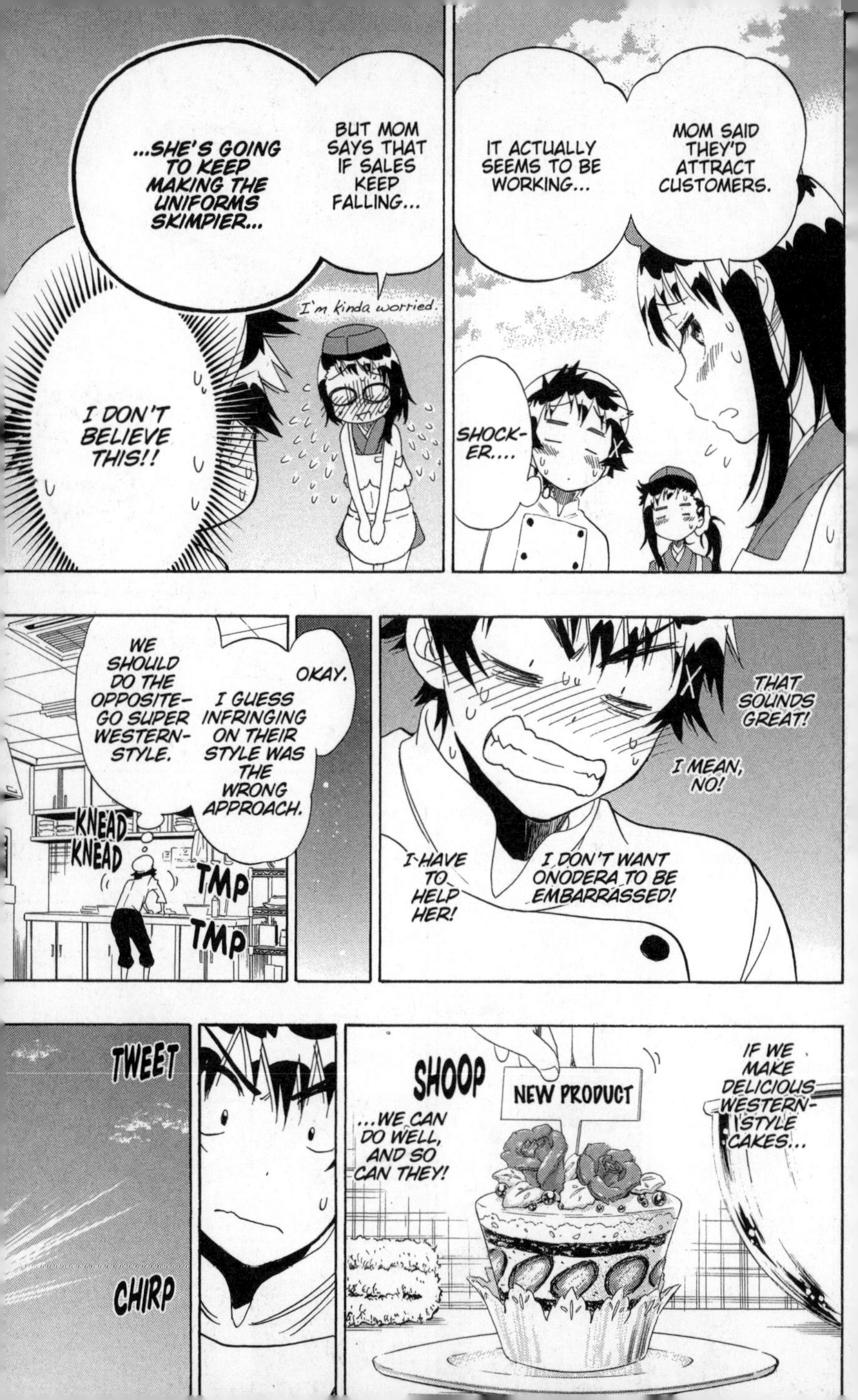
MOM SAID THEY'D ATTRACT CUSTOMERS.
IT ACTUALLY SEEMS TO BE WORKING...
SHOCKER....
BUT MOM SAYS THAT IF SALES KEEP FALLING...
...SHE'S GOING TO KEEP MAKING THE UNIFORMS SKIMPIER...
I'm kinda worried.
I DON'T BELIEVE THIS!!
THAT SOUNDS GREAT!
I MEAN, NO!
I DON'T WANT ONODERA TO BE EMBARRASSED!
I HAVE TO HELP HER!
OKAY.
I GUESS INFRINGING ON THEIR STYLE WAS THE WRONG APPROACH.
WE SHOULD DO THE OPPOSITE- GO SUPER WESTERN-STYLE.
KNEAD KNEAD
TMP
TMP
IF WE MAKE DELICIOUS WESTERN-STYLE CAKES...
SHOOP
NEW PRODUCT
...WE CAN DO WELL, AND SO CAN THEY!
TWEET
CHIRP

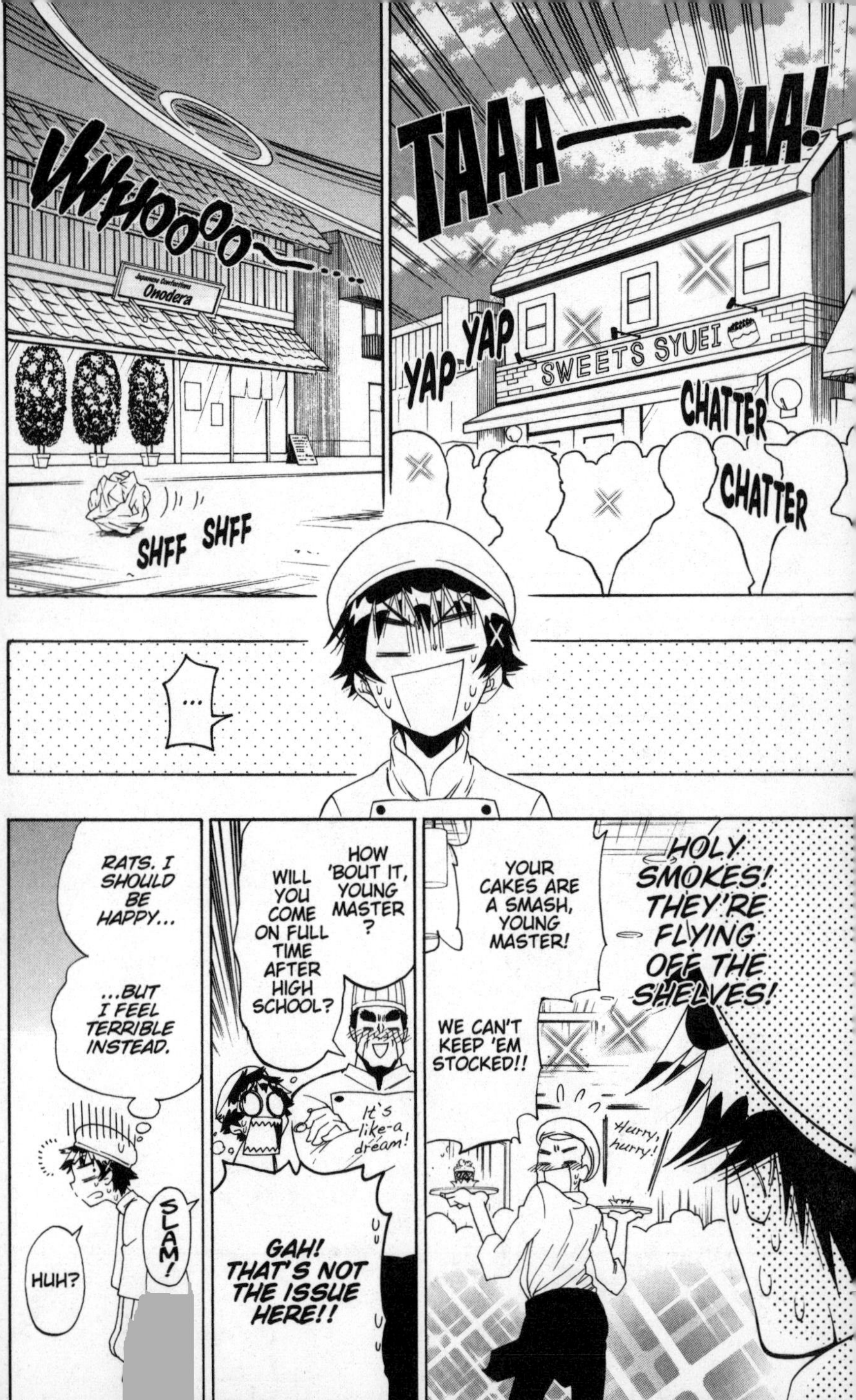
TAAA— DAA!
SWEETS SYUEI
YAP YAP
CHATTER
CHATTER
WHOOOO~...
Japanese Confections
Onodera
SHFF SHFF
...
HOLY SMOKES! THEY'RE FLYING OFF THE SHELVES!
YOUR CAKES ARE A SMASH, YOUNG MASTER!
WE CAN'T KEEP 'EM STOCKED!!
Hurry, hurry!
HOW 'BOUT IT, YOUNG MASTER?
WILL YOU COME ON FULL TIME AFTER HIGH SCHOOL?
It's like-a dream!
GAH! THAT'S NOT THE ISSUE HERE!!
RATS. I SHOULD BE HAPPY...
...BUT I FEEL TERRIBLE INSTEAD.
SLAM!
HUH?

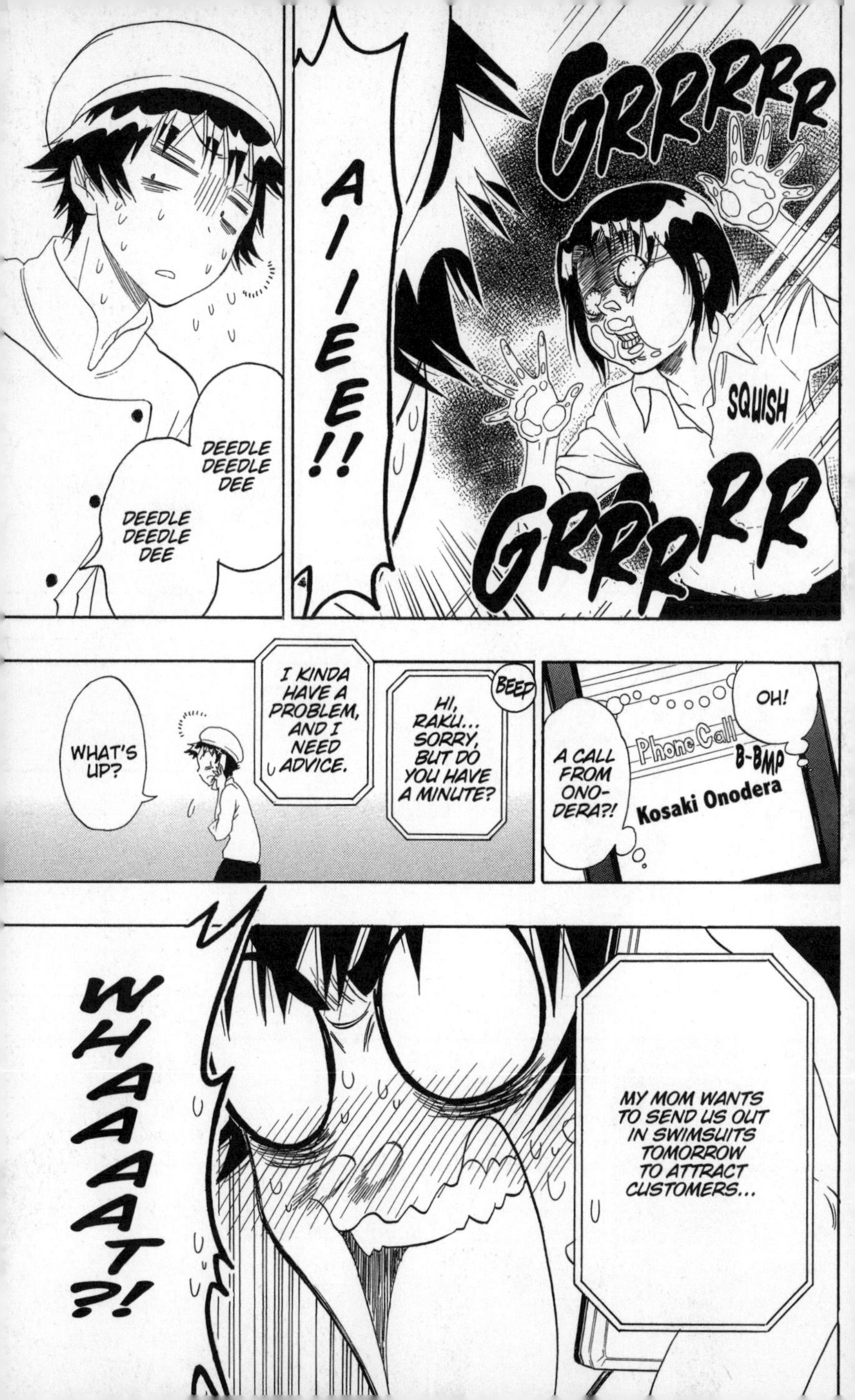
GRRRRR
SQUISH
GRRRRR
AIIEEE!!
DEEDLE DEEDLE DEE
DEEDLE DEEDLE DEE
OH!
Phone Call
B-BMP
Kosaki Onodera
A CALL FROM ONODERA?!
BEEP
HI, RAKU... SORRY, BUT DO YOU HAVE A MINUTE?
I KINDA HAVE A PROBLEM, AND I NEED ADVICE.
WHAT'S UP?
MY MOM WANTS TO SEND US OUT IN SWIMSUITS TOMORROW TO ATTRACT CUSTOMERS...
WHAAAAT?!

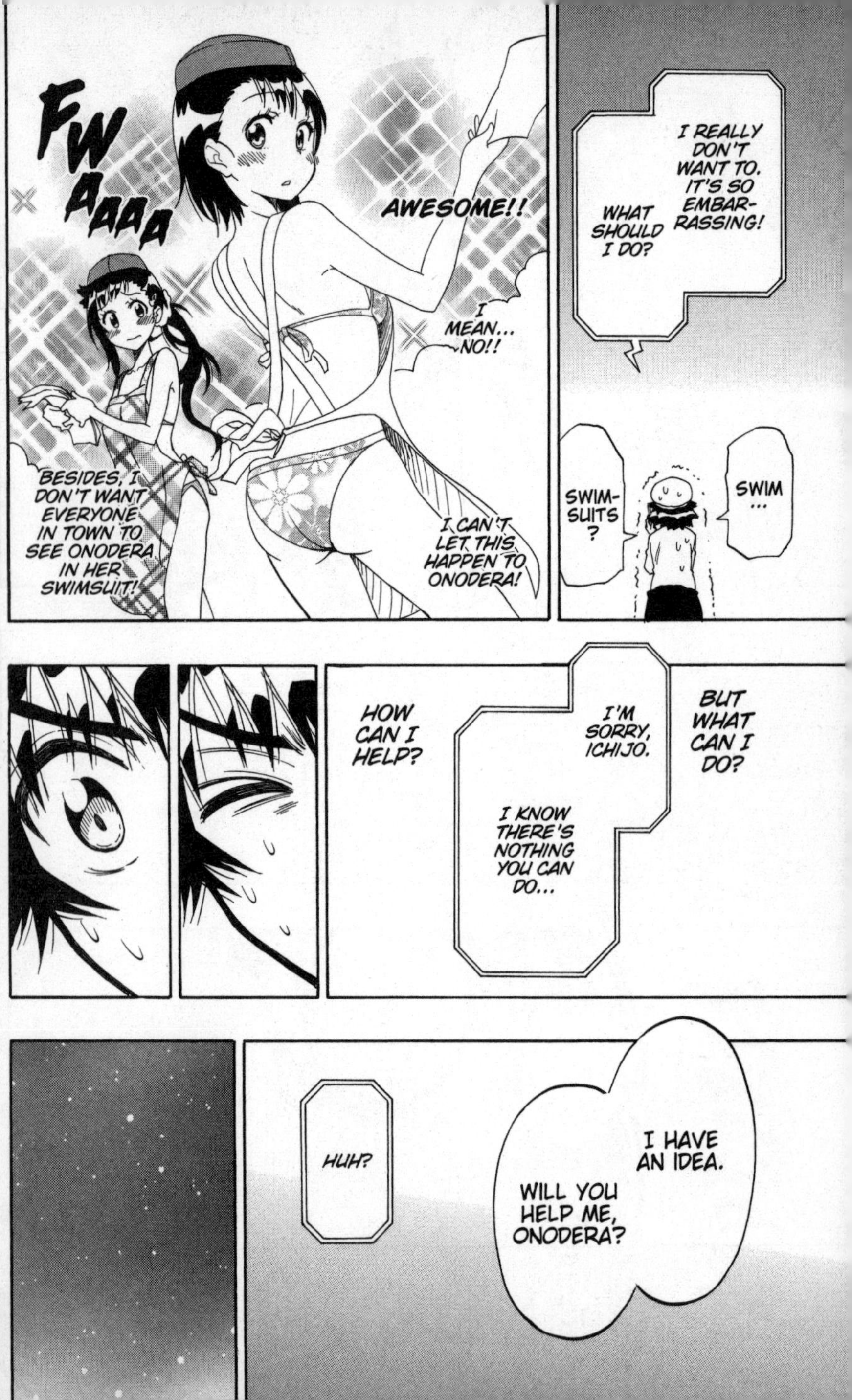
I REALLY DON'T WANT TO. IT'S SO EMBARRASSING!
WHAT SHOULD I DO?
SWIM...
SWIMSUITS?
AWESOME!!
FWAAAA
I MEAN... NO!!
I CAN'T LET THIS HAPPEN TO ONODERA!
BESIDES, I DON'T WANT EVERYONE IN TOWN TO SEE ONODERA IN HER SWIMSUIT!
BUT WHAT CAN I DO?
I'M SORRY, ICHIJO.
I KNOW THERE'S NOTHING YOU CAN DO...
HOW CAN I HELP?
I HAVE AN IDEA.
WILL YOU HELP ME, ONODERA?
HUH?

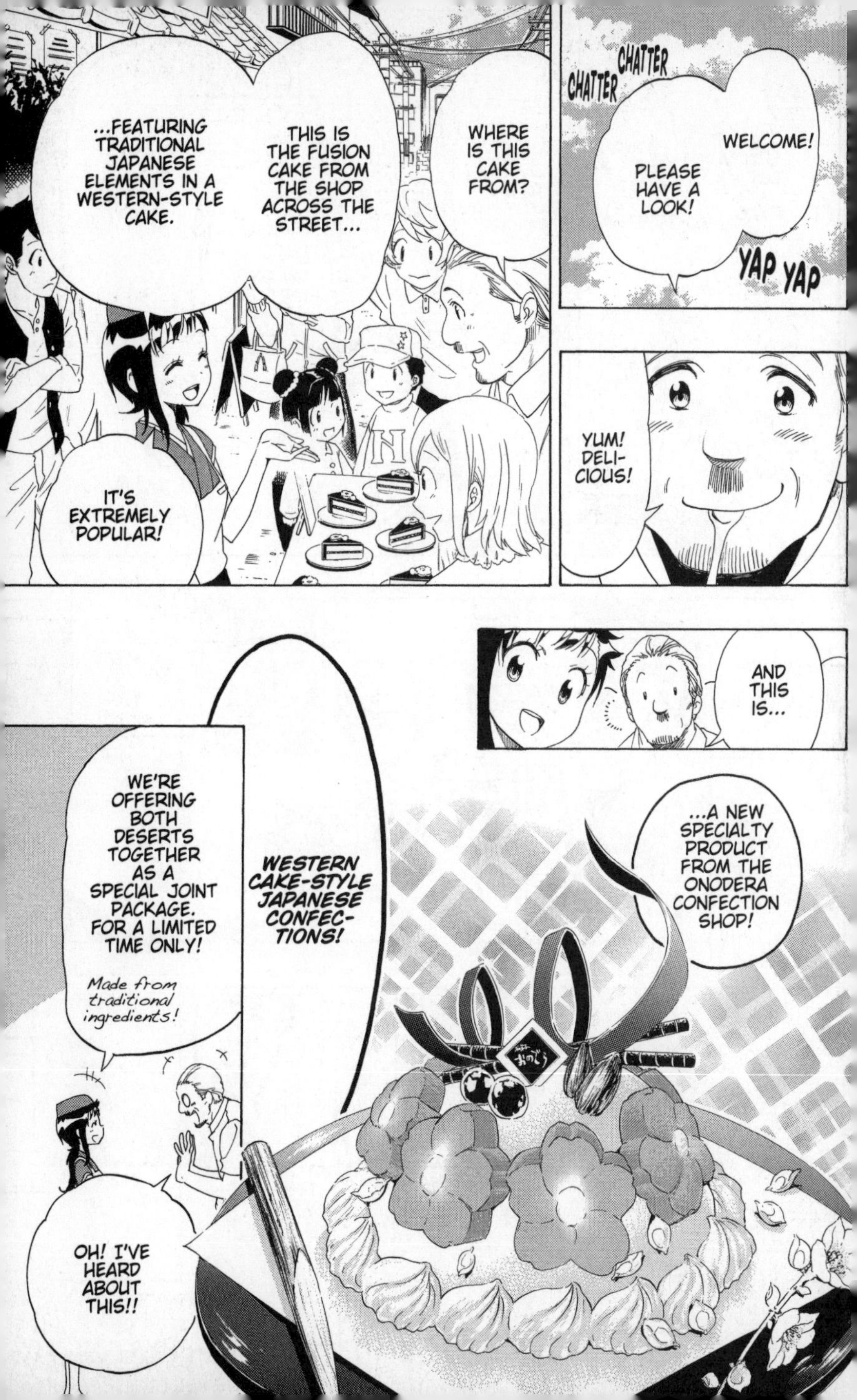
CHATTER CHATTER
WELCOME!
PLEASE HAVE A LOOK!
YAP YAP
YUM! DELI-CIOUS!
WHERE IS THIS CAKE FROM?
THIS IS THE FUSION CAKE FROM THE SHOP ACROSS THE STREET...
...FEATURING TRADITIONAL JAPANESE ELEMENTS IN A WESTERN-STYLE CAKE.
IT'S EXTREMELY POPULAR!
AND THIS IS...
...A NEW SPECIALTY PRODUCT FROM THE ONODERA CONFECTION SHOP!
WESTERN CAKE-STYLE JAPANESE CONFEC-TIONS!
WE'RE OFFERING BOTH DESERTS TOGETHER AS A SPECIAL JOINT PACKAGE. FOR A LIMITED TIME ONLY!
Made from traditional ingredients!
OH! I'VE HEARD ABOUT THIS!!

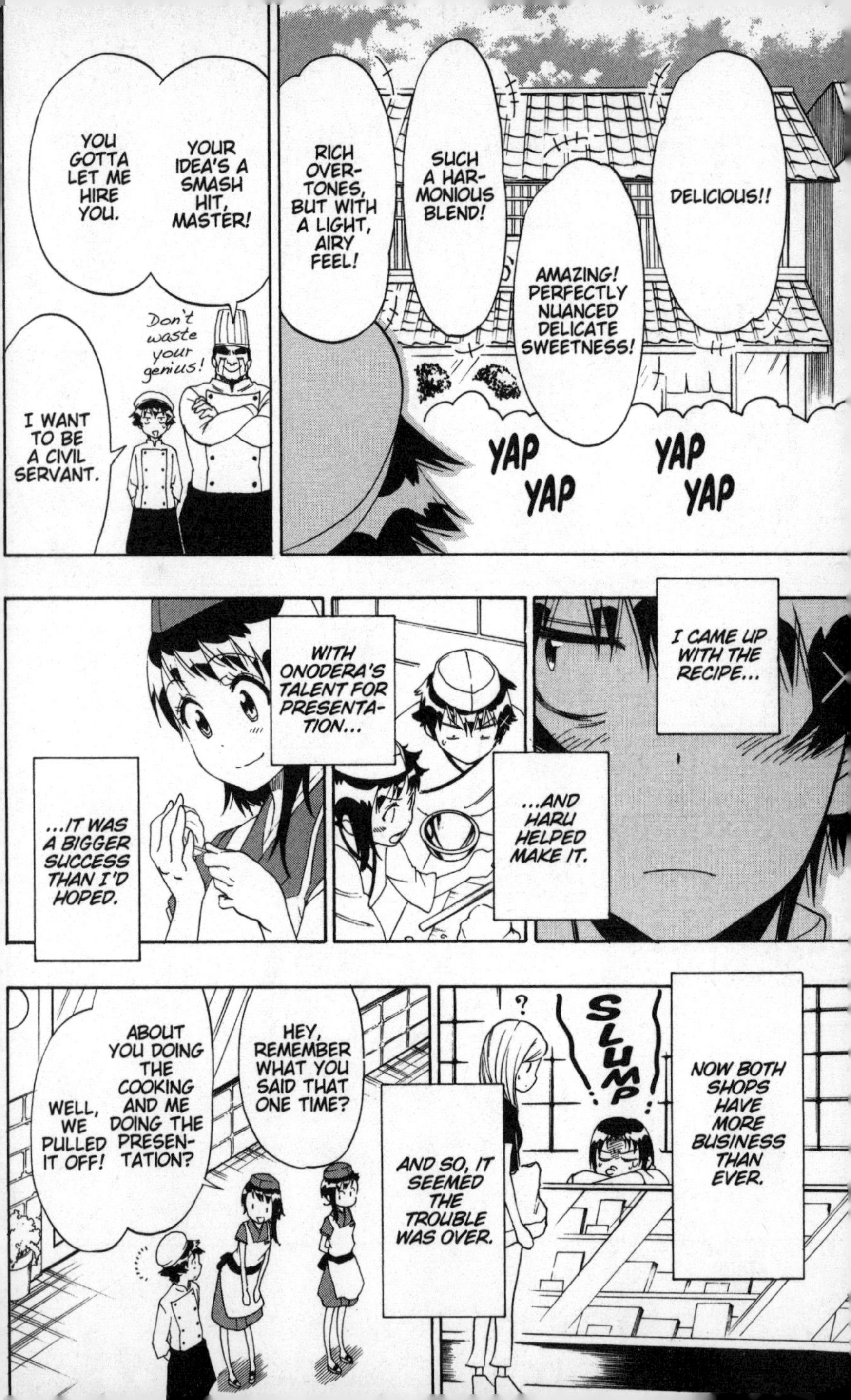
DELICIOUS!!
AMAZING! PERFECTLY NUANCED DELICATE SWEETNESS!
SUCH A HARMONIOUS BLEND!
RICH OVERTONES, BUT WITH A LIGHT, AIRY FEEL!
YAP YAP
YAP YAP
YOUR IDEA'S A SMASH HIT, MASTER!
YOU GOTTA LET ME HIRE YOU.
Don't waste your genius!
I WANT TO BE A CIVIL SERVANT.
I CAME UP WITH THE RECIPE...
WITH ONODERA'S TALENT FOR PRESENTATION...
...AND HARU HELPED MAKE IT.
...IT WAS A BIGGER SUCCESS THAN I'D HOPED.
NOW BOTH SHOPS HAVE MORE BUSINESS THAN EVER.
SLUMP
?
AND SO, IT SEEMED THE TROUBLE WAS OVER.
HEY, REMEMBER WHAT YOU SAID THAT ONE TIME?
ABOUT YOU DOING THE COOKING AND ME DOING THE PRESENTATION?
WELL, WE PULLED IT OFF!

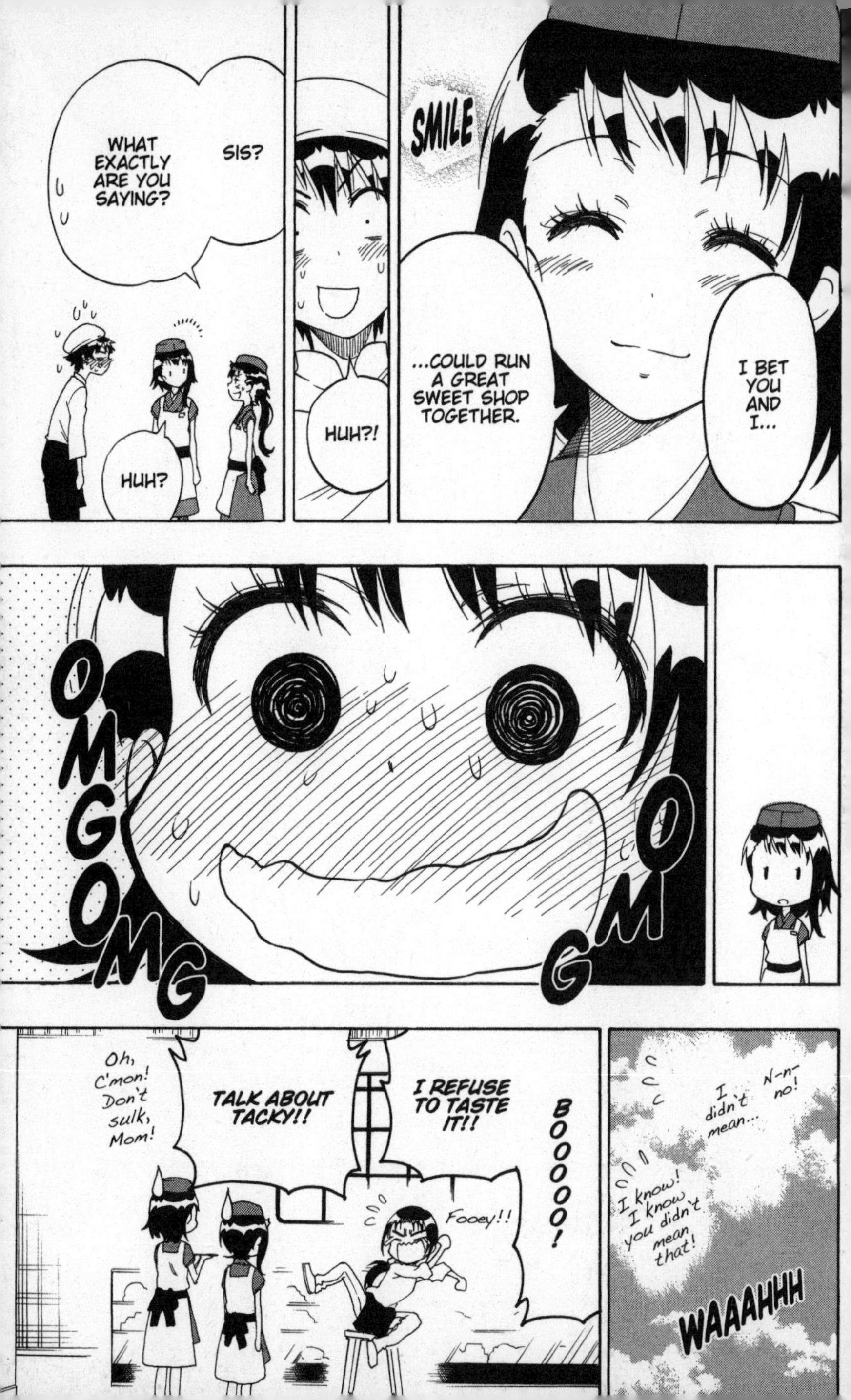
SMILE
I BET YOU AND I...
...COULD RUN A GREAT SWEET SHOP TOGETHER.
HUH?!
SIS?
WHAT EXACTLY ARE YOU SAYING?
HUH?
OMGOMG
OMGOMG
N-n-no!
I didn't mean...
I know! I know you didn't mean that!
WAAAHHH
BOOOOOO!
I REFUSE TO TASTE IT!!
TALK ABOUT TACKY!!
Oh, C'mon! Don't sulk, Mom!
Fooey!!

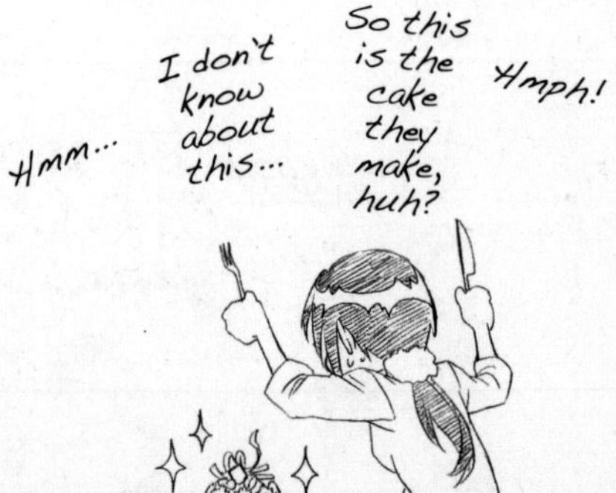
Hmph!
So this is the cake they make, huh?
I don't know about this...
Hmm...

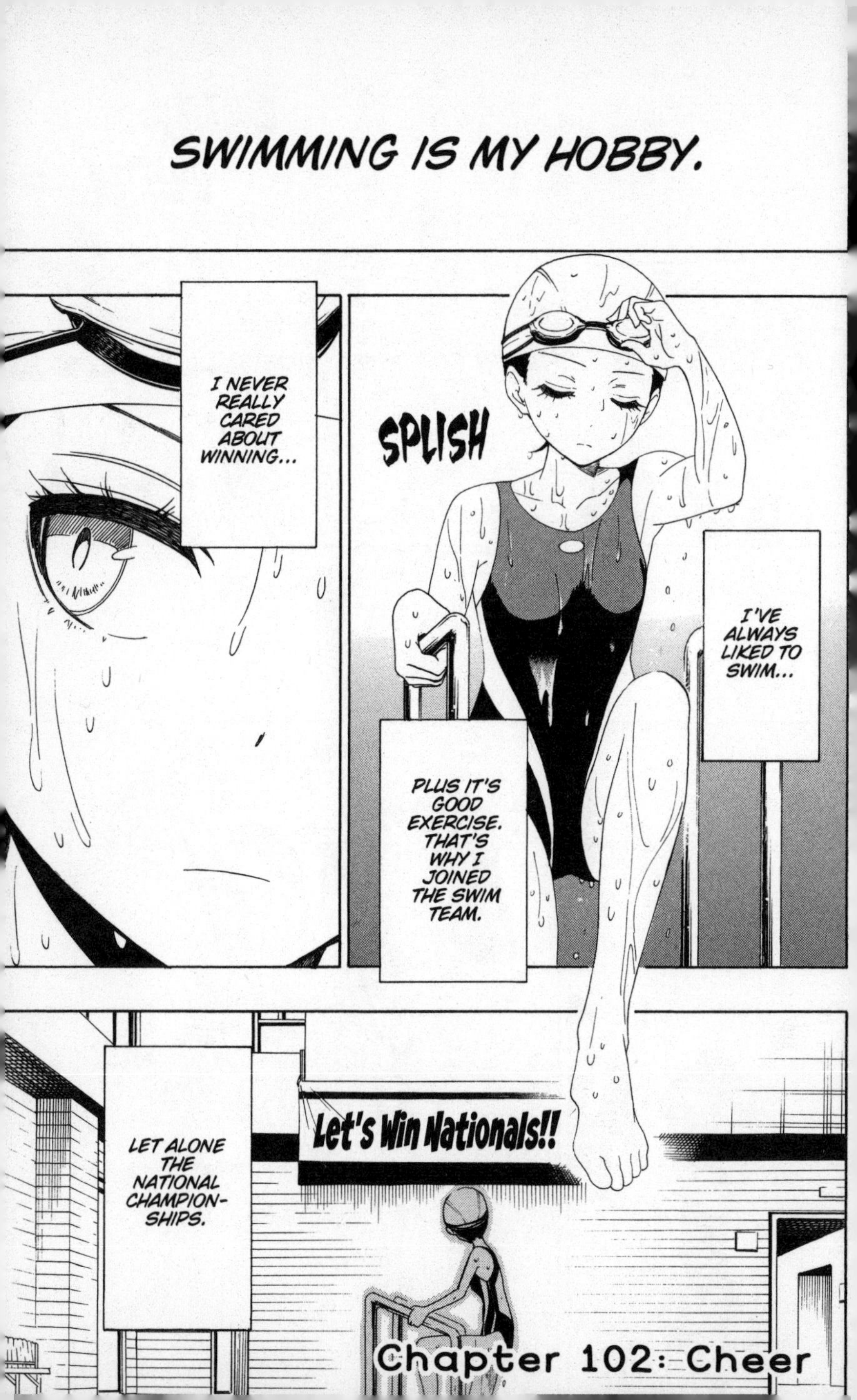
SWIMMING IS MY HOBBY.
SPLISH
I'VE ALWAYS LIKED TO SWIM...
PLUS IT'S GOOD EXERCISE. THAT'S WHY I JOINED THE SWIM TEAM.
I NEVER REALLY CARED ABOUT WINNING...
Let's Win Nationals!!
LET ALONE THE NATIONAL CHAMPION-SHIPS.
Chapter 102: Cheer

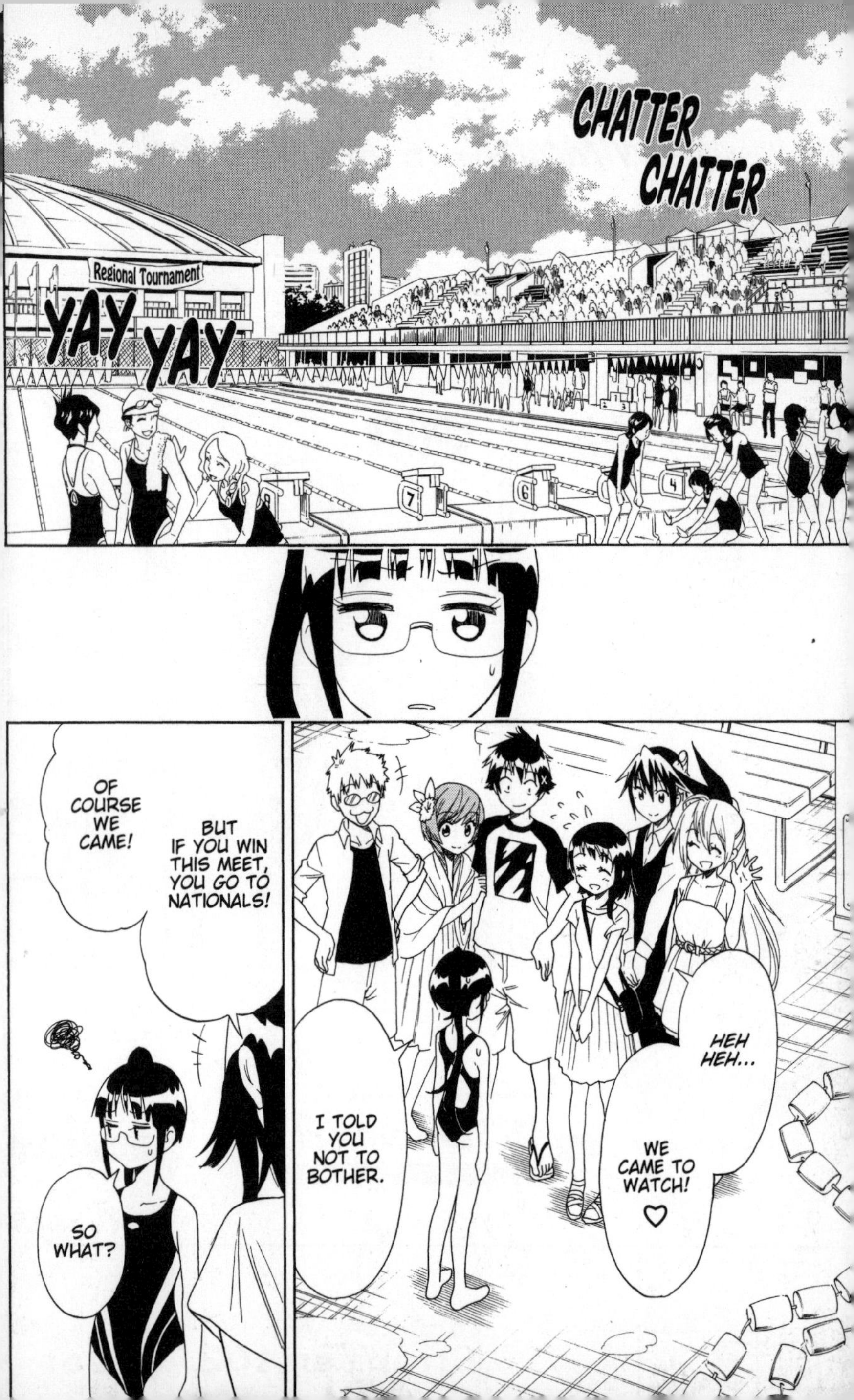
CHATTER CHATTER
Regional Tournament
YAY YAY
HEH HEH...
WE CAME TO WATCH! ♡
I TOLD YOU NOT TO BOTHER.
OF COURSE WE CAME!
BUT IF YOU WIN THIS MEET, YOU GO TO NATIONALS!
SO WHAT?

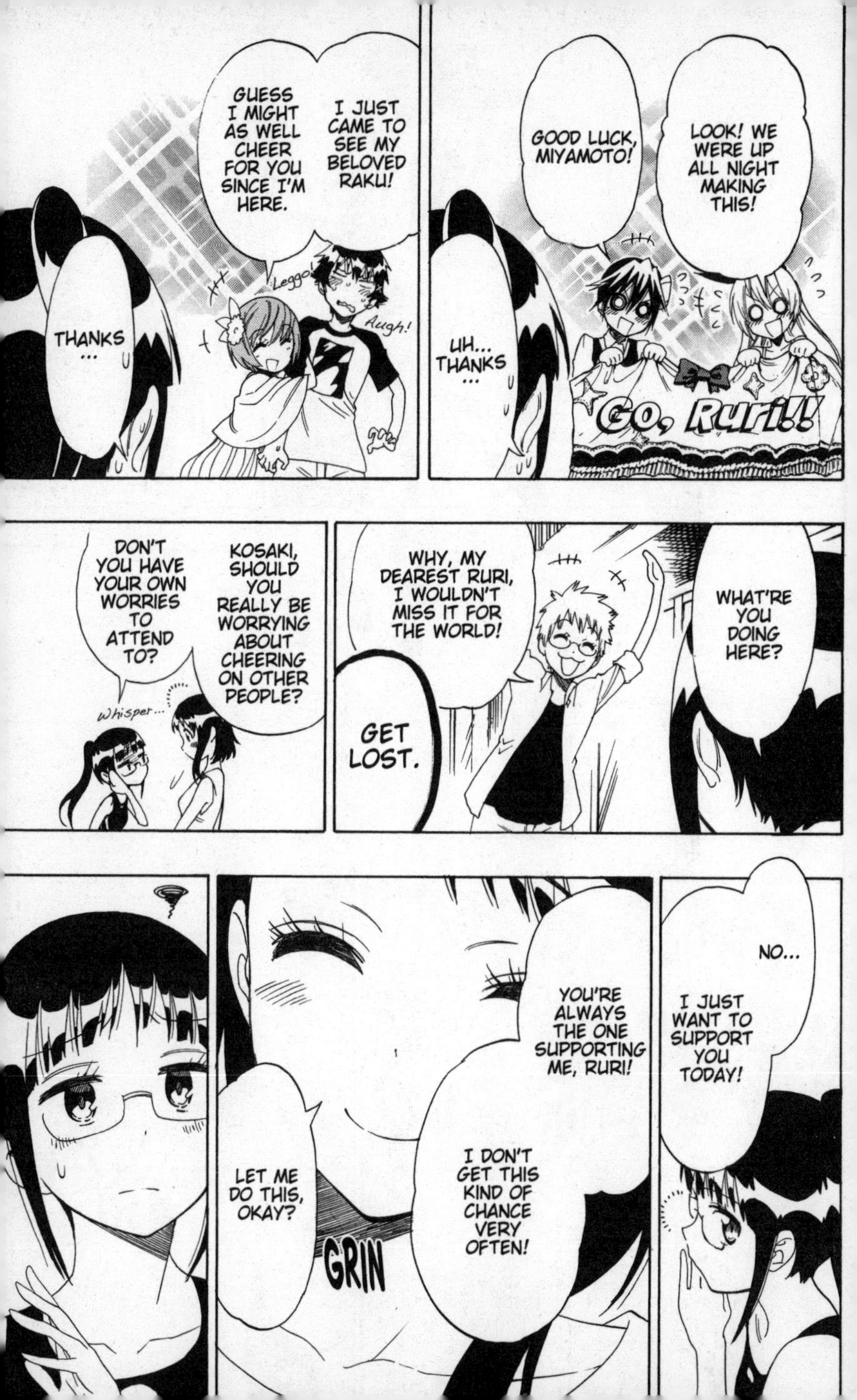
LOOK! WE WERE UP ALL NIGHT MAKING THIS!
GOOD LUCK, MIYAMOTO!
Go, Ruri!!
UH... THANKS...
I JUST CAME TO SEE MY BELOVED RAKU!
GUESS I MIGHT AS WELL CHEER FOR YOU SINCE I'M HERE.
Leggo!
Augh!
THANKS...
WHAT'RE YOU DOING HERE?
WHY, MY DEAREST RURI, I WOULDN'T MISS IT FOR THE WORLD!
GET LOST.
KOSAKI, SHOULD YOU REALLY BE WORRYING ABOUT CHEERING ON OTHER PEOPLE?
DON'T YOU HAVE YOUR OWN WORRIES TO ATTEND TO?
Whisper...
NO...
I JUST WANT TO SUPPORT YOU TODAY!
YOU'RE ALWAYS THE ONE SUPPORTING ME, RURI!
I DON'T GET THIS KIND OF CHANCE VERY OFTEN!
LET ME DO THIS, OKAY?
GRIN

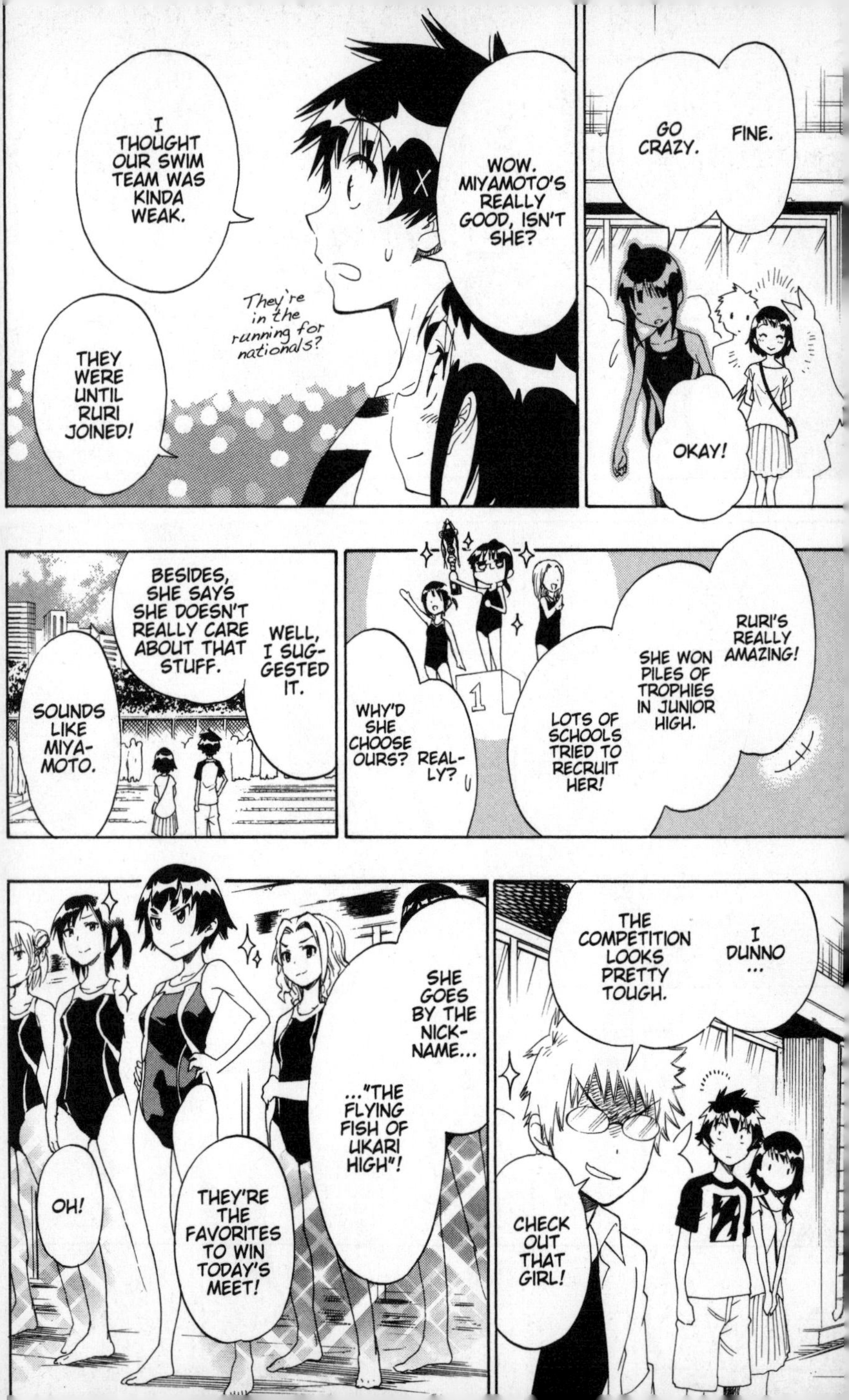
FINE.
GO CRAZY.
OKAY!
WOW. MIYAMOTO'S REALLY GOOD, ISN'T SHE?
I THOUGHT OUR SWIM TEAM WAS KINDA WEAK.
They're in the running for nationals?
THEY WERE UNTIL RURI JOINED!
RURI'S REALLY AMAZING!
SHE WON PILES OF TROPHIES IN JUNIOR HIGH.
LOTS OF SCHOOLS TRIED TO RECRUIT HER!
REAL-LY?
WHY'D SHE CHOOSE OURS?
WELL, I SUG-GESTED IT.
BESIDES, SHE SAYS SHE DOESN'T REALLY CARE ABOUT THAT STUFF.
SOUNDS LIKE MIYA-MOTO.
I DUNNO...
THE COMPETITION LOOKS PRETTY TOUGH.
CHECK OUT THAT GIRL!
SHE GOES BY THE NICK-NAME...
..."THE FLYING FISH OF UKARI HIGH"!
THEY'RE THE FAVORITES TO WIN TODAY'S MEET!
OH!

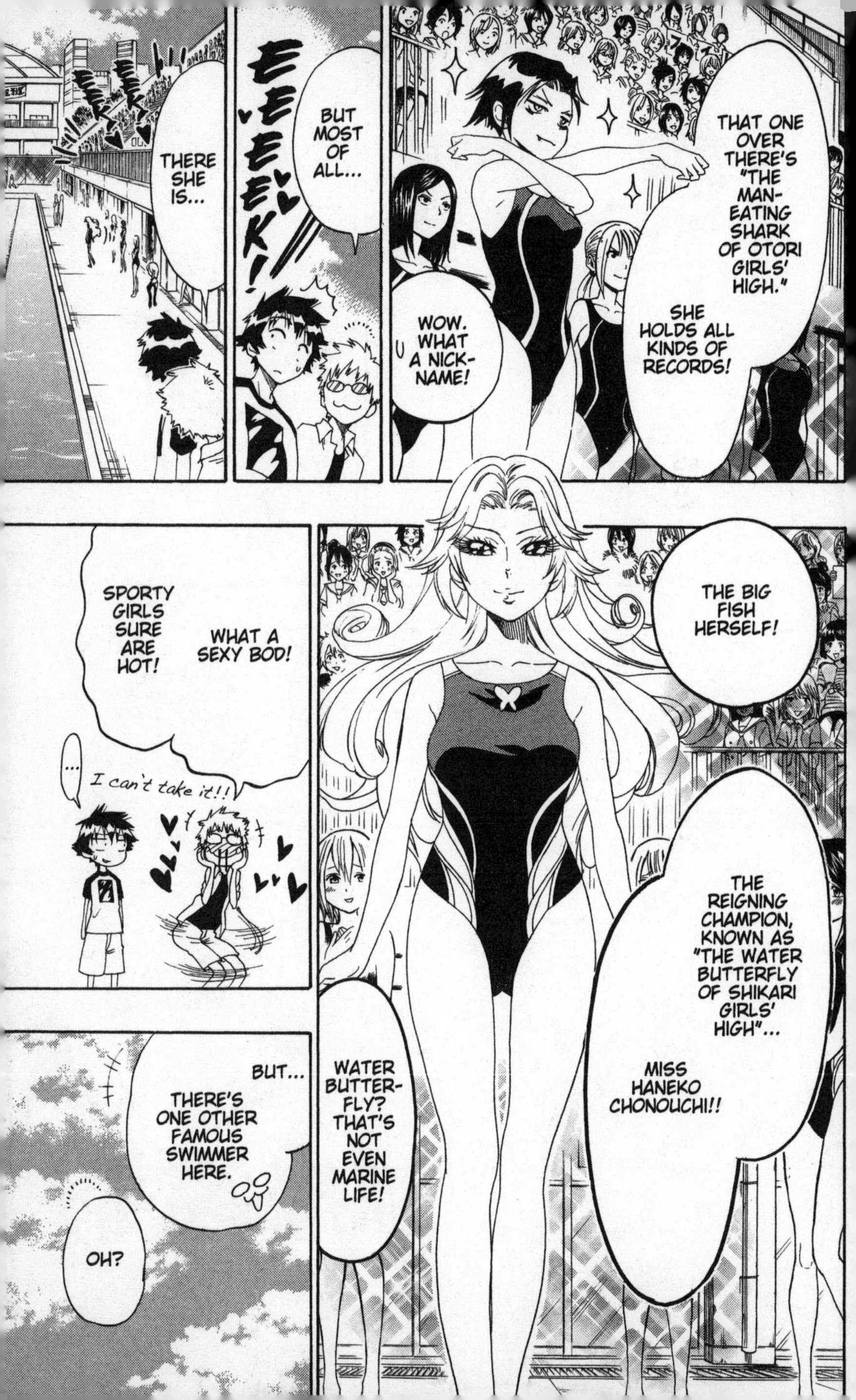

THAT ONE OVER THERE'S "THE MAN-EATING SHARK OF OTORI GIRLS' HIGH."
SHE HOLDS ALL KINDS OF RECORDS!
WOW. WHAT A NICK-NAME!
EEEEK!
BUT MOST OF ALL...
EEEK!
THERE SHE IS...
THE BIG FISH HERSELF!
THE REIGNING CHAMPION, KNOWN AS "THE WATER BUTTERFLY OF SHIKARI GIRLS' HIGH"...
MISS HANEKO CHONOUCHI!!
WATER BUTTER-FLY? THAT'S NOT EVEN MARINE LIFE!
WHAT A SEXY BOD!
SPORTY GIRLS SURE ARE HOT!
...
I can't take it!!
BUT...
THERE'S ONE OTHER FAMOUS SWIMMER HERE.
OH?

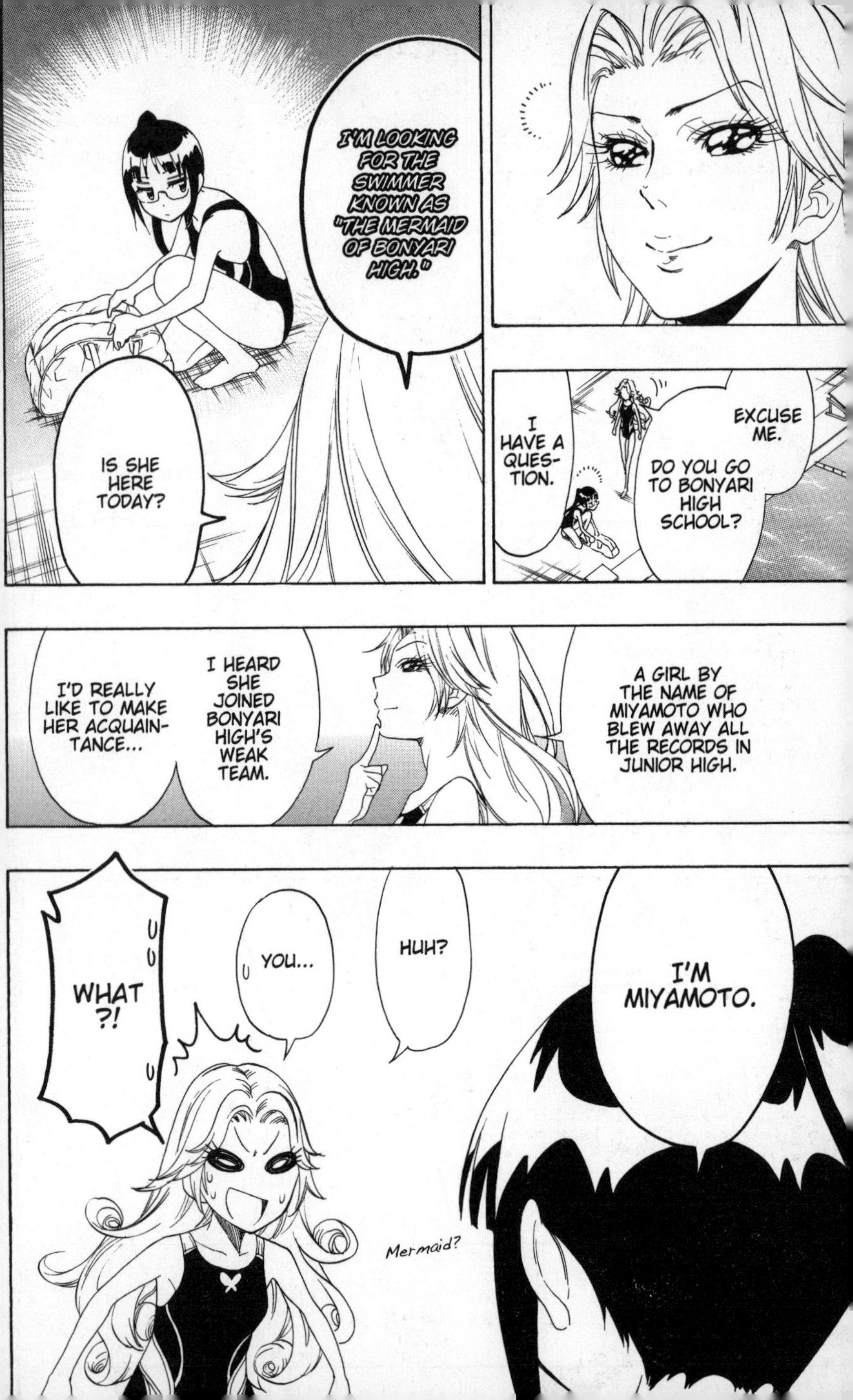
EXCUSE ME.
DO YOU GO TO BONYARI HIGH SCHOOL?
I HAVE A QUES-TION.
I'M LOOKING FOR THE SWIMMER KNOWN AS "THE MERMAID OF BONYARI HIGH."
IS SHE HERE TODAY?
A GIRL BY THE NAME OF MIYAMOTO WHO BLEW AWAY ALL THE RECORDS IN JUNIOR HIGH.
I HEARD SHE JOINED BONYARI HIGH'S WEAK TEAM.
I'D REALLY LIKE TO MAKE HER ACQUAIN-TANCE...
I'M MIYAMOTO.
HUH?
YOU...
WHAT ?!
Mermaid?

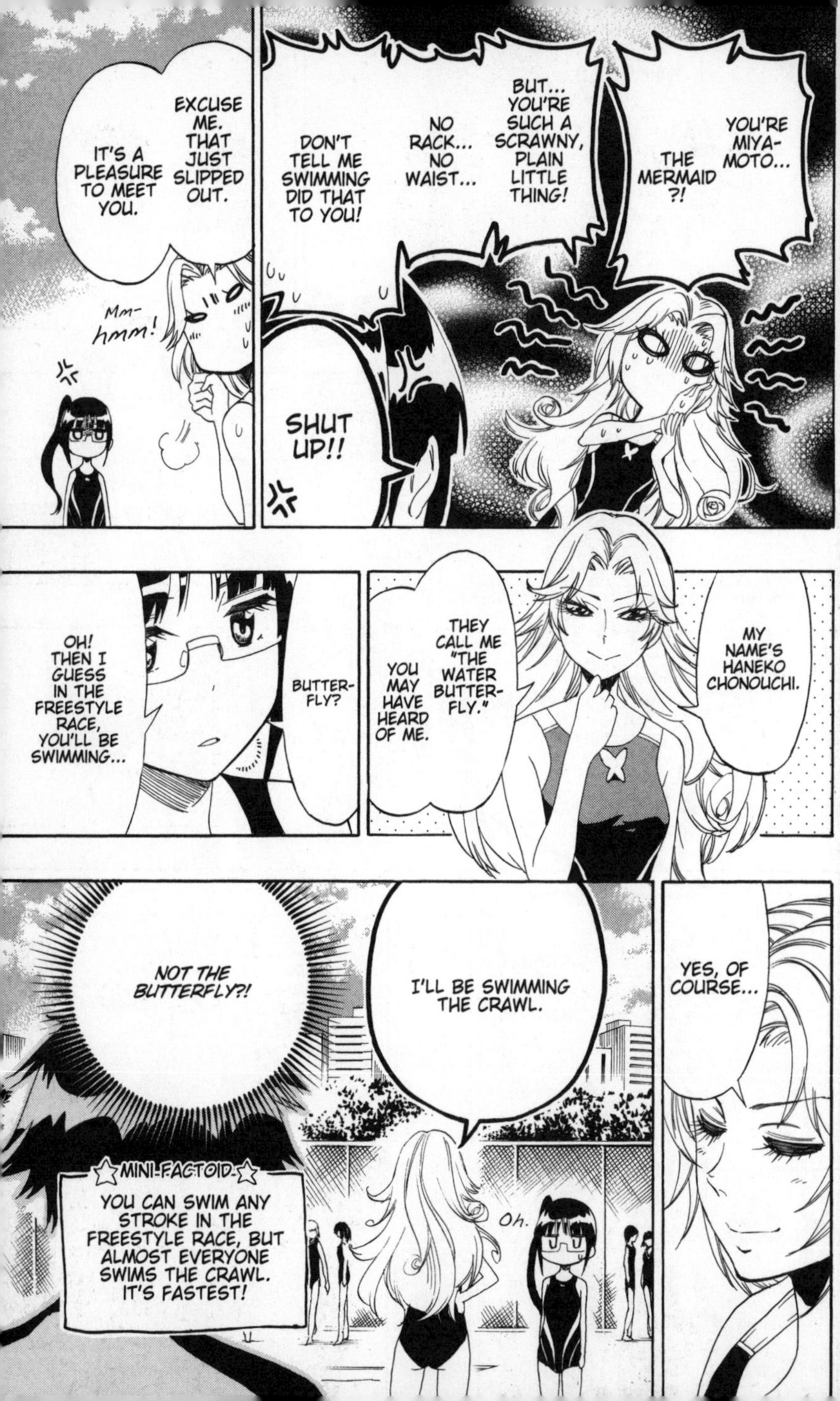
YOU'RE MIYA-MOTO...
THE MERMAID ?!
BUT... YOU'RE SUCH A SCRAWNY, PLAIN LITTLE THING!
NO RACK... NO WAIST...
DON'T TELL ME SWIMMING DID THAT TO YOU!
SHUT UP!!
EXCUSE ME. THAT JUST SLIPPED OUT.
IT'S A PLEASURE TO MEET YOU.
Mm-hmm!
MY NAME'S HANEKO CHONOUCHI.
THEY CALL ME "THE WATER BUTTERFLY."
YOU MAY HAVE HEARD OF ME.
BUTTER-FLY?
OH! THEN I GUESS IN THE FREESTYLE RACE, YOU'LL BE SWIMMING...
YES, OF COURSE...
I'LL BE SWIMMING THE CRAWL.
Oh.
NOT THE BUTTERFLY?!
☆MINI-FACTOID☆
YOU CAN SWIM ANY STROKE IN THE FREESTYLE RACE, BUT ALMOST EVERYONE SWIMS THE CRAWL. IT'S FASTEST!

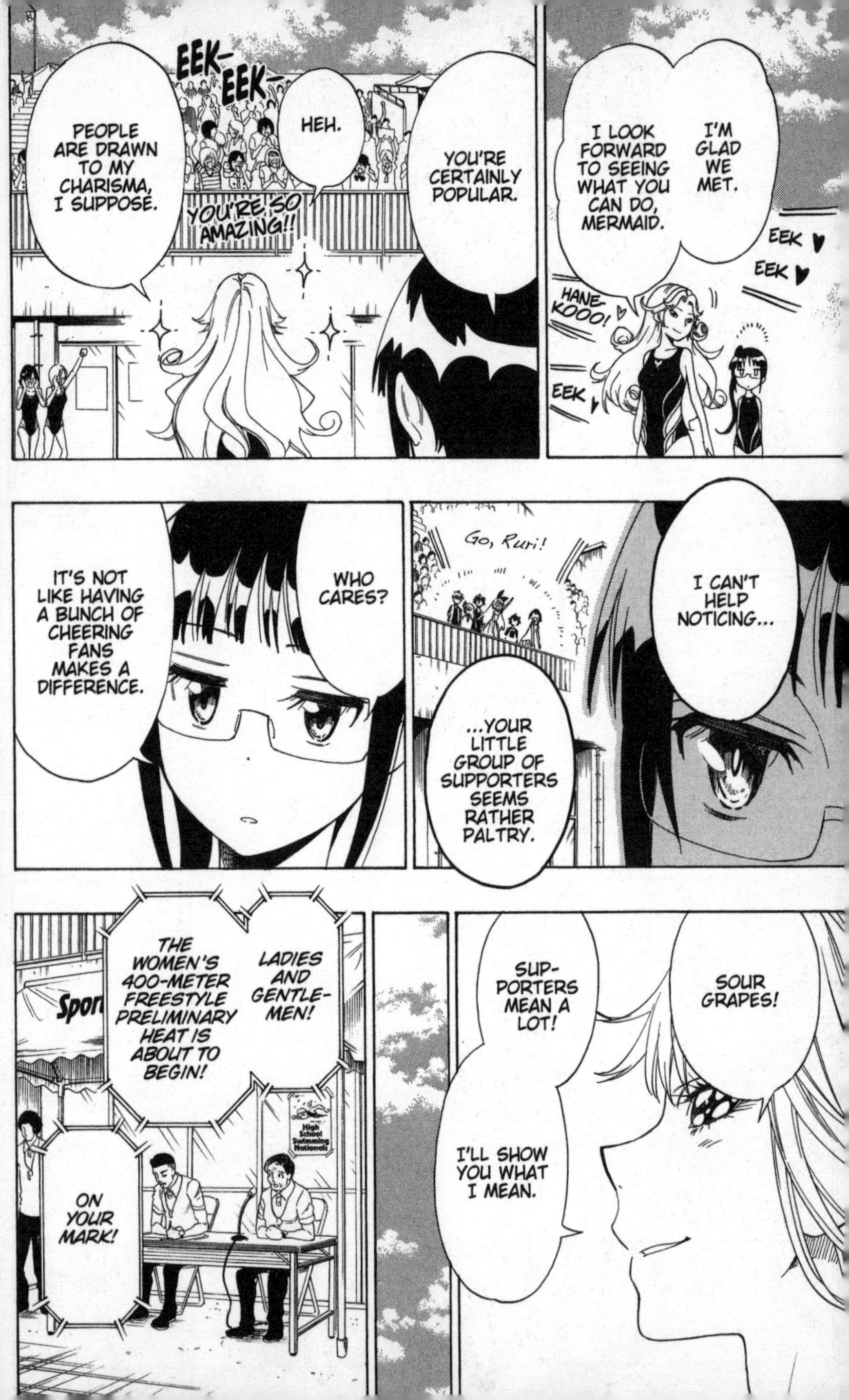
I'M GLAD WE MET.
I LOOK FORWARD TO SEEING WHAT YOU CAN DO, MERMAID.
EEK ♥
EEK ♥
HANE-KOOO! ♥
EEK ♥
YOU'RE CERTAINLY POPULAR.
EEK-
EEK-
HEH.
PEOPLE ARE DRAWN TO MY CHARISMA, I SUPPOSE.
YOU'RE SO AMAZING!!
I CAN'T HELP NOTICING...
Go, Ruri!
...YOUR LITTLE GROUP OF SUPPORTERS SEEMS RATHER PALTRY.
WHO CARES?
IT'S NOT LIKE HAVING A BUNCH OF CHEERING FANS MAKES A DIFFERENCE.
SOUR GRAPES!
SUP-PORTERS MEAN A LOT!
I'LL SHOW YOU WHAT I MEAN.
LADIES AND GENTLE-MEN!
THE WOMEN'S 400-METER FREESTYLE PRELIMINARY HEAT IS ABOUT TO BEGIN!
High School Swimming Nationals
ON YOUR MARK!

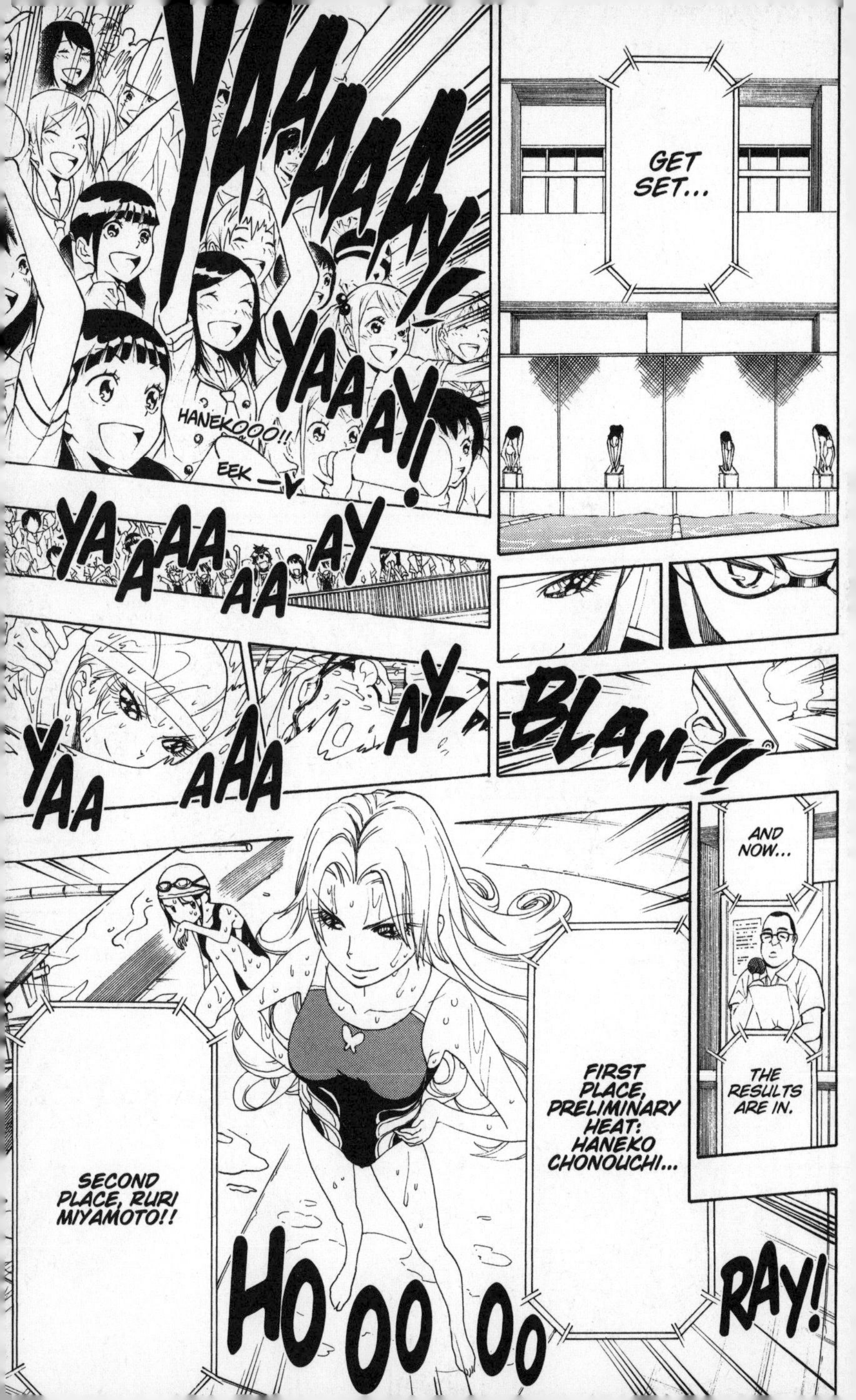

GET SET...
BLAM!!
YAAAAY!
YAAAY!
HANEKOOO!!
EEK
YAAAAAAAAY
YAAAAAAY
AND NOW...
THE RESULTS ARE IN.
FIRST PLACE, PRELIMINARY HEAT: HANEKO CHONOUCHI...
SECOND PLACE, RURI MIYAMOTO!!
HOOOOOORAY!

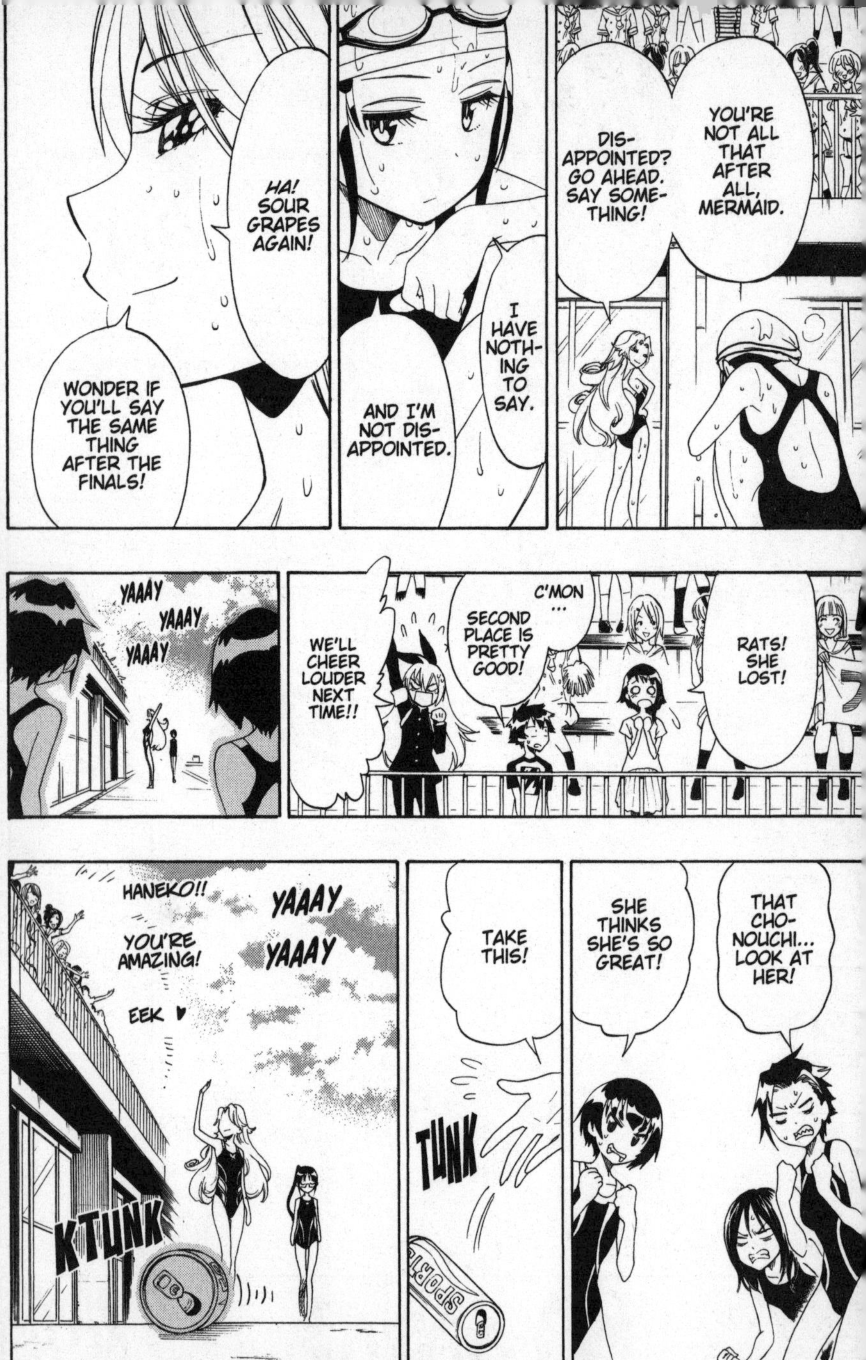

YOU'RE NOT ALL THAT AFTER ALL, MERMAID.
DIS-APPOINTED? GO AHEAD. SAY SOME-THING!
I HAVE NOTH-ING TO SAY.
AND I'M NOT DIS-APPOINTED.
HA! SOUR GRAPES AGAIN!
WONDER IF YOU'LL SAY THE SAME THING AFTER THE FINALS!
RATS! SHE LOST!
C'MON ...
SECOND PLACE IS PRETTY GOOD!
WE'LL CHEER LOUDER NEXT TIME!!
YAAAY
YAAAY
YAAAY
THAT CHO-NOUCHI... LOOK AT HER!
SHE THINKS SHE'S SO GREAT!
TAKE THIS!
TUNK
HANEKO!!
YOU'RE AMAZING!
EEK ♥
YAAAY
YAAAY
KTUNK

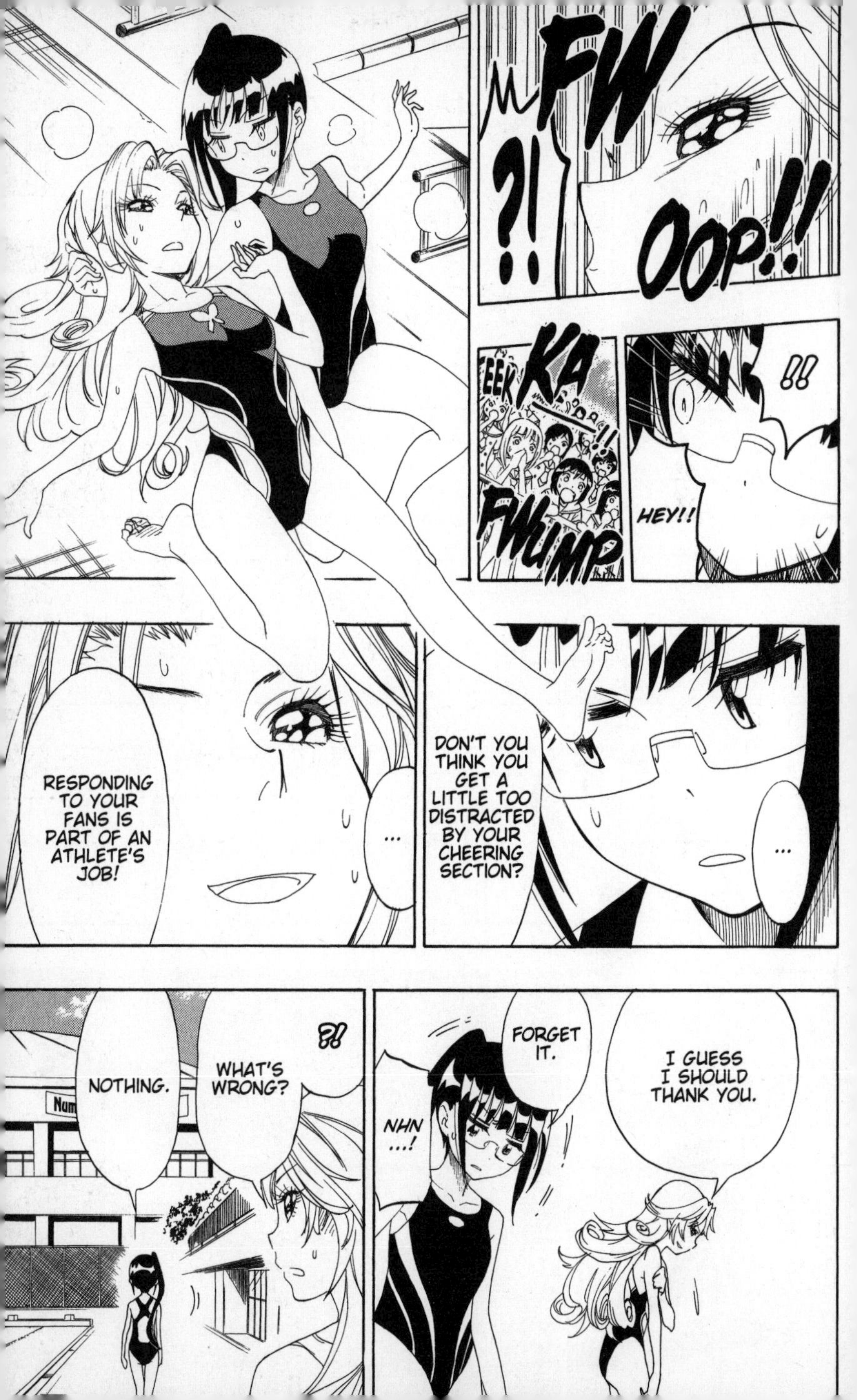
FWOOP!!
?!!
!!
HEY!!
KA
EEEK
FWUMP
...
DON'T YOU THINK YOU GET A LITTLE TOO DISTRACTED BY YOUR CHEERING SECTION?
...
RESPONDING TO YOUR FANS IS PART OF AN ATHLETE'S JOB!
I GUESS I SHOULD THANK YOU.
FORGET IT.
NHN ...!
?!
WHAT'S WRONG?
NOTHING.

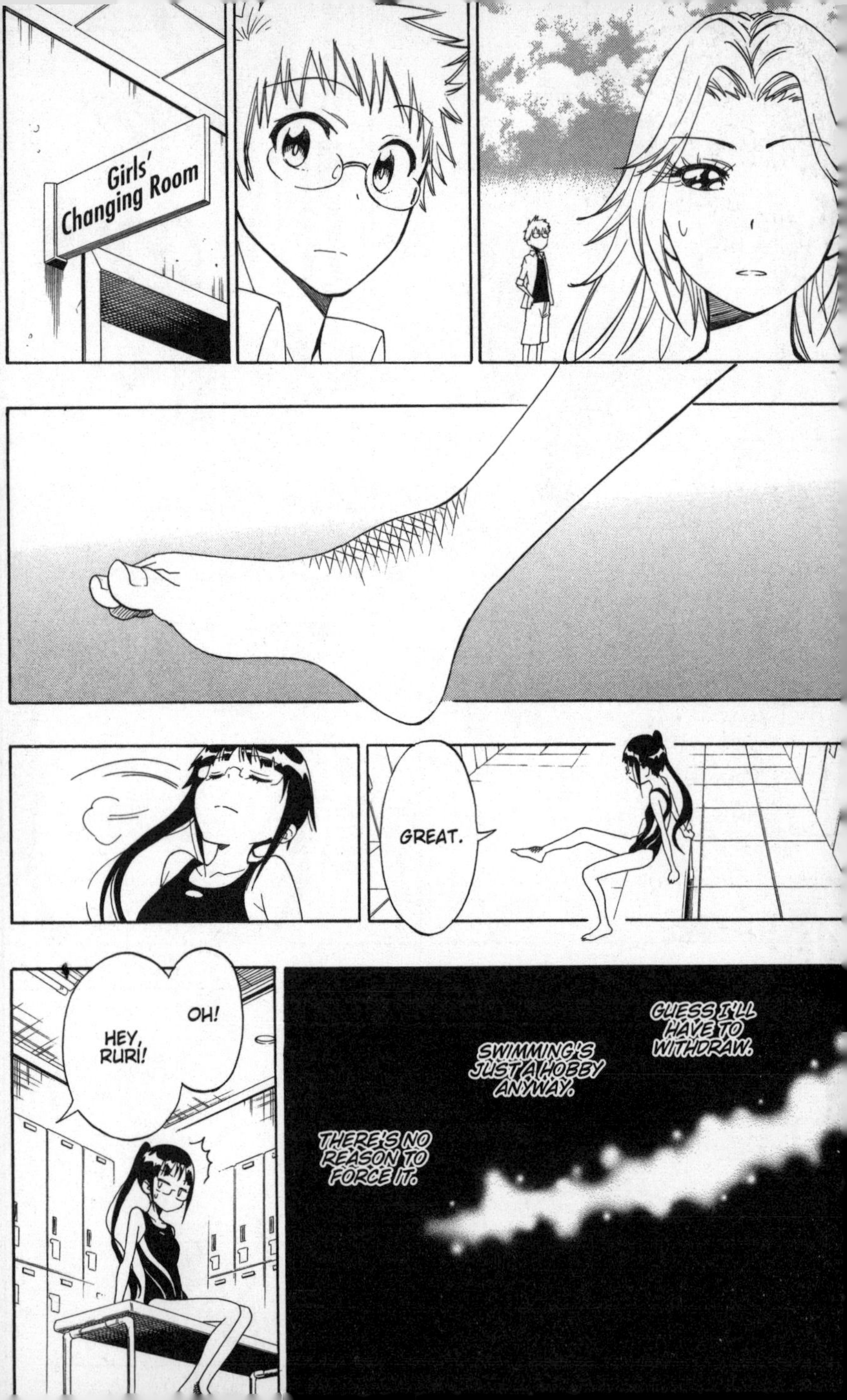
Girls' Changing Room
GREAT.
GUESS I'LL HAVE TO WITHDRAW.
SWIMMING'S JUST A HOBBY ANYWAY.
THERE'S NO REASON TO FORCE IT.
OH!
HEY, RURI!

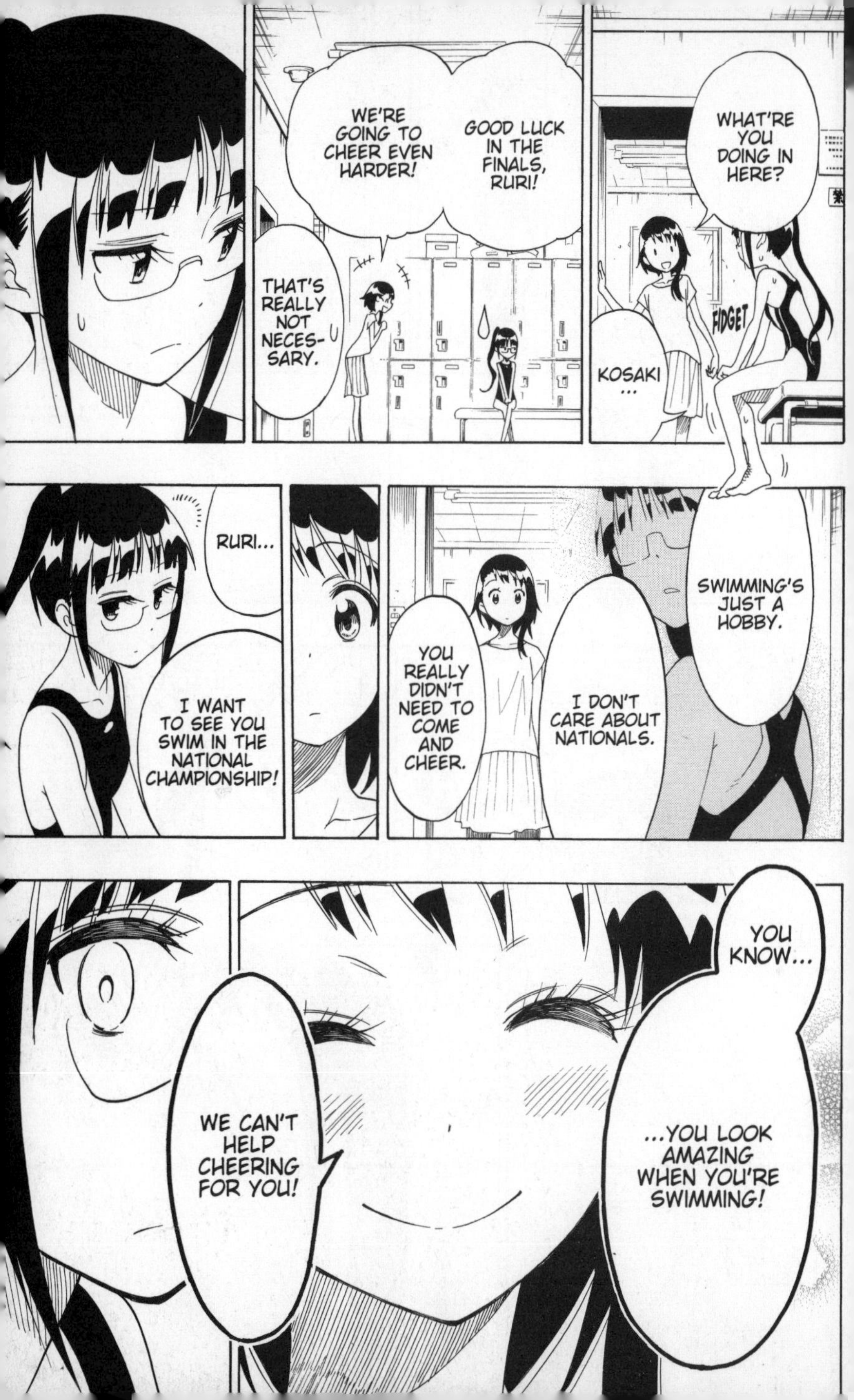
WHAT'RE YOU DOING IN HERE?
KOSAKI ...
FIDGET
GOOD LUCK IN THE FINALS, RURI!
WE'RE GOING TO CHEER EVEN HARDER!
THAT'S REALLY NOT NECES-SARY.
SWIMMING'S JUST A HOBBY.
I DON'T CARE ABOUT NATIONALS.
YOU REALLY DIDN'T NEED TO COME AND CHEER.
RURI...
I WANT TO SEE YOU SWIM IN THE NATIONAL CHAMPIONSHIP!
YOU KNOW...
...YOU LOOK AMAZING WHEN YOU'RE SWIMMING!
WE CAN'T HELP CHEERING FOR YOU!

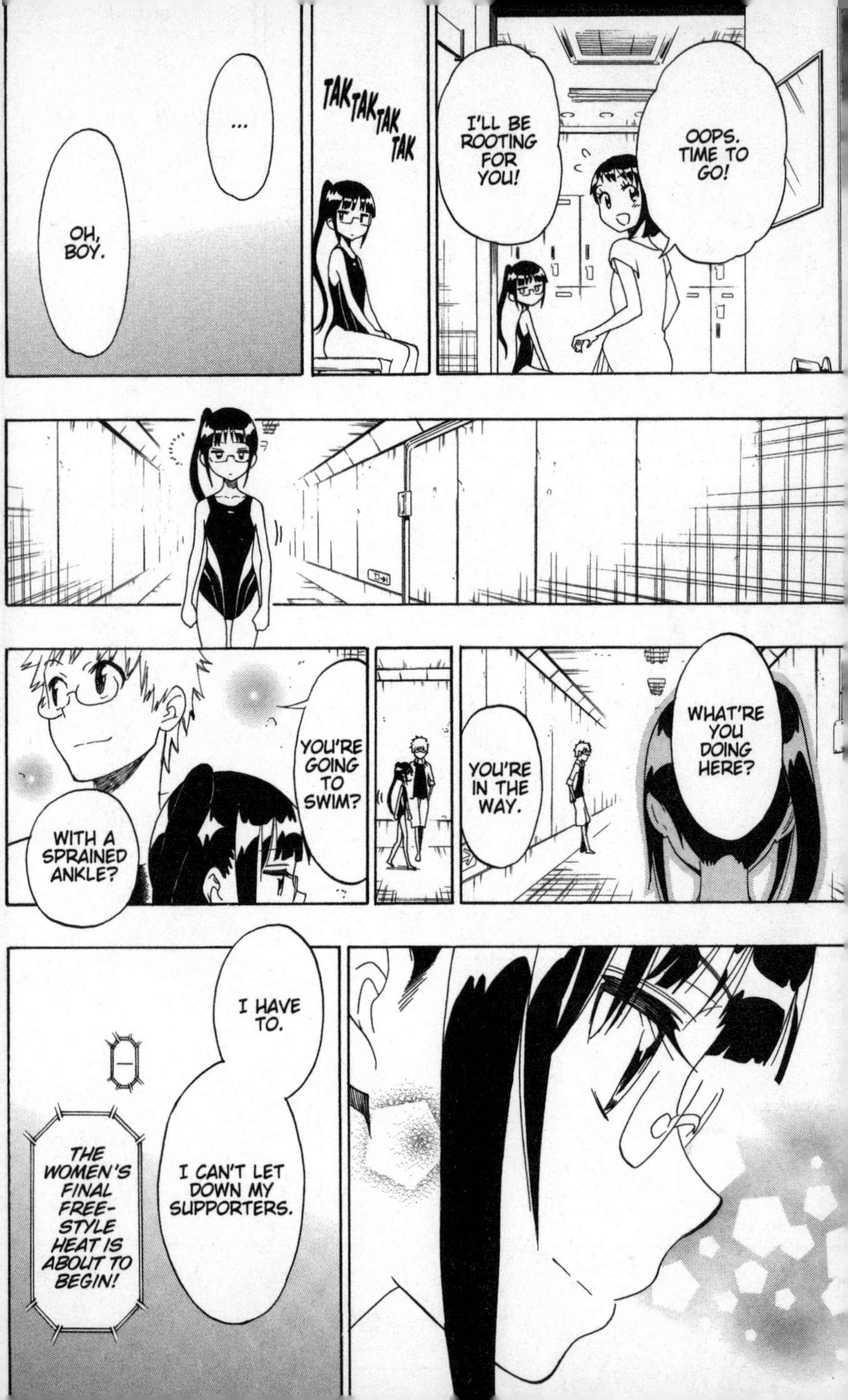
OOPS. TIME TO GO!
I'LL BE ROOTING FOR YOU!
TAK TAK TAK TAK
...
OH, BOY.
WHAT'RE YOU DOING HERE?
YOU'RE IN THE WAY.
YOU'RE GOING TO SWIM?
WITH A SPRAINED ANKLE?
I HAVE TO.
I CAN'T LET DOWN MY SUPPORTERS.
THE WOMEN'S FINAL FREE-STYLE HEAT IS ABOUT TO BEGIN!

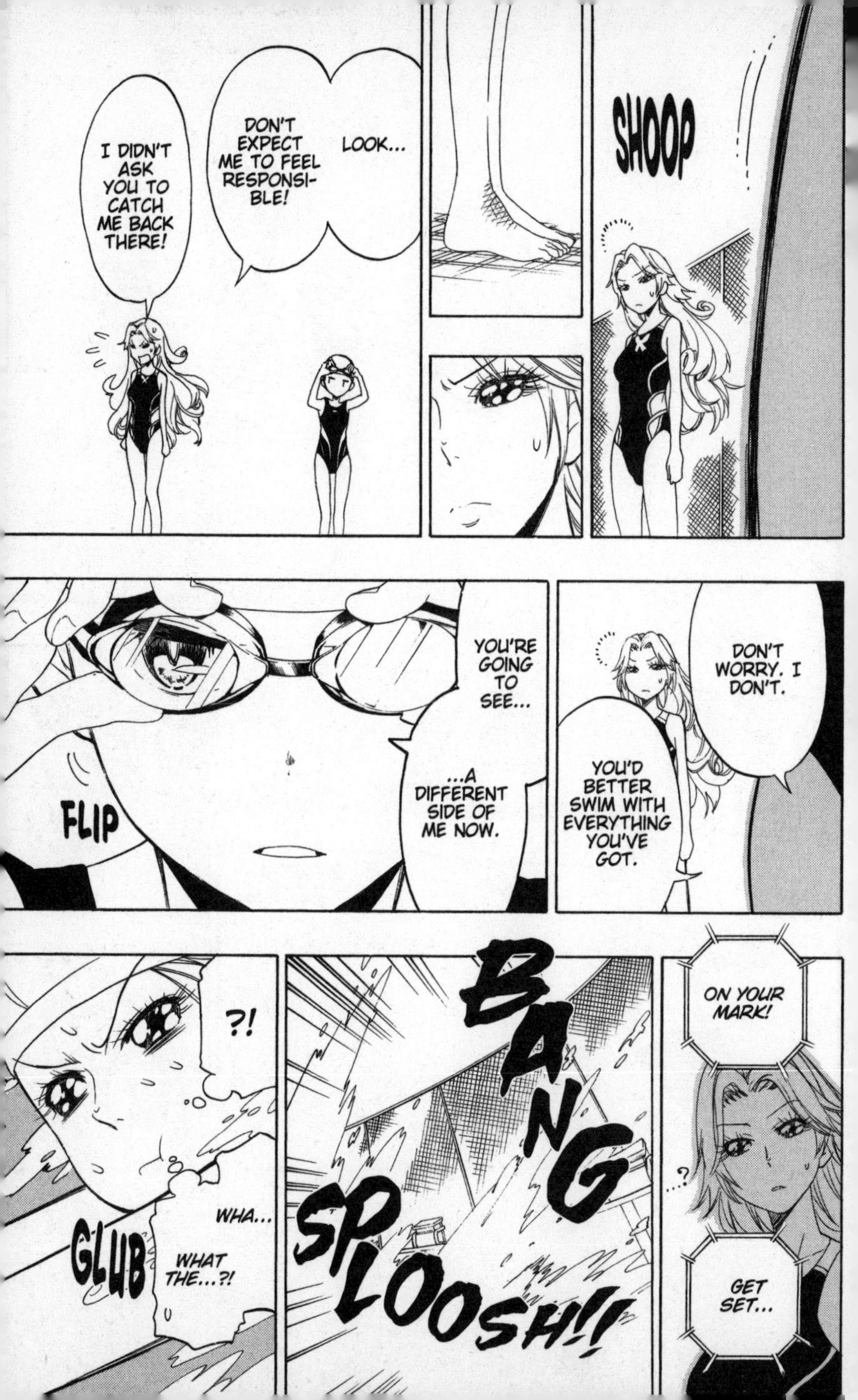
SHOOP
LOOK...
DON'T EXPECT ME TO FEEL RESPONSIBLE!
I DIDN'T ASK YOU TO CATCH ME BACK THERE!
DON'T WORRY. I DON'T.
YOU'D BETTER SWIM WITH EVERYTHING YOU'VE GOT.
YOU'RE GOING TO SEE...
...A DIFFERENT SIDE OF ME NOW.
FLIP
ON YOUR MARK!
...?
GET SET...
BANG
SPLOOSH!!
?!
WHA...
WHAT THE...?!
GLUB

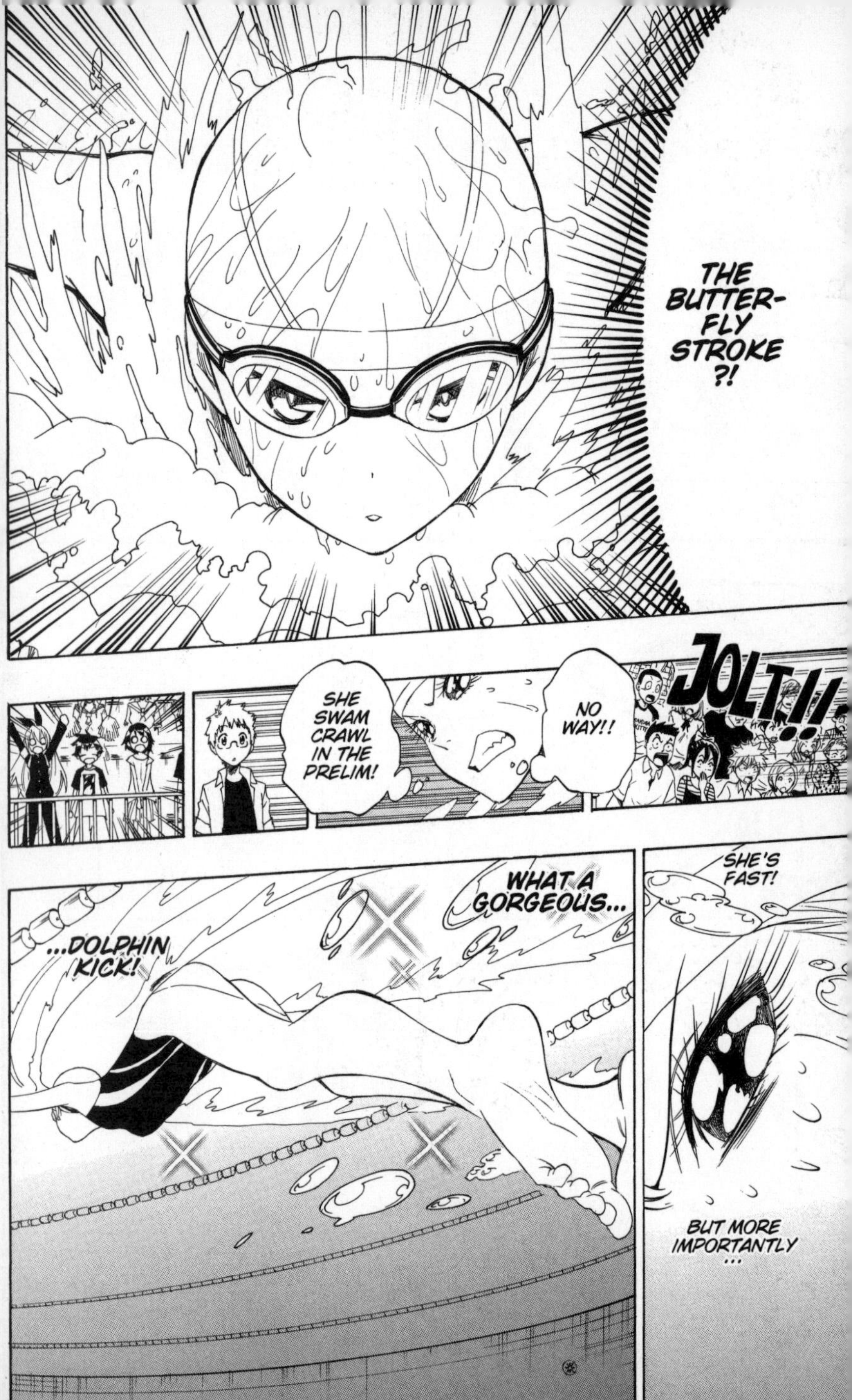
THE BUTTER-FLY STROKE?!
JOLT!!
NO WAY!!
SHE SWAM CRAWL IN THE PRELIM!
SHE'S FAST!
BUT MORE IMPORTANTLY...
WHAT A GORGEOUS...
...DOLPHIN KICK!

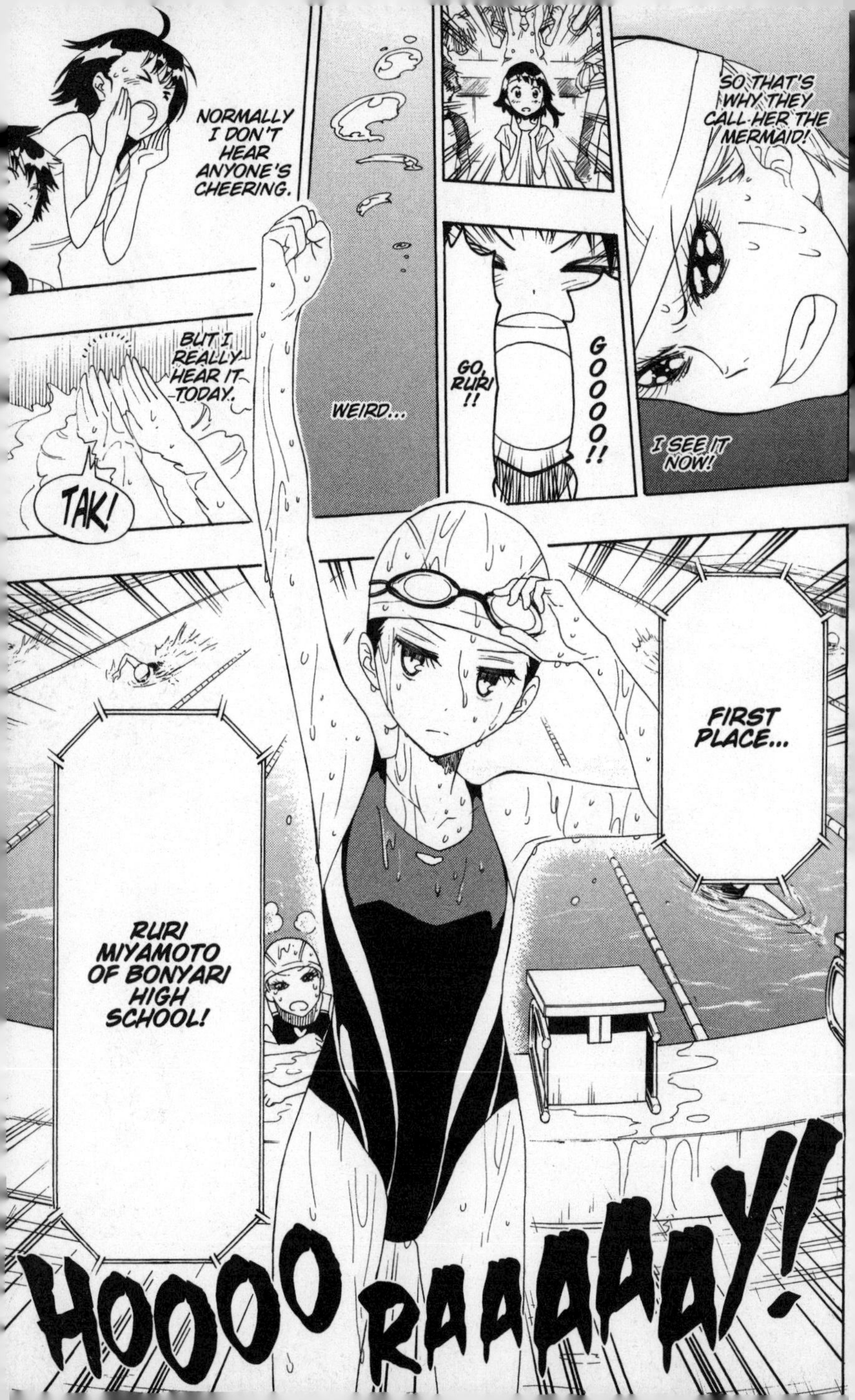
SO THAT'S WHY THEY CALL HER THE MERMAID!
I SEE IT NOW!
GOOOOOO!!
GO, RURI!!
WEIRD...
NORMALLY I DON'T HEAR ANYONE'S CHEERING.
BUT I REALLY HEAR IT TODAY.
TAK!
FIRST PLACE...
RURI MIYAMOTO OF BONYARI HIGH SCHOOL!
HOOOO RAAAAAY!

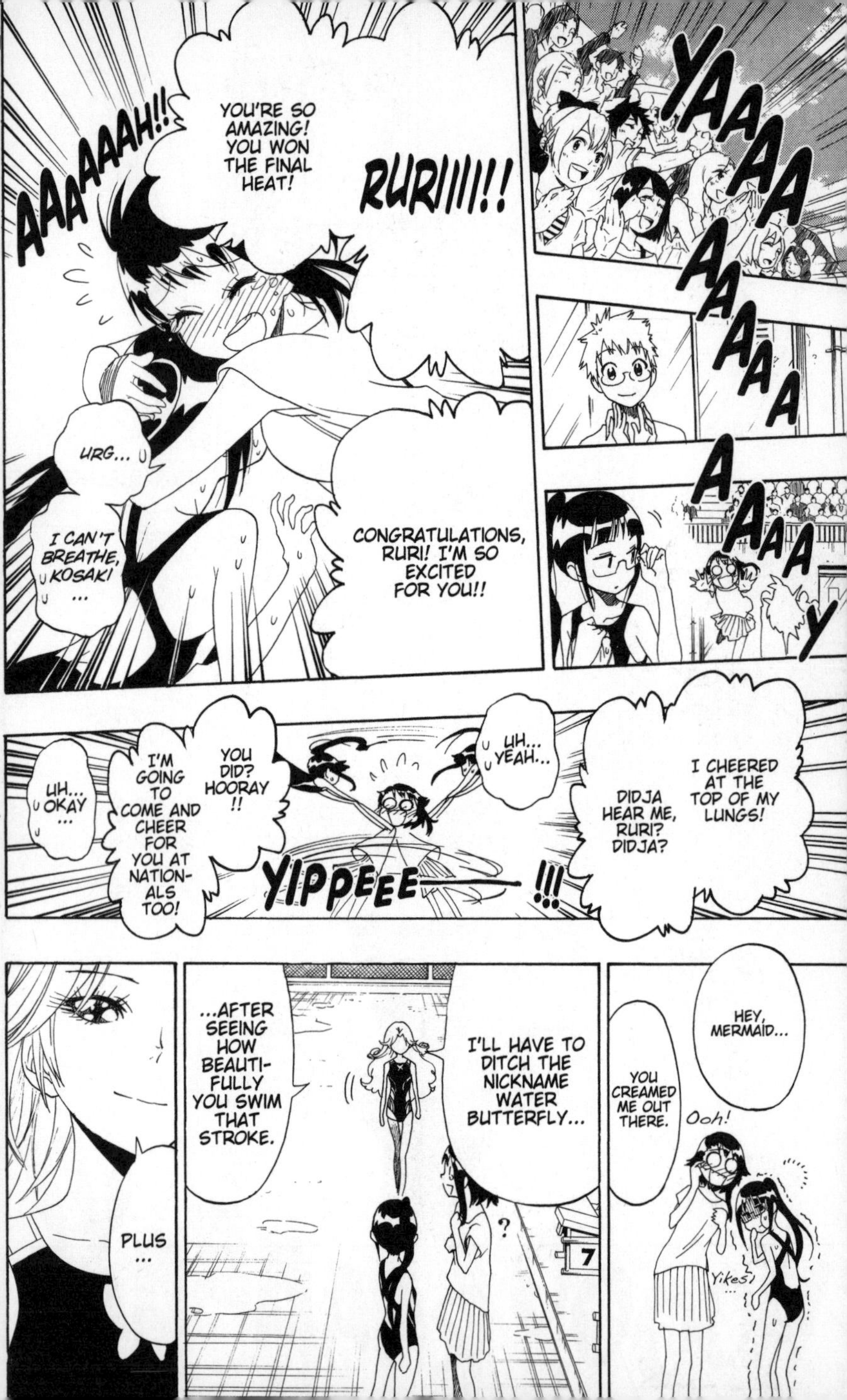

YAAAAAAAAAAAAAAAAY
RURI!!!!!!
YOU'RE SO AMAZING! YOU WON THE FINAL HEAT!
AAAAAAH!!
CONGRATULATIONS, RURI! I'M SO EXCITED FOR YOU!!
URG...
I CAN'T BREATHE, KOSAKI...
I CHEERED AT THE TOP OF MY LUNGS!
DIDJA HEAR ME, RURI? DIDJA?
UH... YEAH...
YIPPEEE—!!!
YOU DID? HOORAY!!
I'M GOING TO COME AND CHEER FOR YOU AT NATIONALS TOO!
UH... OKAY...
HEY, MERMAID...
YOU CREAMED ME OUT THERE.
Ooh!
Yikes!...
I'LL HAVE TO DITCH THE NICKNAME WATER BUTTERFLY...
...AFTER SEEING HOW BEAUTIFULLY YOU SWIM THAT STROKE.
?
7
PLUS...

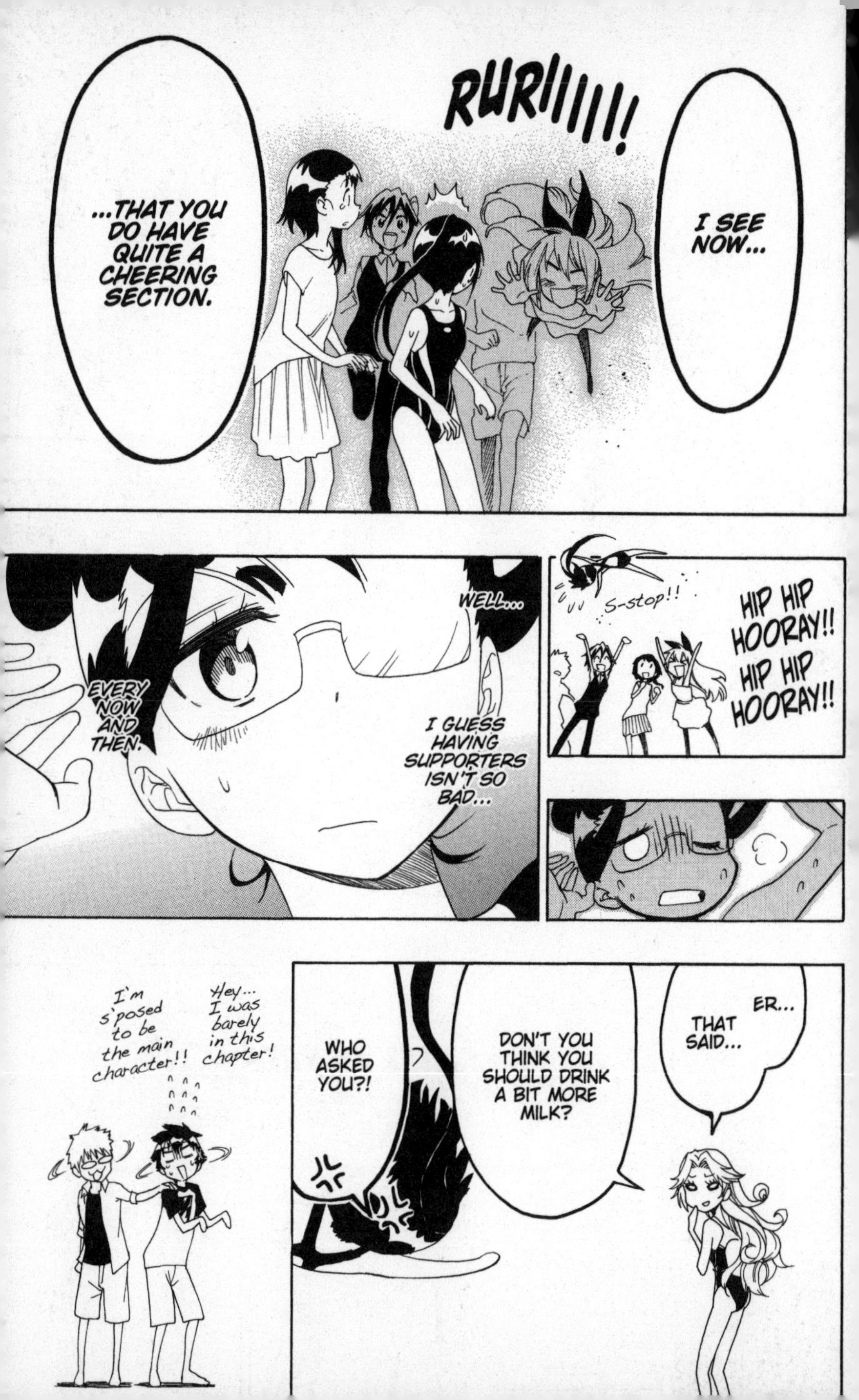
I SEE NOW...
RURI!!!!!!
...THAT YOU DO HAVE QUITE A CHEERING SECTION.
HIP HIP HOORAY!! HIP HIP HOORAY!!
S-stop!!
WELL...
I GUESS HAVING SUPPORTERS ISN'T SO BAD...
EVERY NOW AND THEN.
ER...
THAT SAID...
DON'T YOU THINK YOU SHOULD DRINK A BIT MORE MILK?
WHO ASKED YOU?!
Hey... I was barely in this chapter!
I'm s'posed to be the main character!!

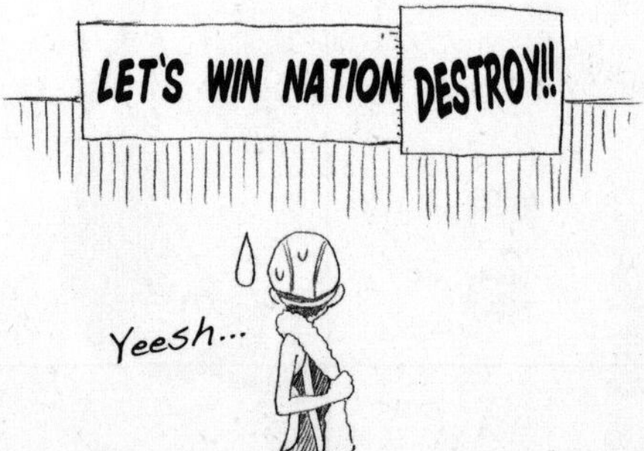
LET'S WIN NATION DESTROY!!
Yeesh...

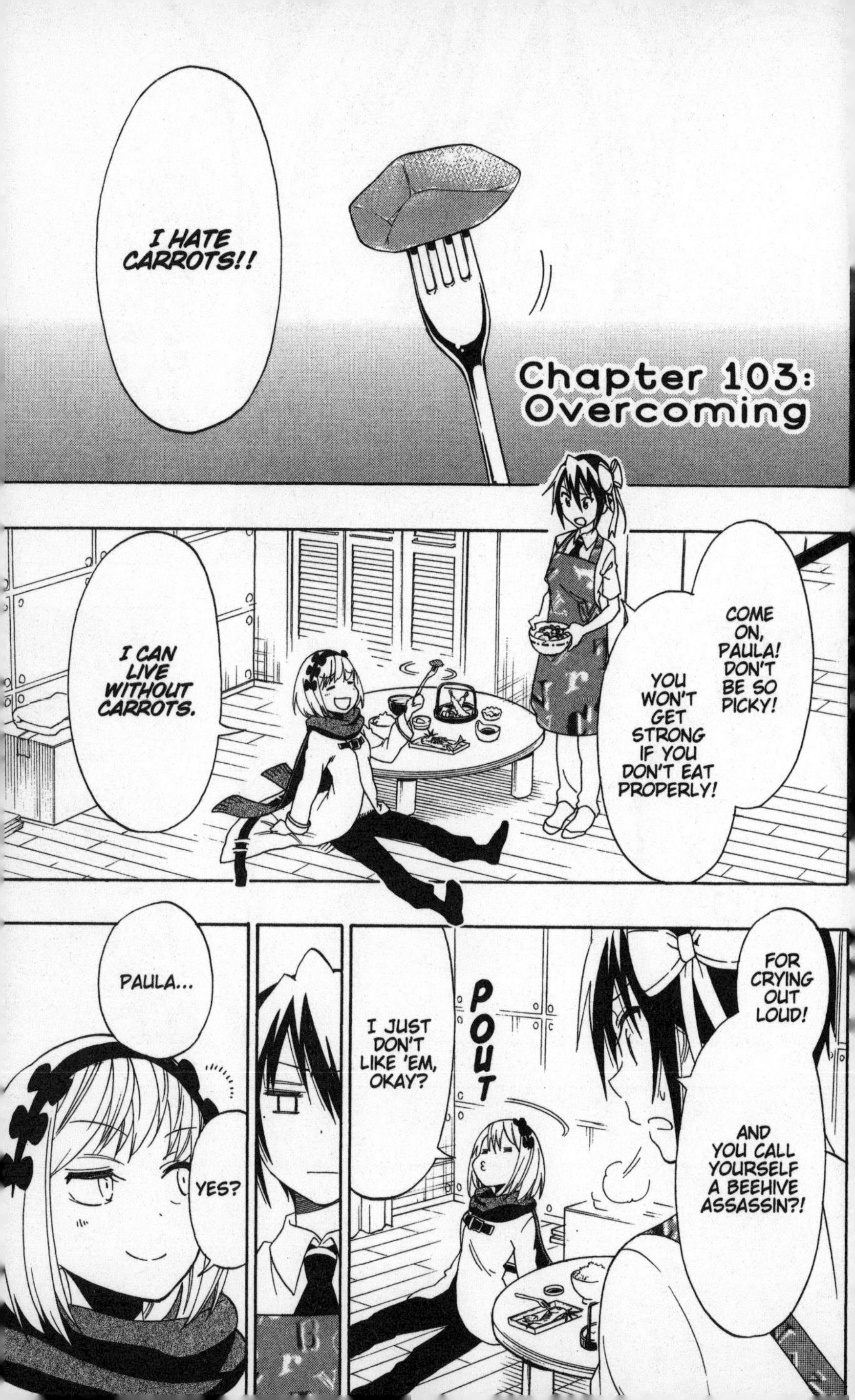
I HATE CARROTS!!
Chapter 103: Overcoming
COME ON, PAULA! DON'T BE SO PICKY!
YOU WON'T GET STRONG IF YOU DON'T EAT PROPERLY!
I CAN LIVE WITHOUT CARROTS.
FOR CRYING OUT LOUD!
AND YOU CALL YOURSELF A BEEHIVE ASSASSIN?!
POUT
I JUST DON'T LIKE 'EM, OKAY?
PAULA...
YES?

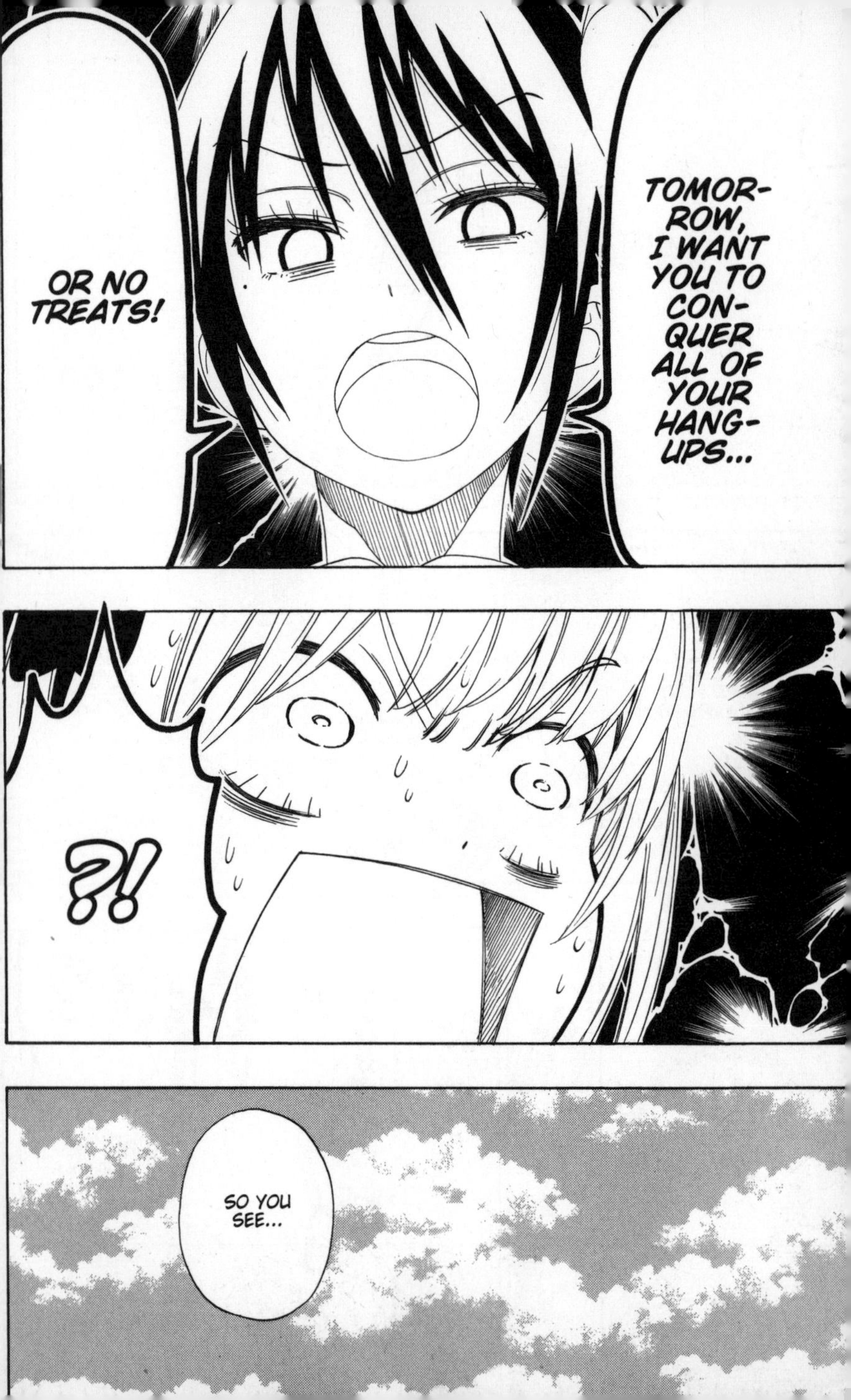
TOMOR-ROW, I WANT YOU TO CON-QUER ALL OF YOUR HANG-UPS...
OR NO TREATS!
?!
SO YOU SEE...

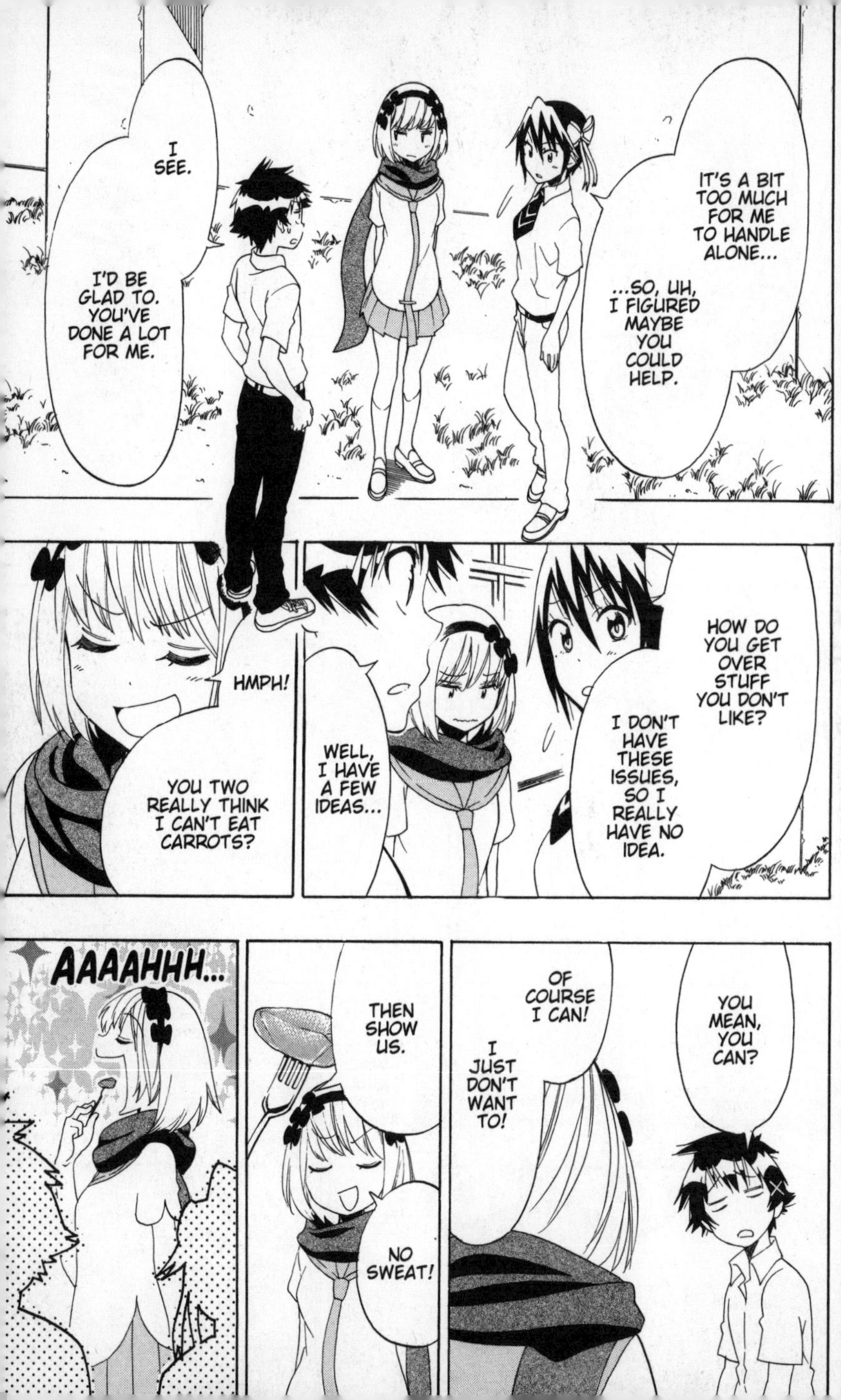
IT'S A BIT TOO MUCH FOR ME TO HANDLE ALONE...
...SO, UH, I FIGURED MAYBE YOU COULD HELP.
I SEE.
I'D BE GLAD TO. YOU'VE DONE A LOT FOR ME.
HOW DO YOU GET OVER STUFF YOU DON'T LIKE?
I DON'T HAVE THESE ISSUES, SO I REALLY HAVE NO IDEA.
WELL, I HAVE A FEW IDEAS...
HMPH!
YOU TWO REALLY THINK I CAN'T EAT CARROTS?
YOU MEAN, YOU CAN?
OF COURSE I CAN!
I JUST DON'T WANT TO!
THEN SHOW US.
NO SWEAT!
AAAAHHH...

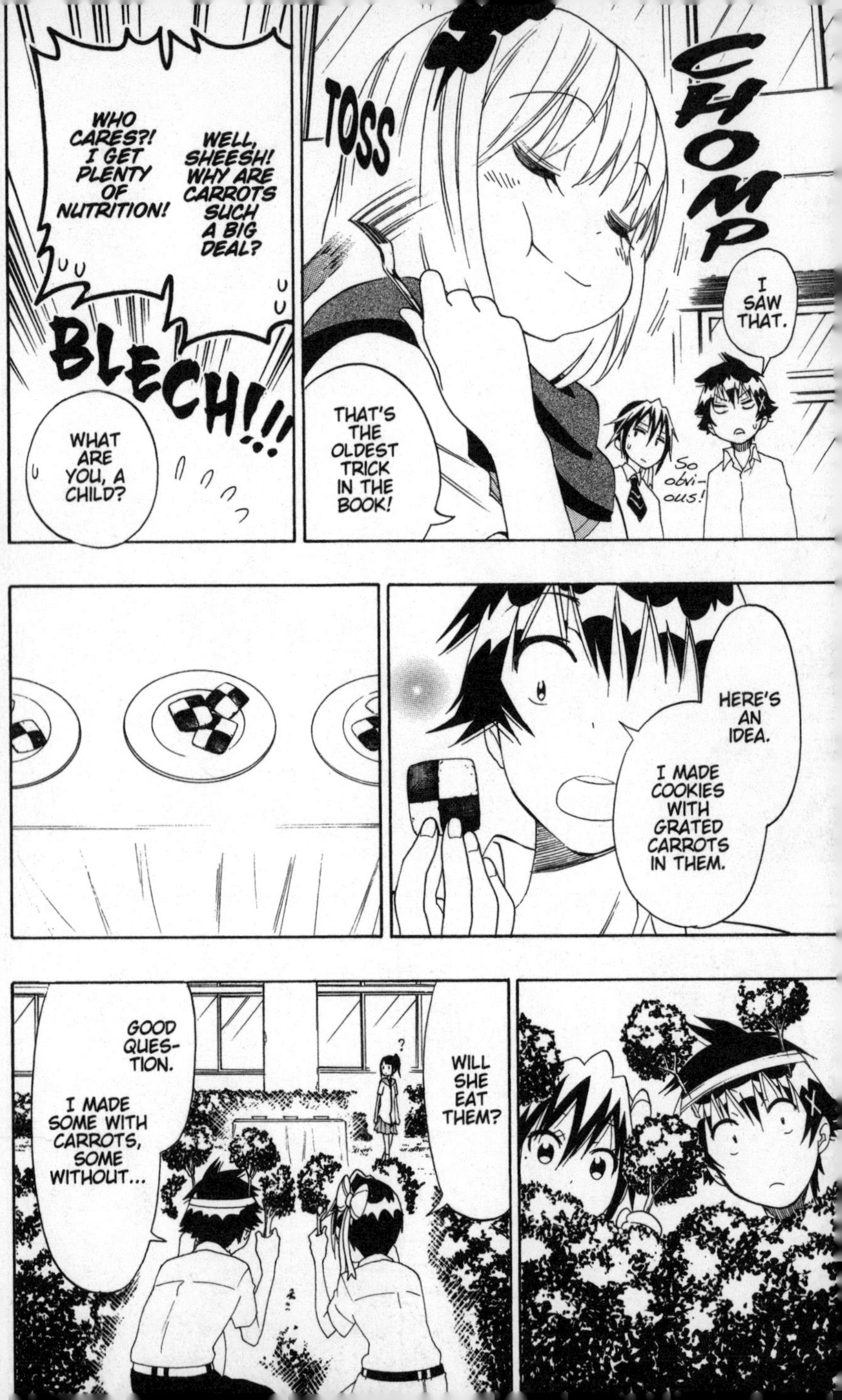
CHOMP
TOSS
I SAW THAT.
So obvi-ous!
THAT'S THE OLDEST TRICK IN THE BOOK!
WELL, SHEESH! WHY ARE CARROTS SUCH A BIG DEAL?
WHO CARES?! I GET PLENTY OF NUTRITION!
BLECH!!!
WHAT ARE YOU, A CHILD?
HERE'S AN IDEA.
I MADE COOKIES WITH GRATED CARROTS IN THEM.
WILL SHE EAT THEM?
?
GOOD QUES-TION.
I MADE SOME WITH CARROTS, SOME WITHOUT...

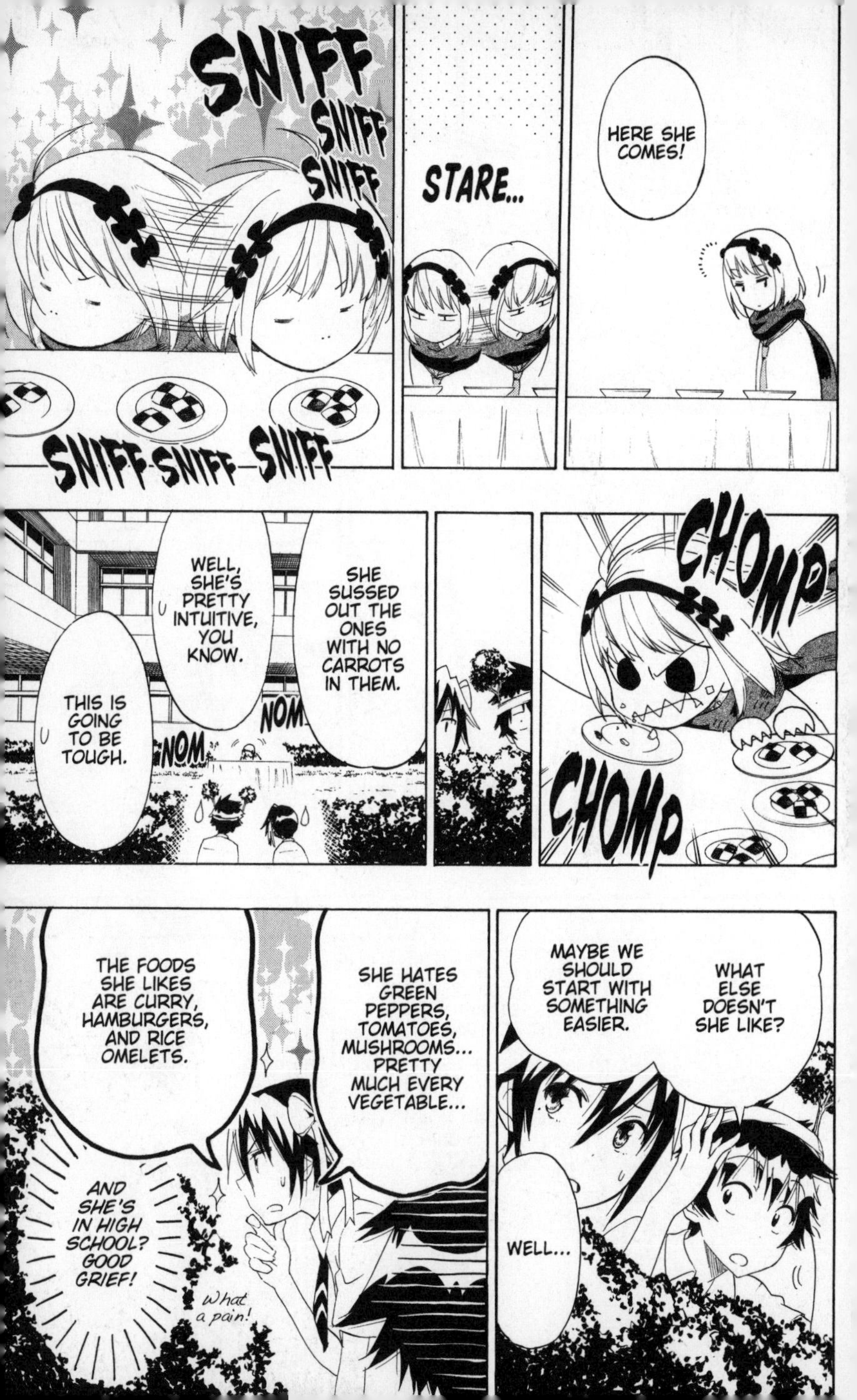
HERE SHE COMES!
STARE...
SNIFF
SNIFF
SNIFF
SNIFF SNIFF SNIFF
CHOMP
CHOMP
SHE SUSSED OUT THE ONES WITH NO CARROTS IN THEM.
WELL, SHE'S PRETTY INTUITIVE, YOU KNOW.
NOM
NOM
THIS IS GOING TO BE TOUGH.
WHAT ELSE DOESN'T SHE LIKE?
MAYBE WE SHOULD START WITH SOMETHING EASIER.
WELL...
SHE HATES GREEN PEPPERS, TOMATOES, MUSHROOMS... PRETTY MUCH EVERY VEGETABLE...
THE FOODS SHE LIKES ARE CURRY, HAMBURGERS, AND RICE OMELETS.
AND SHE'S IN HIGH SCHOOL? GOOD GRIEF!
What a pain!

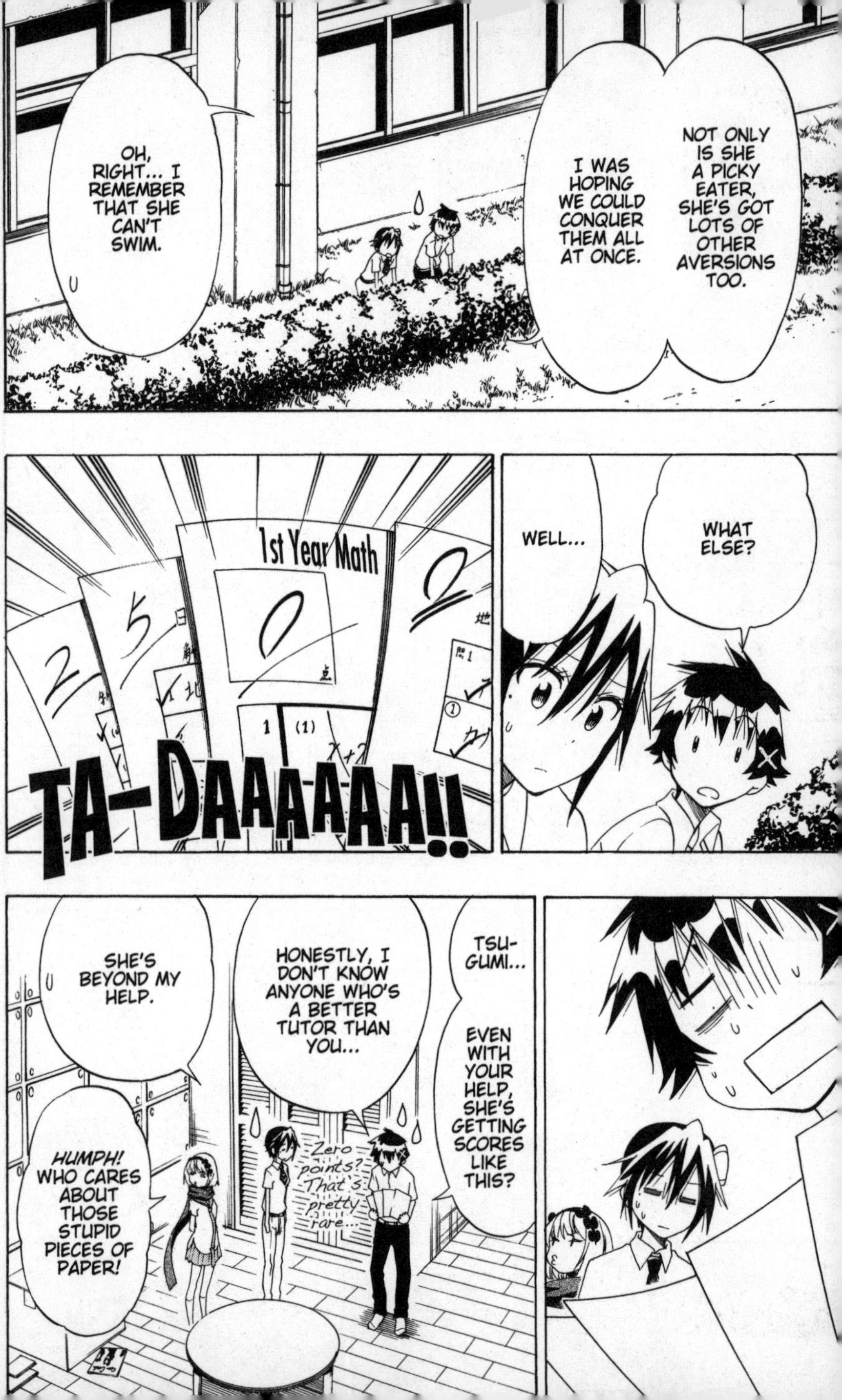
NOT ONLY IS SHE A PICKY EATER, SHE'S GOT LOTS OF OTHER AVERSIONS TOO.
I WAS HOPING WE COULD CONQUER THEM ALL AT ONCE.
OH, RIGHT... I REMEMBER THAT SHE CAN'T SWIM.
WHAT ELSE?
WELL...
1st Year Math
TA-DAAAAAA!!
TSU-GUMI...
EVEN WITH YOUR HELP, SHE'S GETTING SCORES LIKE THIS?
HONESTLY, I DON'T KNOW ANYONE WHO'S A BETTER TUTOR THAN YOU...
Zero points? That's pretty rare...
SHE'S BEYOND MY HELP.
HUMPH! WHO CARES ABOUT THOSE STUPID PIECES OF PAPER!

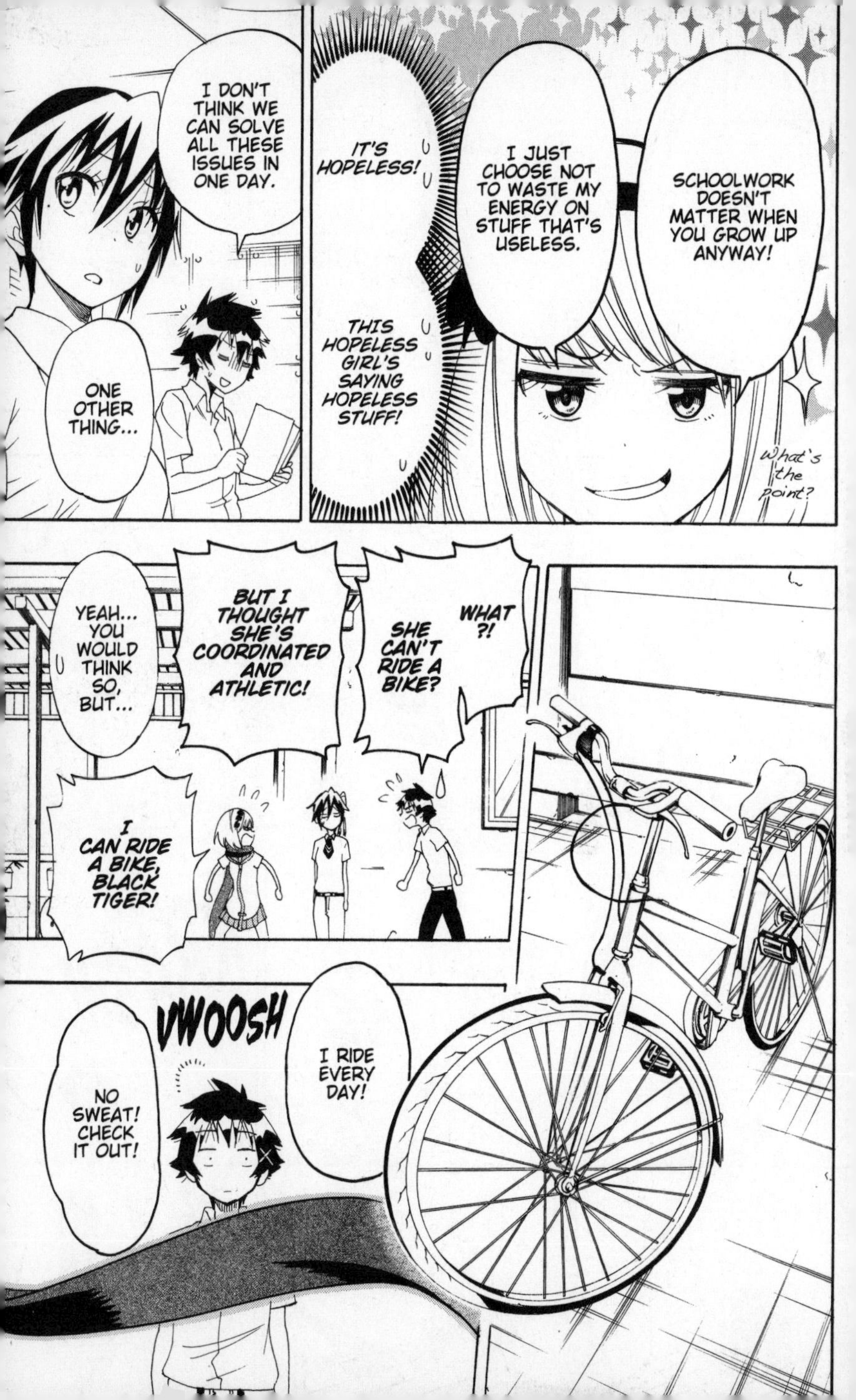
SCHOOLWORK DOESN'T MATTER WHEN YOU GROW UP ANYWAY!
I JUST CHOOSE NOT TO WASTE MY ENERGY ON STUFF THAT'S USELESS.
What's the point?
IT'S HOPELESS!
THIS HOPELESS GIRL'S SAYING HOPELESS STUFF!
I DON'T THINK WE CAN SOLVE ALL THESE ISSUES IN ONE DAY.
ONE OTHER THING...
WHAT?!
SHE CAN'T RIDE A BIKE?
BUT I THOUGHT SHE'S COORDINATED AND ATHLETIC!
YEAH... YOU WOULD THINK SO, BUT...
I CAN RIDE A BIKE, BLACK TIGER!
I RIDE EVERY DAY!
VWOOSH
NO SWEAT! CHECK IT OUT!

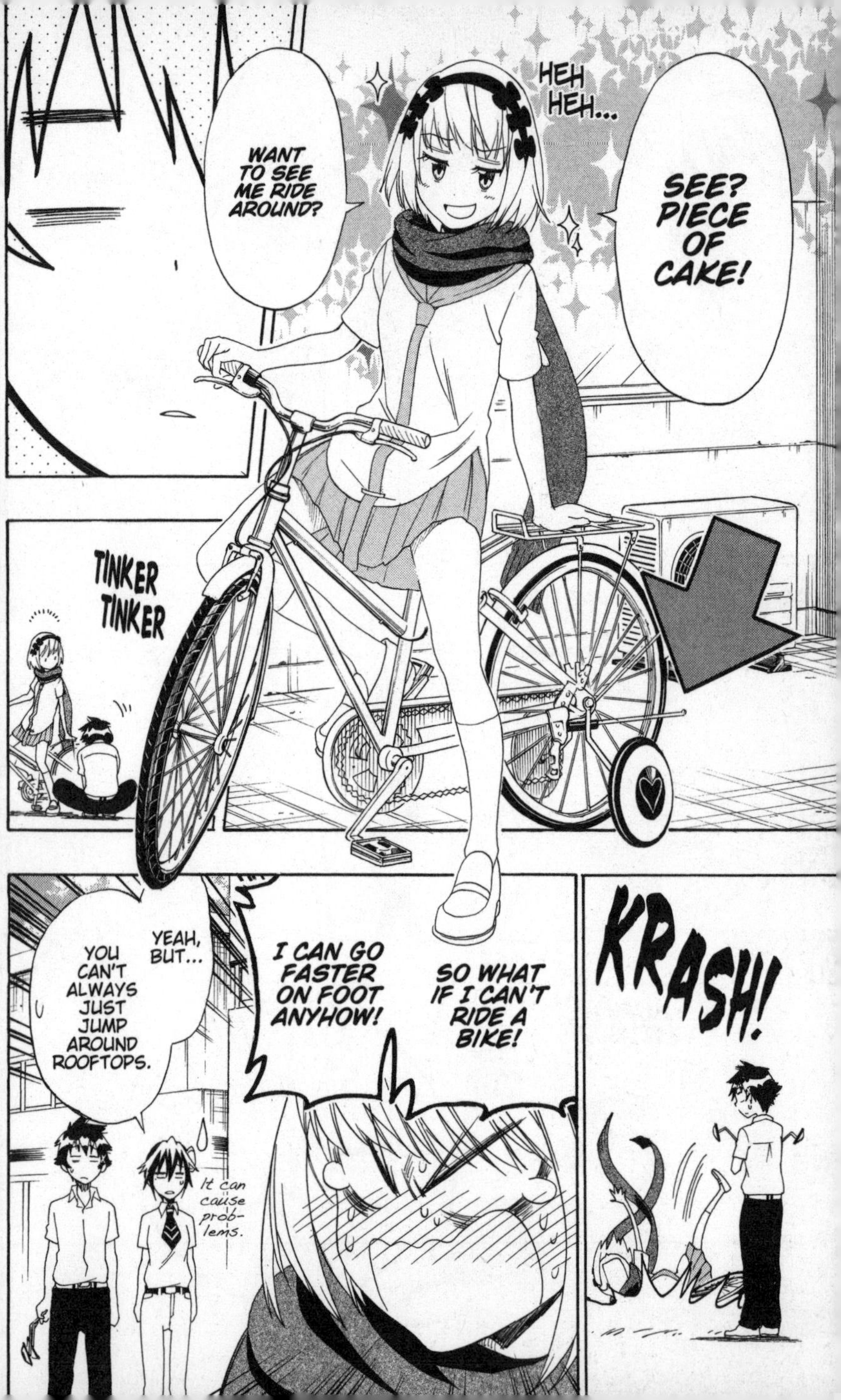
HEH HEH...
SEE? PIECE OF CAKE!
WANT TO SEE ME RIDE AROUND?
TINKER TINKER
KRASH!
SO WHAT IF I CAN'T RIDE A BIKE!
I CAN GO FASTER ON FOOT ANYHOW!
YEAH, BUT...
YOU CAN'T ALWAYS JUST JUMP AROUND ROOFTOPS.
It can cause prob-lems.

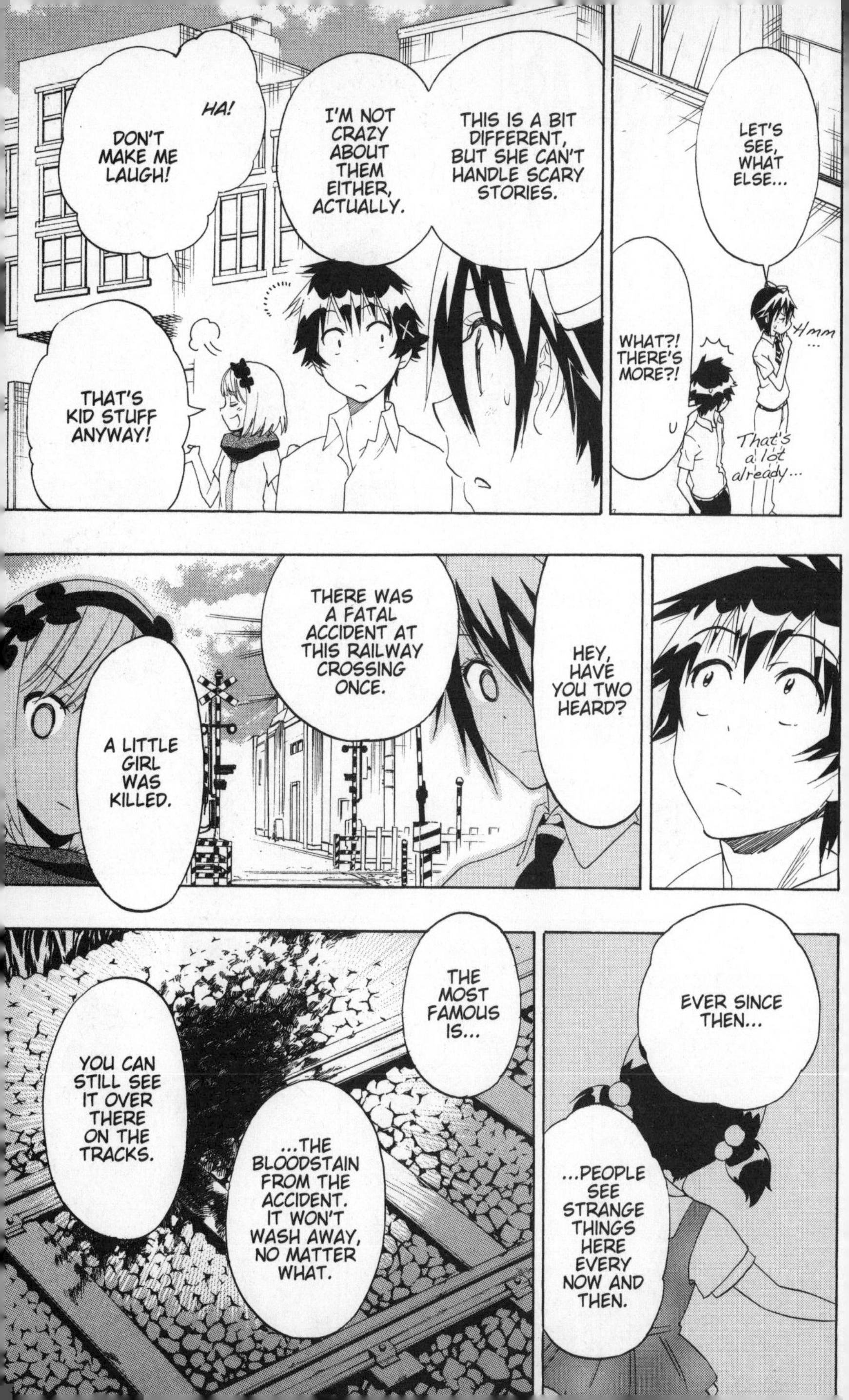
LET'S SEE, WHAT ELSE...
Hmm...
WHAT?! THERE'S MORE?!
That's a lot already...
THIS IS A BIT DIFFERENT, BUT SHE CAN'T HANDLE SCARY STORIES.
I'M NOT CRAZY ABOUT THEM EITHER, ACTUALLY.
HA! DON'T MAKE ME LAUGH!
THAT'S KID STUFF ANYWAY!
HEY, HAVE YOU TWO HEARD?
THERE WAS A FATAL ACCIDENT AT THIS RAILWAY CROSSING ONCE.
A LITTLE GIRL WAS KILLED.
EVER SINCE THEN...
...PEOPLE SEE STRANGE THINGS HERE EVERY NOW AND THEN.
THE MOST FAMOUS IS...
...THE BLOODSTAIN FROM THE ACCIDENT. IT WON'T WASH AWAY, NO MATTER WHAT.
YOU CAN STILL SEE IT OVER THERE ON THE TRACKS.

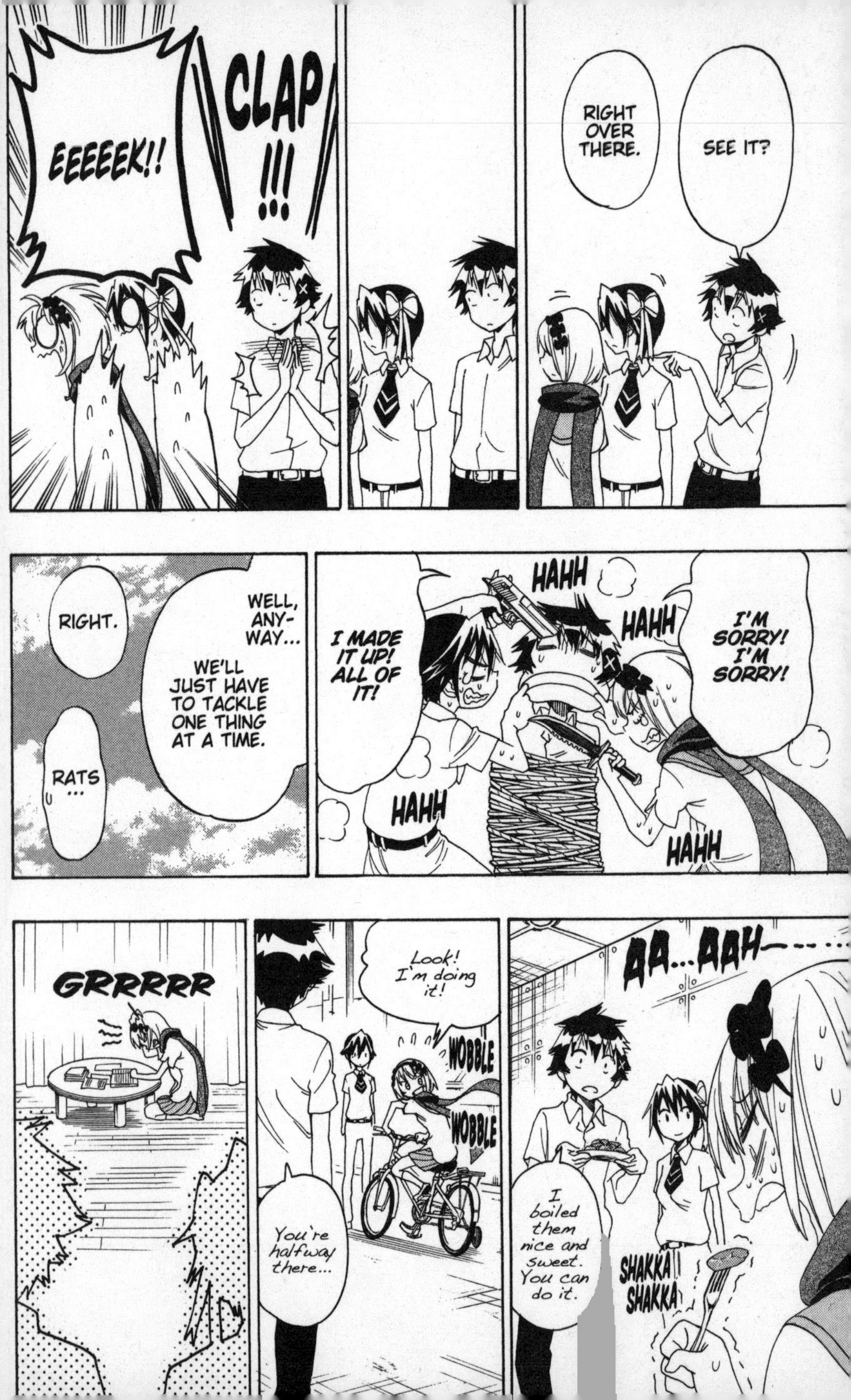
SEE IT?
RIGHT OVER THERE.
CLAP!!!
EEEEEK!!
I'M SORRY! I'M SORRY!
HAHH
HAHH
I MADE IT UP! ALL OF IT!
HAHH
HAHH
WELL, ANY-WAY...
WE'LL JUST HAVE TO TACKLE ONE THING AT A TIME.
RIGHT.
RATS...
AA...AAH—
I boiled them nice and sweet. You can do it.
SHAKKA SHAKKA
Look! I'm doing it!
WOBBLE
WOBBLE
You're halfway there...
GRRRRR

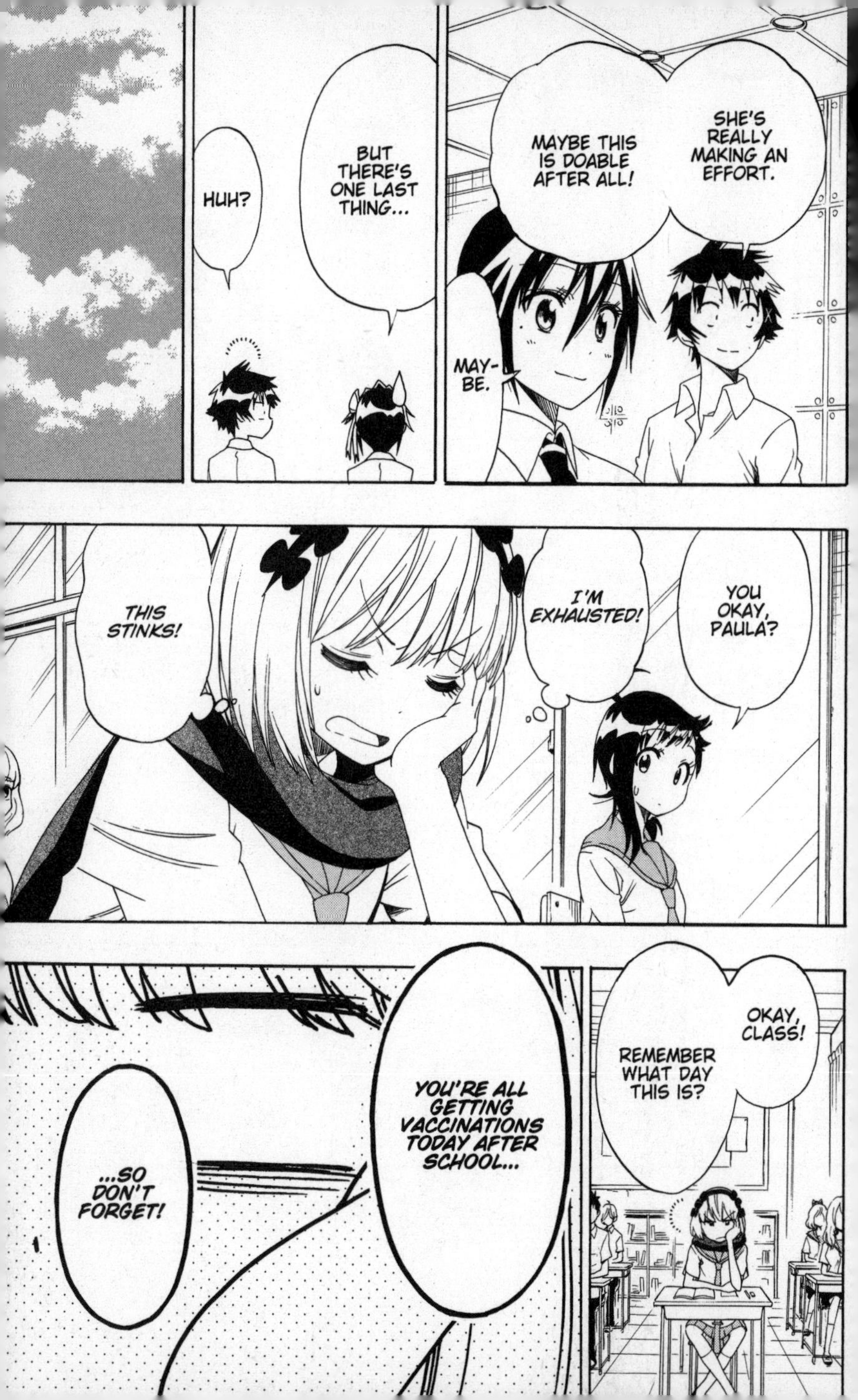
SHE'S REALLY MAKING AN EFFORT.
MAYBE THIS IS DOABLE AFTER ALL!
MAY-BE.
BUT THERE'S ONE LAST THING...
HUH?
YOU OKAY, PAULA?
I'M EXHAUSTED!
THIS STINKS!
OKAY, CLASS!
REMEMBER WHAT DAY THIS IS?
YOU'RE ALL GETTING VACCINATIONS TODAY AFTER SCHOOL...
...SO DON'T FORGET!

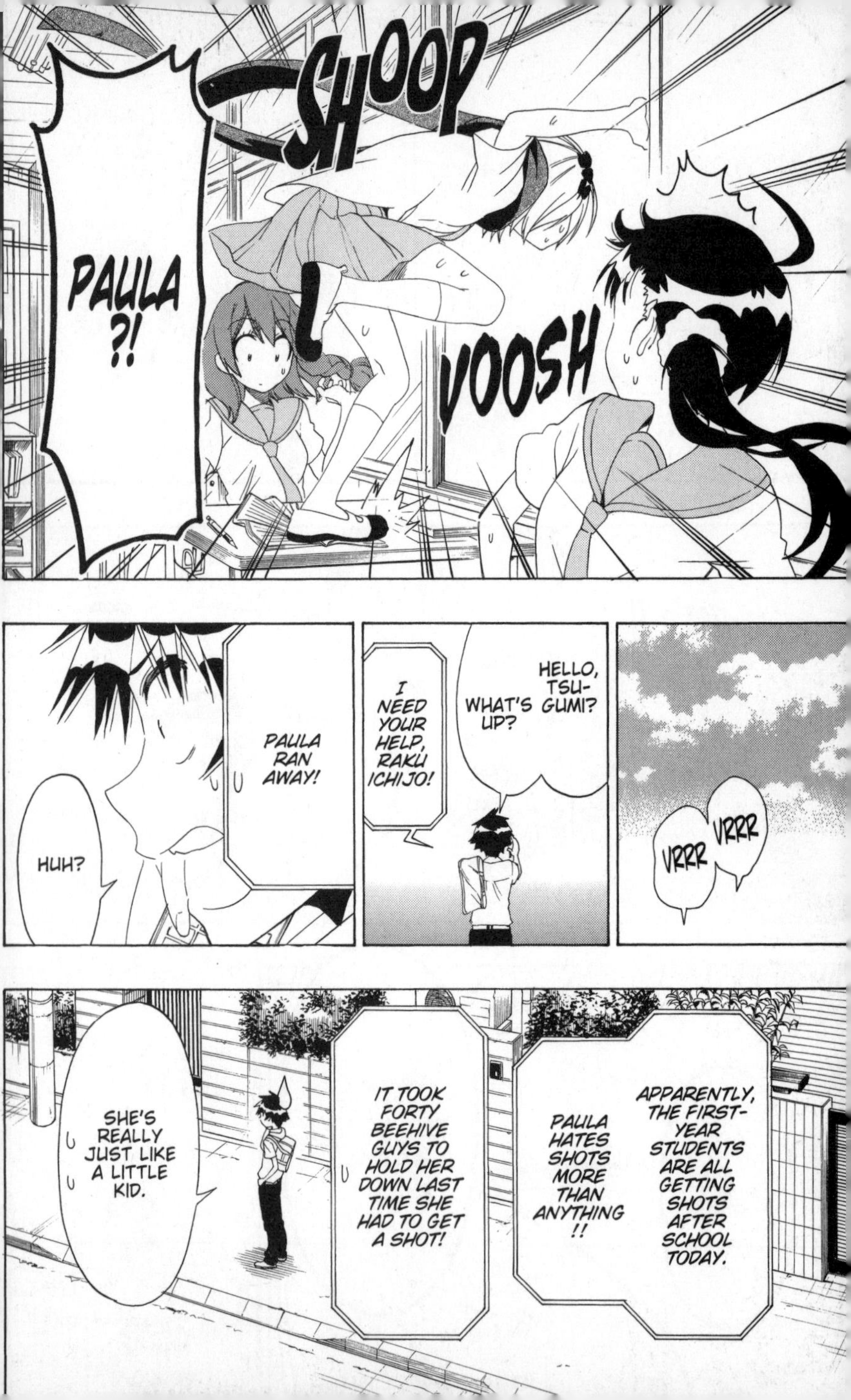
SHOOP
VOOSH
PAULA ?!
VRRR
VRRR
HELLO, TSUGUMI? WHAT'S UP?
I NEED YOUR HELP, RAKU ICHIJO!
PAULA RAN AWAY!
HUH?
APPARENTLY, THE FIRST-YEAR STUDENTS ARE ALL GETTING SHOTS AFTER SCHOOL TODAY.
PAULA HATES SHOTS MORE THAN ANYTHING!!
IT TOOK FORTY BEEHIVE GUYS TO HOLD HER DOWN LAST TIME SHE HAD TO GET A SHOT!
SHE'S REALLY JUST LIKE A LITTLE KID.

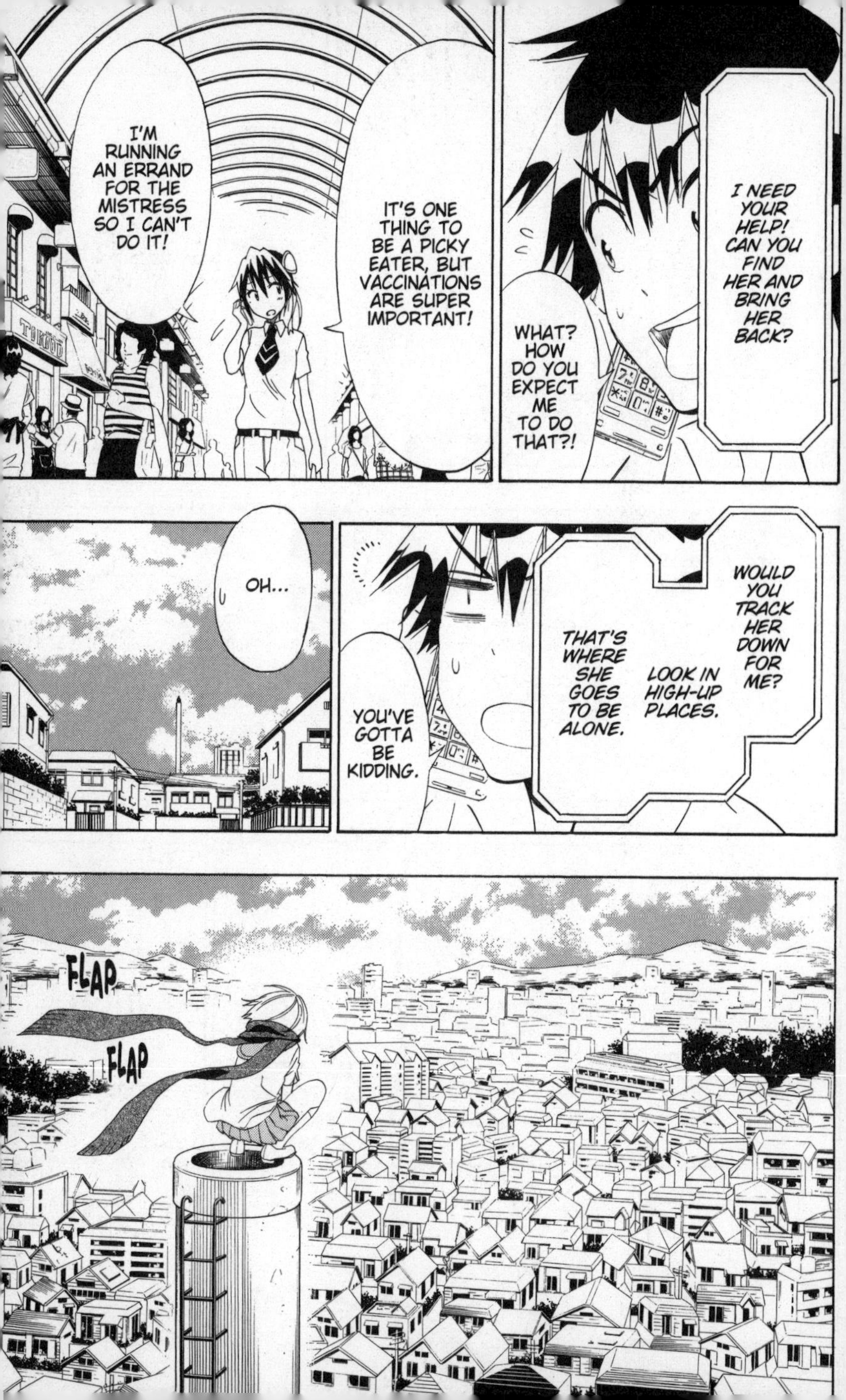
I NEED YOUR HELP! CAN YOU FIND HER AND BRING HER BACK?
WHAT? HOW DO YOU EXPECT ME TO DO THAT?!
IT'S ONE THING TO BE A PICKY EATER, BUT VACCINATIONS ARE SUPER IMPORTANT!
I'M RUNNING AN ERRAND FOR THE MISTRESS SO I CAN'T DO IT!
WOULD YOU TRACK HER DOWN FOR ME?
LOOK IN HIGH-UP PLACES.
THAT'S WHERE SHE GOES TO BE ALONE.
YOU'VE GOTTA BE KIDDING.
OH...
FLAP
FLAP

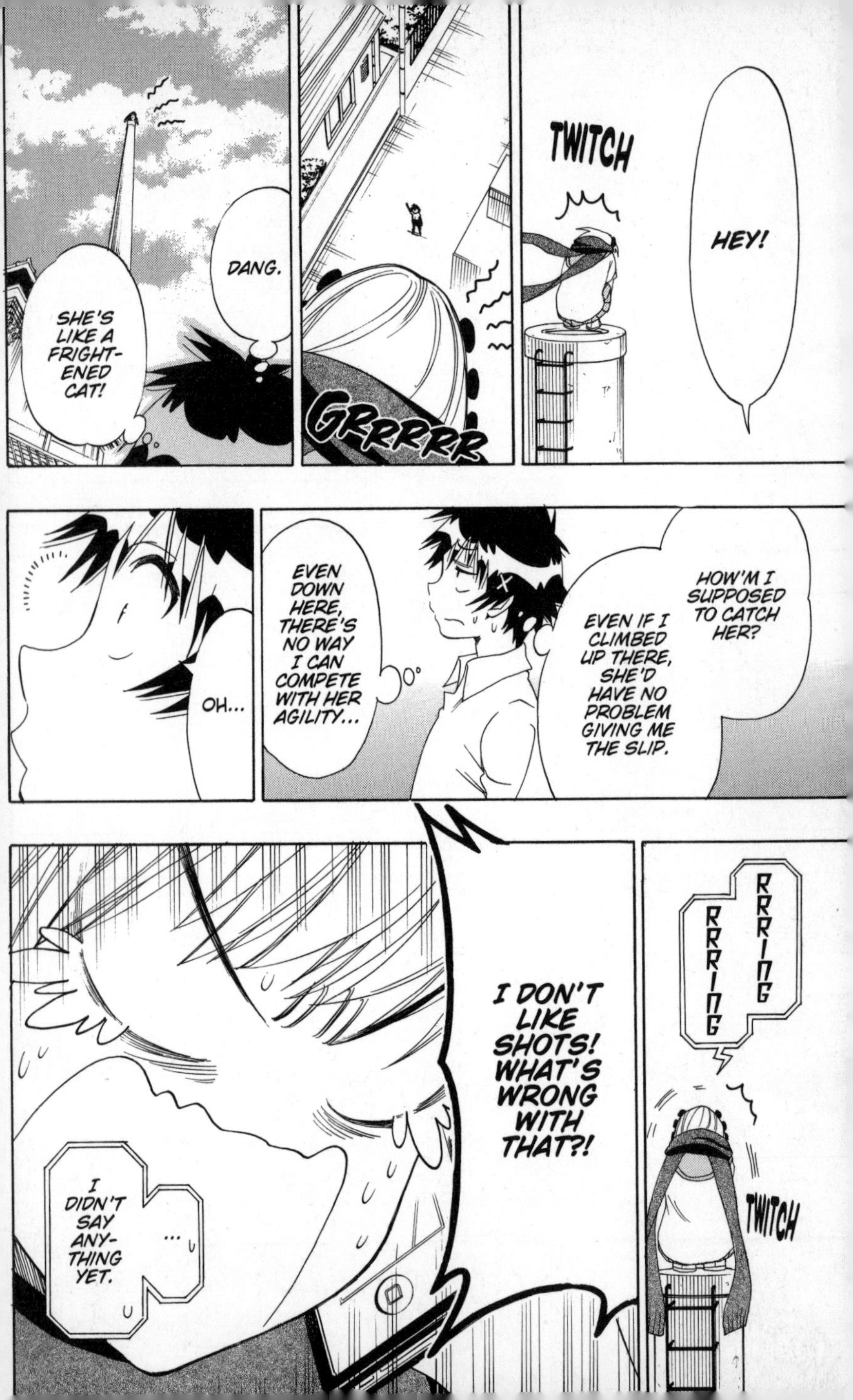
HEY!
TWITCH
GRRRRRR
DANG.
SHE'S LIKE A FRIGHT-ENED CAT!
HOW'M I SUPPOSED TO CATCH HER?
EVEN IF I CLIMBED UP THERE, SHE'D HAVE NO PROBLEM GIVING ME THE SLIP.
EVEN DOWN HERE, THERE'S NO WAY I CAN COMPETE WITH HER AGILITY...
OH...
RRRING
RRRING
TWITCH
I DON'T LIKE SHOTS! WHAT'S WRONG WITH THAT?!
...
I DIDN'T SAY ANY-THING YET.

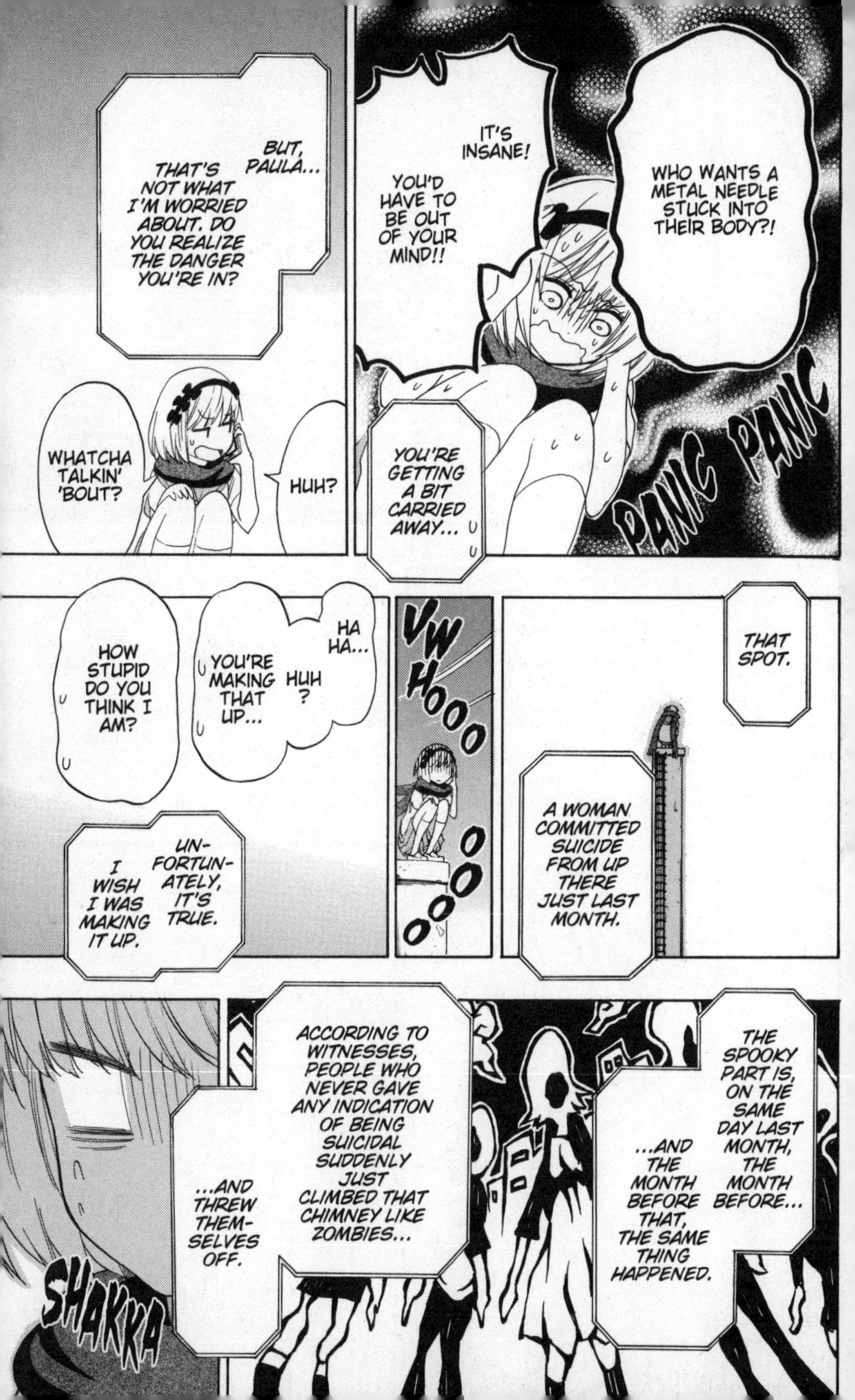
WHO WANTS A METAL NEEDLE STUCK INTO THEIR BODY?!
IT'S INSANE!
YOU'D HAVE TO BE OUT OF YOUR MIND!!
PANIC PANIC
YOU'RE GETTING A BIT CARRIED AWAY...
BUT, PAULA...
THAT'S NOT WHAT I'M WORRIED ABOUT. DO YOU REALIZE THE DANGER YOU'RE IN?
HUH?
WHATCHA TALKIN' 'BOUT?
THAT SPOT.
A WOMAN COMMITTED SUICIDE FROM UP THERE JUST LAST MONTH.
VWHOOOOOOOOO
HA HA...
HUH?
YOU'RE MAKING THAT UP...
HOW STUPID DO YOU THINK I AM?
UN-FORTUN-ATELY, IT'S TRUE.
I WISH I WAS MAKING IT UP.
THE SPOOKY PART IS, ON THE SAME DAY LAST MONTH, THE MONTH BEFORE...
...AND THE MONTH BEFORE THAT, THE SAME THING HAPPENED.
ACCORDING TO WITNESSES, PEOPLE WHO NEVER GAVE ANY INDICATION OF BEING SUICIDAL SUDDENLY JUST CLIMBED THAT CHIMNEY LIKE ZOMBIES...
...AND THREW THEM-SELVES OFF.
SHAKKA

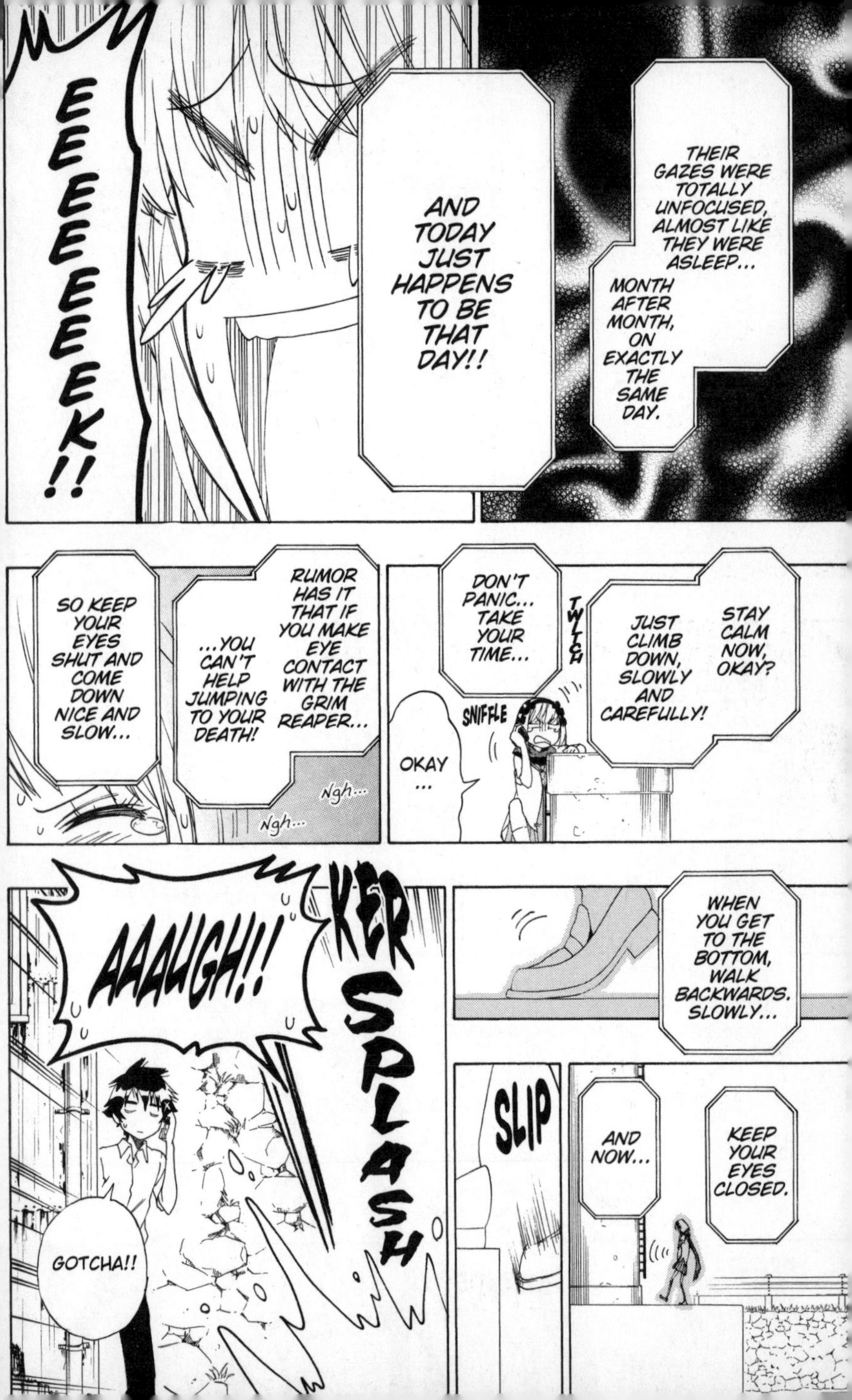
THEIR GAZES WERE TOTALLY UNFOCUSED, ALMOST LIKE THEY WERE ASLEEP...
MONTH AFTER MONTH, ON EXACTLY THE SAME DAY.
AND TODAY JUST HAPPENS TO BE THAT DAY!!
EEEEEEEK!!
STAY CALM NOW, OKAY?
JUST CLIMB DOWN, SLOWLY AND CAREFULLY!
DON'T PANIC... TAKE YOUR TIME...
TWITCH
SNIFFLE
OKAY...
RUMOR HAS IT THAT IF YOU MAKE EYE CONTACT WITH THE GRIM REAPER...
...YOU CAN'T HELP JUMPING TO YOUR DEATH!
SO KEEP YOUR EYES SHUT AND COME DOWN NICE AND SLOW...
Ngh...
Ngh...
WHEN YOU GET TO THE BOTTOM, WALK BACKWARDS. SLOWLY...
KEEP YOUR EYES CLOSED.
AND NOW...
SLIP
KER SPLASH
AAAUGH!!
GOTCHA!!

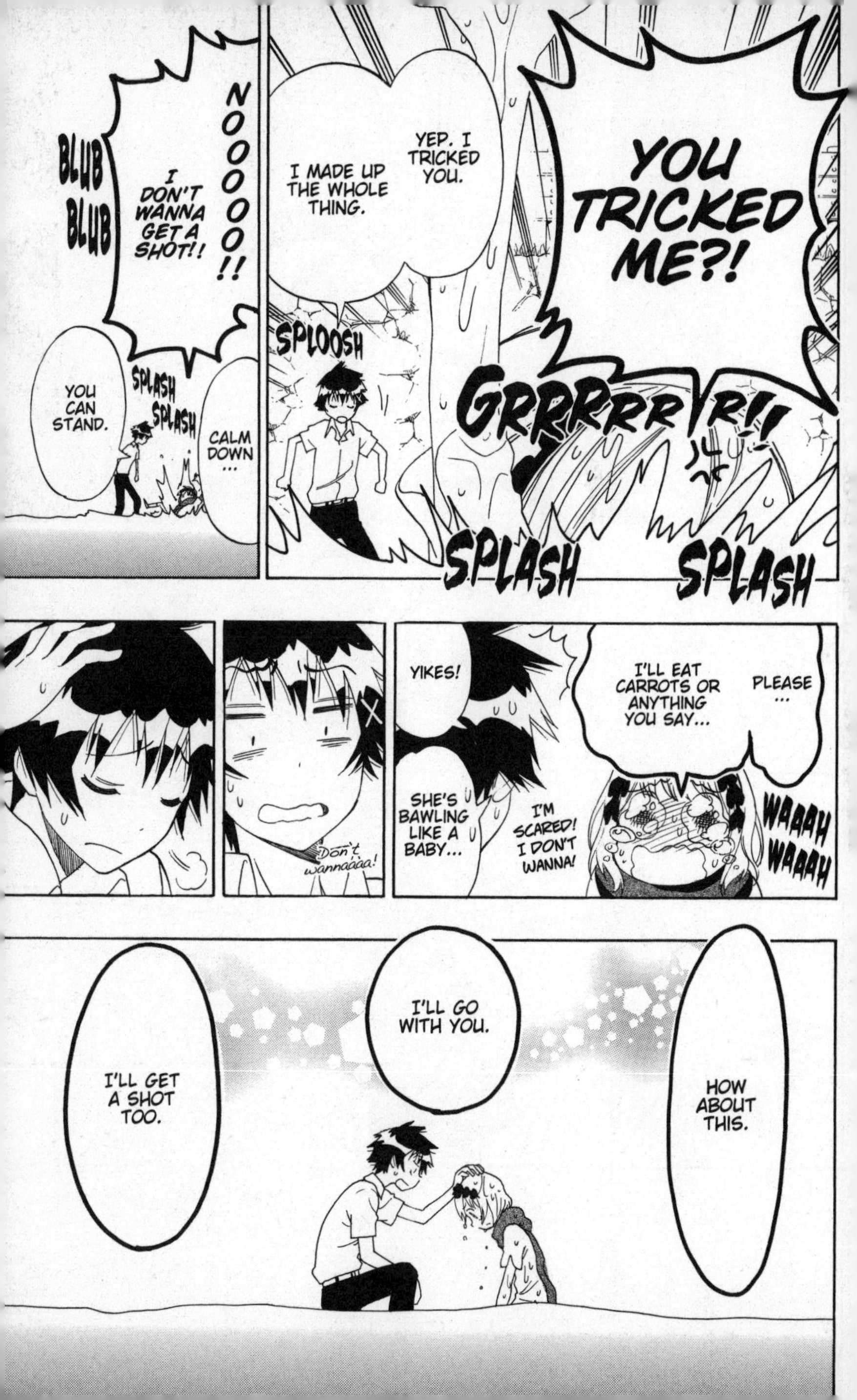
YOU TRICKED ME?!
GRRRRRR!!
SPLASH
SPLASH
YEP. I TRICKED YOU.
I MADE UP THE WHOLE THING.
SPLOOSH
NOOOOOO!!
I DON'T WANNA GET A SHOT!!
BLUB BLUB
CALM DOWN...
SPLASH SPLASH
YOU CAN STAND.
PLEASE...
I'LL EAT CARROTS OR ANYTHING YOU SAY...
WAAAH WAAAH
YIKES!
I'M SCARED! I DON'T WANNA!
SHE'S BAWLING LIKE A BABY...
Don't wannaaaa!
HOW ABOUT THIS.
I'LL GO WITH YOU.
I'LL GET A SHOT TOO.

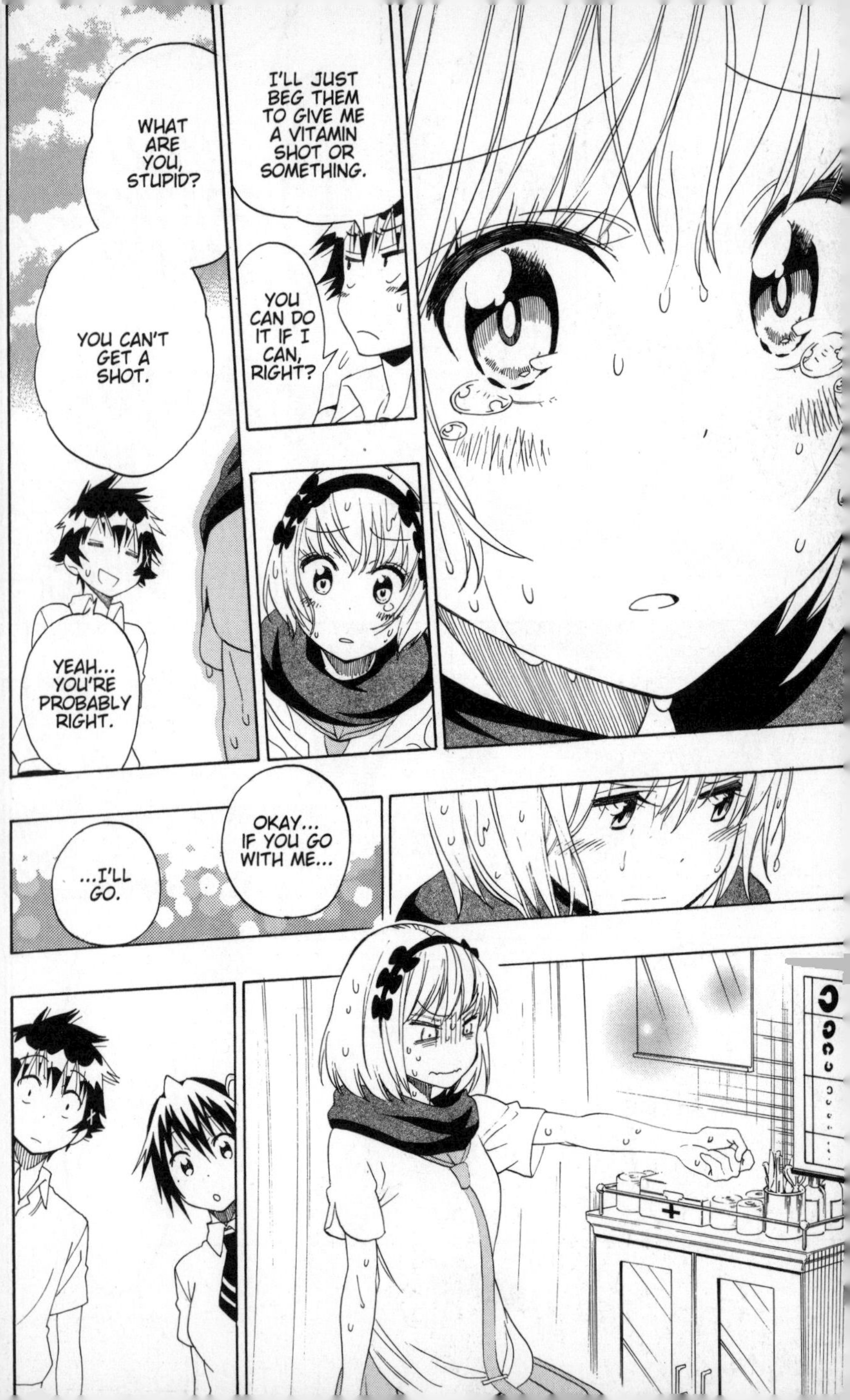

I'LL JUST BEG THEM TO GIVE ME A VITAMIN SHOT OR SOMETHING.
YOU CAN DO IT IF I CAN, RIGHT?
WHAT ARE YOU, STUPID?
YOU CAN'T GET A SHOT.
YEAH... YOU'RE PROBABLY RIGHT.
OKAY... IF YOU GO WITH ME...
...I'LL GO.

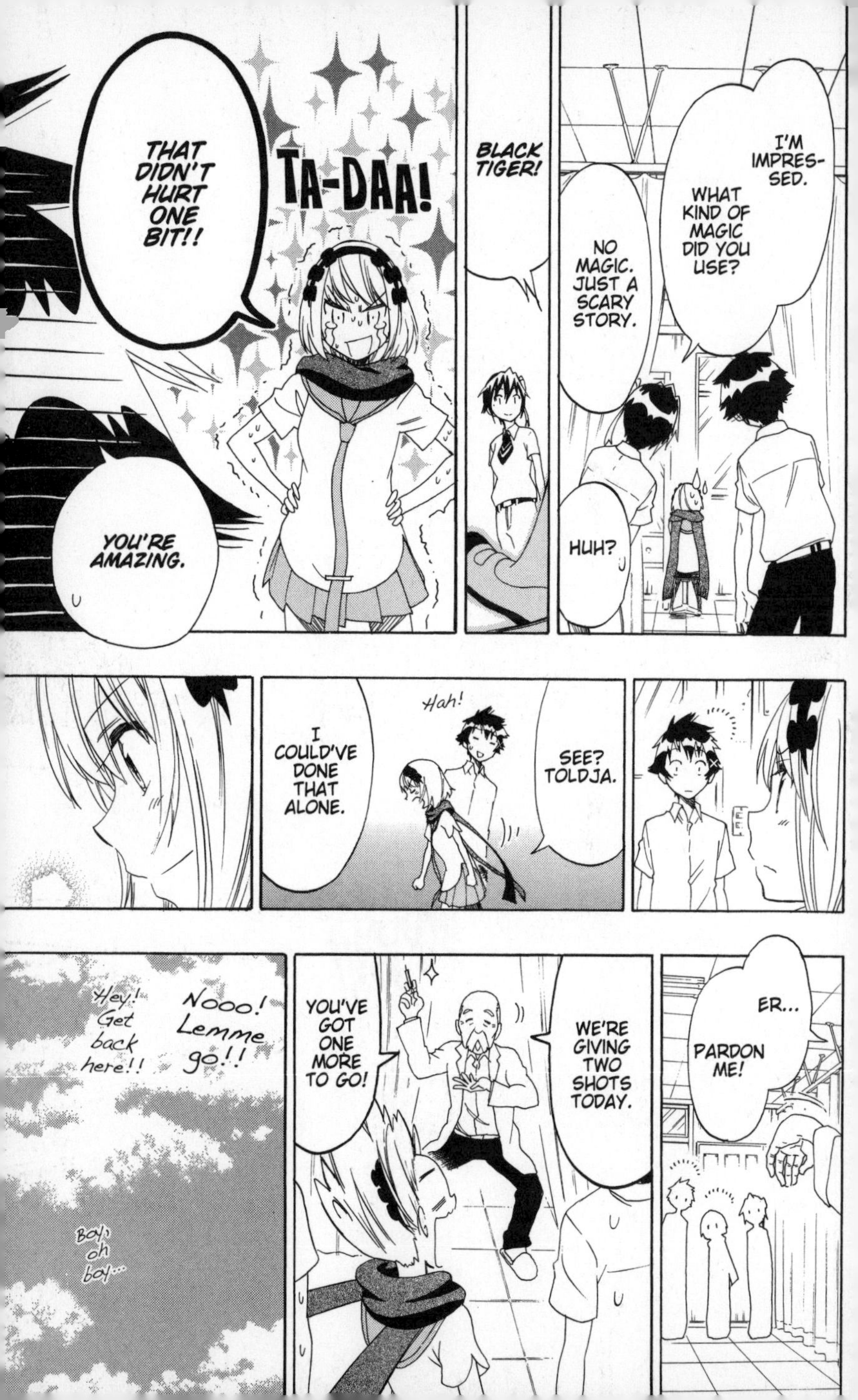
I'M IMPRESSED.
WHAT KIND OF MAGIC DID YOU USE?
NO MAGIC. JUST A SCARY STORY.
HUH?
BLACK TIGER!
TA-DAA!
THAT DIDN'T HURT ONE BIT!!
YOU'RE AMAZING.
SEE? TOLDJA.
Hah!
I COULD'VE DONE THAT ALONE.
ER...
PARDON ME!
WE'RE GIVING TWO SHOTS TODAY.
YOU'VE GOT ONE MORE TO GO!
Nooo! Lemme go!!
Hey! Get back here!!
Boy, oh boy...

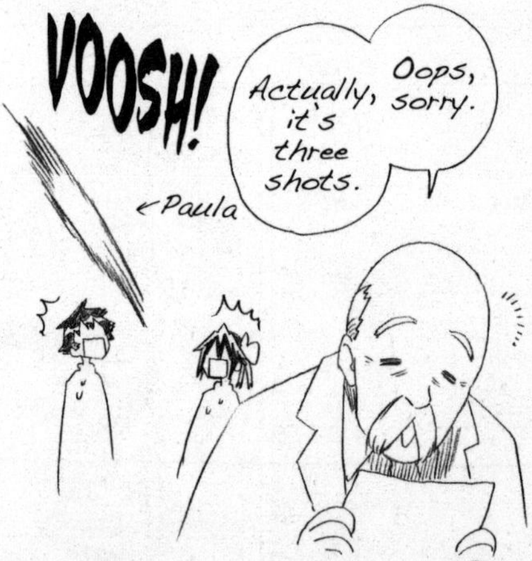
Oops, sorry.
Actually, it's three shots.
VOOSH!
←Paula

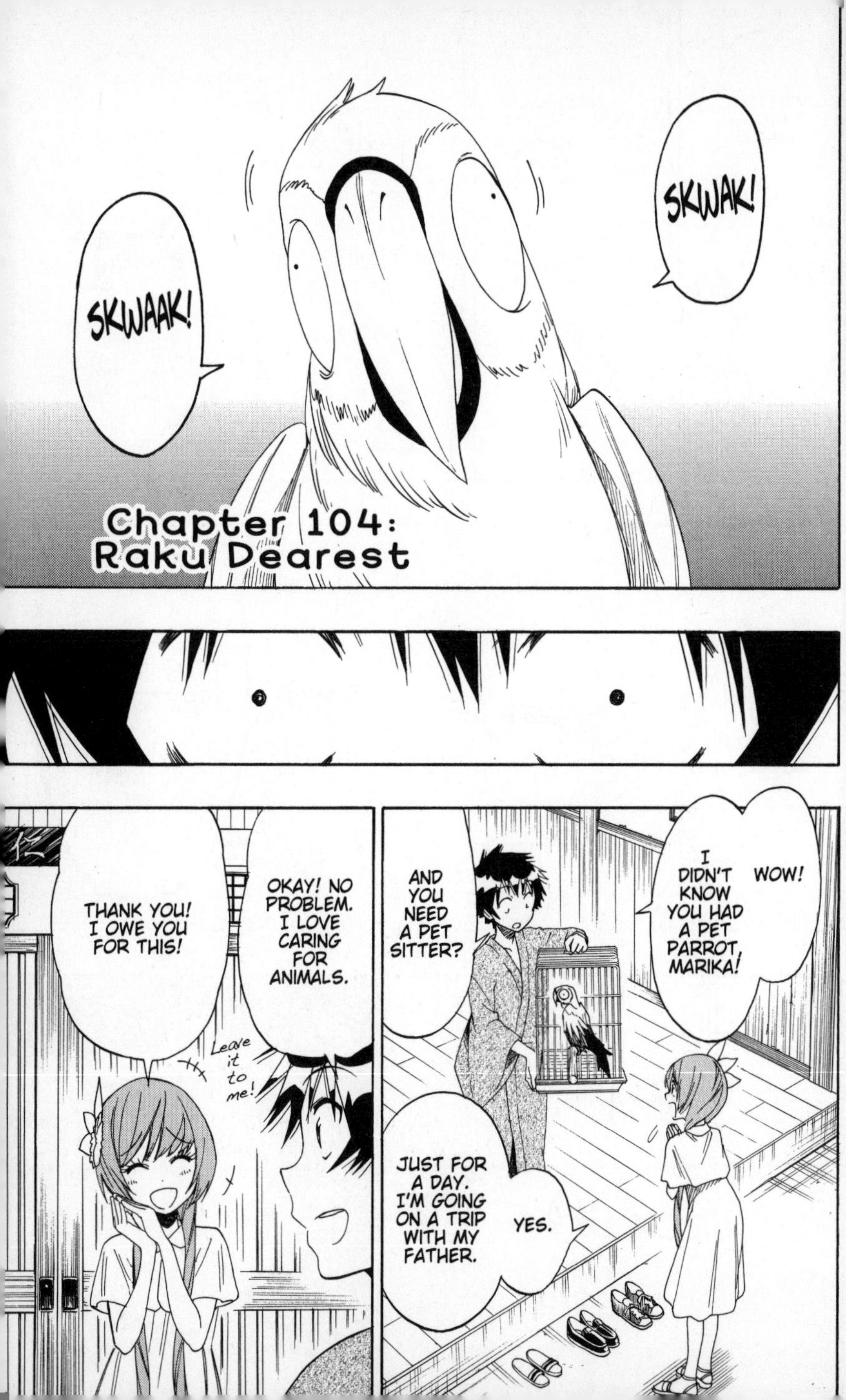
SKWAK!
SKWAAK!
Chapter 104: Raku Dearest
WOW! I DIDN'T KNOW YOU HAD A PET PARROT, MARIKA!
AND YOU NEED A PET SITTER?
YES.
JUST FOR A DAY. I'M GOING ON A TRIP WITH MY FATHER.
OKAY! NO PROBLEM. I LOVE CARING FOR ANIMALS.
Leave it to me!
THANK YOU! I OWE YOU FOR THIS!

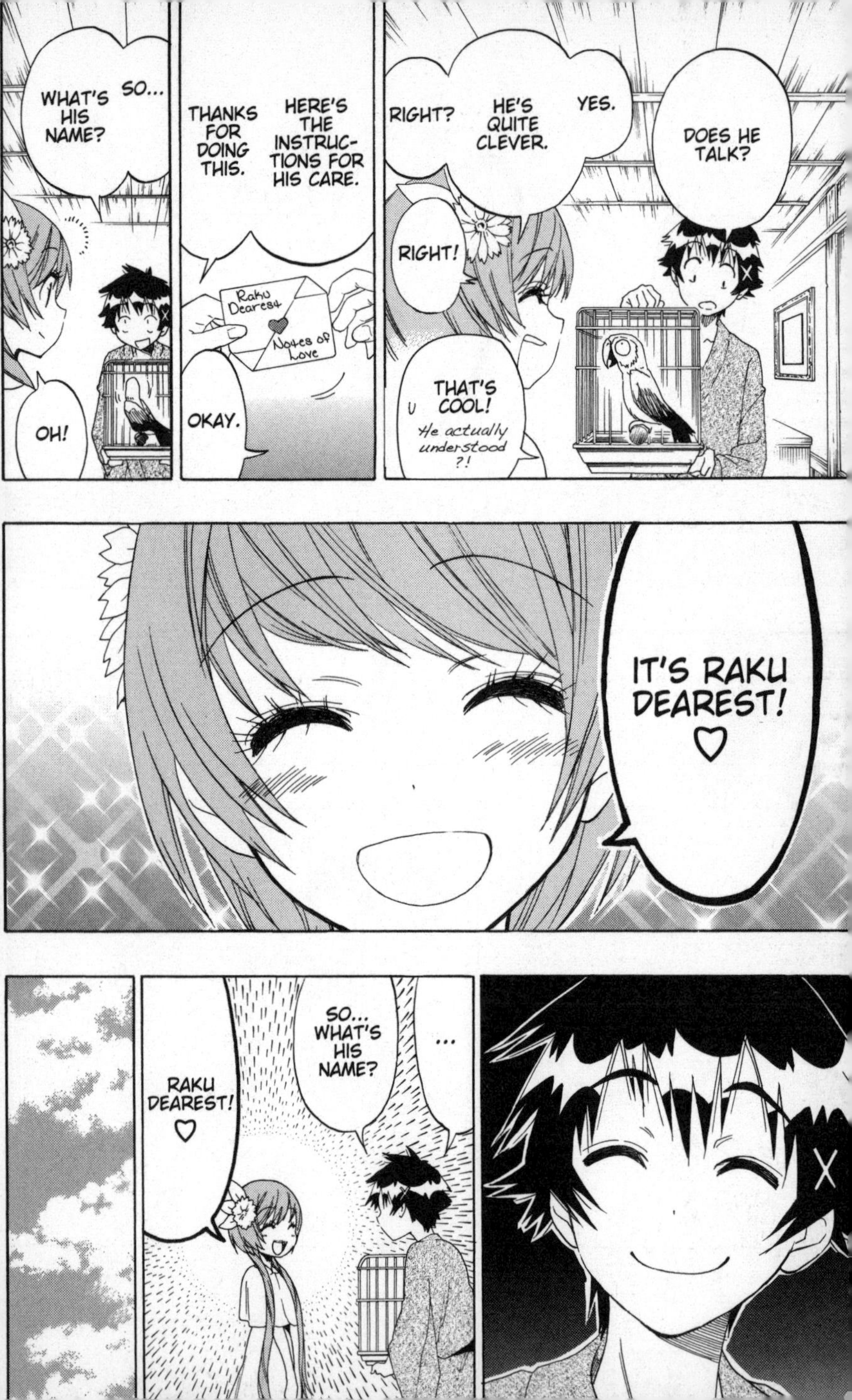
DOES HE TALK?
YES.
HE'S QUITE CLEVER.
RIGHT?
RIGHT!
THAT'S COOL!
He actually understood?!
HERE'S THE INSTRUCTIONS FOR HIS CARE.
THANKS FOR DOING THIS.
Raku Dearest ♡ Notes of Love
OKAY.
SO...
WHAT'S HIS NAME?
OH!
IT'S RAKU DEAREST! ♡
...
SO... WHAT'S HIS NAME?
RAKU DEAREST! ♡

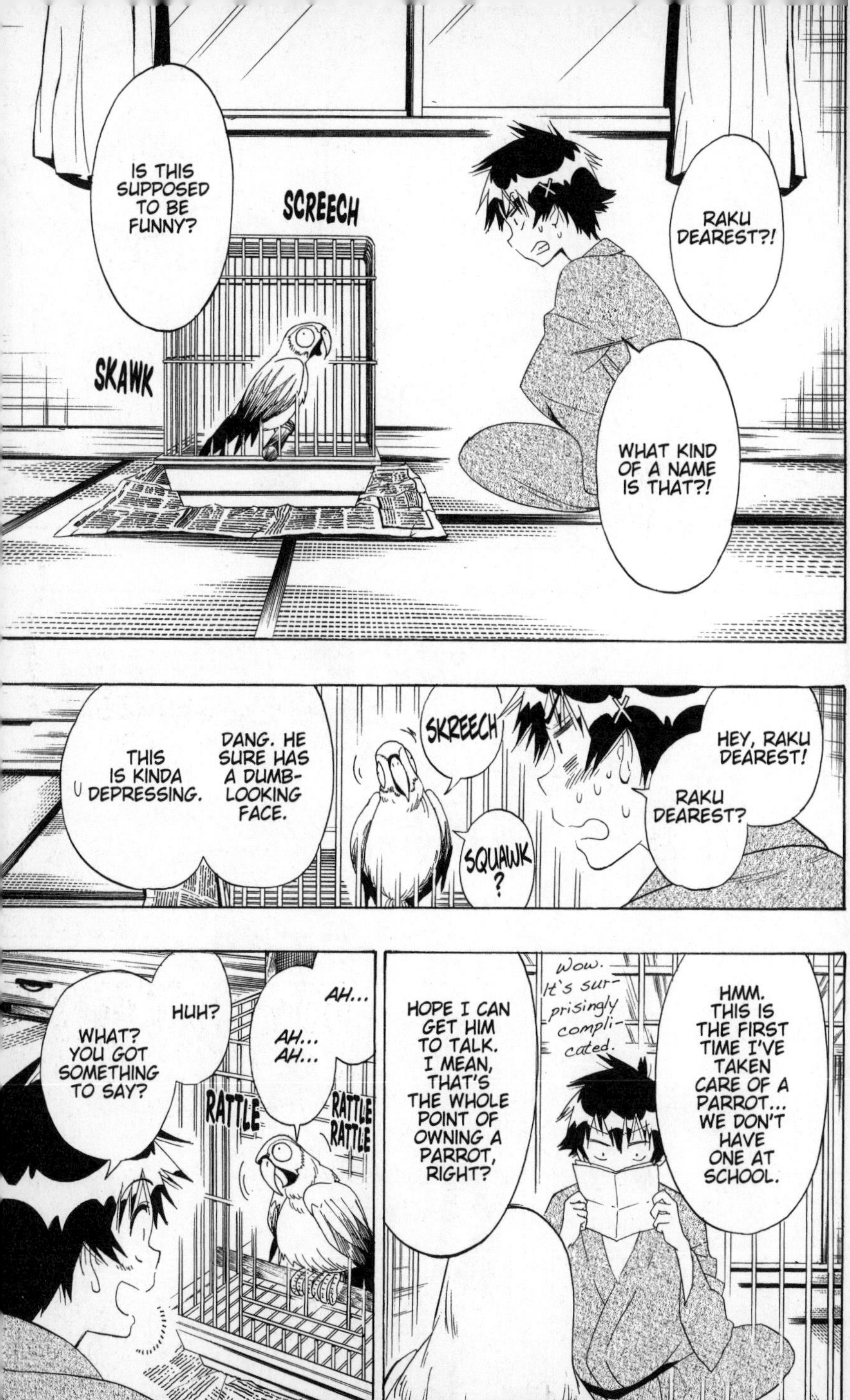
RAKU DEAREST?!
WHAT KIND OF A NAME IS THAT?!
SCREECH
IS THIS SUPPOSED TO BE FUNNY?
SKAWK
HEY, RAKU DEAREST!
RAKU DEAREST?
SKREECH
SQUAWK ?
DANG. HE SURE HAS A DUMB-LOOKING FACE.
THIS IS KINDA DEPRESSING.
HMM. THIS IS THE FIRST TIME I'VE TAKEN CARE OF A PARROT... WE DON'T HAVE ONE AT SCHOOL.
Wow. It's surprisingly complicated.
HOPE I CAN GET HIM TO TALK. I MEAN, THAT'S THE WHOLE POINT OF OWNING A PARROT, RIGHT?
AH... AH... AH...
RATTLE RATTLE
RATTLE
HUH?
WHAT? YOU GOT SOMETHING TO SAY?

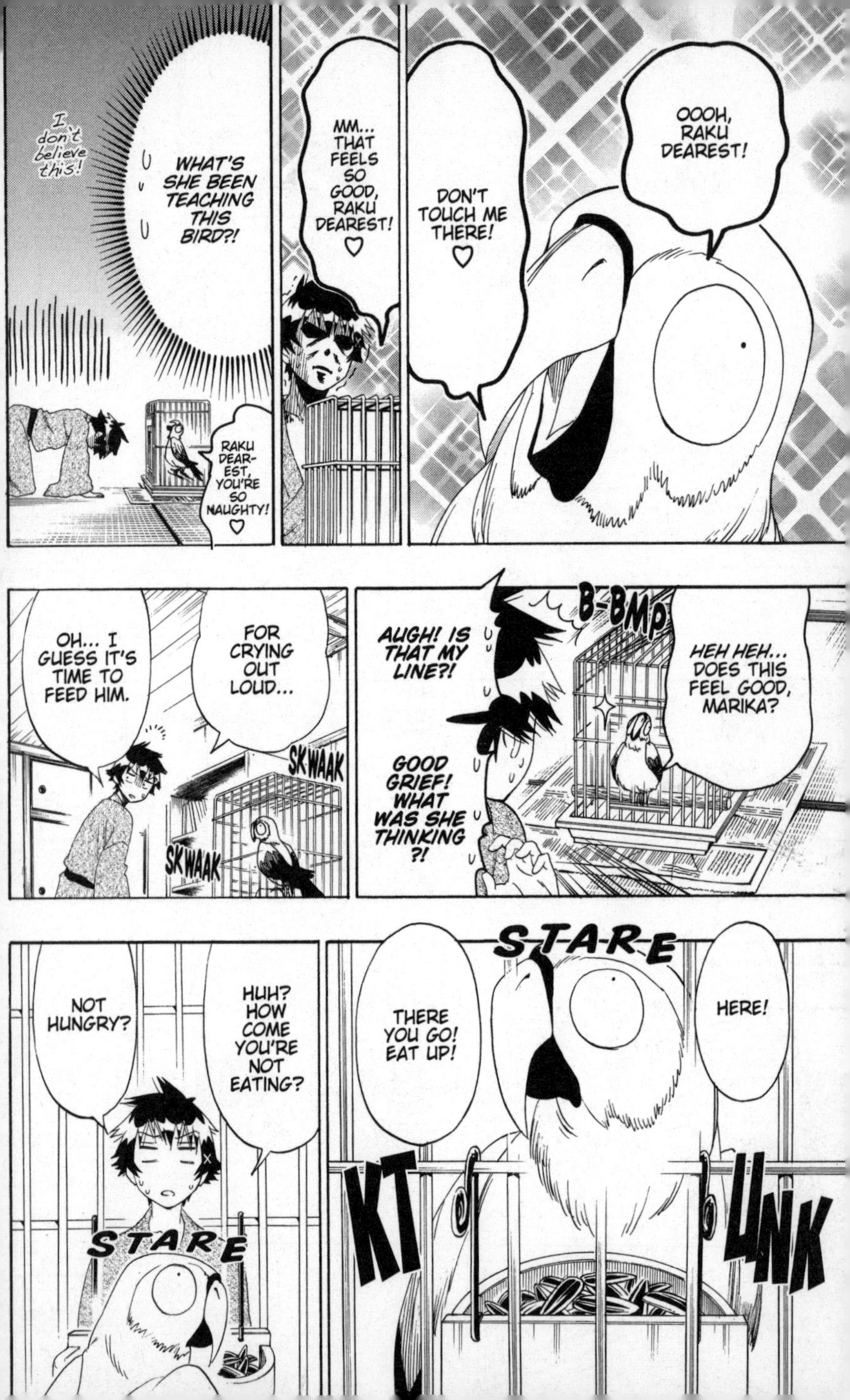
OOOH, RAKU DEAREST!
DON'T TOUCH ME THERE! ♡
MM... THAT FEELS SO GOOD, RAKU DEAREST! ♡
WHAT'S SHE BEEN TEACHING THIS BIRD?!
I don't believe this!
RAKU DEAREST, YOU'RE SO NAUGHTY! ♡
B-BMP
HEH HEH... DOES THIS FEEL GOOD, MARIKA?
AUGH! IS THAT MY LINE?!
GOOD GRIEF! WHAT WAS SHE THINKING?!
FOR CRYING OUT LOUD...
OH... I GUESS IT'S TIME TO FEED HIM.
SKWAAK
SKWAAK
HERE!
STARE
THERE YOU GO! EAT UP!
KT
UNK
HUH? HOW COME YOU'RE NOT EATING?
NOT HUNGRY?
STARE

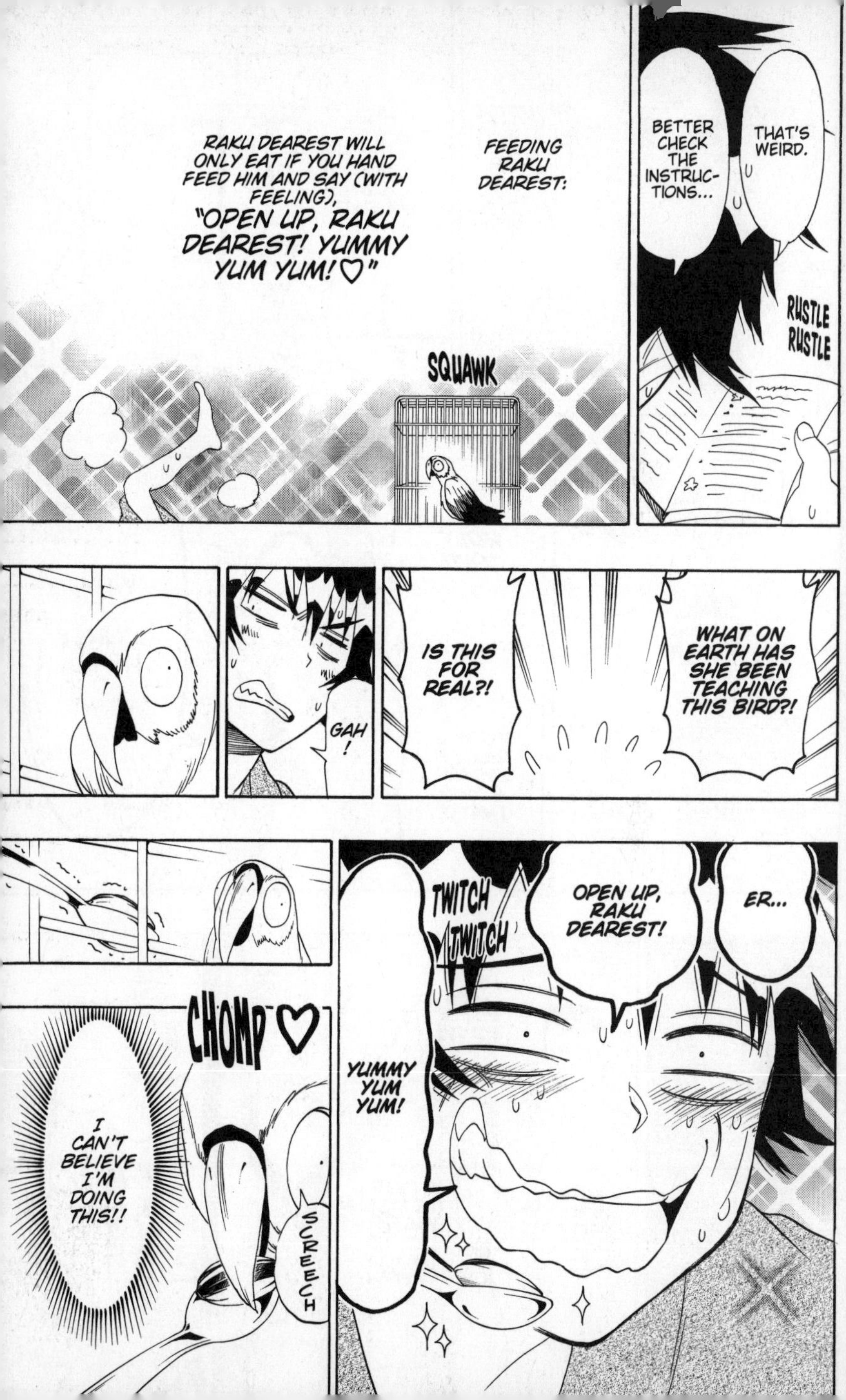
THAT'S WEIRD.
BETTER CHECK THE INSTRUCTIONS...
RUSTLE RUSTLE
FEEDING RAKU DEAREST:
RAKU DEAREST WILL ONLY EAT IF YOU HAND FEED HIM AND SAY (WITH FEELING), "OPEN UP, RAKU DEAREST! YUMMY YUM YUM! ♡"
SQUAWK
WHAT ON EARTH HAS SHE BEEN TEACHING THIS BIRD?!
IS THIS FOR REAL?!
GAH!
ER...
OPEN UP, RAKU DEAREST!
TWITCH TWITCH
YUMMY YUM YUM!
CHOMP ♡
SCREECH
I CAN'T BELIEVE I'M DOING THIS!!

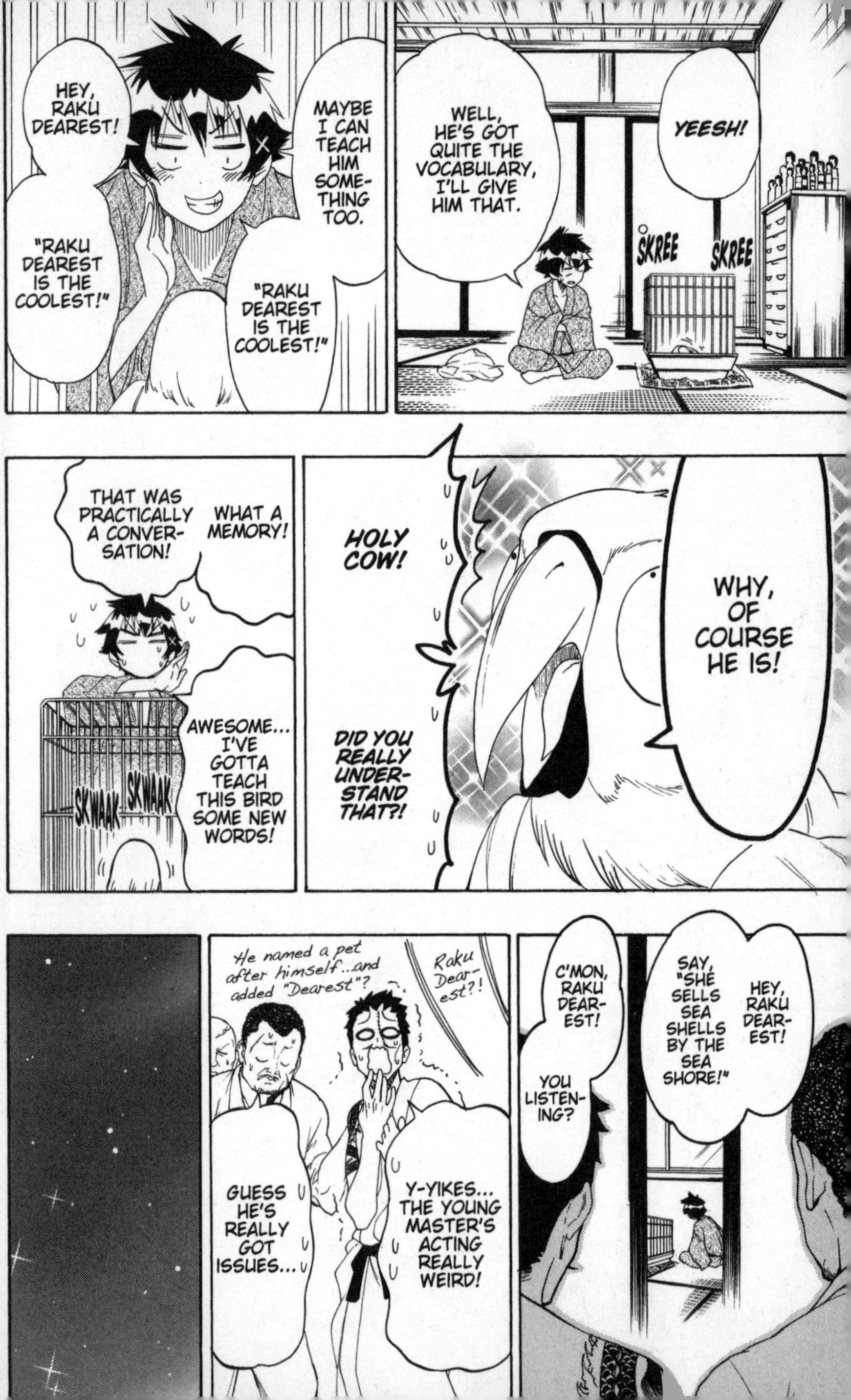
YEESH!
WELL, HE'S GOT QUITE THE VOCABULARY, I'LL GIVE HIM THAT.
SKREE
SKREE
MAYBE I CAN TEACH HIM SOMETHING TOO.
HEY, RAKU DEAREST!
"RAKU DEAREST IS THE COOLEST!"
"RAKU DEAREST IS THE COOLEST!"
WHY, OF COURSE HE IS!
HOLY COW!
DID YOU REALLY UNDERSTAND THAT?!
WHAT A MEMORY!
THAT WAS PRACTICALLY A CONVERSATION!
AWESOME... I'VE GOTTA TEACH THIS BIRD SOME NEW WORDS!
SKWAAK
SKWAAK
HEY, RAKU DEAREST!
SAY, "SHE SELLS SEA SHELLS BY THE SEA SHORE!"
C'MON, RAKU DEAREST!
YOU LISTENING?
Raku Dearest?!
He named a pet after himself...and added "Dearest"?
Y-YIKES... THE YOUNG MASTER'S ACTING REALLY WEIRD!
GUESS HE'S REALLY GOT ISSUES...

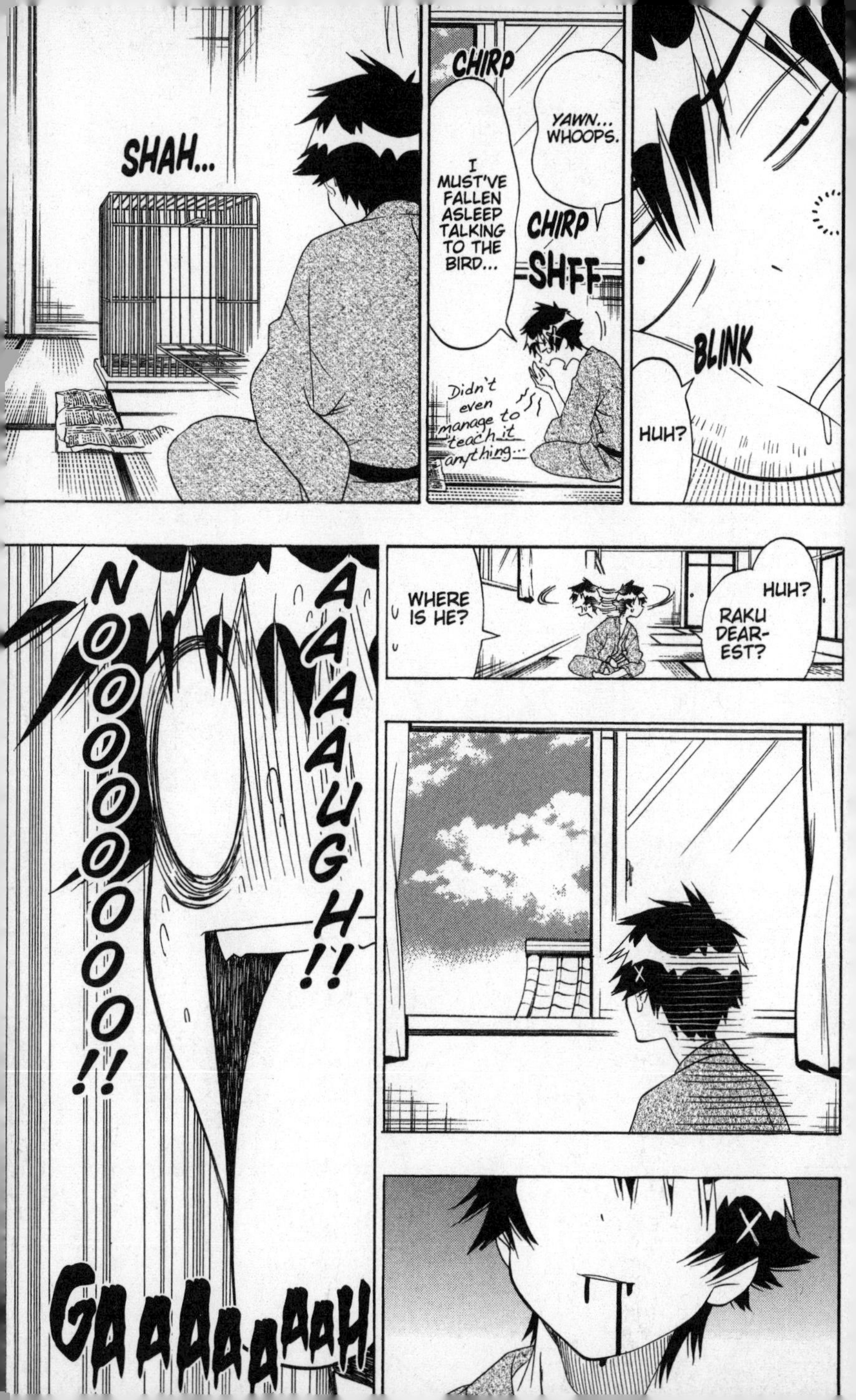
BLINK
HUH?
CHIRP
YAWN... WHOOPS.
I MUST'VE FALLEN ASLEEP TALKING TO THE BIRD...
CHIRP
SHFF
Didn't even manage to teach it anything...
SHAH...
HUH? RAKU DEAREST?
WHERE IS HE?
AAAAAUGH!!
NOOOOOOOOOOOO!!
GAAAA-AAAH

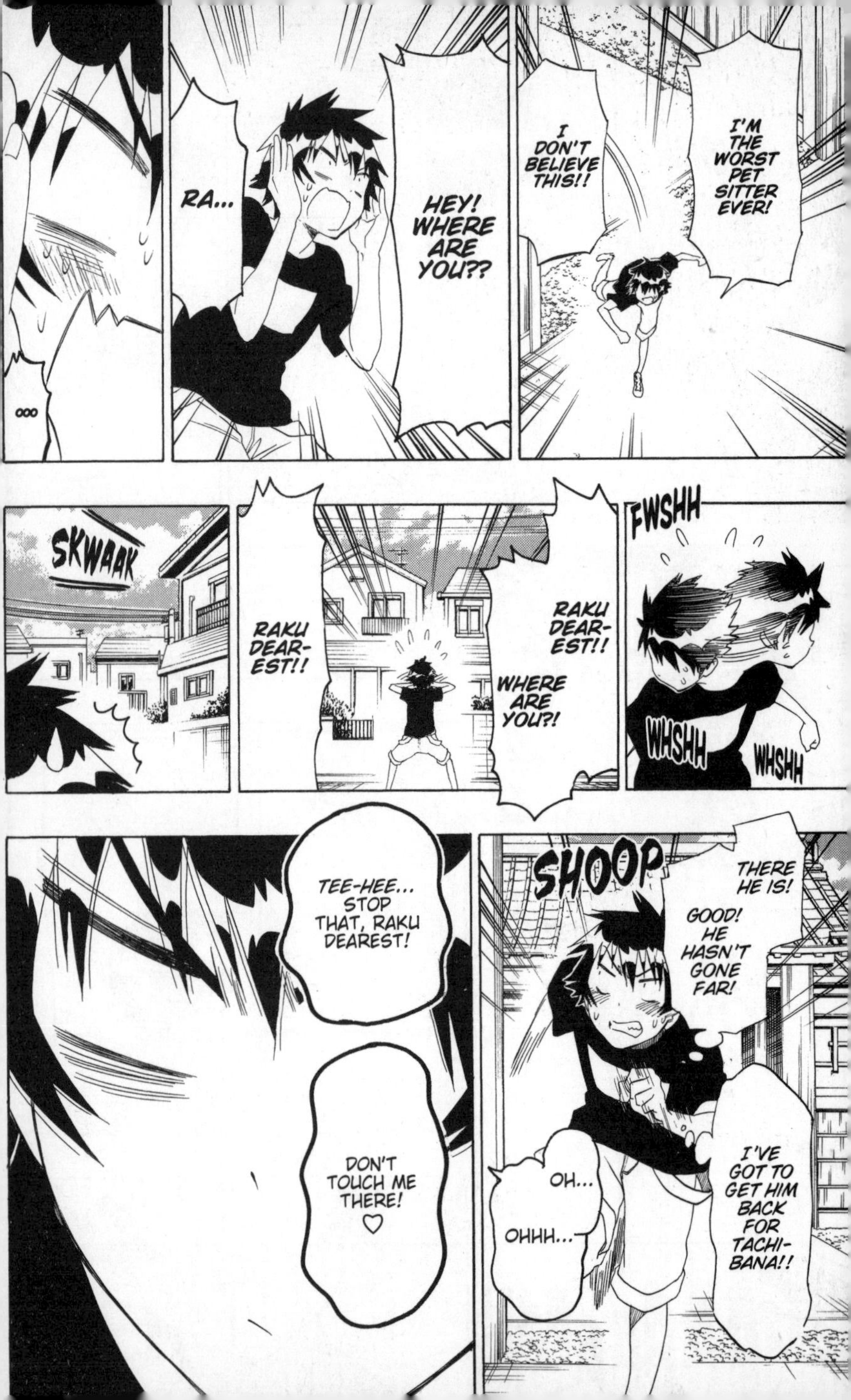
I'M THE WORST PET SITTER EVER!
I DON'T BELIEVE THIS!!
HEY! WHERE ARE YOU??
RA...
ooo
FWSHH
WHSHH
WHSHH
RAKU DEAREST!!
WHERE ARE YOU?!
RAKU DEAREST!!
SKWAAK
THERE HE IS!
SHOOP
GOOD! HE HASN'T GONE FAR!
I'VE GOT TO GET HIM BACK FOR TACHIBANA!!
OH...
OHHH...
TEE-HEE... STOP THAT, RAKU DEAREST!
DON'T TOUCH ME THERE! ♡

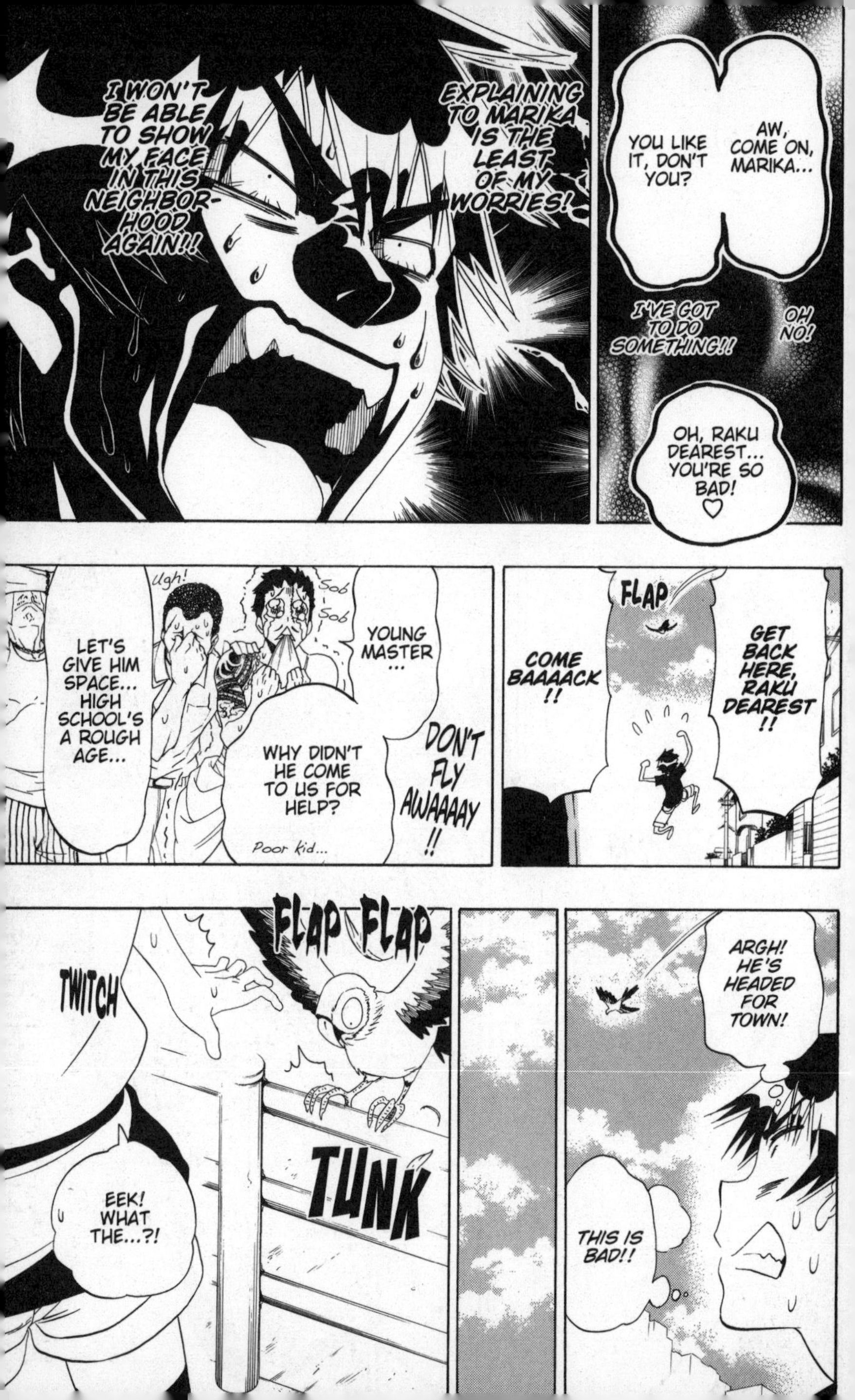
AW, COME ON, MARIKA...
YOU LIKE IT, DON'T YOU?
OH NO!
I'VE GOT TO DO SOMETHING!!
OH, RAKU DEAREST... YOU'RE SO BAD! ♡
EXPLAINING TO MARIKA IS THE LEAST OF MY WORRIES!
I WON'T BE ABLE TO SHOW MY FACE IN THIS NEIGHBOR-HOOD AGAIN!!
FLAP
GET BACK HERE, RAKU DEAREST!!
COME BAAAACK!!
YOUNG MASTER...
Sob Sob
DON'T FLY AWAAAAY!!
WHY DIDN'T HE COME TO US FOR HELP?
Ugh!
LET'S GIVE HIM SPACE... HIGH SCHOOL'S A ROUGH AGE...
Poor kid...
ARGH! HE'S HEADED FOR TOWN!
THIS IS BAD!!
FLAP FLAP
TWITCH
TUNK
EEK! WHAT THE...?!

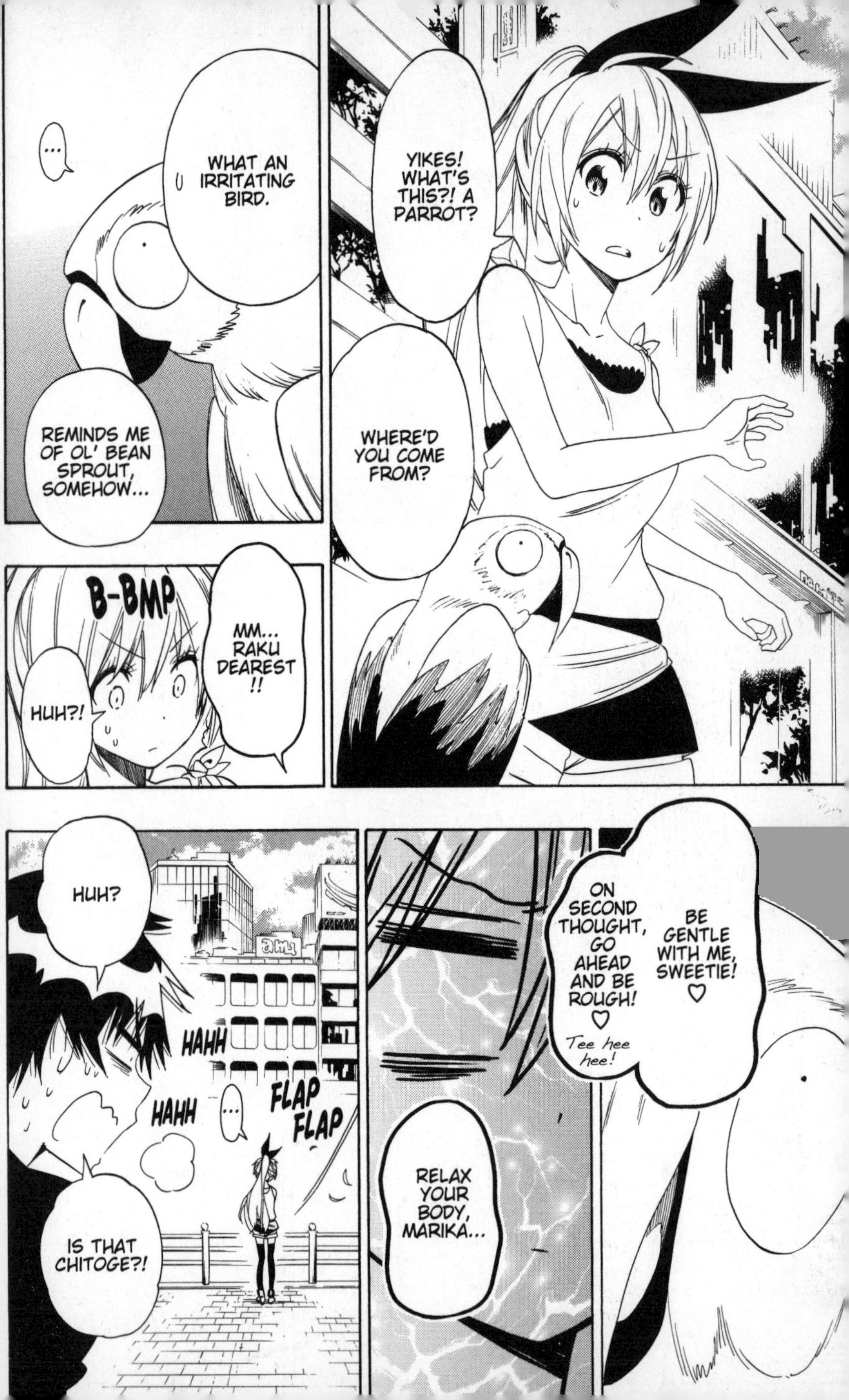
YIKES! WHAT'S THIS?! A PARROT?
WHERE'D YOU COME FROM?
WHAT AN IRRITATING BIRD.
...
REMINDS ME OF OL' BEAN SPROUT, SOMEHOW...
B-BMP
MM... RAKU DEAREST!!
HUH?!
BE GENTLE WITH ME, SWEETIE! ♡
ON SECOND THOUGHT, GO AHEAD AND BE ROUGH! ♡
Tee hee hee!
RELAX YOUR BODY, MARIKA...
HUH?
FLAP FLAP
HAHH
HAHH
...
IS THAT CHITOGE?!

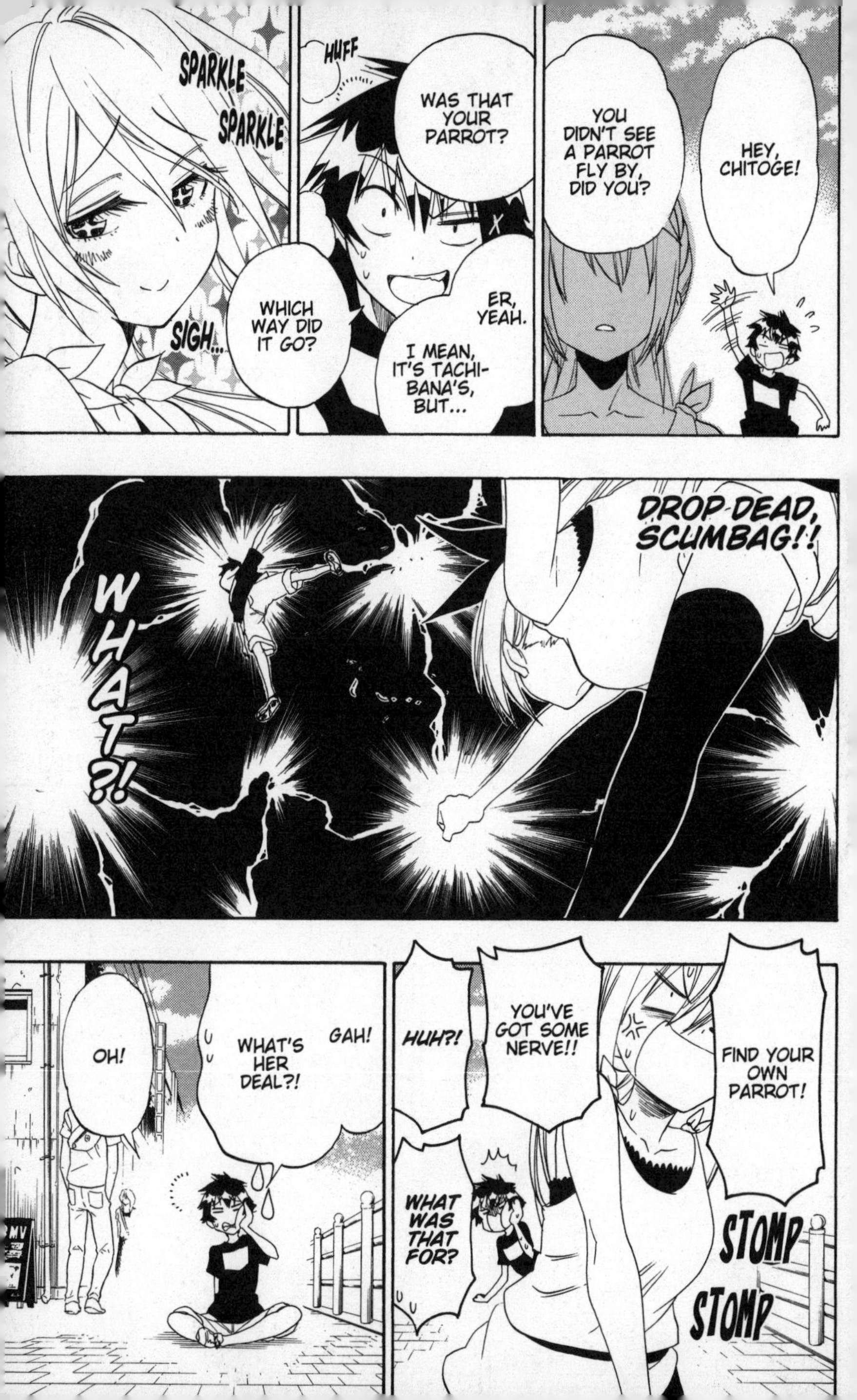
HEY, CHITOGE!
YOU DIDN'T SEE A PARROT FLY BY, DID YOU?
HUFF
WAS THAT YOUR PARROT?
ER, YEAH.
I MEAN, IT'S TACHIBANA'S, BUT...
SPARKLE
SPARKLE
WHICH WAY DID IT GO?
SIGH...
DROP-DEAD, SCUMBAG!!
WHAT?!
FIND YOUR OWN PARROT!
YOU'VE GOT SOME NERVE!!
HUH?!
STOMP
STOMP
WHAT WAS THAT FOR?
GAH!
WHAT'S HER DEAL?!
OH!

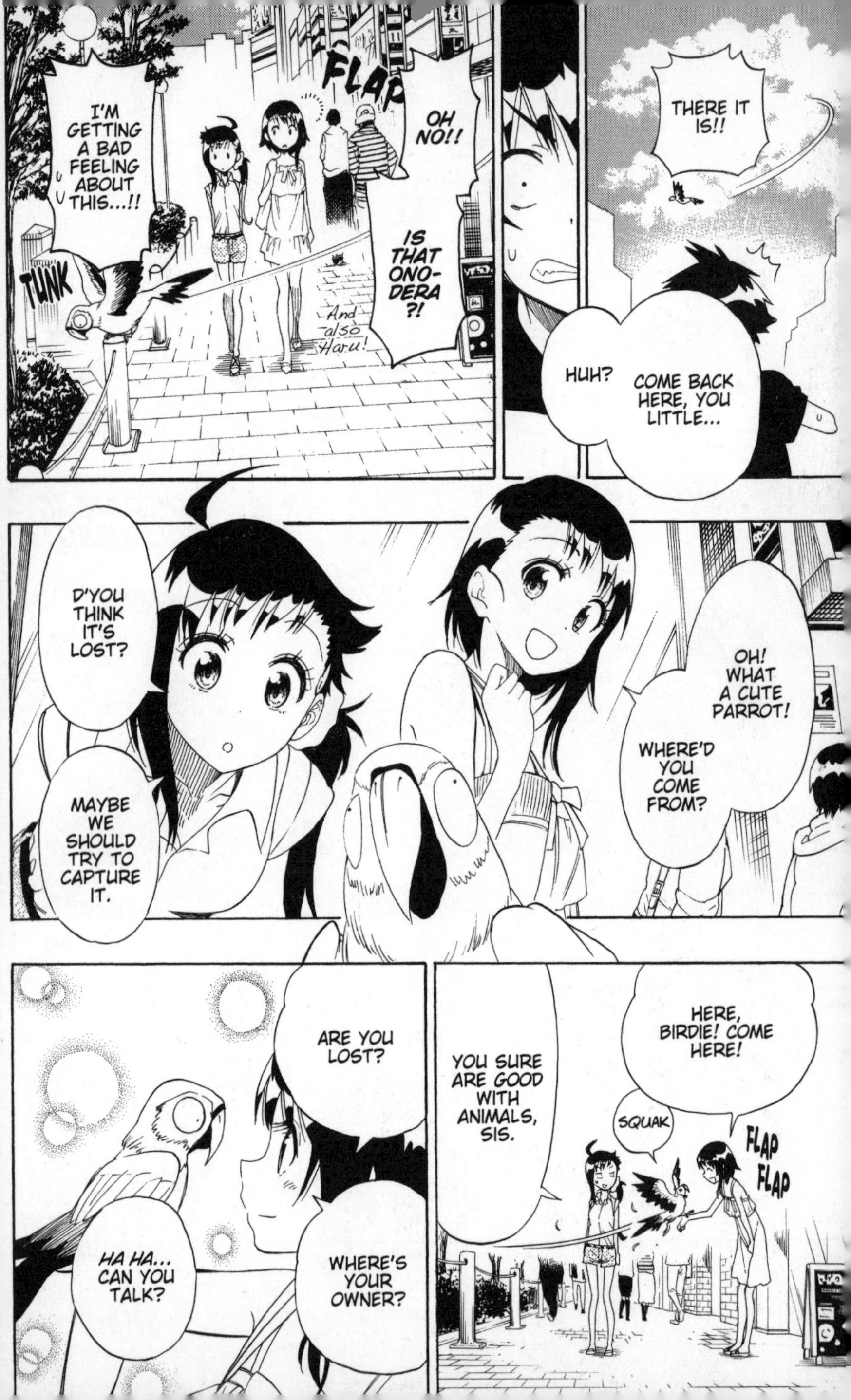
THERE IT IS!!
COME BACK HERE, YOU LITTLE...
HUH?
FLAP
OH NO!!
IS THAT ONODERA?!
And also Haru!
I'M GETTING A BAD FEELING ABOUT THIS...!!
TUNK
OH! WHAT A CUTE PARROT!
WHERE'D YOU COME FROM?
D'YOU THINK IT'S LOST?
MAYBE WE SHOULD TRY TO CAPTURE IT.
HERE, BIRDIE! COME HERE!
FLAP FLAP
SQUAK
YOU SURE ARE GOOD WITH ANIMALS, SIS.
ARE YOU LOST?
WHERE'S YOUR OWNER?
HA HA... CAN YOU TALK?

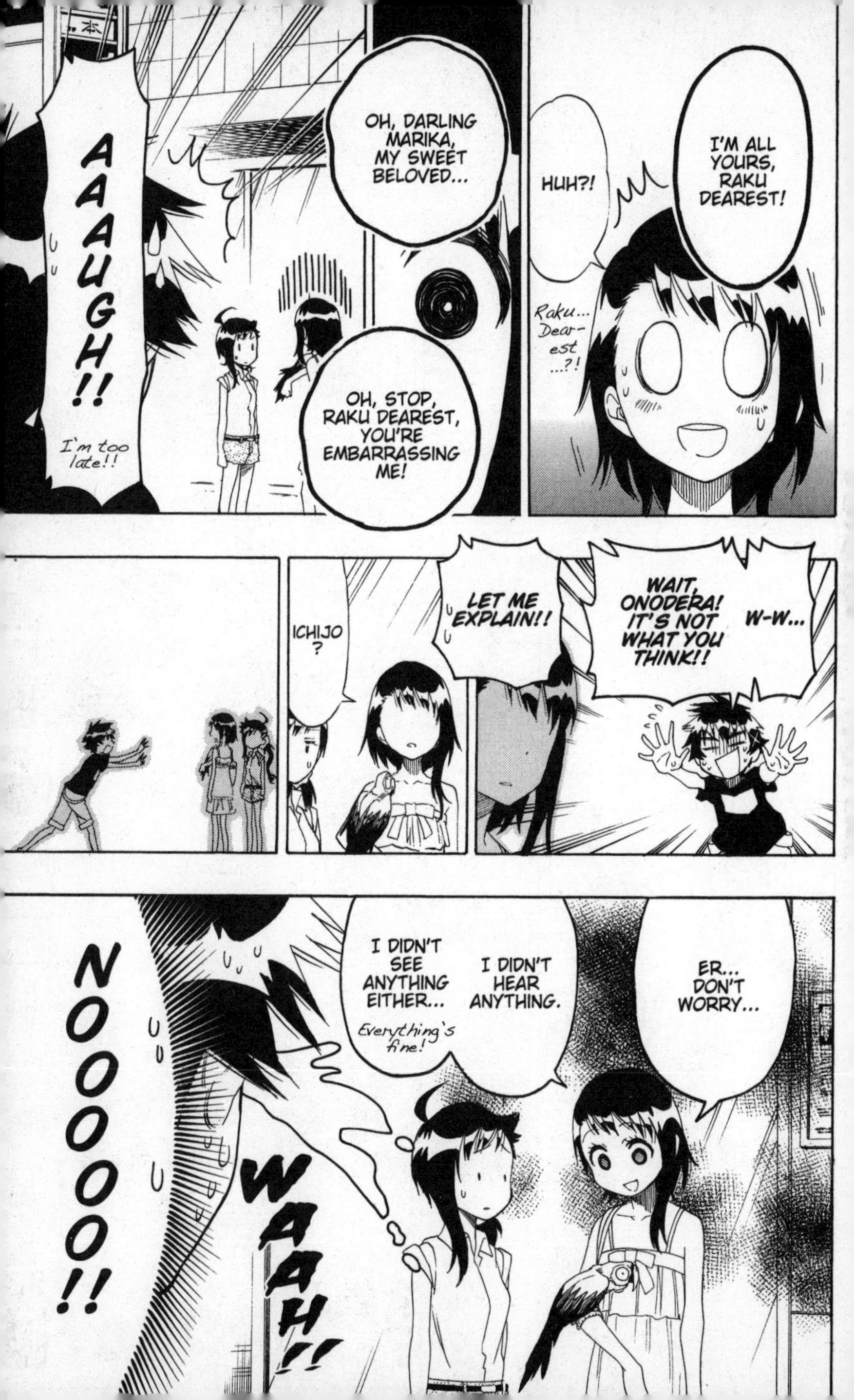
I'M ALL YOURS, RAKU DEAREST!
HUH?!
Raku... Dear-est ...?!
OH, DARLING MARIKA, MY SWEET BELOVED...
OH, STOP, RAKU DEAREST, YOU'RE EMBARRASSING ME!
AAAAUGH!!
I'm too late!!
W-W...
WAIT, ONODERA! IT'S NOT WHAT YOU THINK!!
LET ME EXPLAIN!!
ICHIJO?
ER... DON'T WORRY...
I DIDN'T HEAR ANYTHING.
I DIDN'T SEE ANYTHING EITHER...
Everything's fine!
WAAH!!
NOOOOOO!!

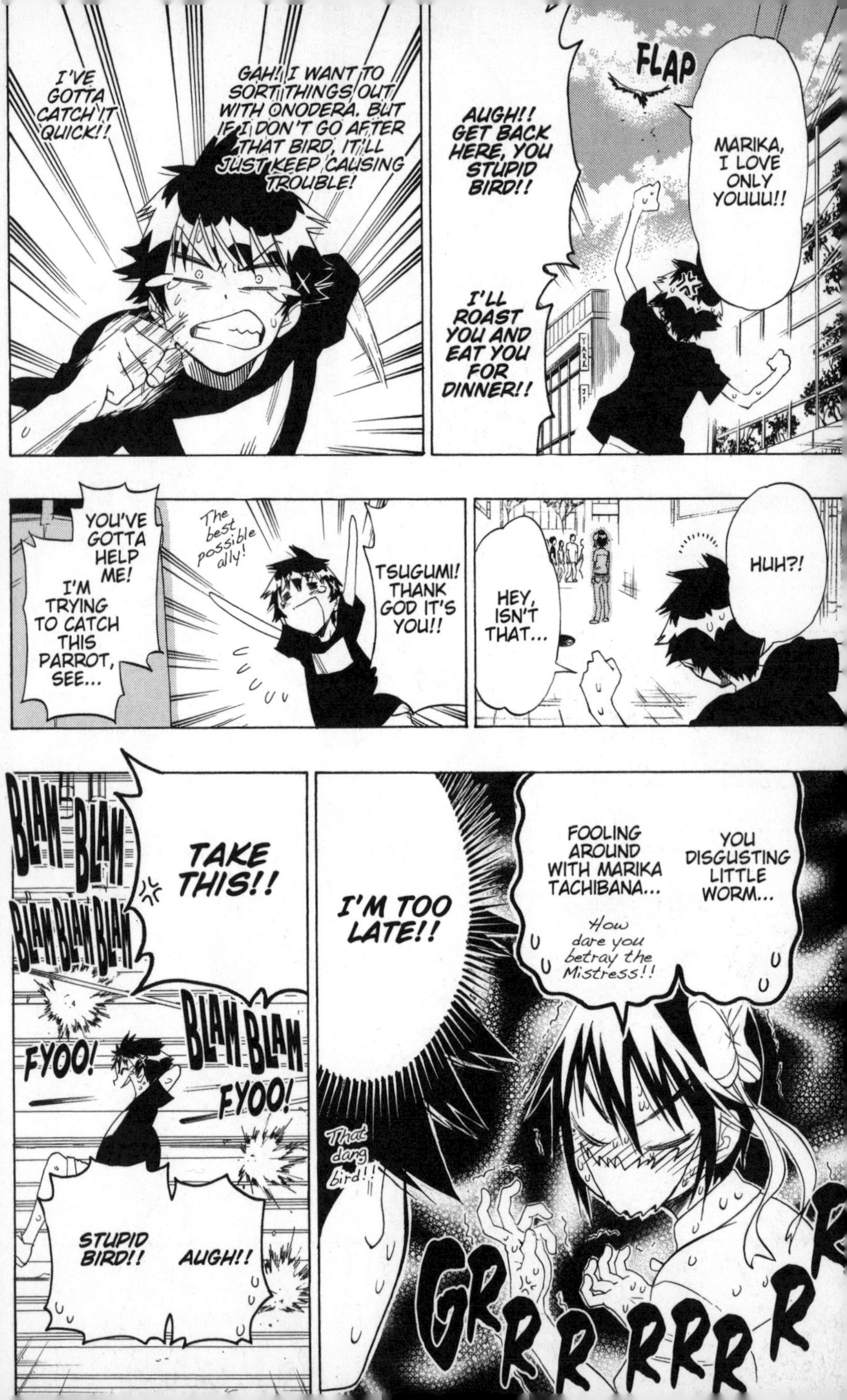
FLAP
MARIKA, I LOVE ONLY YOUUU!!
AUGH!! GET BACK HERE, YOU STUPID BIRD!!
I'LL ROAST YOU AND EAT YOU FOR DINNER!!
GAH! I WANT TO SORT THINGS OUT WITH ONODERA. BUT IF I DON'T GO AFTER THAT BIRD, IT'LL JUST KEEP CAUSING TROUBLE!
I'VE GOTTA CATCH IT QUICK!!
HUH?!
HEY, ISN'T THAT...
TSUGUMI! THANK GOD IT'S YOU!!
The best possible ally!
YOU'VE GOTTA HELP ME! I'M TRYING TO CATCH THIS PARROT, SEE...
YOU DISGUSTING LITTLE WORM...
FOOLING AROUND WITH MARIKA TACHIBANA...
How dare you betray the Mistress!!
I'M TOO LATE!!
That dang bird!!
GRRRRRRRR
TAKE THIS!!
BLAM BLAM
BLAM BLAM BLAM
BLAM BLAM
FYOO!
FYOO!
AUGH!!
STUPID BIRD!!

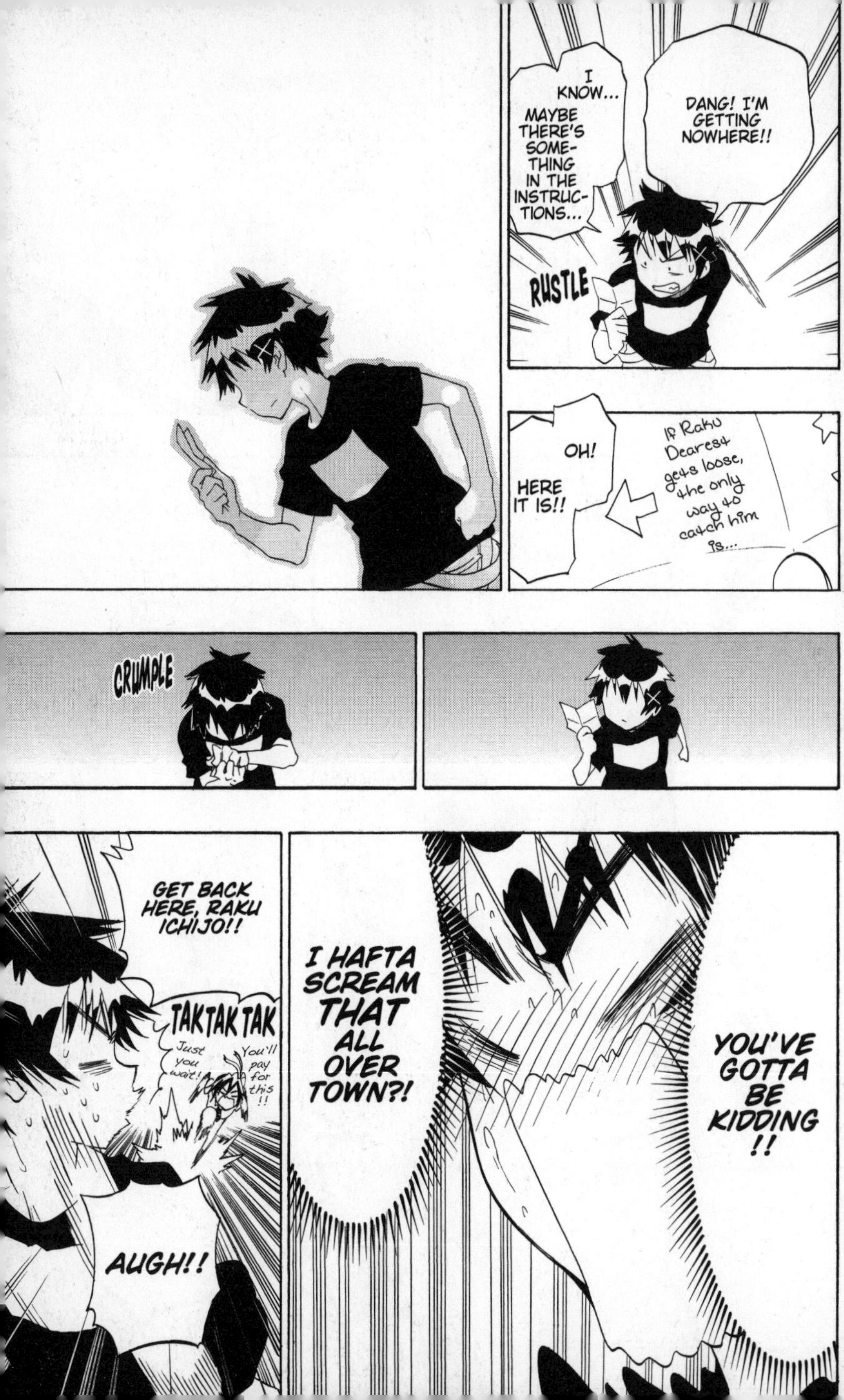
DANG! I'M GETTING NOWHERE!!
I KNOW... MAYBE THERE'S SOME-THING IN THE INSTRUC-TIONS...
RUSTLE
If Raku Dearest gets loose, the only way to catch him is...
OH!
HERE IT IS!!
CRUMPLE
YOU'VE GOTTA BE KIDDING!!
I HAFTA SCREAM THAT ALL OVER TOWN?!
GET BACK HERE, RAKU ICHIJO!!
TAKTAK TAK
You'll pay for this!!
Just you wait!
AUGH!!

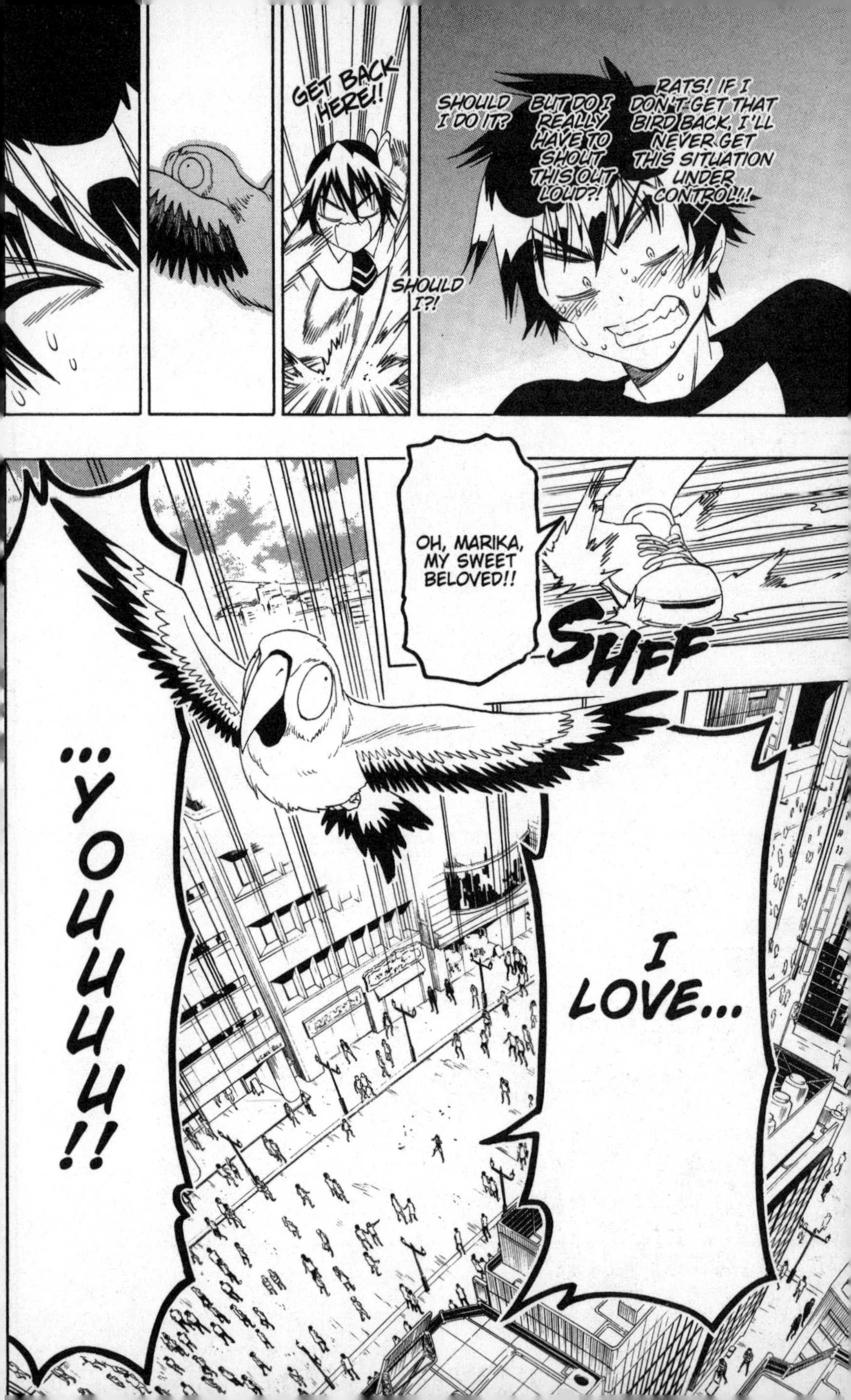
RATS! IF I DON'T GET THAT BIRD BACK, I'LL NEVER GET THIS SITUATION UNDER CONTROL!!
BUT DO I REALLY HAVE TO SHOUT THIS OUT LOUD?!
SHOULD I DO IT?
SHOULD I?!
GET BACK HERE!!
OH, MARIKA, MY SWEET BELOVED!!
SHFF
I LOVE...
...YOUUUUU!!

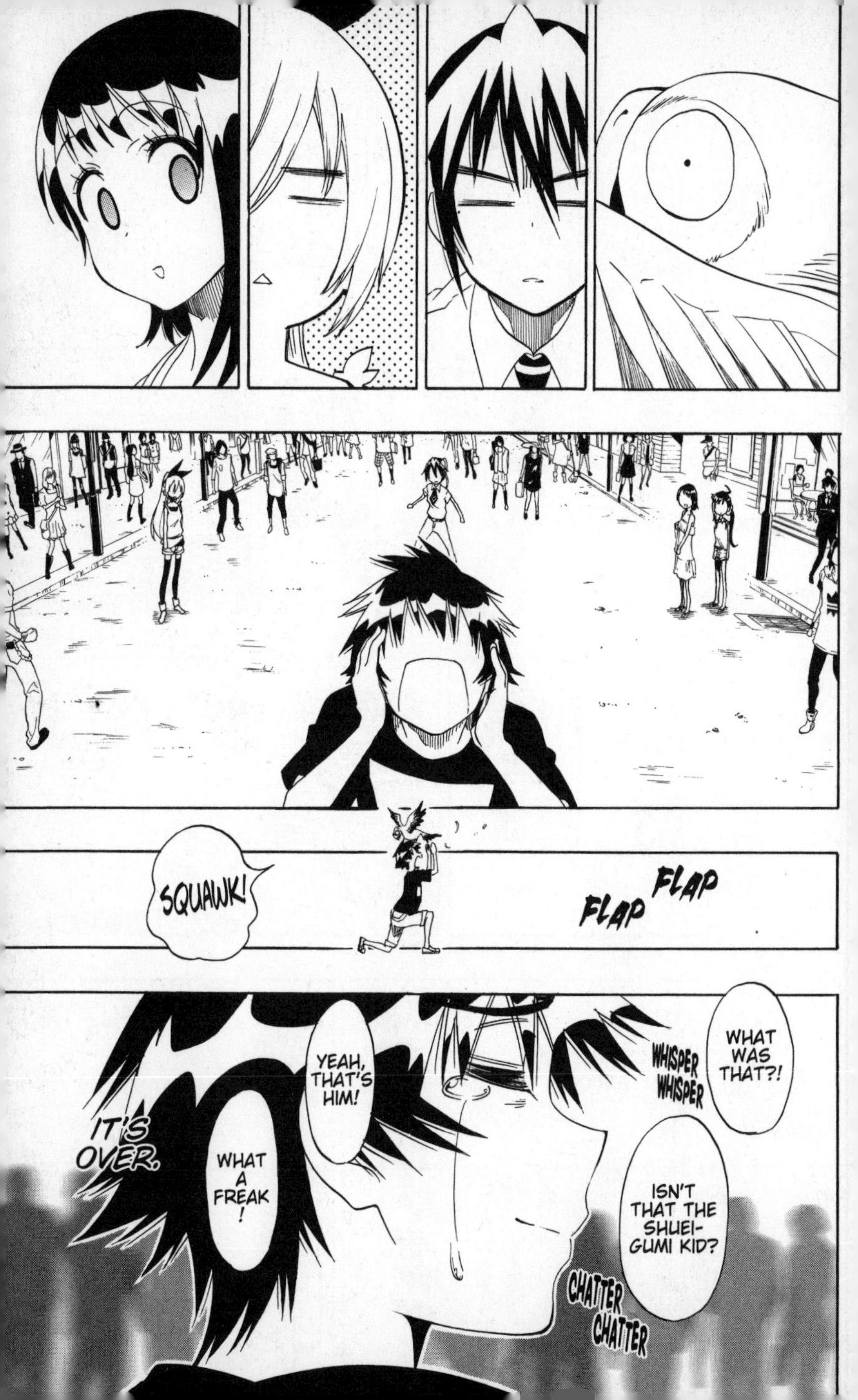
FLAP
FLAP
SQUAWK!
WHAT WAS THAT?!
WHISPER WHISPER
ISN'T THAT THE SHUEI-GUMI KID?
CHATTER CHATTER
YEAH, THAT'S HIM!
WHAT A FREAK!
IT'S OVER.

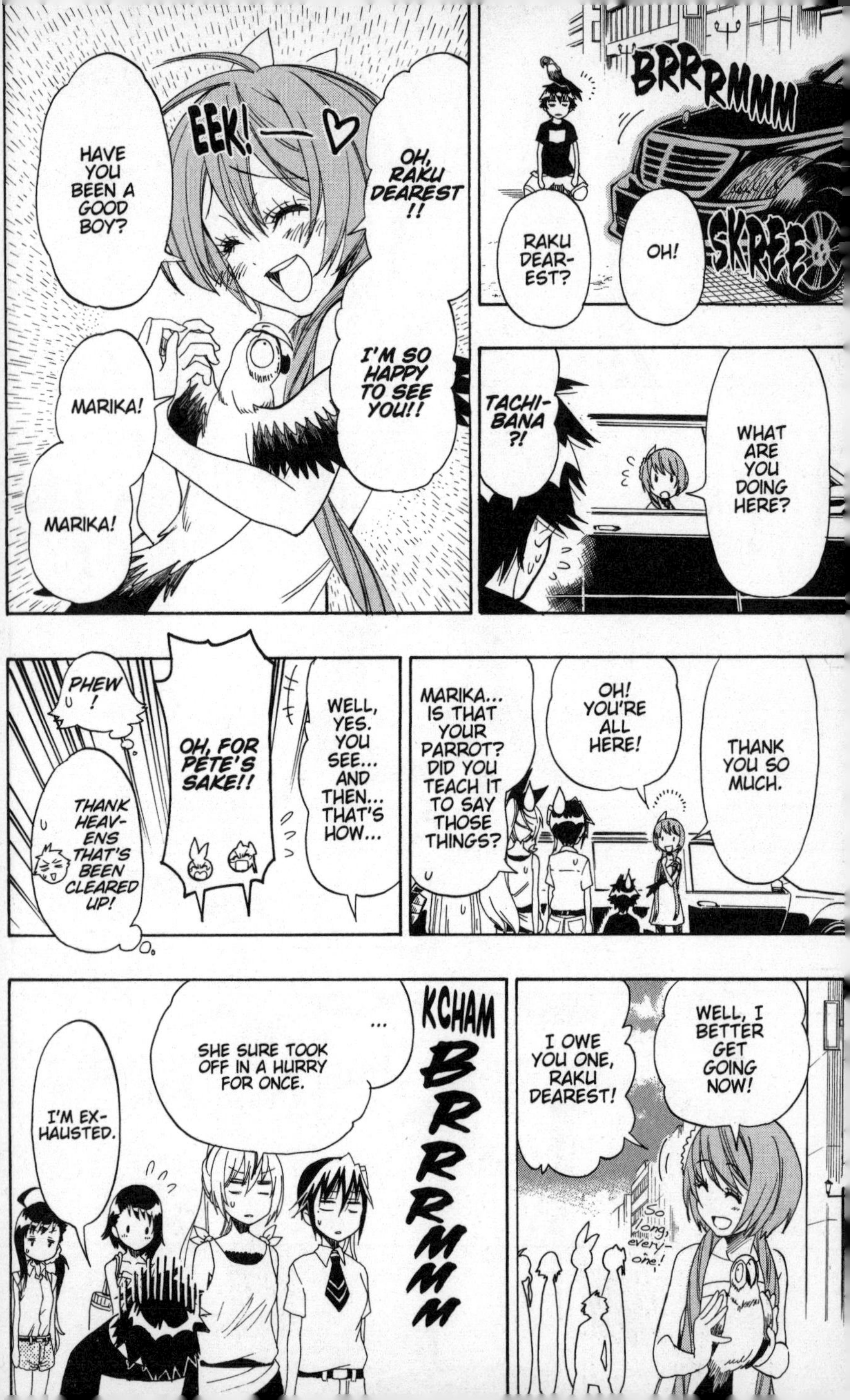
BRRRMMM
SKREE
OH!
RAKU DEAREST?
WHAT ARE YOU DOING HERE?
TACHIBANA?!
OH, RAKU DEAREST!!
EEK!—♥
HAVE YOU BEEN A GOOD BOY?
I'M SO HAPPY TO SEE YOU!!
MARIKA!
MARIKA!
THANK YOU SO MUCH.
OH! YOU'RE ALL HERE!
MARIKA... IS THAT YOUR PARROT? DID YOU TEACH IT TO SAY THOSE THINGS?
WELL, YES. YOU SEE... AND THEN... THAT'S HOW...
OH, FOR PETE'S SAKE!!
PHEW!
THANK HEAVENS THAT'S BEEN CLEARED UP!
WELL, I BETTER GET GOING NOW!
I OWE YOU ONE, RAKU DEAREST!
So long, everyone!
KCHAM
BRRRRMMM
...
SHE SURE TOOK OFF IN A HURRY FOR ONCE.
I'M EXHAUSTED.

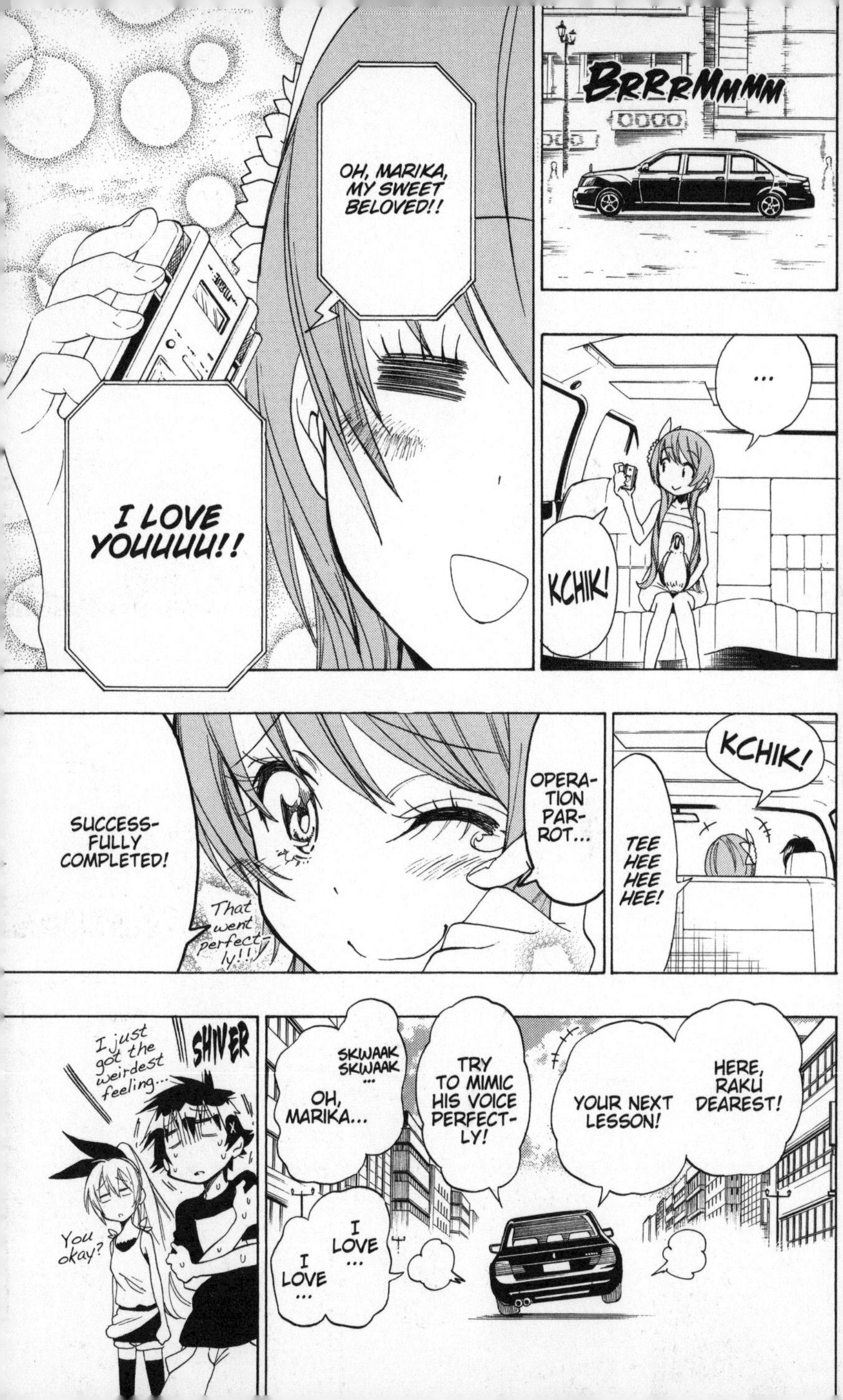
BRRRMMMM
...
KCHIK!
OH, MARIKA, MY SWEET BELOVED!!
I LOVE YOUUUU!!
KCHIK!
TEE HEE HEE HEE!
OPERATION PARROT...
SUCCESSFULLY COMPLETED!
That went perfectly!!
HERE, RAKU DEAREST!
YOUR NEXT LESSON!
TRY TO MIMIC HIS VOICE PERFECTLY!
SKWAAK SKWAAK ...
OH, MARIKA...
I LOVE ...
I LOVE ...
SHIVER
I just got the weirdest feeling...
You okay?

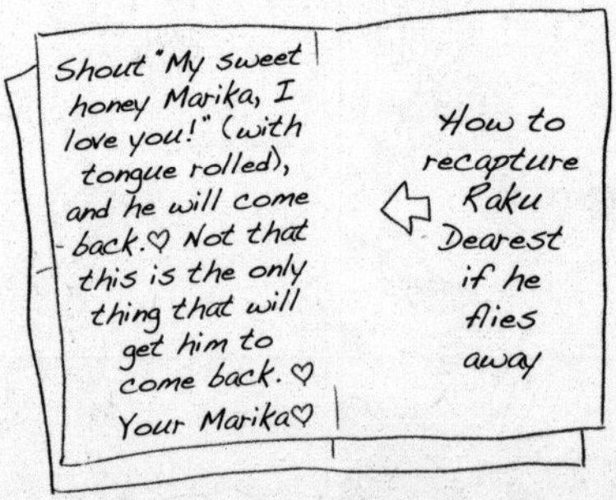
How to recapture Raku Dearest if he flies away
Shout "My sweet honey Marika, I love you!" (with tongue rolled), and he will come back.♡ Not that this is the only thing that will get him to come back.♡
Your Marika♡

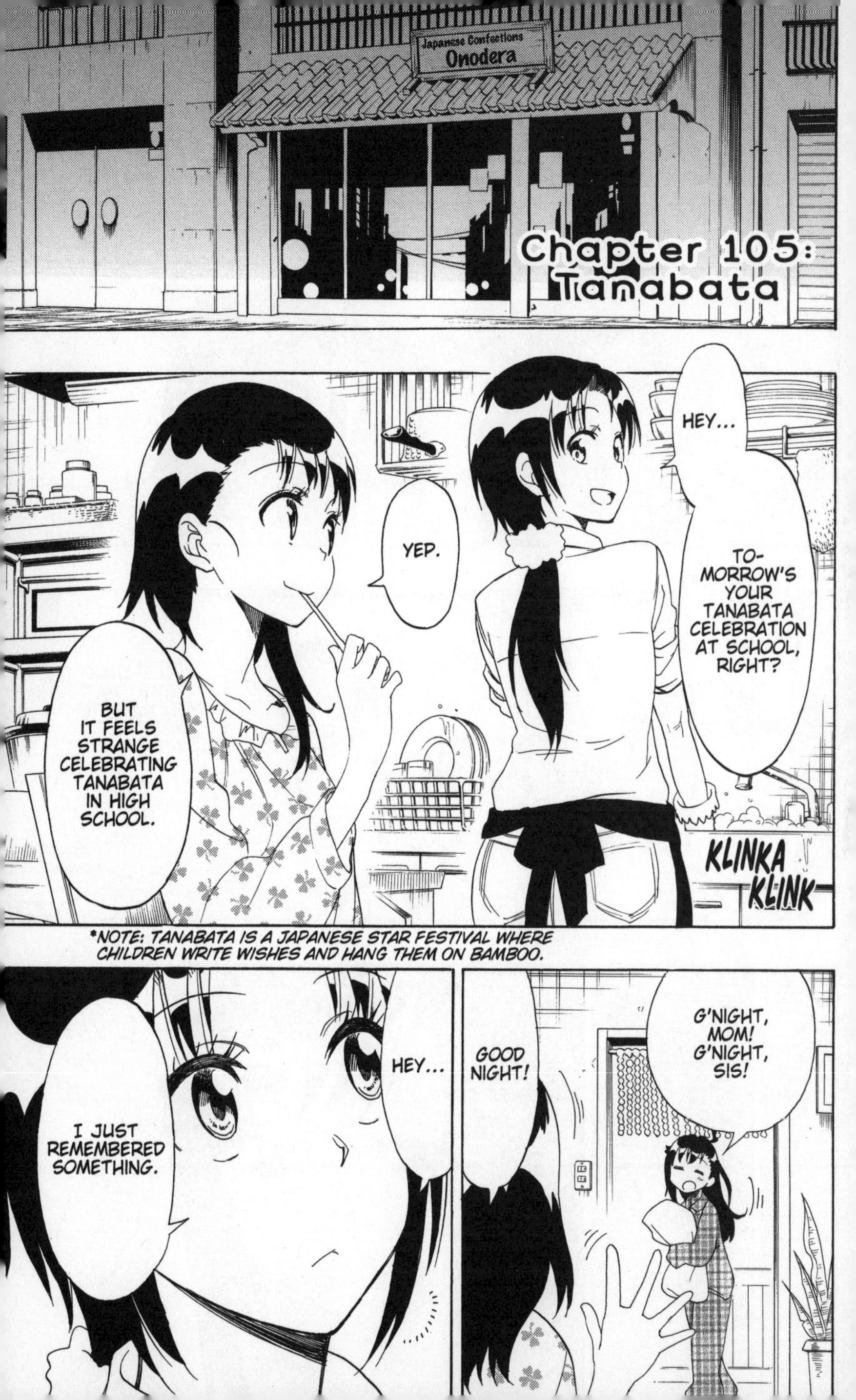
Japanese Confections
Onodera
Chapter 105: Tanabata
HEY...
TO-MORROW'S YOUR TANABATA CELEBRATION AT SCHOOL, RIGHT?
YEP.
BUT IT FEELS STRANGE CELEBRATING TANABATA IN HIGH SCHOOL.
KLINKA KLINK
*NOTE: TANABATA IS A JAPANESE STAR FESTIVAL WHERE CHILDREN WRITE WISHES AND HANG THEM ON BAMBOO.
G'NIGHT, MOM! G'NIGHT, SIS!
GOOD NIGHT!
HEY...
I JUST REMEMBERED SOMETHING.

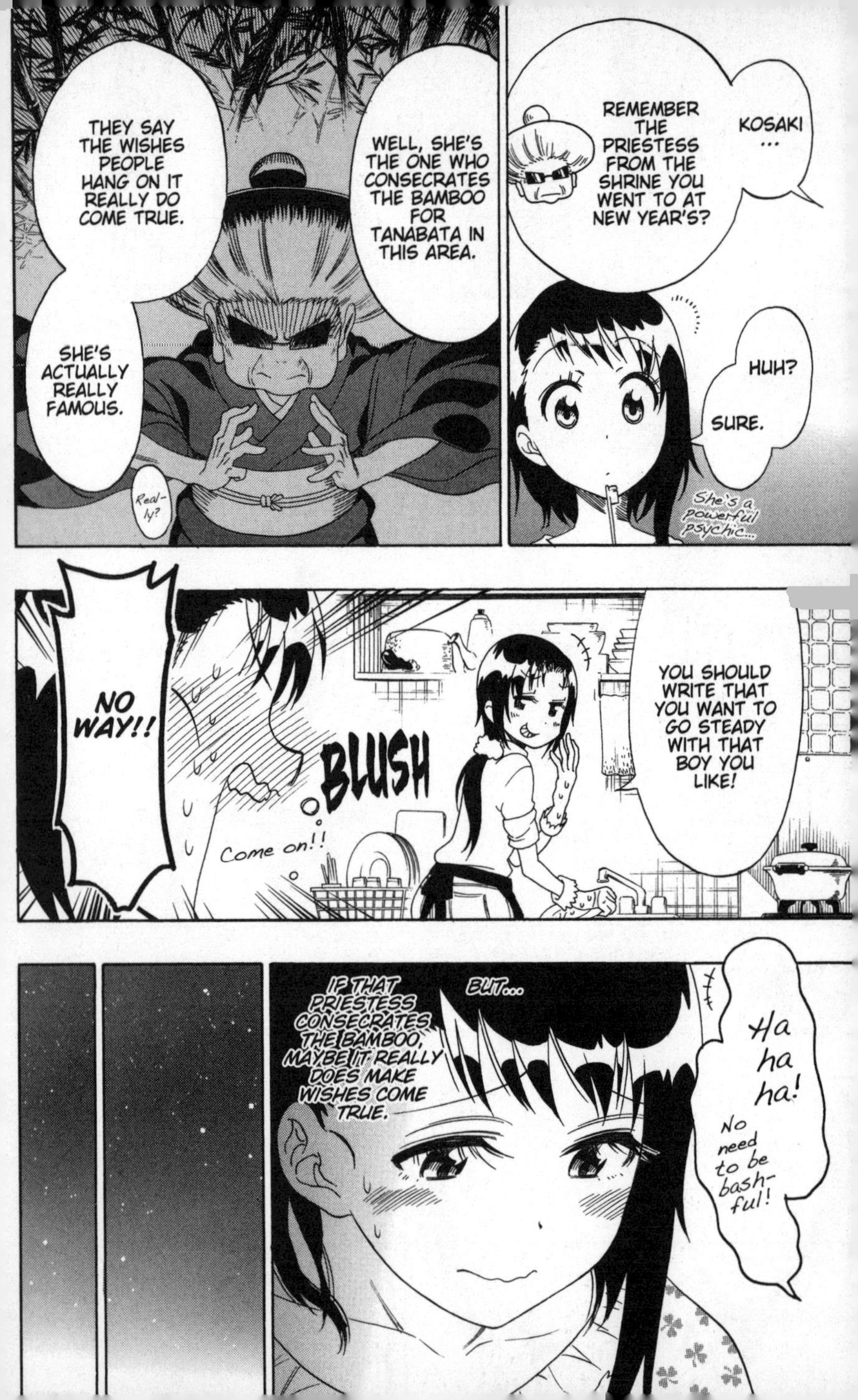
Kosaki...
Remember the priestess from the shrine you went to at New Year's?
Huh?
Sure.
She's a powerful psychic...
Well, she's the one who consecrates the bamboo for Tanabata in this area.
They say the wishes people hang on it really do come true.
She's actually really famous.
Real-ly?
You should write that you want to go steady with that boy you like!
BLUSH
Come on!!
NO WAY!!
Ha ha ha!
No need to be bash-ful!
But...
If that priestess consecrates the bamboo, maybe it really does make wishes come true.

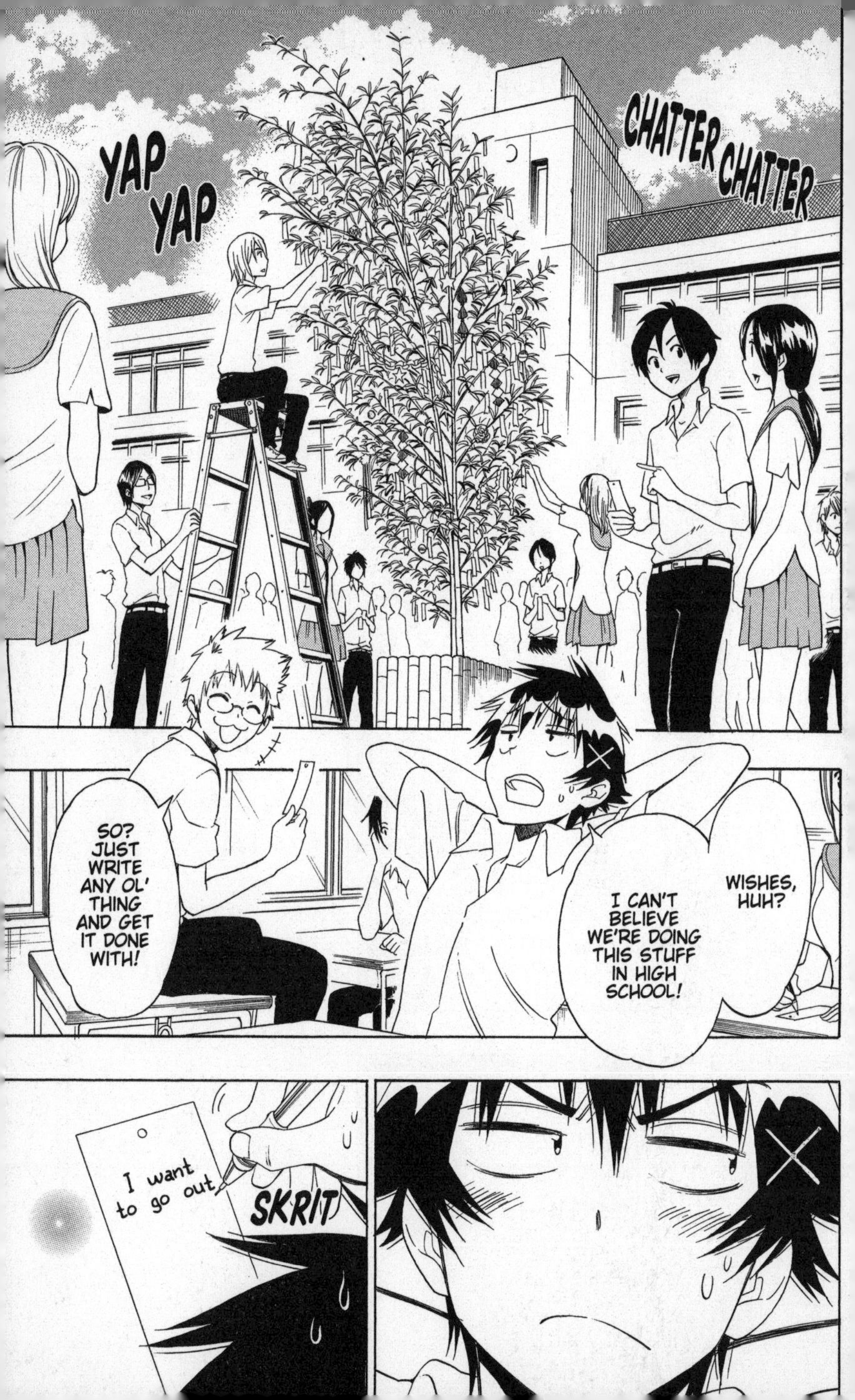
CHATTER CHATTER
YAP YAP
WISHES, HUH?
I CAN'T BELIEVE WE'RE DOING THIS STUFF IN HIGH SCHOOL!
SO? JUST WRITE ANY OL' THING AND GET IT DONE WITH!
SKRIT
I want to go out

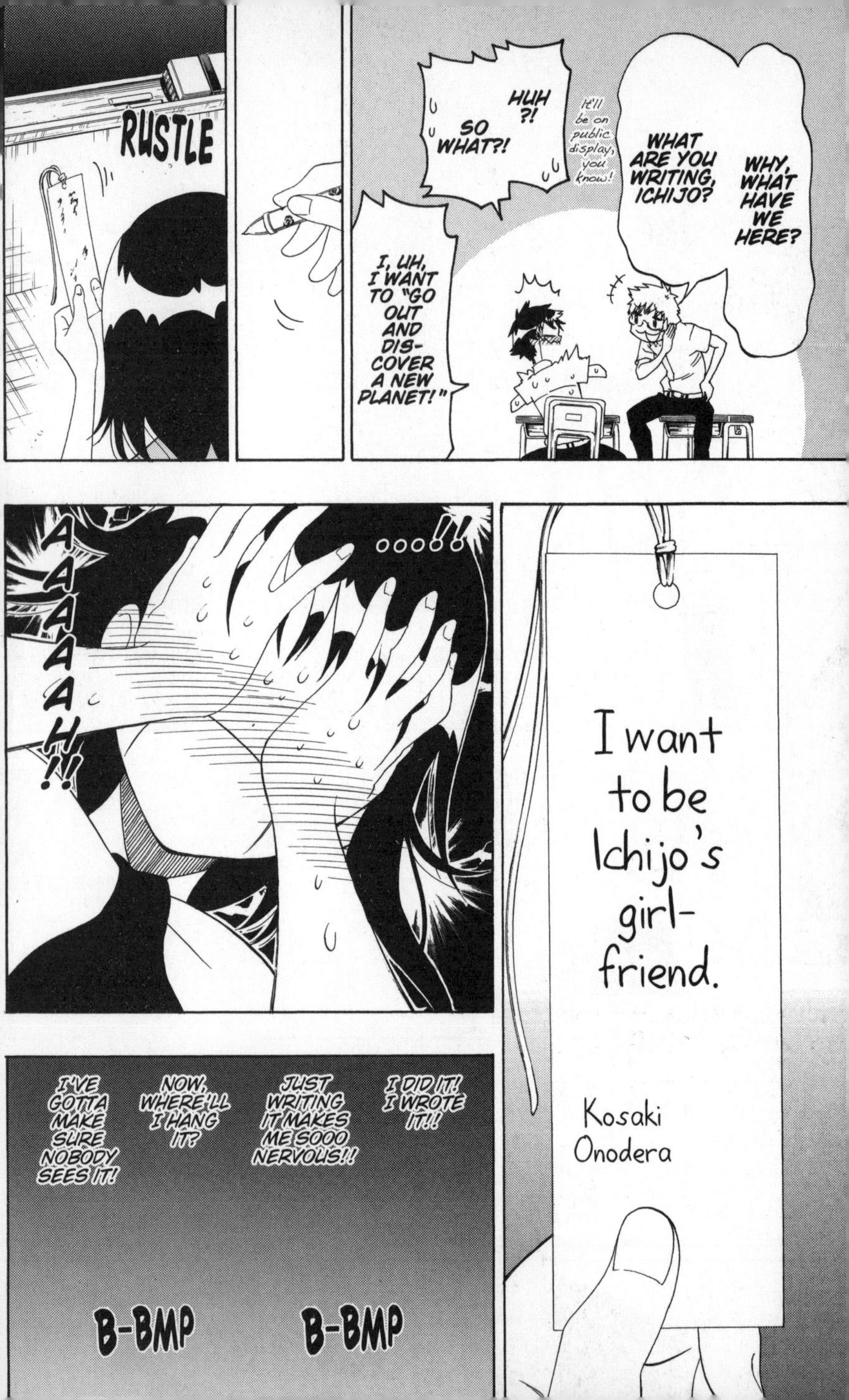
WHY, WHAT HAVE WE HERE?
WHAT ARE YOU WRITING, ICHIJO?
It'll be on public display, you know!
HUH?! SO WHAT?!
I, UH, I WANT TO "GO OUT AND DISCOVER A NEW PLANET!"
RUSTLE
I want to be Ichijo's girlfriend.
Kosaki Onodera
ooo!!
AAAAAAH!!
I DID IT! I WROTE IT!!
JUST WRITING IT MAKES ME SOOO NERVOUS!!
NOW, WHERE'LL I HANG IT?
I'VE GOTTA MAKE SURE NOBODY SEES IT!
B-BMP
B-BMP

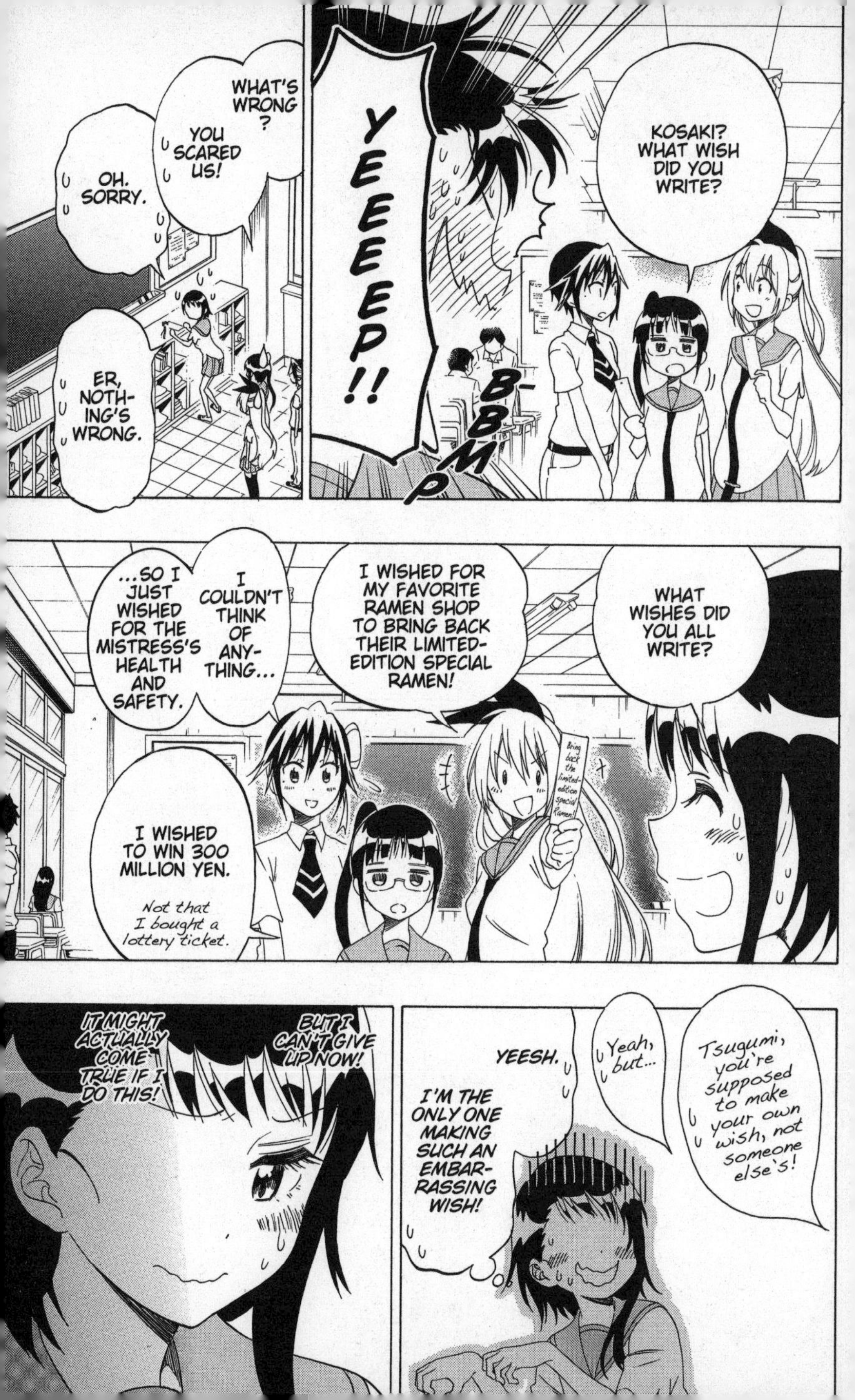
KOSAKI? WHAT WISH DID YOU WRITE?
YEEEEEP!!
B-BBMP
WHAT'S WRONG? YOU SCARED US!
OH. SORRY.
ER, NOTHING'S WRONG.
WHAT WISHES DID YOU ALL WRITE?
I WISHED FOR MY FAVORITE RAMEN SHOP TO BRING BACK THEIR LIMITED-EDITION SPECIAL RAMEN!
Bring back the limited-edition special Ramen!
I COULDN'T THINK OF ANYTHING...
...SO I JUST WISHED FOR THE MISTRESS'S HEALTH AND SAFETY.
I WISHED TO WIN 300 MILLION YEN.
Not that I bought a lottery ticket.
Tsugumi, you're supposed to make your own wish, not someone else's!
Yeah, but...
YEESH.
I'M THE ONLY ONE MAKING SUCH AN EMBARRASSING WISH!
BUT I CAN'T GIVE UP NOW!
IT MIGHT ACTUALLY COME TRUE IF I DO THIS!

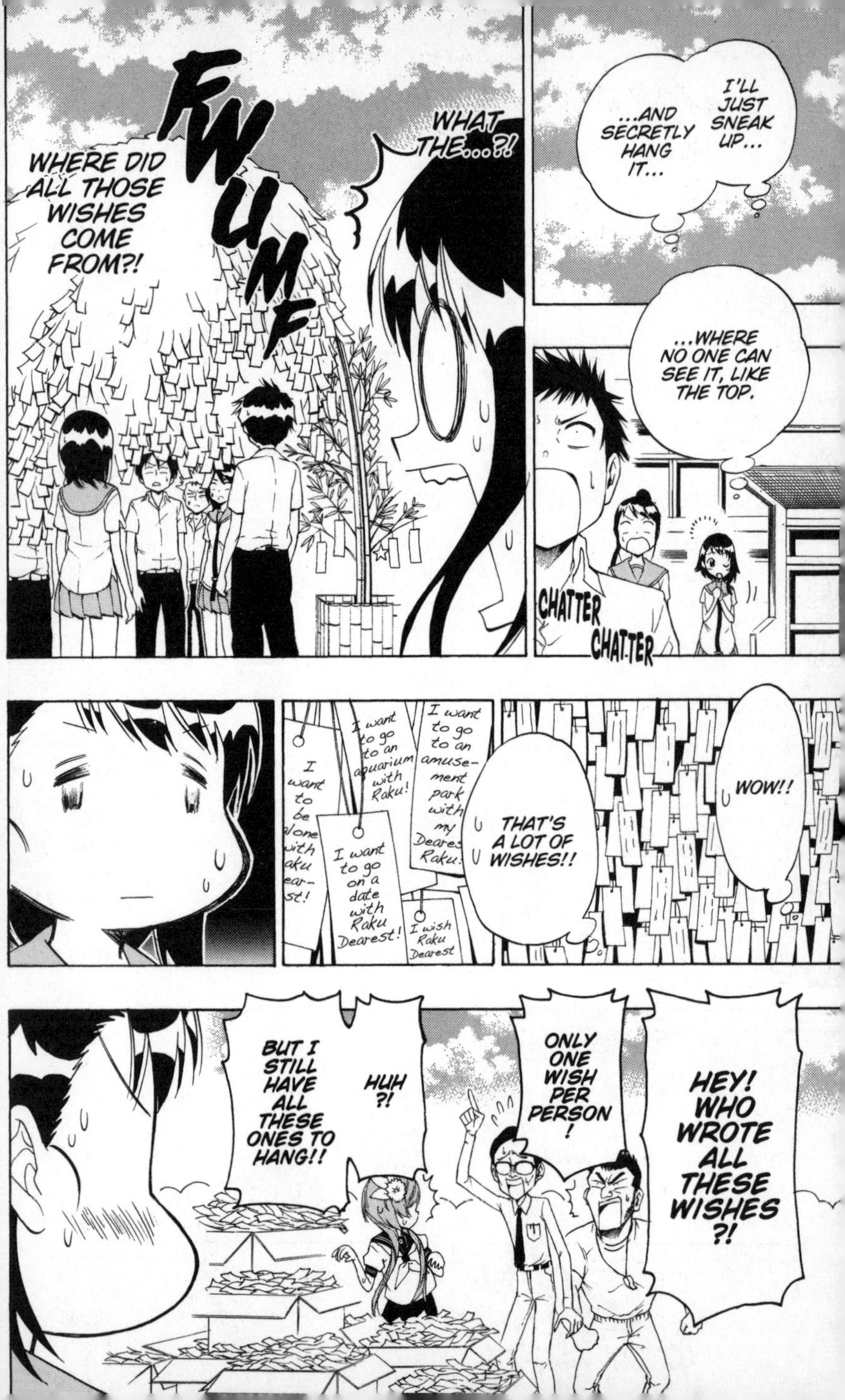
I'LL JUST SNEAK UP...
...AND SECRETLY HANG IT...
...WHERE NO ONE CAN SEE IT, LIKE THE TOP.
CHATTER
CHATTER
WHAT THE...?!
FWUMF
WHERE DID ALL THOSE WISHES COME FROM?!
WOW!!
THAT'S A LOT OF WISHES!!
I want to go to an amusement park with my Dearest Raku!
I want to go to an aquarium with Raku!
I want to be alone with aku ear- st!
I want to go on a date with Raku Dearest!
I wish Raku Dearest
HEY! WHO WROTE ALL THESE WISHES?!
ONLY ONE WISH PER PERSON!
HUH?!
BUT I STILL HAVE ALL THESE ONES TO HANG!!

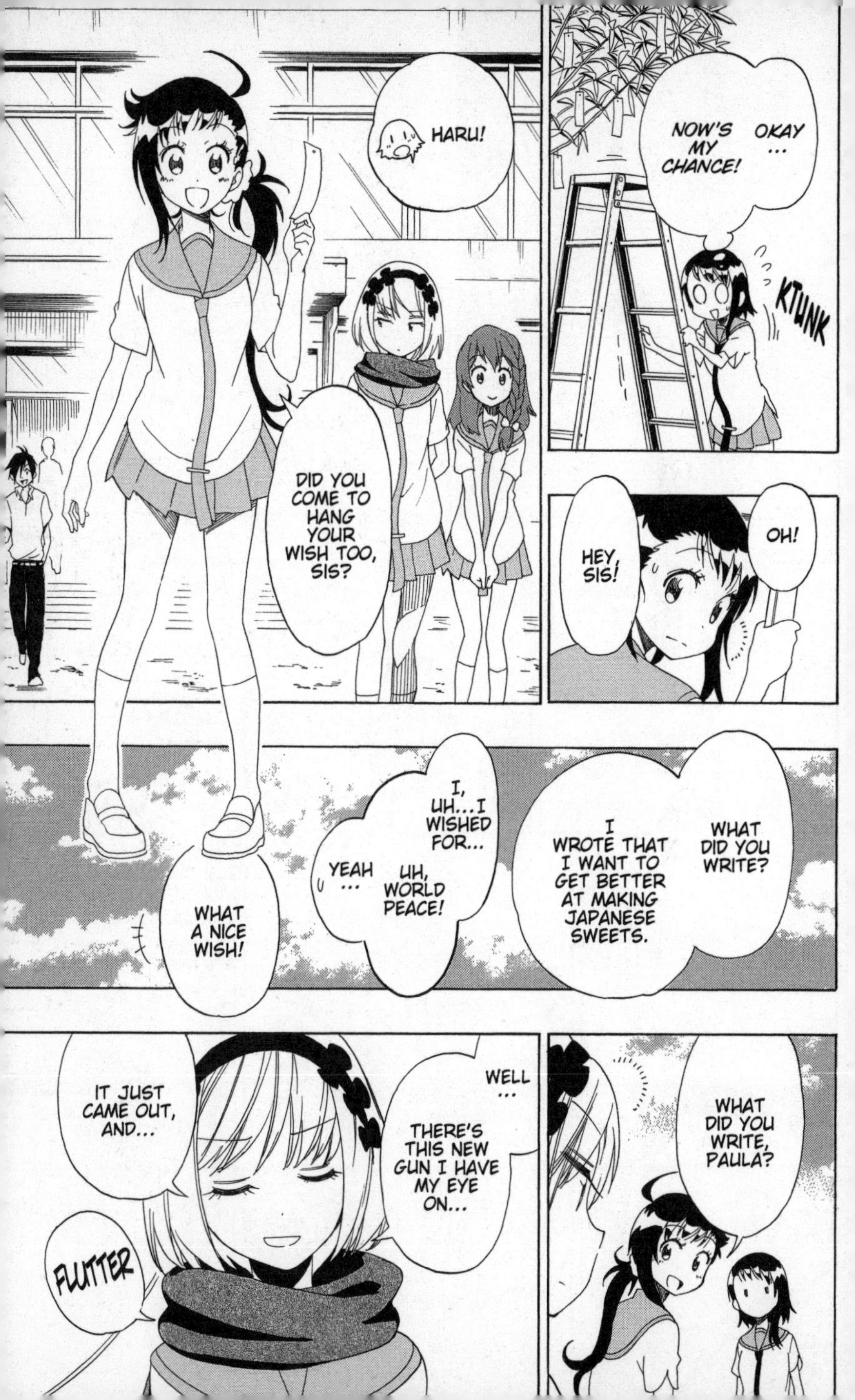
OKAY...
NOW'S MY CHANCE!
KTUNK
OH!
HEY, SIS!
HARU!
DID YOU COME TO HANG YOUR WISH TOO, SIS?
WHAT DID YOU WRITE?
I WROTE THAT I WANT TO GET BETTER AT MAKING JAPANESE SWEETS.
I, UH...I WISHED FOR...
UH, WORLD PEACE!
YEAH...
WHAT A NICE WISH!
WHAT DID YOU WRITE, PAULA?
WELL...
THERE'S THIS NEW GUN I HAVE MY EYE ON...
IT JUST CAME OUT, AND...
FLUTTER

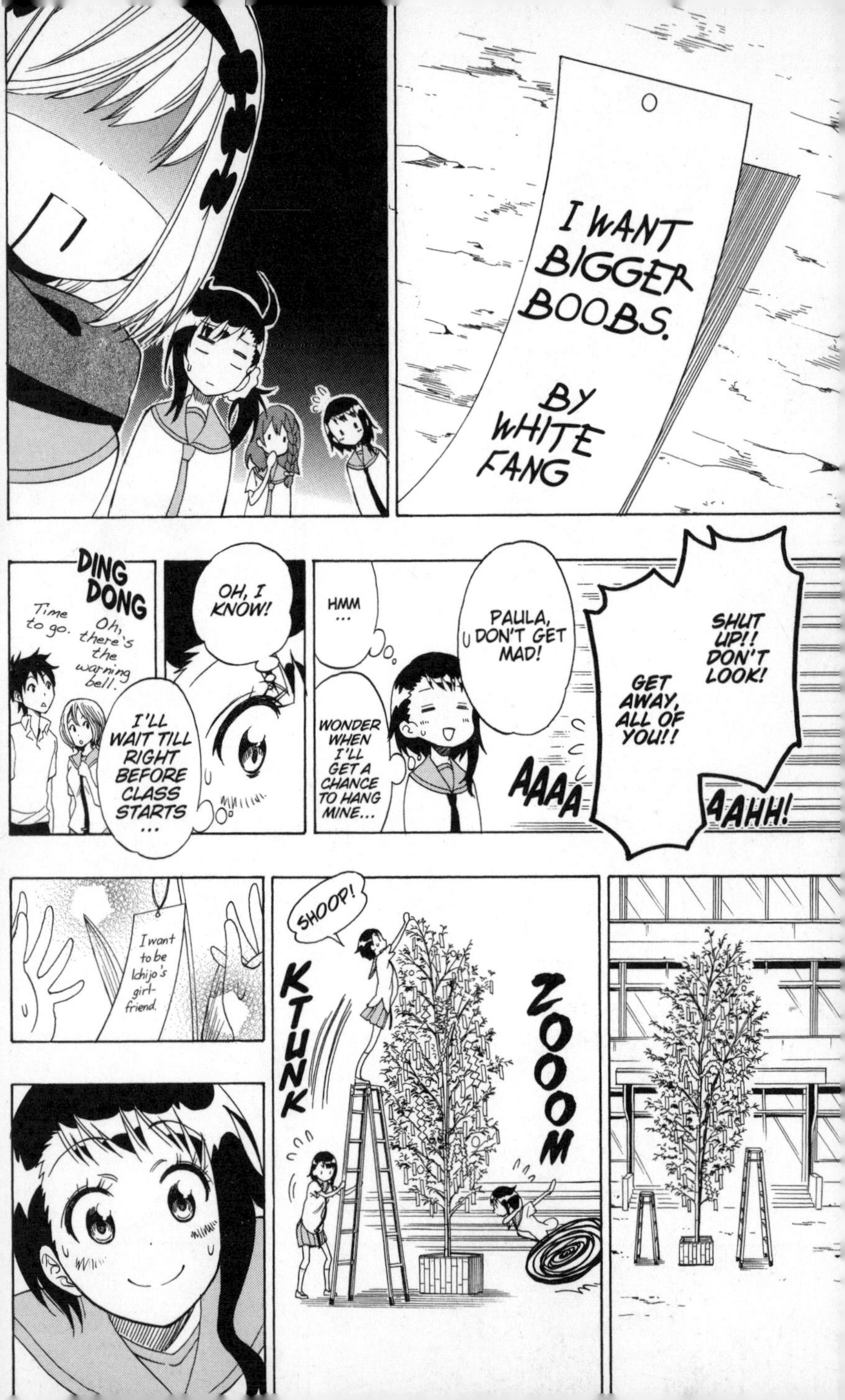
I WANT BIGGER BOOBS.
BY WHITE FANG
SHUT UP!! DON'T LOOK!
GET AWAY, ALL OF YOU!!
AAAA AAHH!
PAULA, DON'T GET MAD!
HMM ...
WONDER WHEN I'LL GET A CHANCE TO HANG MINE...
OH, I KNOW!
I'LL WAIT TILL RIGHT BEFORE CLASS STARTS ...
DING DONG
Oh, there's the warning bell.
Time to go.
ZOOOOM
SHOOP!
KTUNK
I want to be Ichijo's girlfriend.

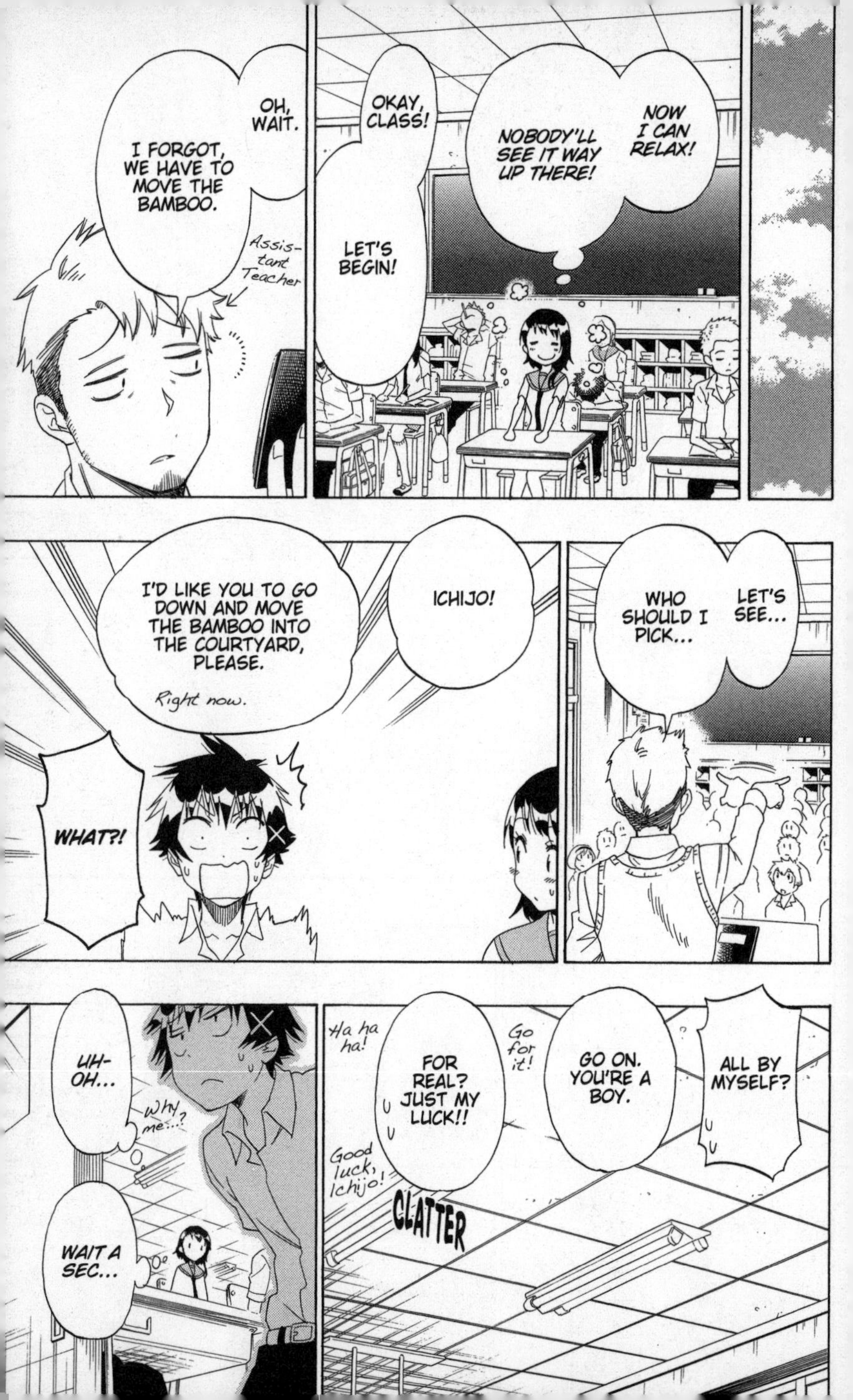
NOW I CAN RELAX!
NOBODY'LL SEE IT WAY UP THERE!
OKAY, CLASS!
LET'S BEGIN!
OH, WAIT.
I FORGOT, WE HAVE TO MOVE THE BAMBOO.
Assis-tant Teacher
LET'S SEE...
WHO SHOULD I PICK...
ICHIJO!
I'D LIKE YOU TO GO DOWN AND MOVE THE BAMBOO INTO THE COURTYARD, PLEASE.
Right now.
WHAT?!
ALL BY MYSELF?
GO ON. YOU'RE A BOY.
Go for it!
FOR REAL? JUST MY LUCK!!
Ha ha ha!
Good luck, Ichijo!
CLATTER
UH-OH...
Why me...?
WAIT A SEC...

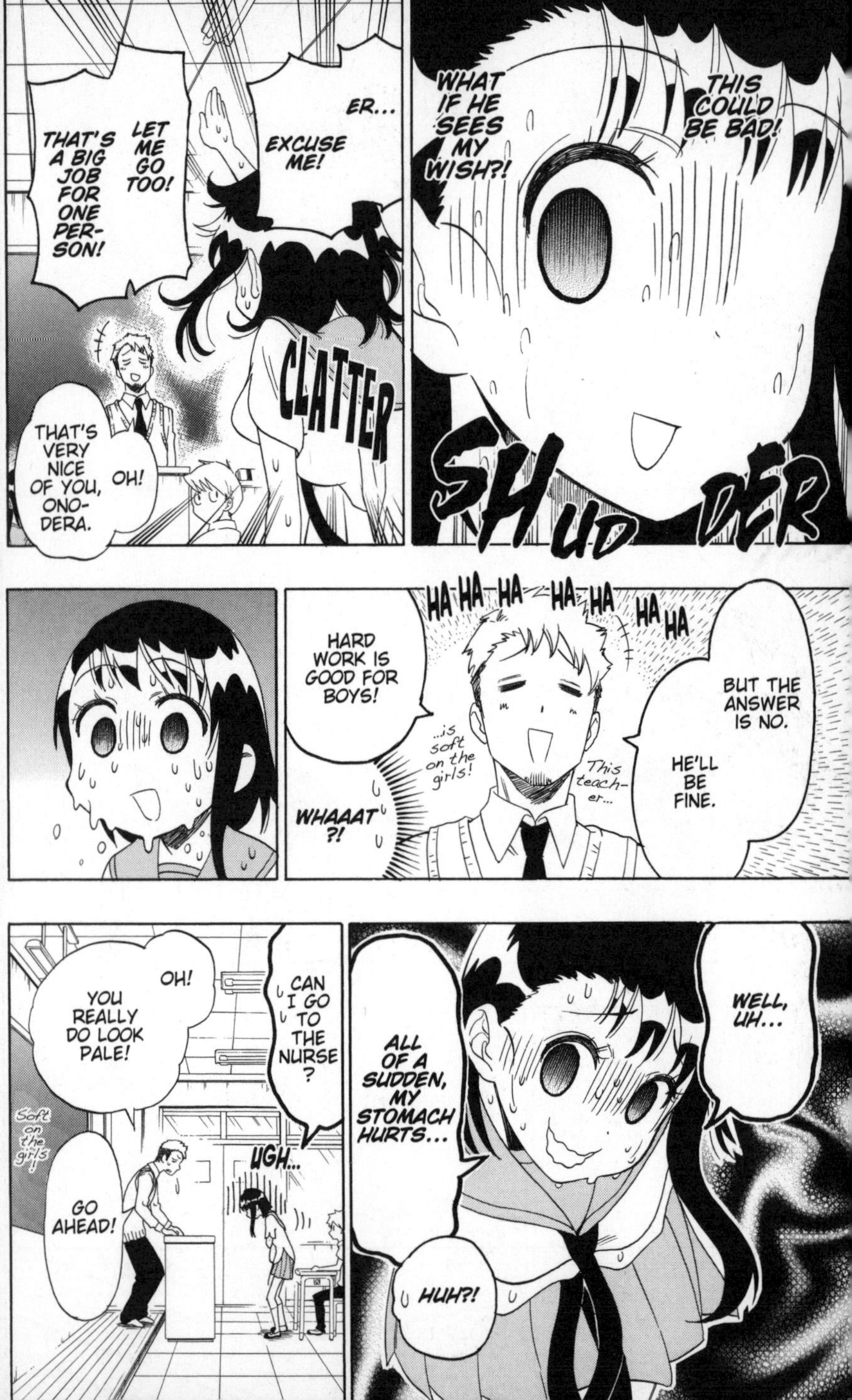
THIS COULD BE BAD!
WHAT IF HE SEES MY WISH?!
SHUDDER
ER... EXCUSE ME!
LET ME GO TOO!
THAT'S A BIG JOB FOR ONE PER-SON!
CLATTER
OH!
THAT'S VERY NICE OF YOU, ONO-DERA.
HA HA HA HA HA HA HA
BUT THE ANSWER IS NO.
HE'LL BE FINE.
HARD WORK IS GOOD FOR BOYS!
This teach-er...
...is soft on the girls!
WHAAAT?!
WELL, UH...
ALL OF A SUDDEN, MY STOMACH HURTS...
HUH?!
CAN I GO TO THE NURSE?
UGH...
OH!
YOU REALLY DO LOOK PALE!
Soft on the girls!
GO AHEAD!

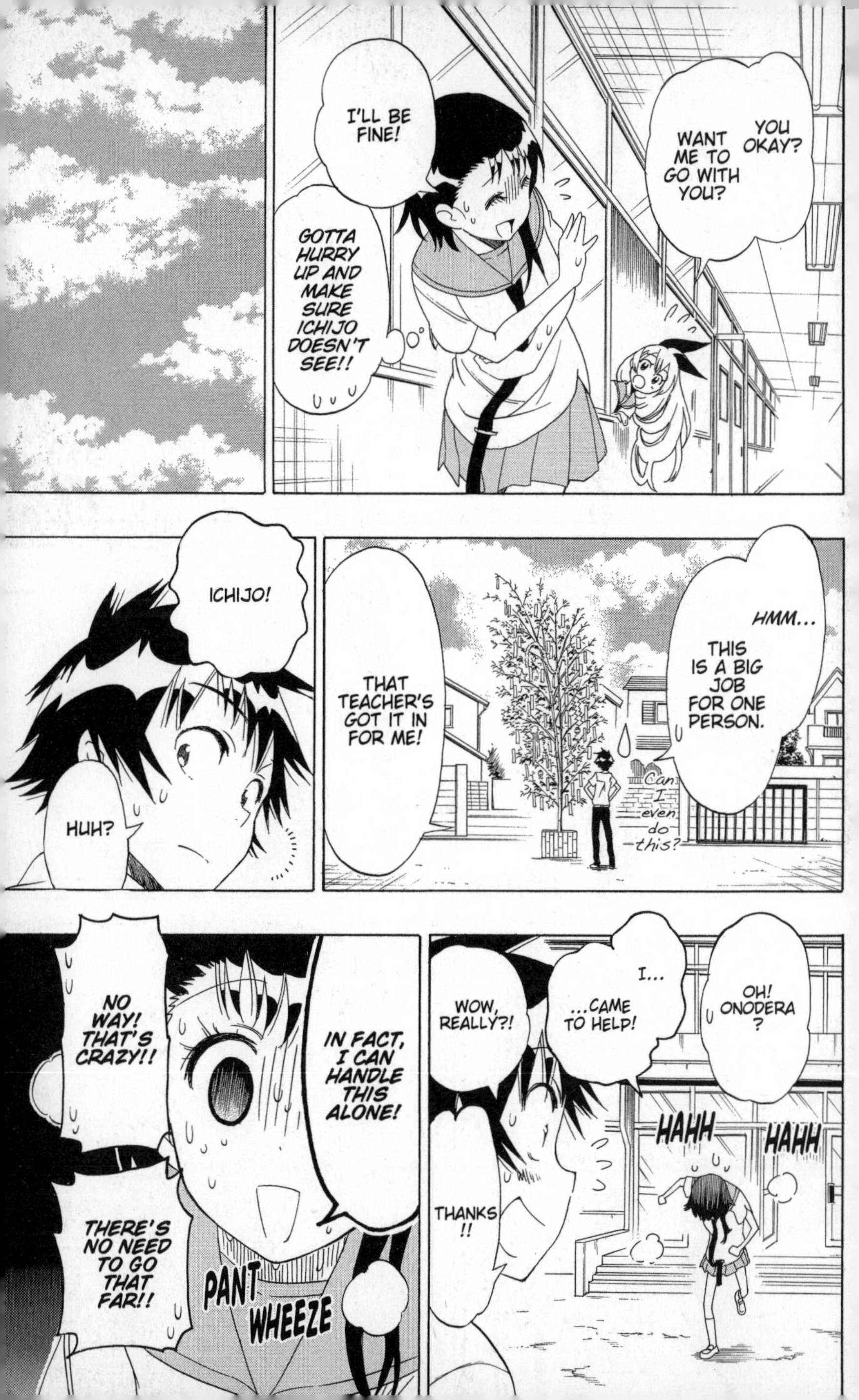
YOU OKAY? WANT ME TO GO WITH YOU?
I'LL BE FINE!
GOTTA HURRY UP AND MAKE SURE ICHIJO DOESN'T SEE!!
HMM... THIS IS A BIG JOB FOR ONE PERSON.
Can I even do this?
THAT TEACHER'S GOT IT IN FOR ME!
ICHIJO!
HUH?
OH! ONODERA?
HAHH HAHH
I... ...CAME TO HELP!
WOW, REALLY?!
THANKS!!
IN FACT, I CAN HANDLE THIS ALONE!
NO WAY! THAT'S CRAZY!!
THERE'S NO NEED TO GO THAT FAR!!
PANT WHEEZE

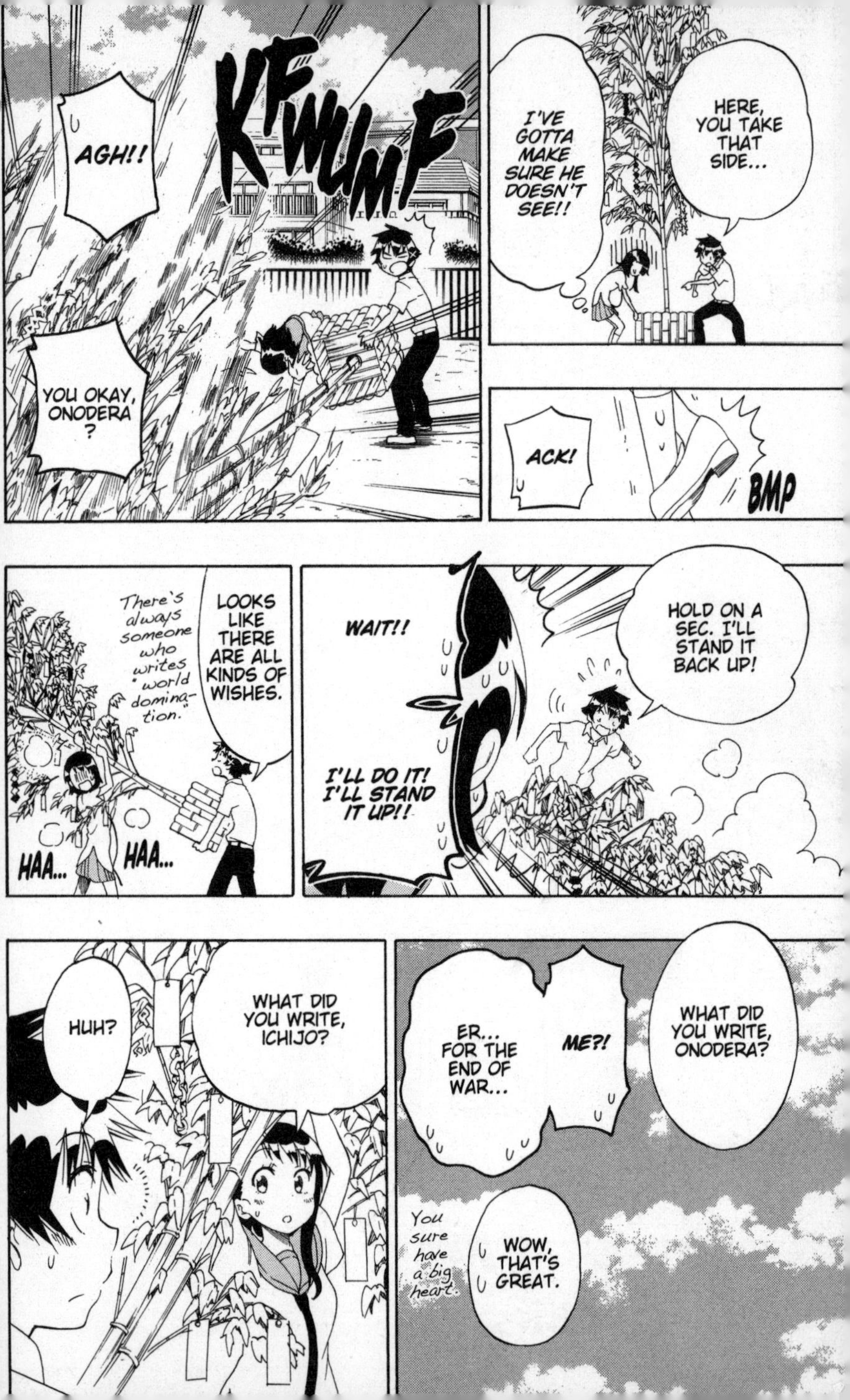
HERE, YOU TAKE THAT SIDE...
I'VE GOTTA MAKE SURE HE DOESN'T SEE!!
ACK!
BMP
KFWUMF
AGH!!
YOU OKAY, ONODERA?
HOLD ON A SEC. I'LL STAND IT BACK UP!
WAIT!!
I'LL DO IT! I'LL STAND IT UP!!
LOOKS LIKE THERE ARE ALL KINDS OF WISHES.
There's always someone who writes "world domination."
HAA... HAA...
WHAT DID YOU WRITE, ONODERA?
ME?!
ER... FOR THE END OF WAR...
WOW, THAT'S GREAT.
You sure have a big heart.
WHAT DID YOU WRITE, ICHIJO?
HUH?

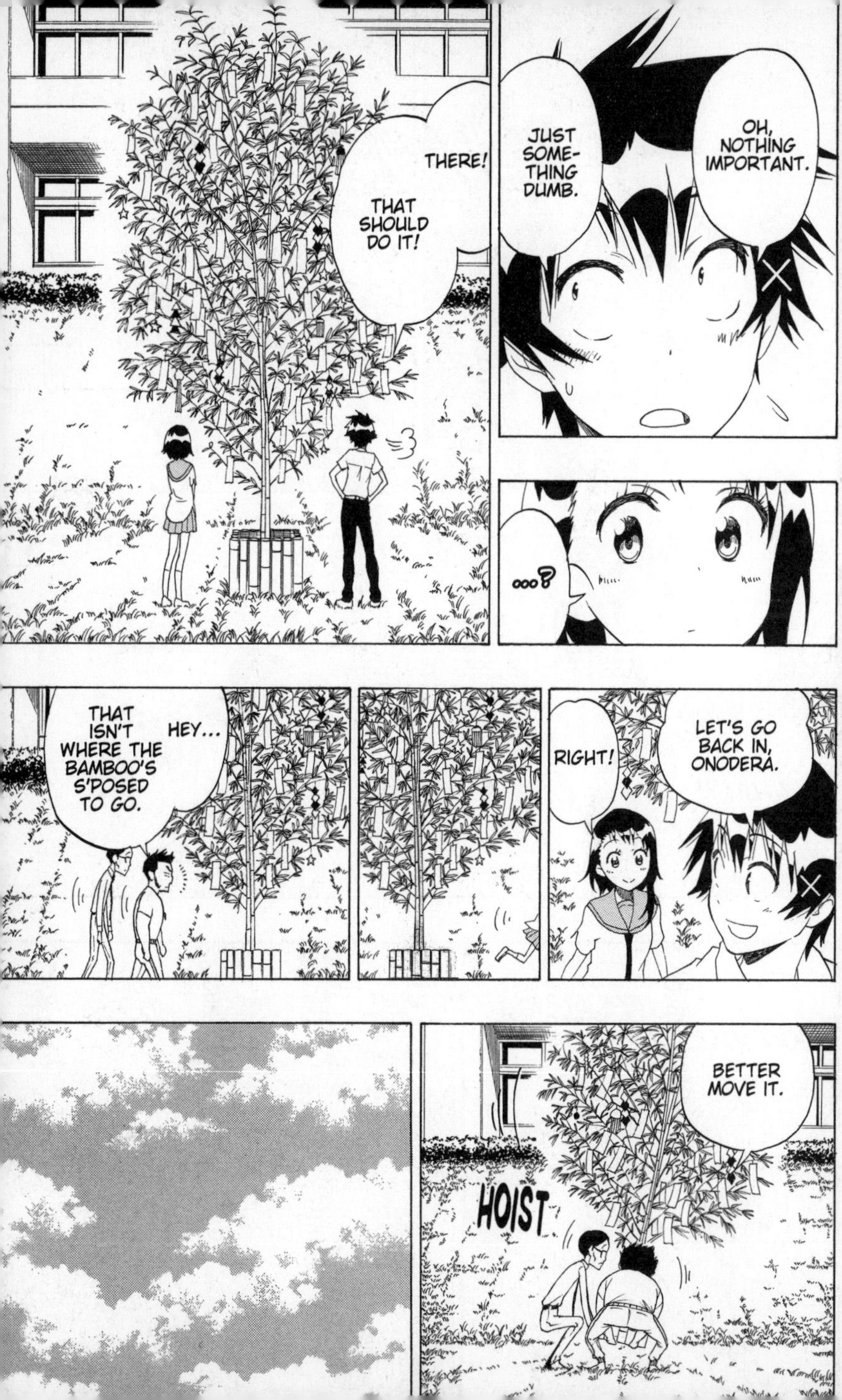
OH, NOTHING IMPORTANT.
JUST SOME-THING DUMB.
...?
THERE!
THAT SHOULD DO IT!
LET'S GO BACK IN, ONODERA.
RIGHT!
HEY...
THAT ISN'T WHERE THE BAMBOO'S S'POSED TO GO.
BETTER MOVE IT.
HOIST

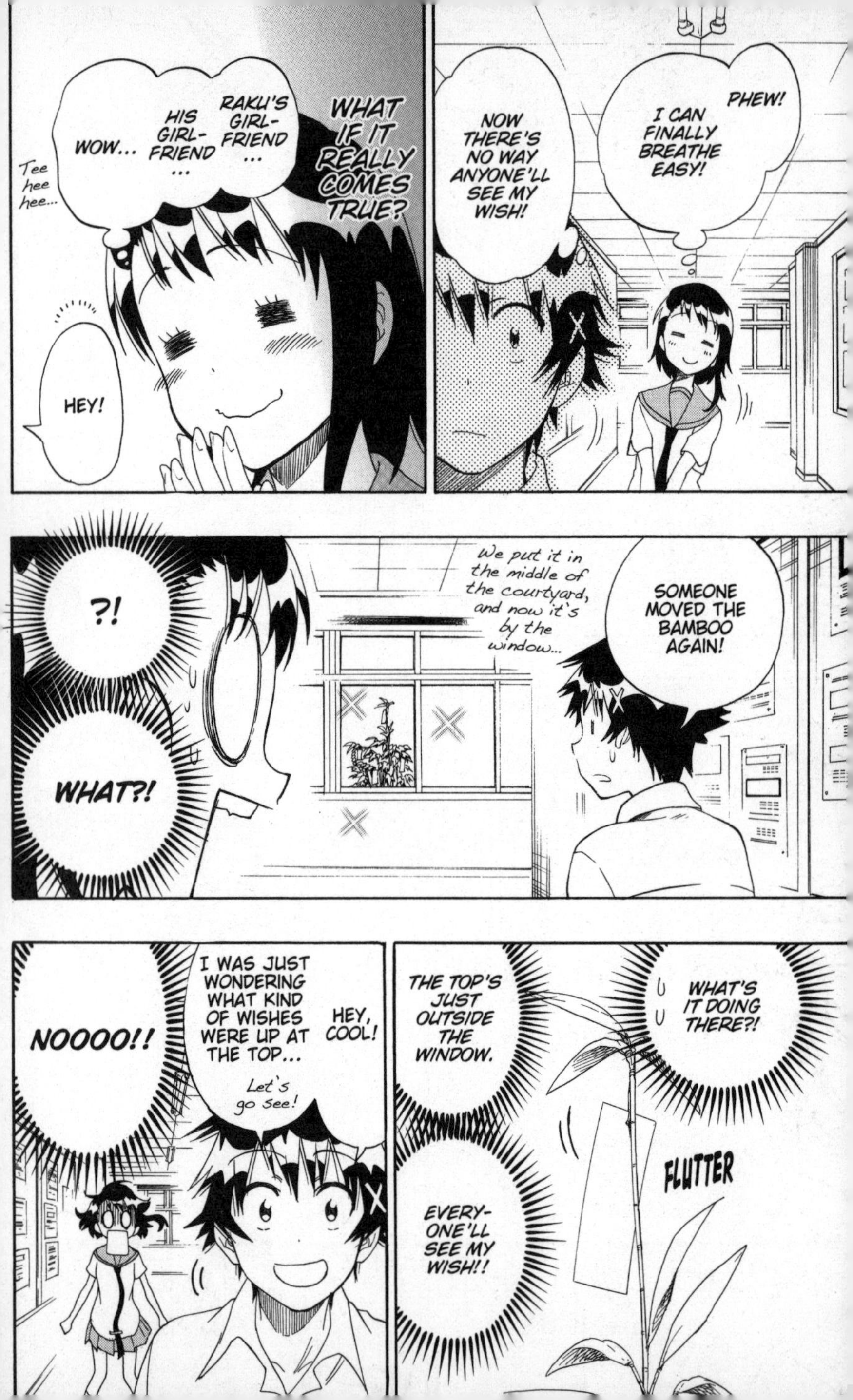
PHEW! I CAN FINALLY BREATHE EASY!
NOW THERE'S NO WAY ANYONE'LL SEE MY WISH!
WHAT IF IT REALLY COMES TRUE?
RAKU'S GIRL-FRIEND...
HIS GIRL-FRIEND...
WOW...
Tee hee hee...
HEY!
SOMEONE MOVED THE BAMBOO AGAIN!
We put it in the middle of the courtyard, and now it's by the window...
?!
WHAT?!
WHAT'S IT DOING THERE?!
THE TOP'S JUST OUTSIDE THE WINDOW.
FLUTTER
EVERY-ONE'LL SEE MY WISH!!
HEY, COOL!
I WAS JUST WONDERING WHAT KIND OF WISHES WERE UP AT THE TOP...
Let's go see!
NOOOO!!

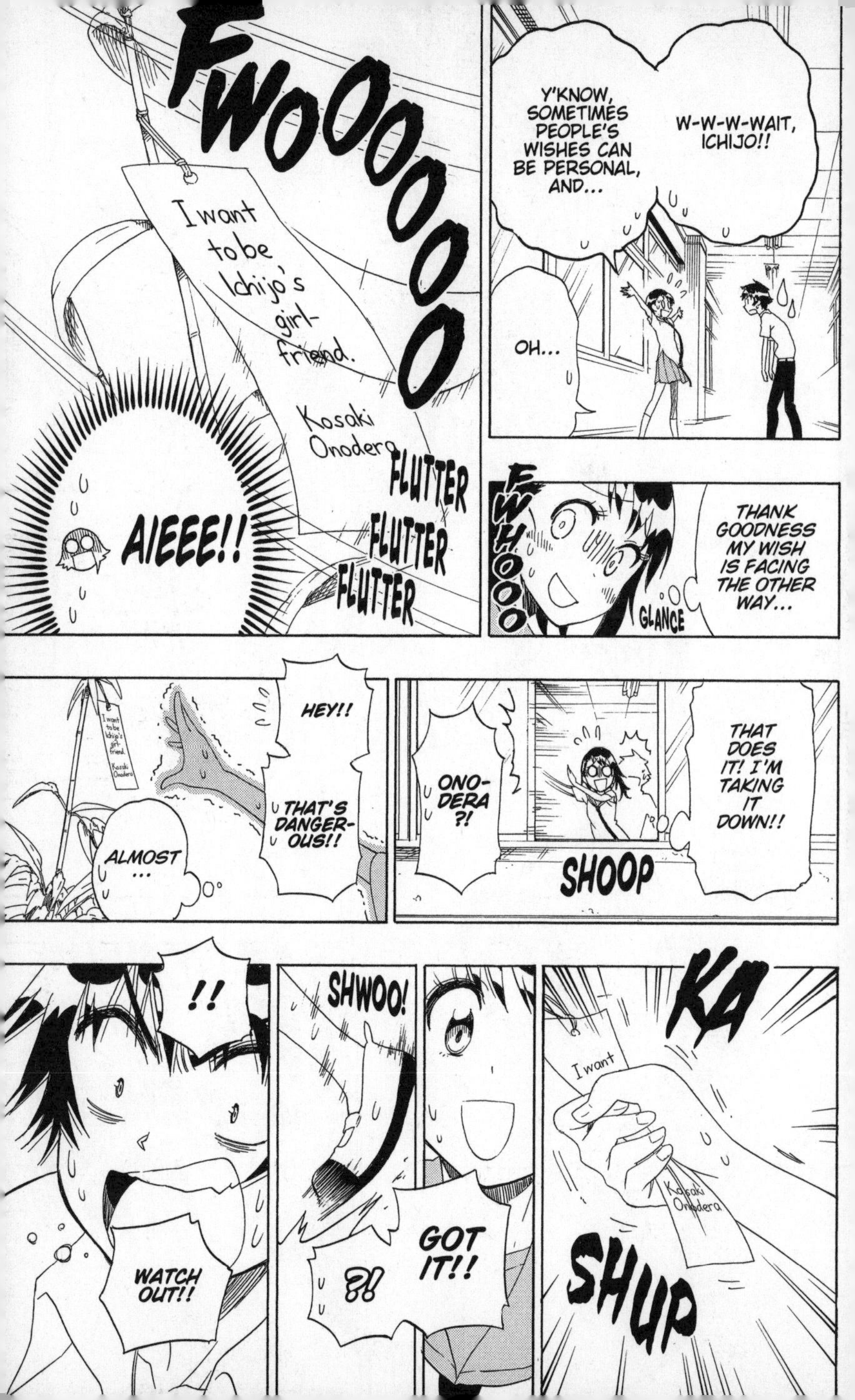
W-W-W-WAIT, ICHIJO!!
Y'KNOW, SOMETIMES PEOPLE'S WISHES CAN BE PERSONAL, AND...
OH...
THANK GOODNESS MY WISH IS FACING THE OTHER WAY...
FWHOOO
GLANCE
FWOOOOOOO
I want to be Ichijo's girl-friend.
Kosaki Onodera
FLUTTER
FLUTTER
FLUTTER
AIEEE!!
THAT DOES IT! I'M TAKING IT DOWN!!
ONO-DERA?!
SHOOP
HEY!!
THAT'S DANGER-OUS!!
ALMOST...
KA
I want
Kosaki Onodera
SHUP
SHWOO!
GOT IT!!
?!
!!
WATCH OUT!!

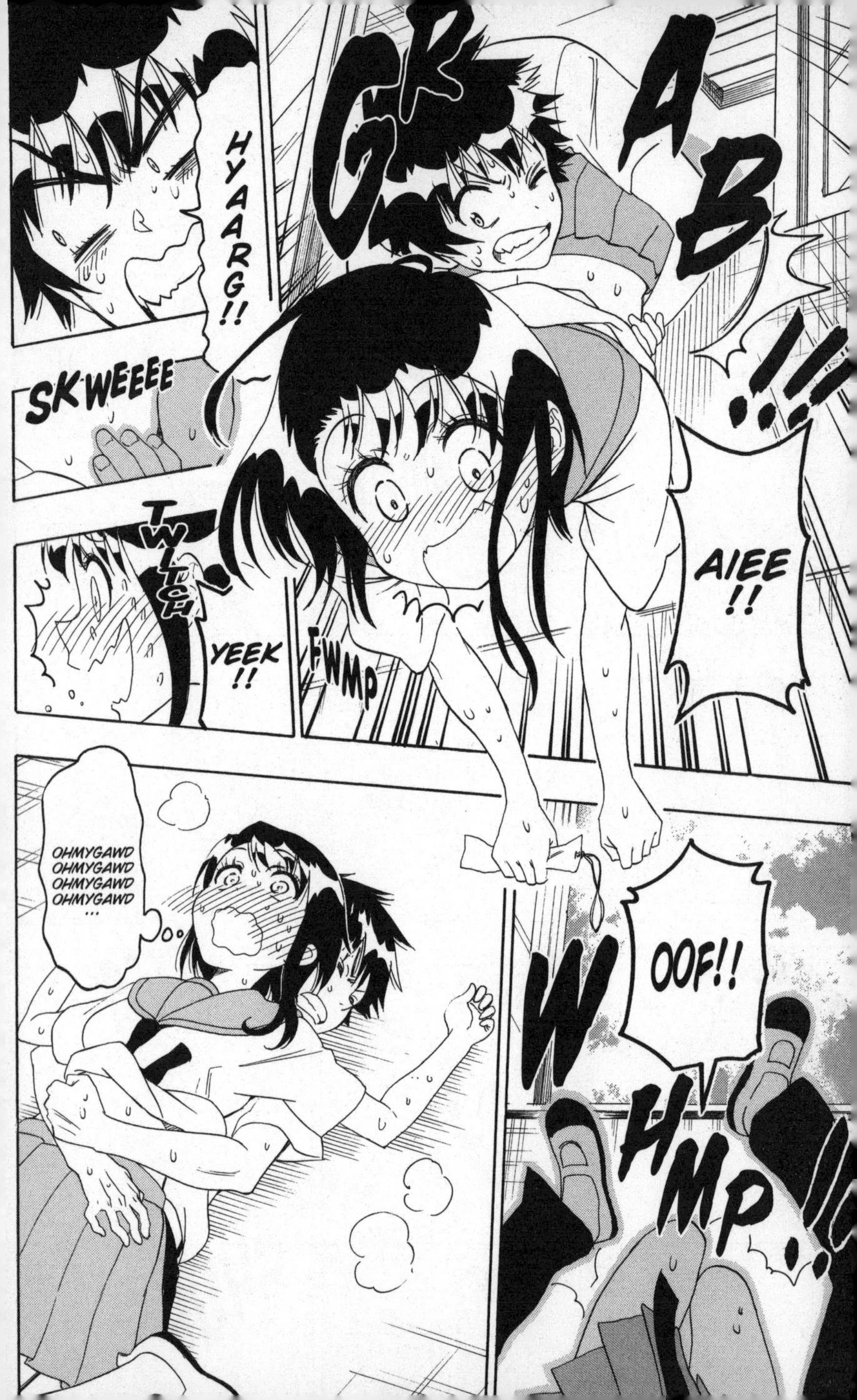
GRAB..!!!
AIEE!!
FWMP
HYAARG!!
SK-WEEEE
TWITCH
YEEK!!
WHUMP..!!!
OOF!!
OHMYGAWD
OHMYGAWD
OHMYGAWD
OHMYGAWD
...

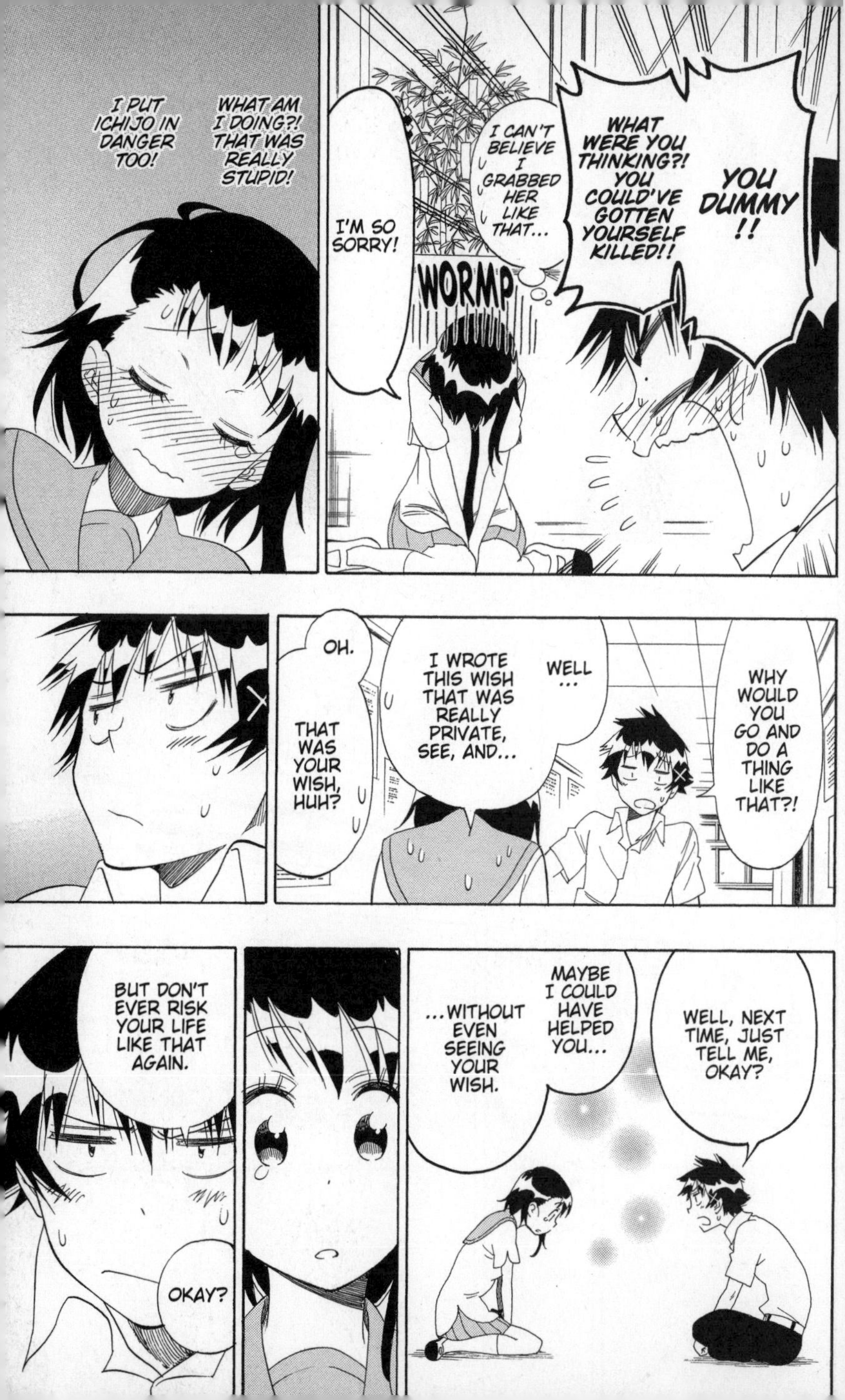
YOU DUMMY!!
WHAT WERE YOU THINKING?! YOU COULD'VE GOTTEN YOURSELF KILLED!!
I CAN'T BELIEVE I GRABBED HER LIKE THAT...
WORMP
I'M SO SORRY!
WHAT AM I DOING?! THAT WAS REALLY STUPID!
I PUT ICHIJO IN DANGER TOO!
WHY WOULD YOU GO AND DO A THING LIKE THAT?!
WELL...
I WROTE THIS WISH THAT WAS REALLY PRIVATE, SEE, AND...
OH.
THAT WAS YOUR WISH, HUH?
WELL, NEXT TIME, JUST TELL ME, OKAY?
MAYBE I COULD HAVE HELPED YOU...
...WITHOUT EVEN SEEING YOUR WISH.
BUT DON'T EVER RISK YOUR LIFE LIKE THAT AGAIN.
OKAY?

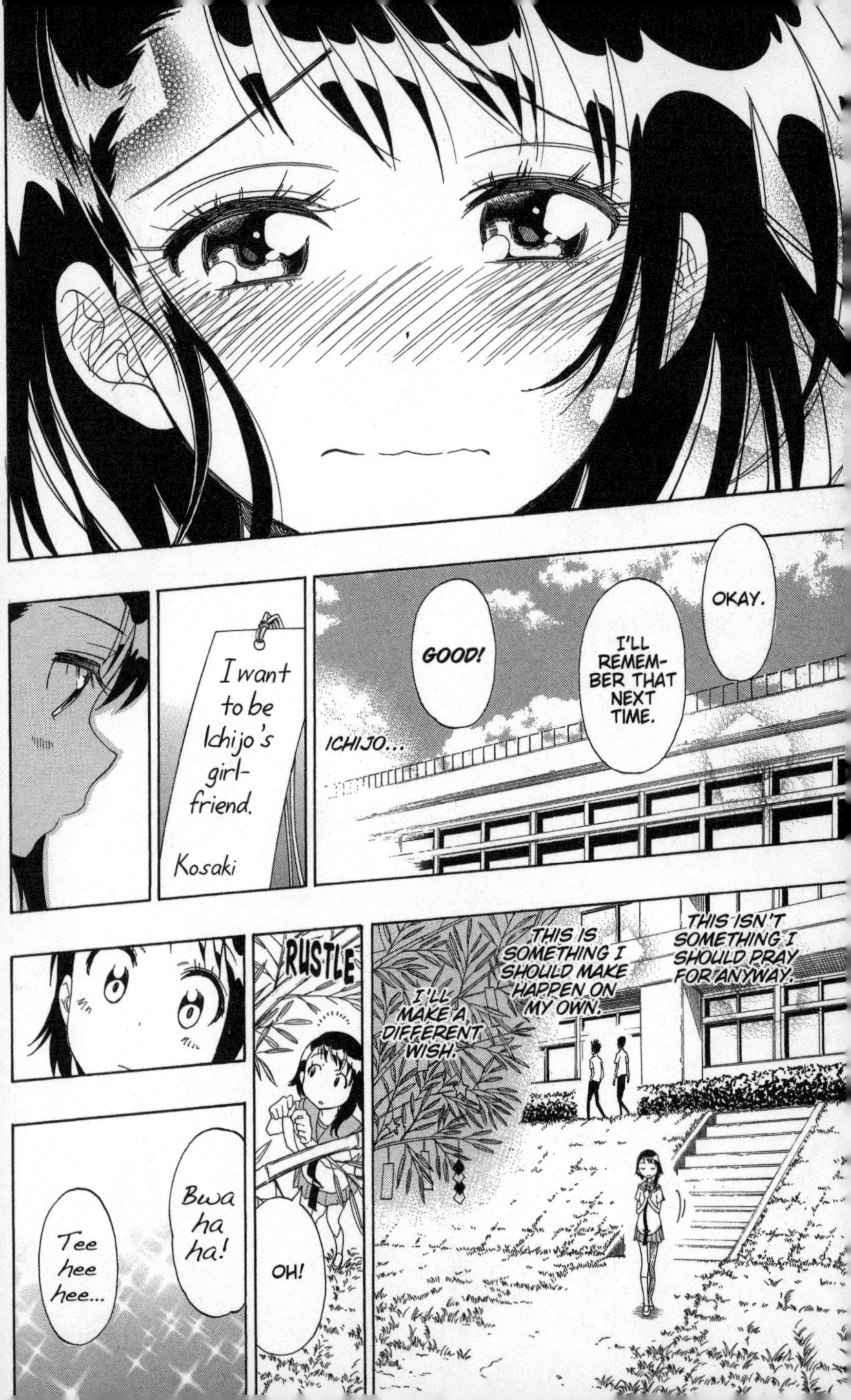

OKAY.
I'LL REMEMBER THAT NEXT TIME.
GOOD!
ICHIJO...
I want to be Ichijo's girlfriend.
Kosaki
THIS ISN'T SOMETHING I SHOULD PRAY FOR ANYWAY.
THIS IS SOMETHING I SHOULD MAKE HAPPEN ON MY OWN.
I'LL MAKE A DIFFERENT WISH.
RUSTLE
OH!
Bwa ha ha!
Tee hee hee...

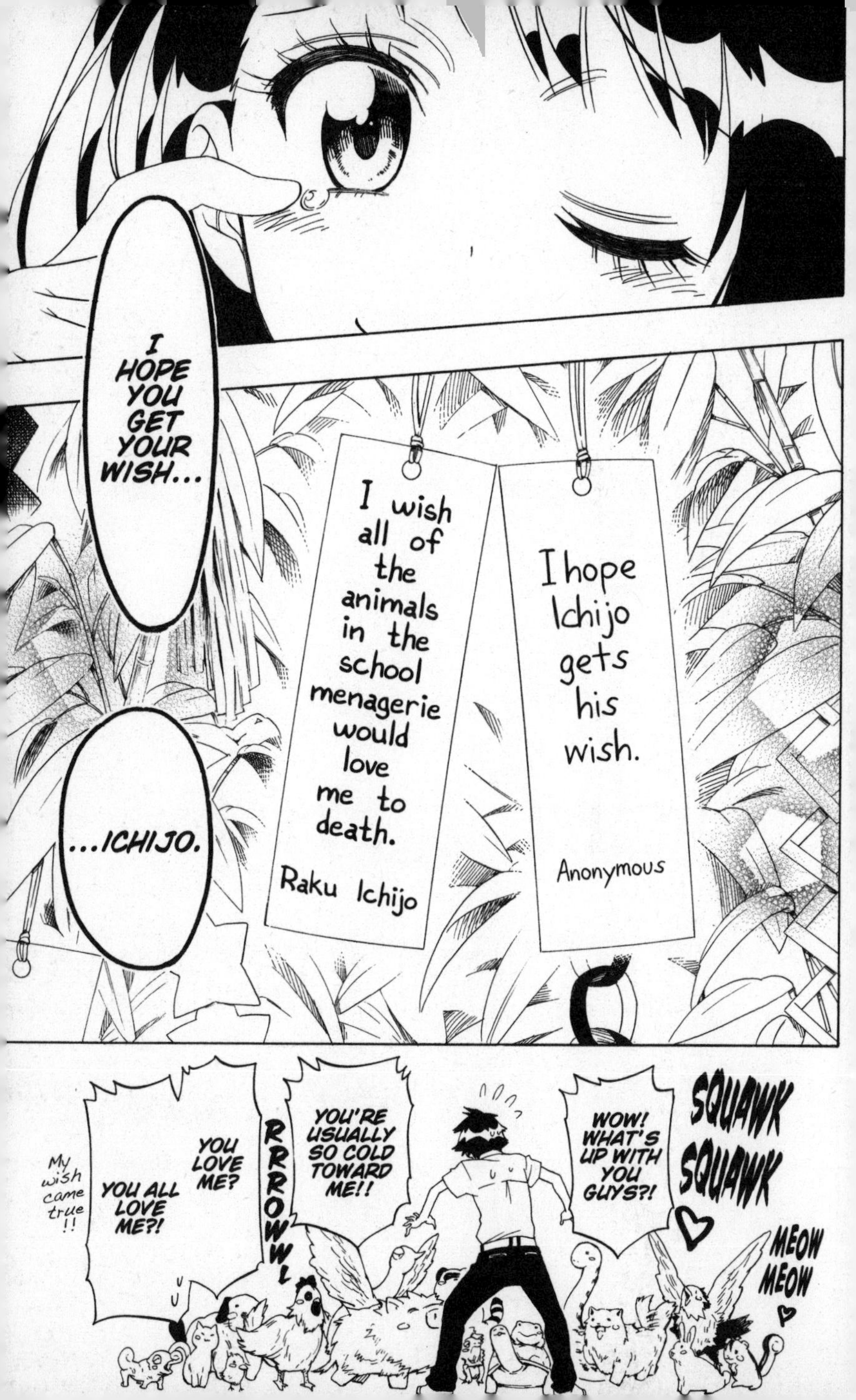
I HOPE YOU GET YOUR WISH...
I hope Ichijo gets his wish.
Anonymous
I wish all of the animals in the school menagerie would love me to death.
Raku Ichijo
...ICHIJO.
SQUAWK
SQUAWK
MEOW
MEOW
WOW! WHAT'S UP WITH YOU GUYS?!
YOU'RE USUALLY SO COLD TOWARD ME!!
RRROWWL
YOU LOVE ME?
YOU ALL LOVE ME?!
My wish came true!!

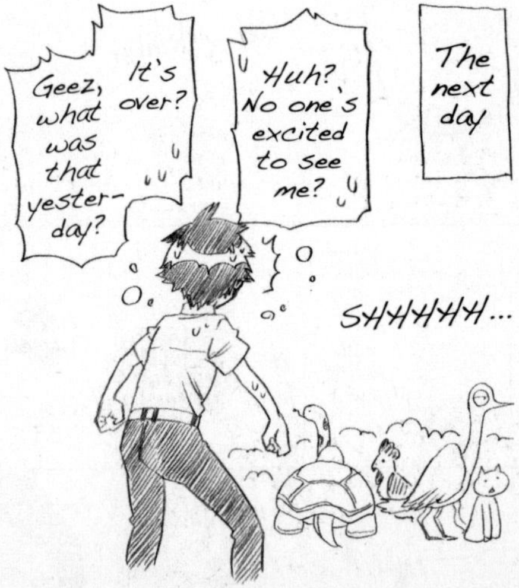
The next day
Huh? No one's excited to see me?
It's over?
Geez, what was that yesterday?
SHHHHH...

Chapter 106: Search

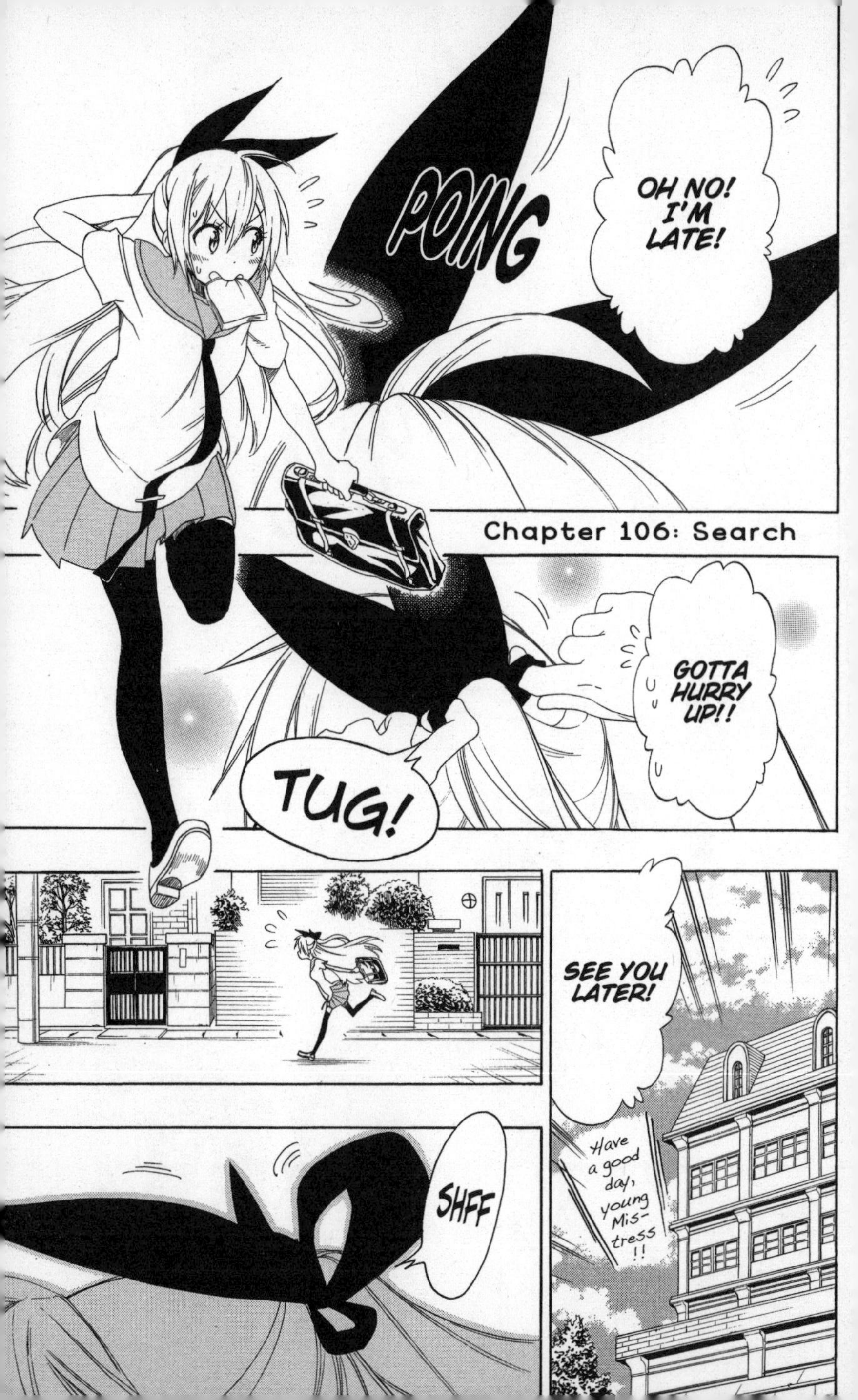
POING
OH NO! I'M LATE!
GOTTA HURRY UP!!
TUG!
SEE YOU LATER!
Have a good day, young Mistress!!
SHFF

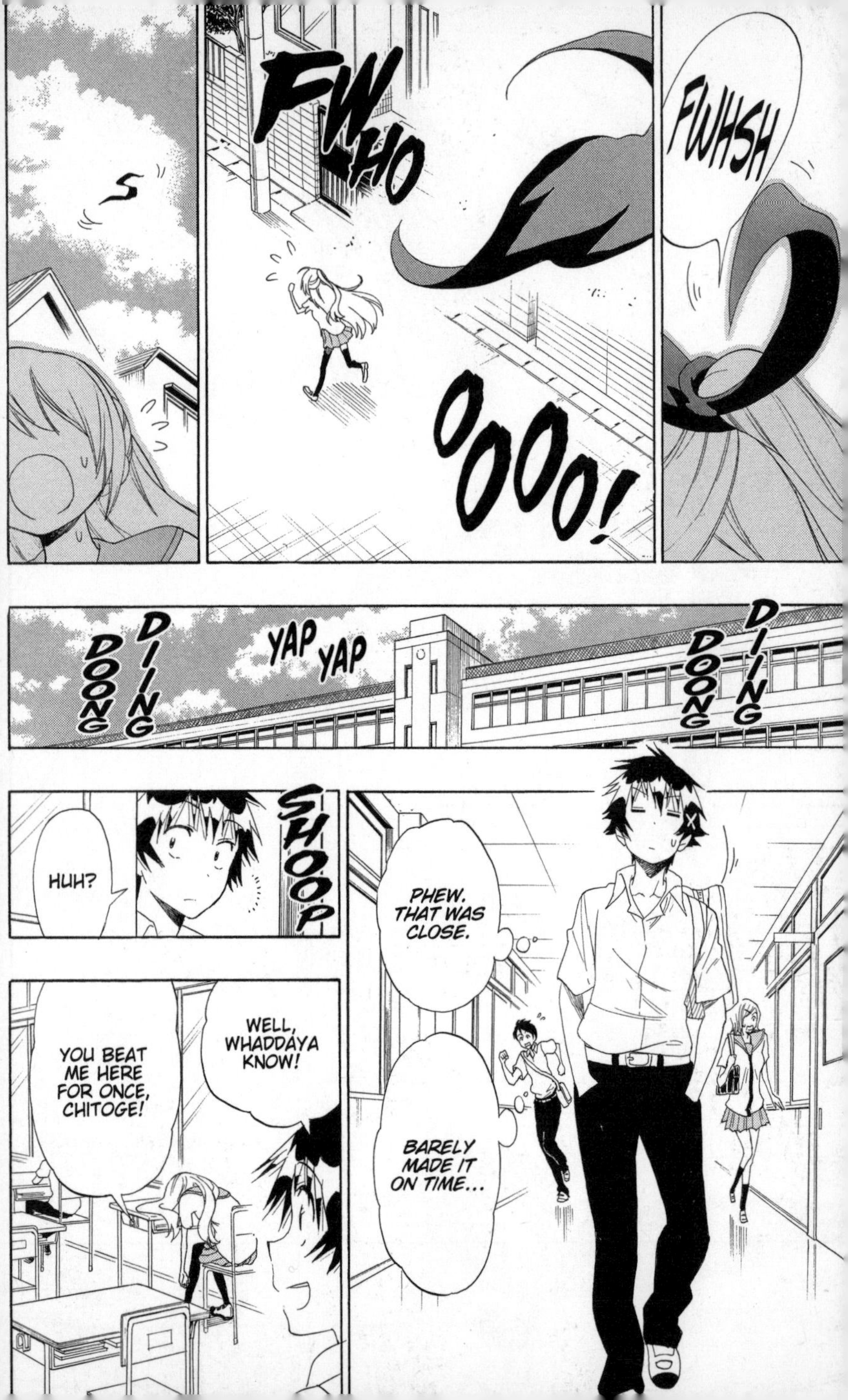

FWHSH
FWHO
OOOO!
S
DIING
DOONG
YAP YAP
DIING
DOONG
PHEW. THAT WAS CLOSE.
BARELY MADE IT ON TIME...
SHOOP
HUH?
WELL, WHADDAYA KNOW!
YOU BEAT ME HERE FOR ONCE, CHITOGE!

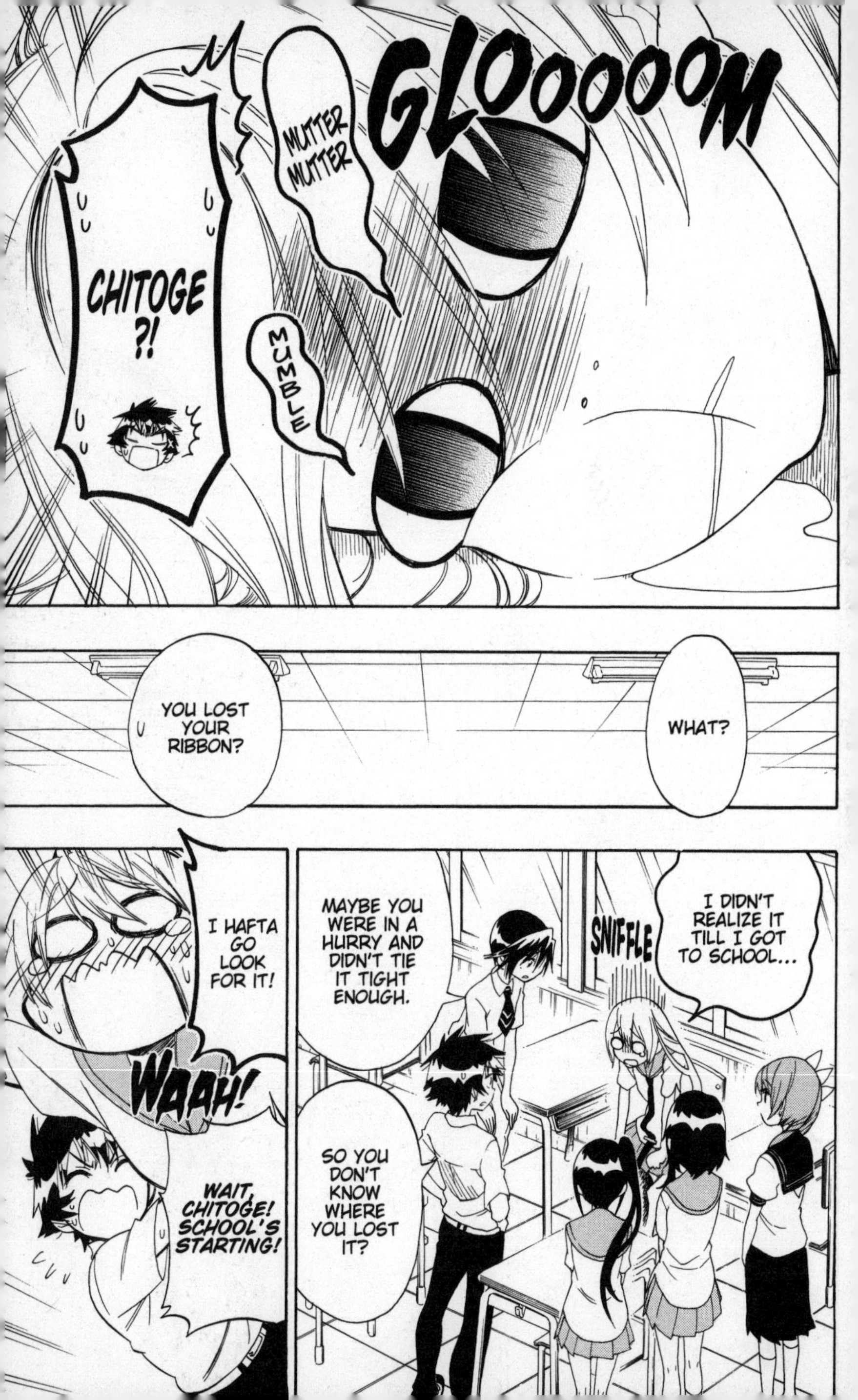
GLOOOOOM
MUTTER MUTTER
MUMBLE
CHITOGE ?!
WHAT?
YOU LOST YOUR RIBBON?
SNIFFLE
I DIDN'T REALIZE IT TILL I GOT TO SCHOOL...
MAYBE YOU WERE IN A HURRY AND DIDN'T TIE IT TIGHT ENOUGH.
SO YOU DON'T KNOW WHERE YOU LOST IT?
I HAFTA GO LOOK FOR IT!
WAAH!
WAIT, CHITOGE! SCHOOL'S STARTING!

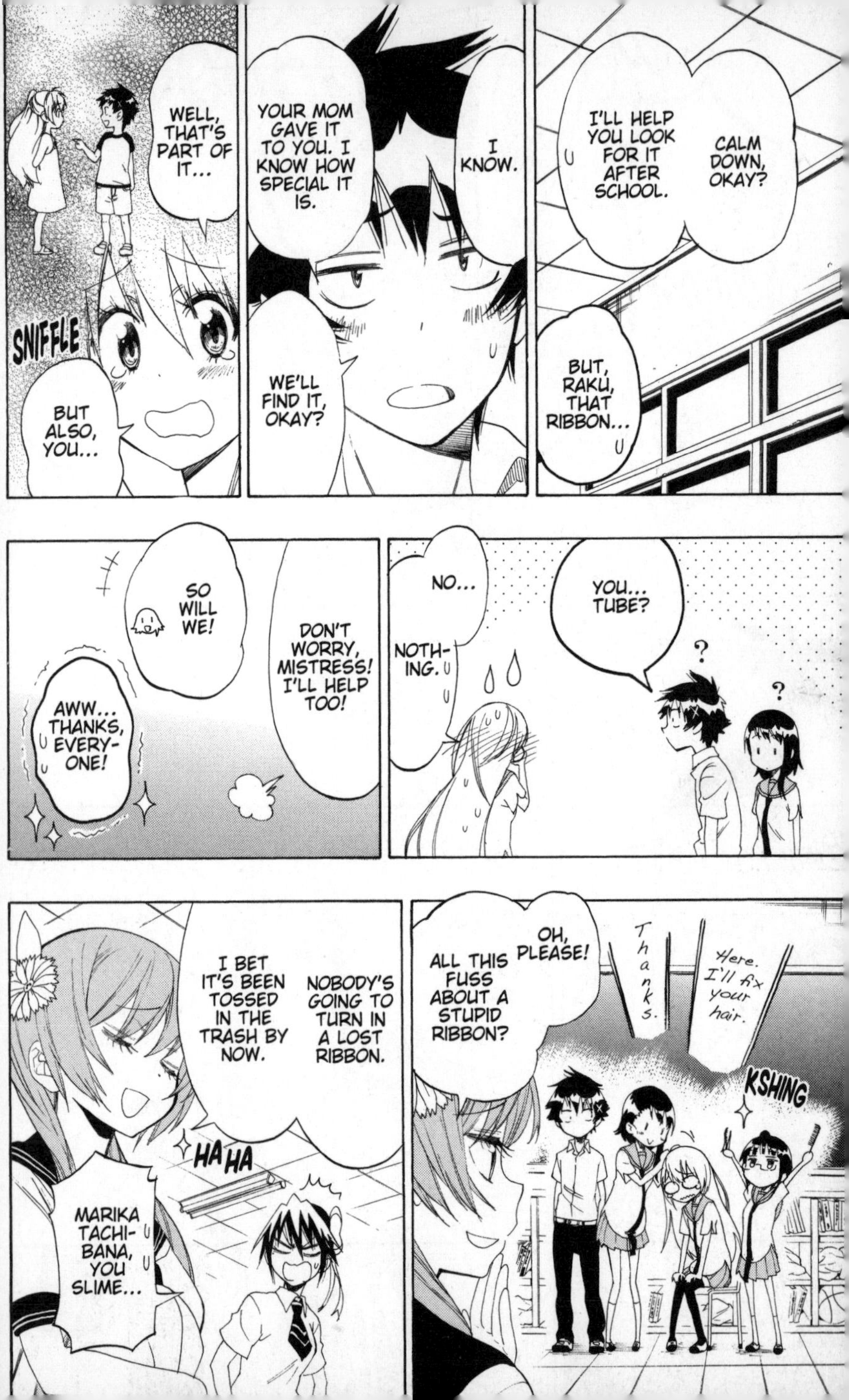
CALM DOWN, OKAY?
I'LL HELP YOU LOOK FOR IT AFTER SCHOOL.
BUT, RAKU, THAT RIBBON...
I KNOW.
YOUR MOM GAVE IT TO YOU. I KNOW HOW SPECIAL IT IS.
WE'LL FIND IT, OKAY?
WELL, THAT'S PART OF IT...
SNIFFLE
BUT ALSO, YOU...
YOU... TUBE?
NO...
NOTH-ING.
DON'T WORRY, MISTRESS! I'LL HELP TOO!
SO WILL WE!
AWW... THANKS, EVERY-ONE!
Here. I'll fix your hair.
Thanks.
OH, PLEASE!
ALL THIS FUSS ABOUT A STUPID RIBBON?
KSHING
NOBODY'S GOING TO TURN IN A LOST RIBBON.
I BET IT'S BEEN TOSSED IN THE TRASH BY NOW.
HA HA
MARIKA TACHI-BANA, YOU SLIME...

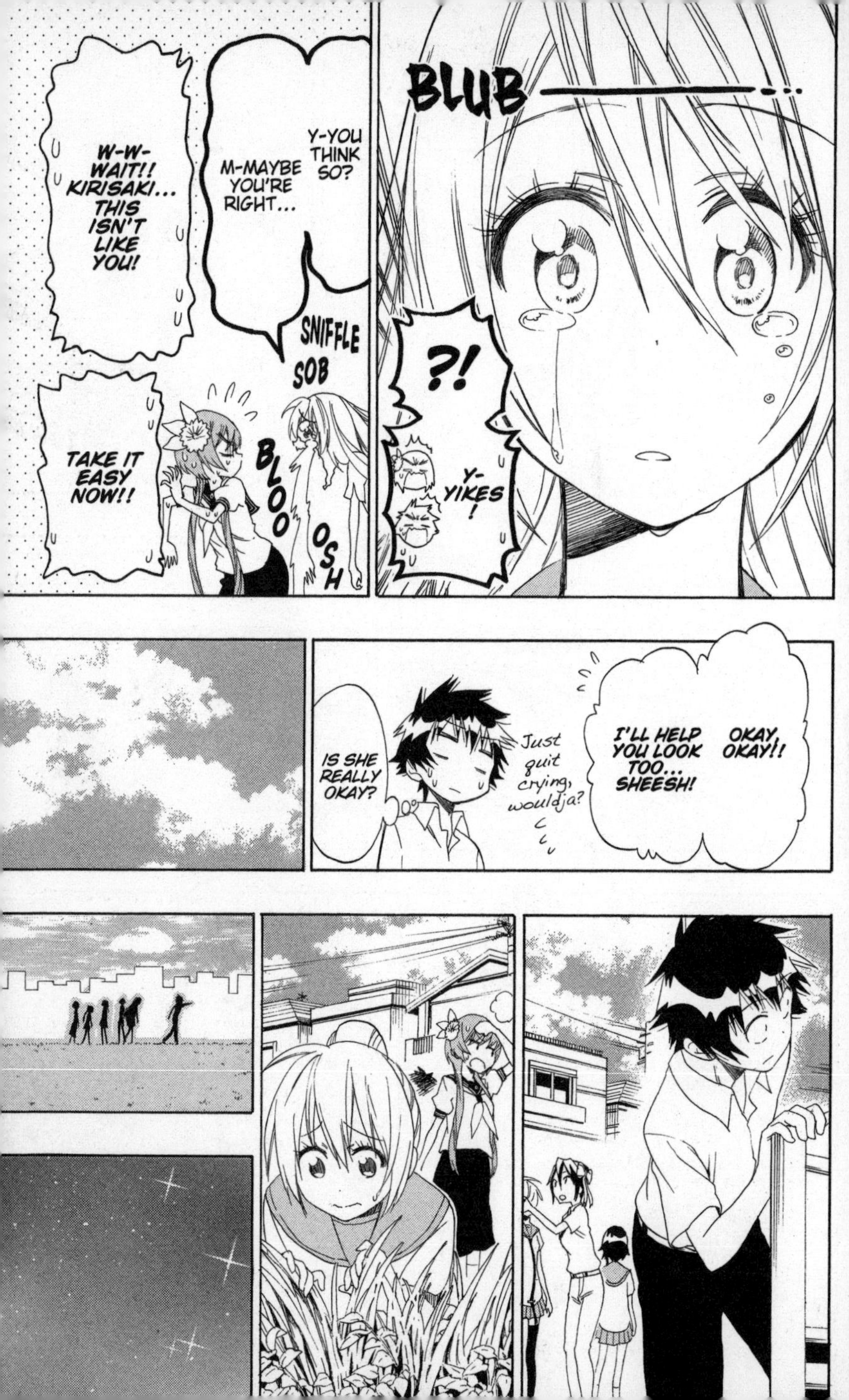
BLUB———...
?!
Y-YIKES!
Y-YOU THINK SO?
M-MAYBE YOU'RE RIGHT...
SNIFFLE
SOB
BLOOOSH
W-W-WAIT!! KIRISAKI... THIS ISN'T LIKE YOU!
TAKE IT EASY NOW!!
OKAY, OKAY!!
I'LL HELP YOU LOOK TOO... SHEESH!
Just quit crying, wouldja?
IS SHE REALLY OKAY?

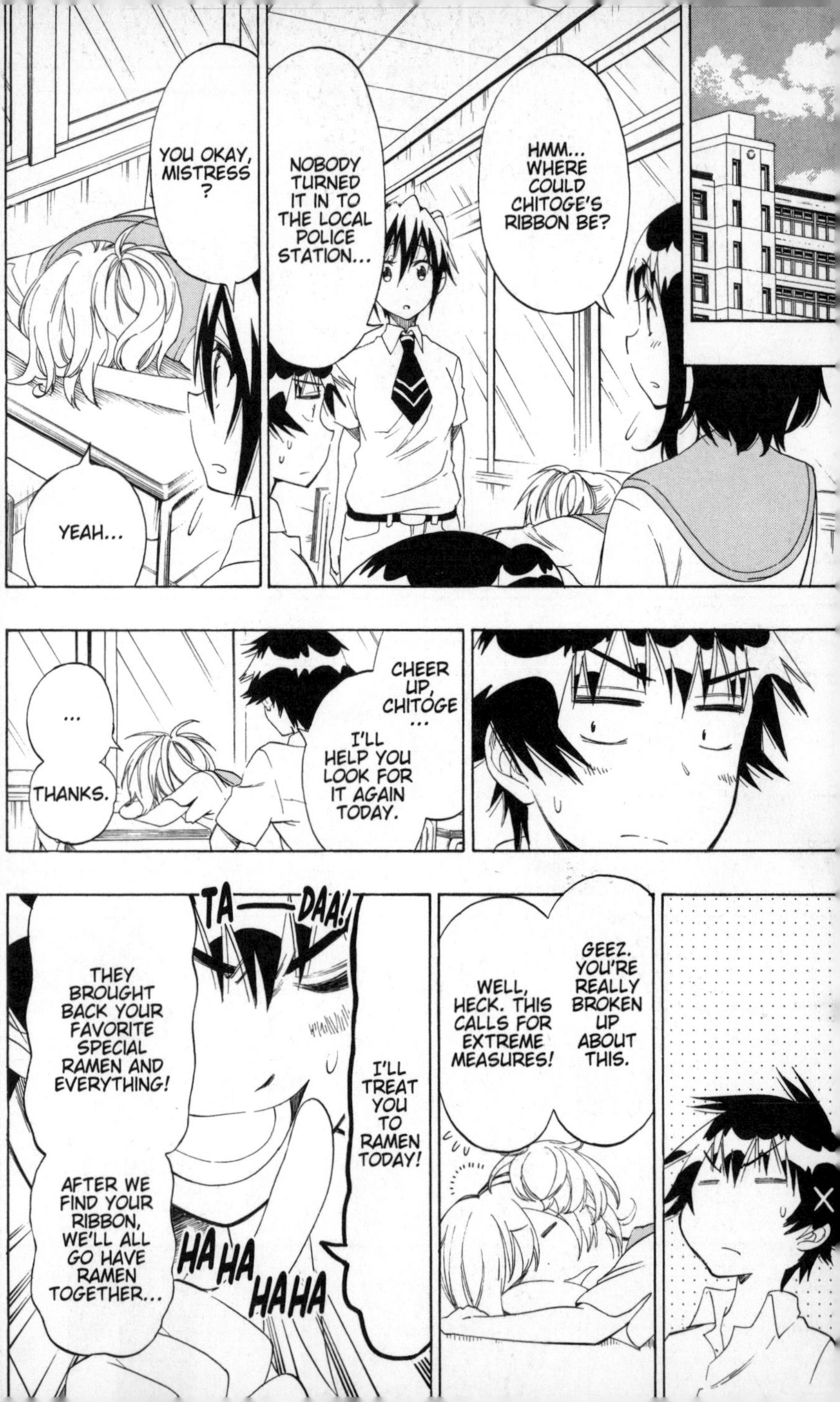
HMM... WHERE COULD CHITOGE'S RIBBON BE?
NOBODY TURNED IT IN TO THE LOCAL POLICE STATION...
YOU OKAY, MISTRESS?
YEAH...
CHEER UP, CHITOGE...
I'LL HELP YOU LOOK FOR IT AGAIN TODAY.
...
THANKS.
GEEZ. YOU'RE REALLY BROKEN UP ABOUT THIS.
WELL, HECK. THIS CALLS FOR EXTREME MEASURES!
TA—DAA!
I'LL TREAT YOU TO RAMEN TODAY!
THEY BROUGHT BACK YOUR FAVORITE SPECIAL RAMEN AND EVERYTHING!
AFTER WE FIND YOUR RIBBON, WE'LL ALL GO HAVE RAMEN TOGETHER...
HA HA HAHA

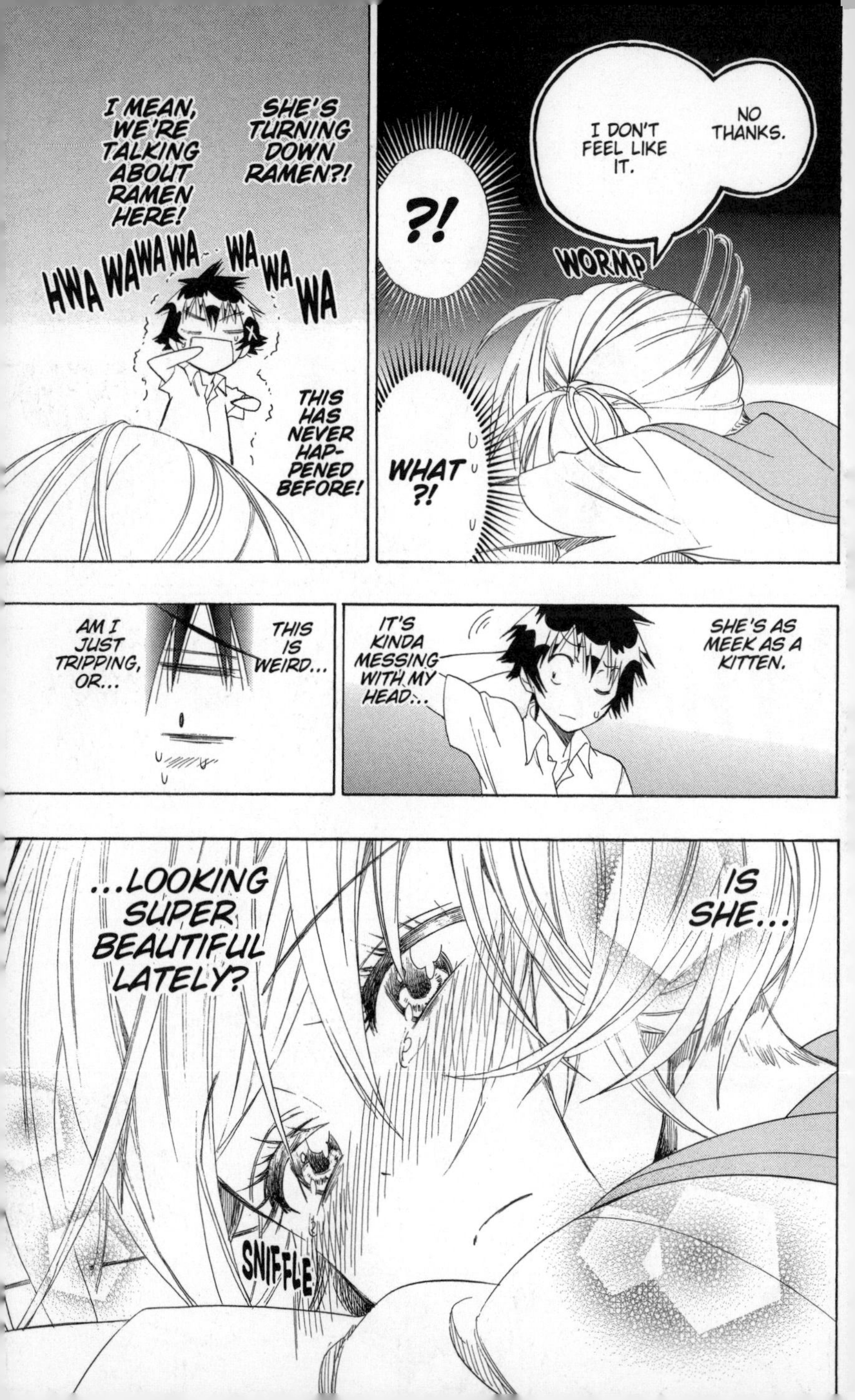
NO THANKS.
I DON'T FEEL LIKE IT.
WORMP
?!
WHAT?!
SHE'S TURNING DOWN RAMEN?!
I MEAN, WE'RE TALKING ABOUT RAMEN HERE!
HWA WAWAWA WA WA WA WA
THIS HAS NEVER HAP-PENED BEFORE!
SHE'S AS MEEK AS A KITTEN.
IT'S KINDA MESSING WITH MY HEAD...
THIS IS WEIRD...
AM I JUST TRIPPING, OR...
IS SHE...
...LOOKING SUPER BEAUTIFUL LATELY?
SNIFFLE

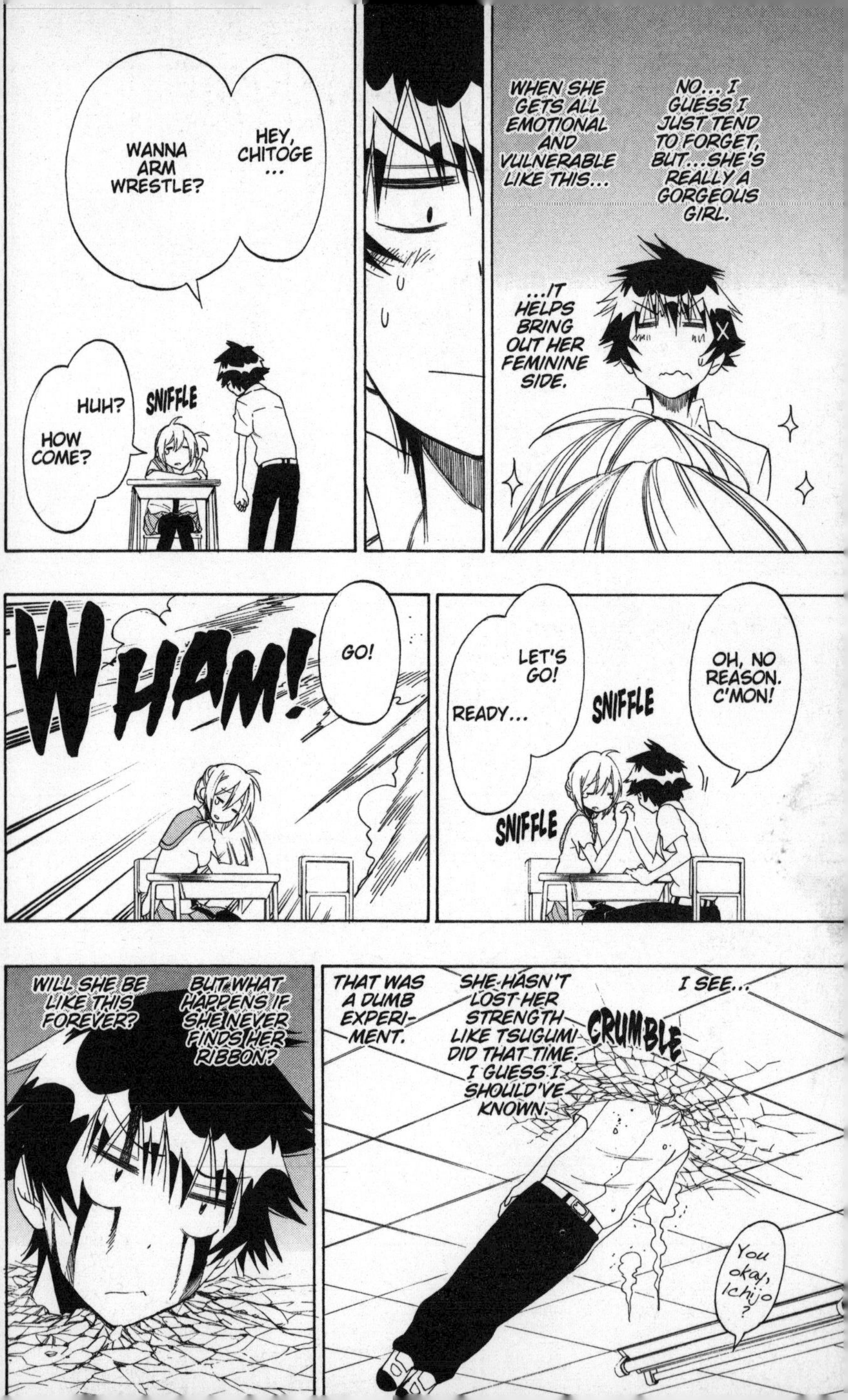
NO... I GUESS I JUST TEND TO FORGET, BUT...SHE'S REALLY A GORGEOUS GIRL.
WHEN SHE GETS ALL EMOTIONAL AND VULNERABLE LIKE THIS...
...IT HELPS BRING OUT HER FEMININE SIDE.
HEY, CHITOGE...
WANNA ARM WRESTLE?
SNIFFLE
HUH? HOW COME?
OH, NO REASON. C'MON!
SNIFFLE
LET'S GO! READY...
SNIFFLE
GO!
WHAM!
I SEE...
CRUMBLE
SHE HASN'T LOST HER STRENGTH LIKE TSUGUMI DID THAT TIME. I GUESS I SHOULD'VE KNOWN.
THAT WAS A DUMB EXPERIMENT.
You okay, Ichijo?
BUT WHAT HAPPENS IF SHE NEVER FINDS HER RIBBON?
WILL SHE BE LIKE THIS FOREVER?

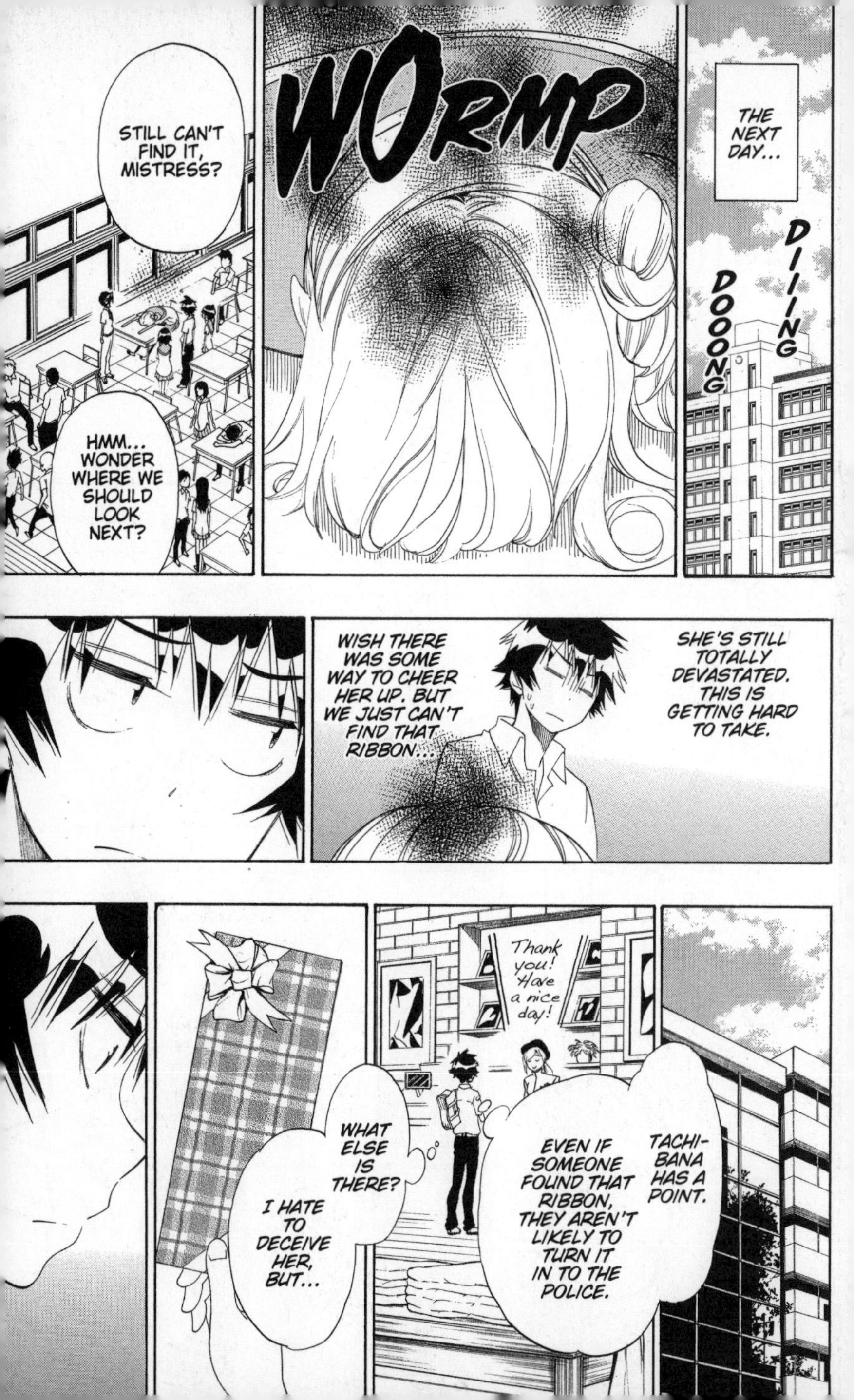
THE NEXT DAY...
DIIING
DOOOONG
WORMP
STILL CAN'T FIND IT, MISTRESS?
HMM... WONDER WHERE WE SHOULD LOOK NEXT?
SHE'S STILL TOTALLY DEVASTATED. THIS IS GETTING HARD TO TAKE.
WISH THERE WAS SOME WAY TO CHEER HER UP. BUT WE JUST CAN'T FIND THAT RIBBON...
TACHIBANA HAS A POINT.
EVEN IF SOMEONE FOUND THAT RIBBON, THEY AREN'T LIKELY TO TURN IT IN TO THE POLICE.
Thank you! Have a nice day!
WHAT ELSE IS THERE?
I HATE TO DECEIVE HER, BUT...

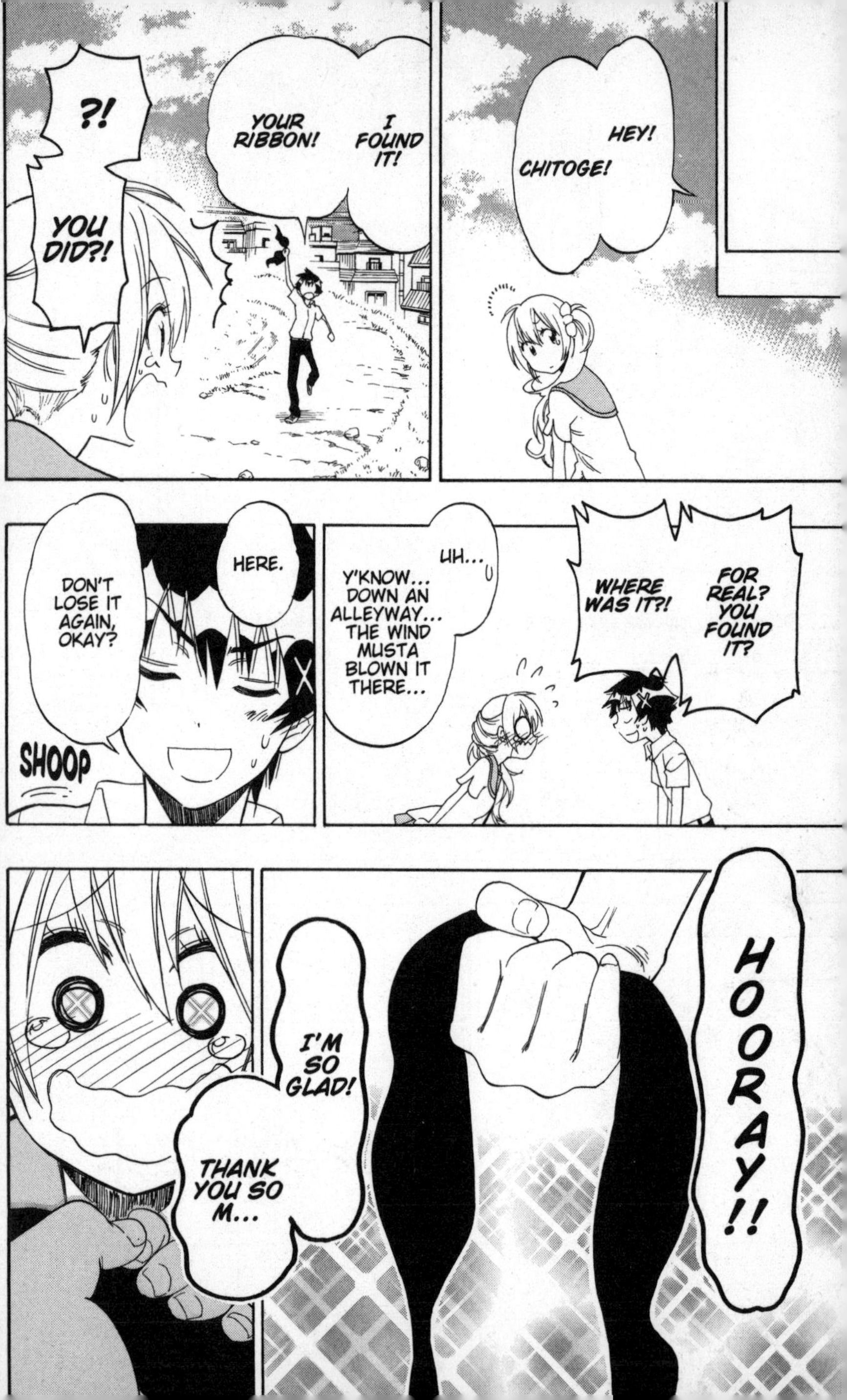
HEY!
CHITOGE!
I FOUND IT!
YOUR RIBBON!
?!
YOU DID?!
FOR REAL? YOU FOUND IT?
WHERE WAS IT?!
UH...
Y'KNOW... DOWN AN ALLEYWAY... THE WIND MUSTA BLOWN IT THERE...
HERE.
DON'T LOSE IT AGAIN, OKAY?
SHOOP
HOORAY!!
I'M SO GLAD!
THANK YOU SO M...

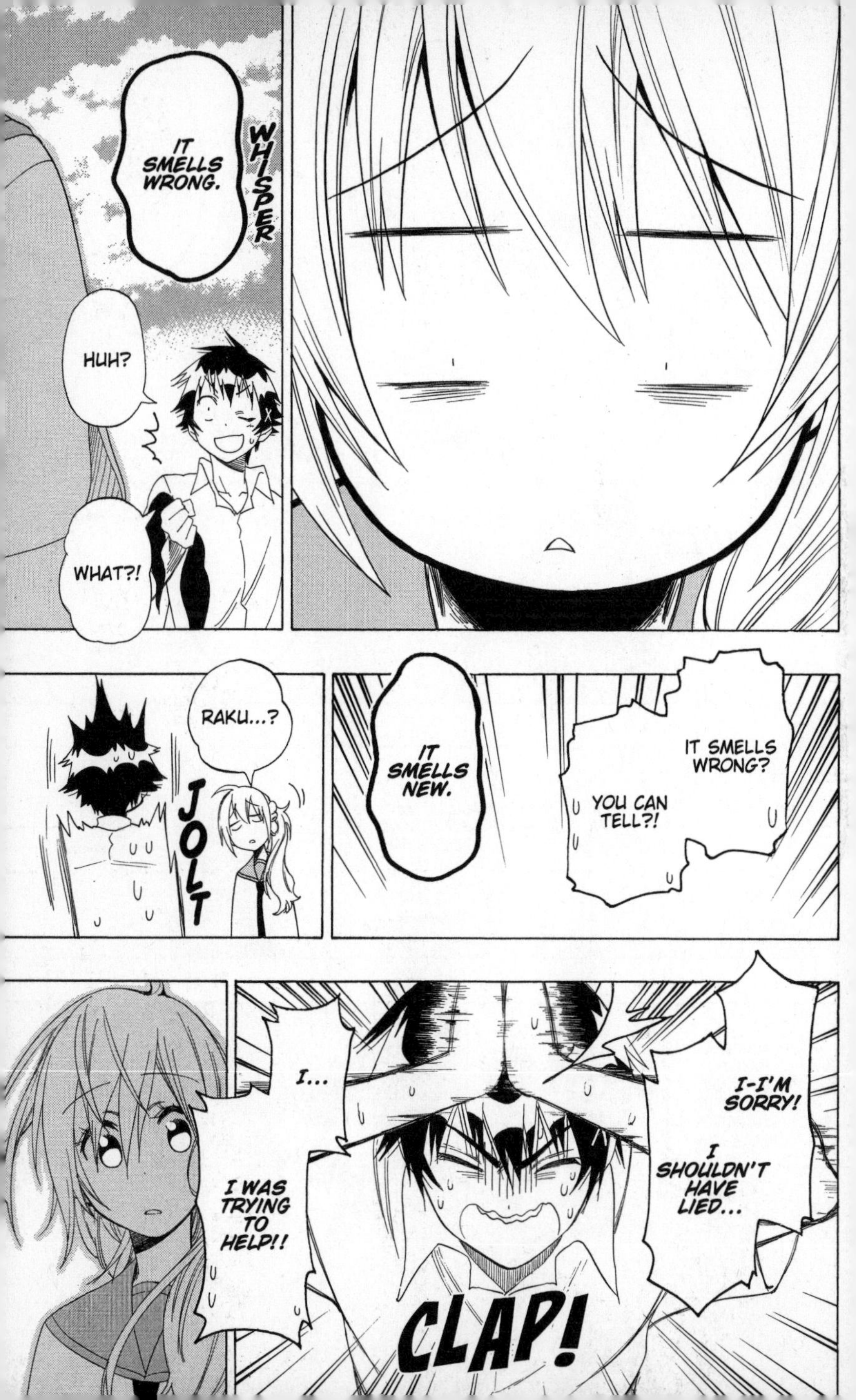
IT SMELLS WRONG.
WHISPER
HUH?
WHAT?!
IT SMELLS WRONG?
YOU CAN TELL?!
IT SMELLS NEW.
RAKU...?
JOLT
I-I'M SORRY!
I SHOULDN'T HAVE LIED...
I...
I WAS TRYING TO HELP!!
CLAP!

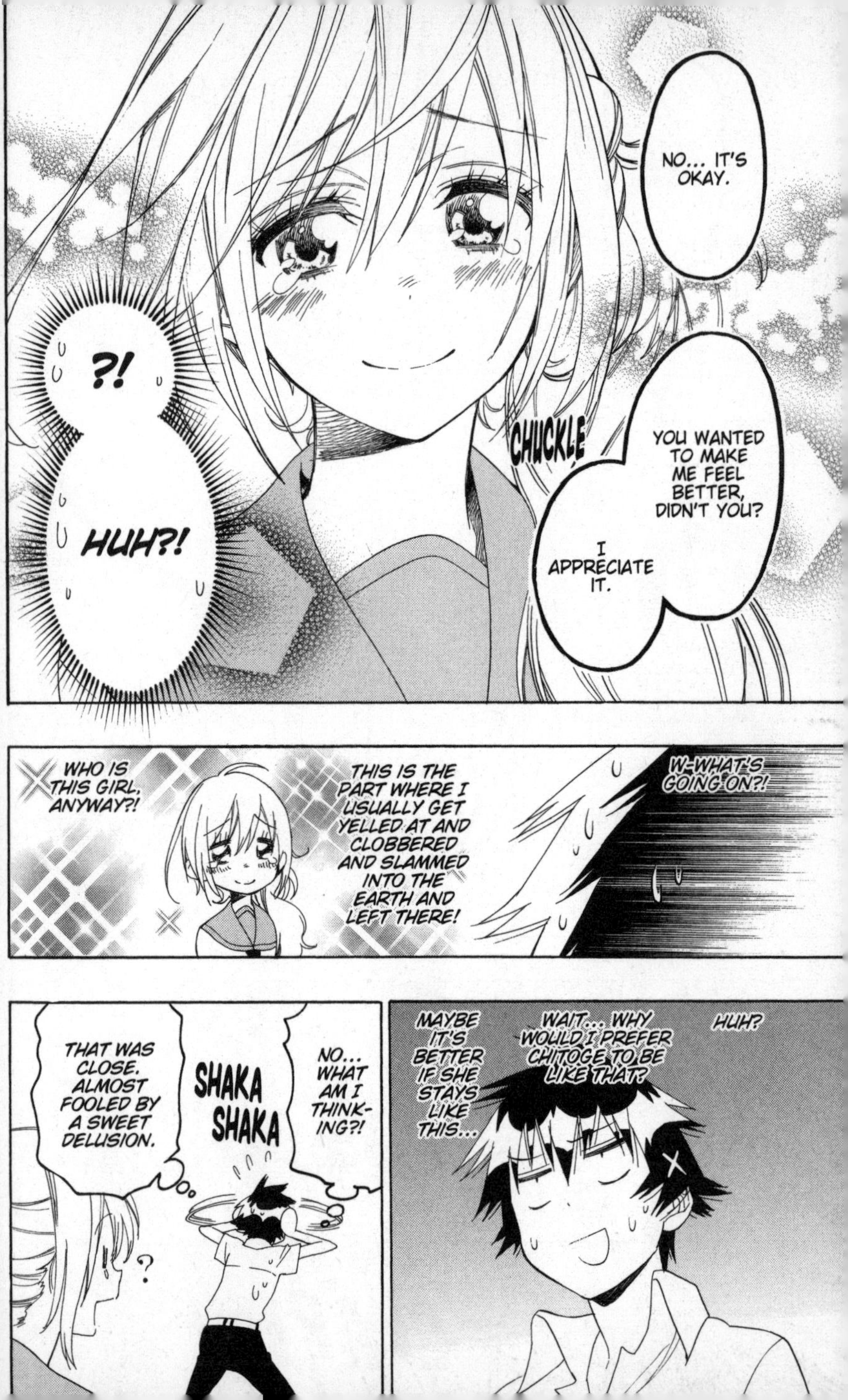
NO... IT'S OKAY.
CHUCKLE
YOU WANTED TO MAKE ME FEEL BETTER, DIDN'T YOU?
I APPRECIATE IT.
?!
HUH?!
W-WHAT'S GOING ON?!
THIS IS THE PART WHERE I USUALLY GET YELLED AT AND CLOBBERED AND SLAMMED INTO THE EARTH AND LEFT THERE!
WHO IS THIS GIRL, ANYWAY?!
HUH?
WAIT... WHY WOULD I PREFER CHITOGE TO BE LIKE THAT?
MAYBE IT'S BETTER IF SHE STAYS LIKE THIS...
NO... WHAT AM I THINKING?!
SHAKA SHAKA
THAT WAS CLOSE. ALMOST FOOLED BY A SWEET DELUSION.

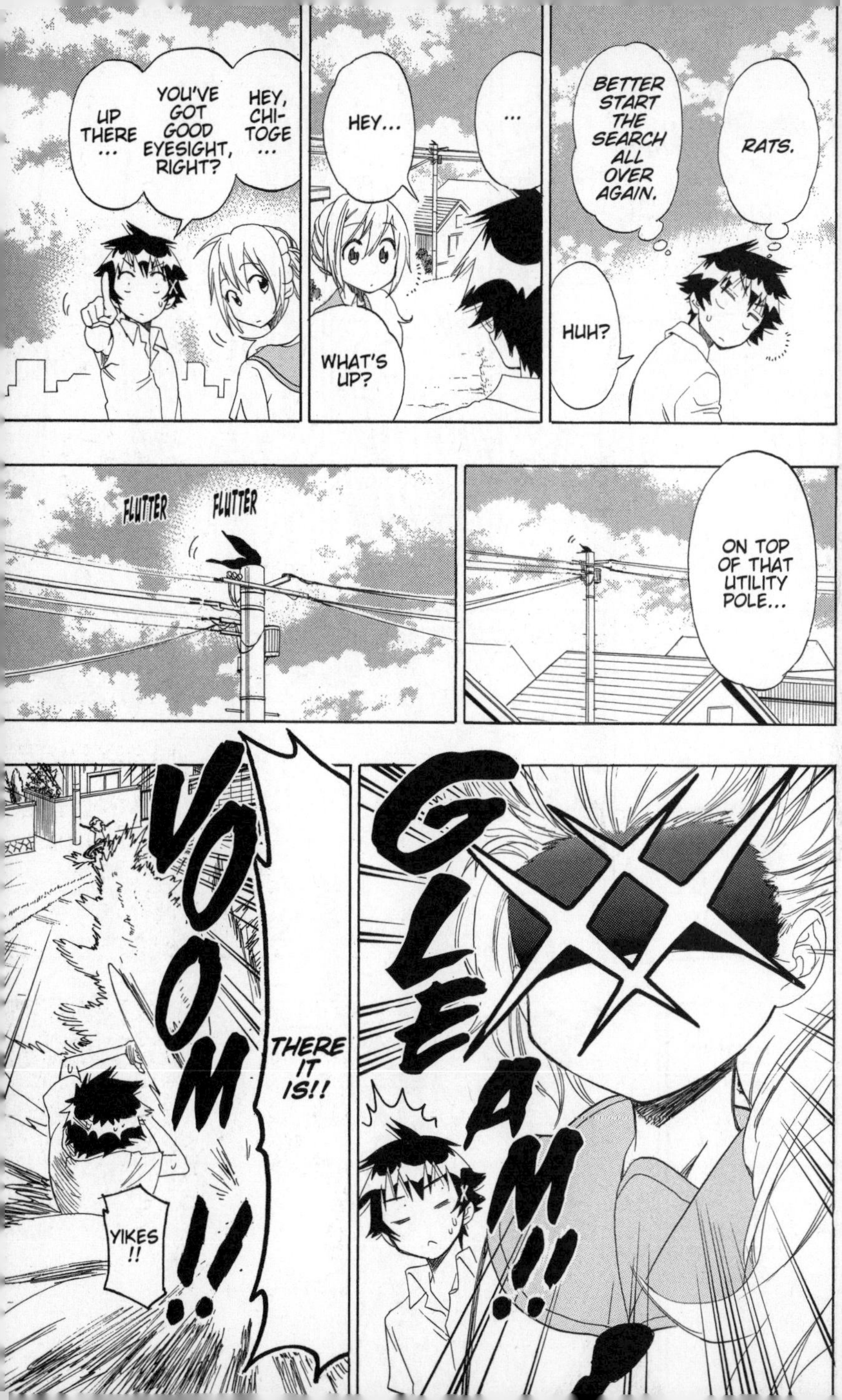

RATS.
BETTER START THE SEARCH ALL OVER AGAIN.
HUH?
...
HEY...
WHAT'S UP?
HEY, CHI-TOGE...
YOU'VE GOT GOOD EYESIGHT, RIGHT?
UP THERE...
ON TOP OF THAT UTILITY POLE...
FLUTTER
FLUTTER
GLEAM!!
VOOM!!
THERE IT IS!!
YIKES!!

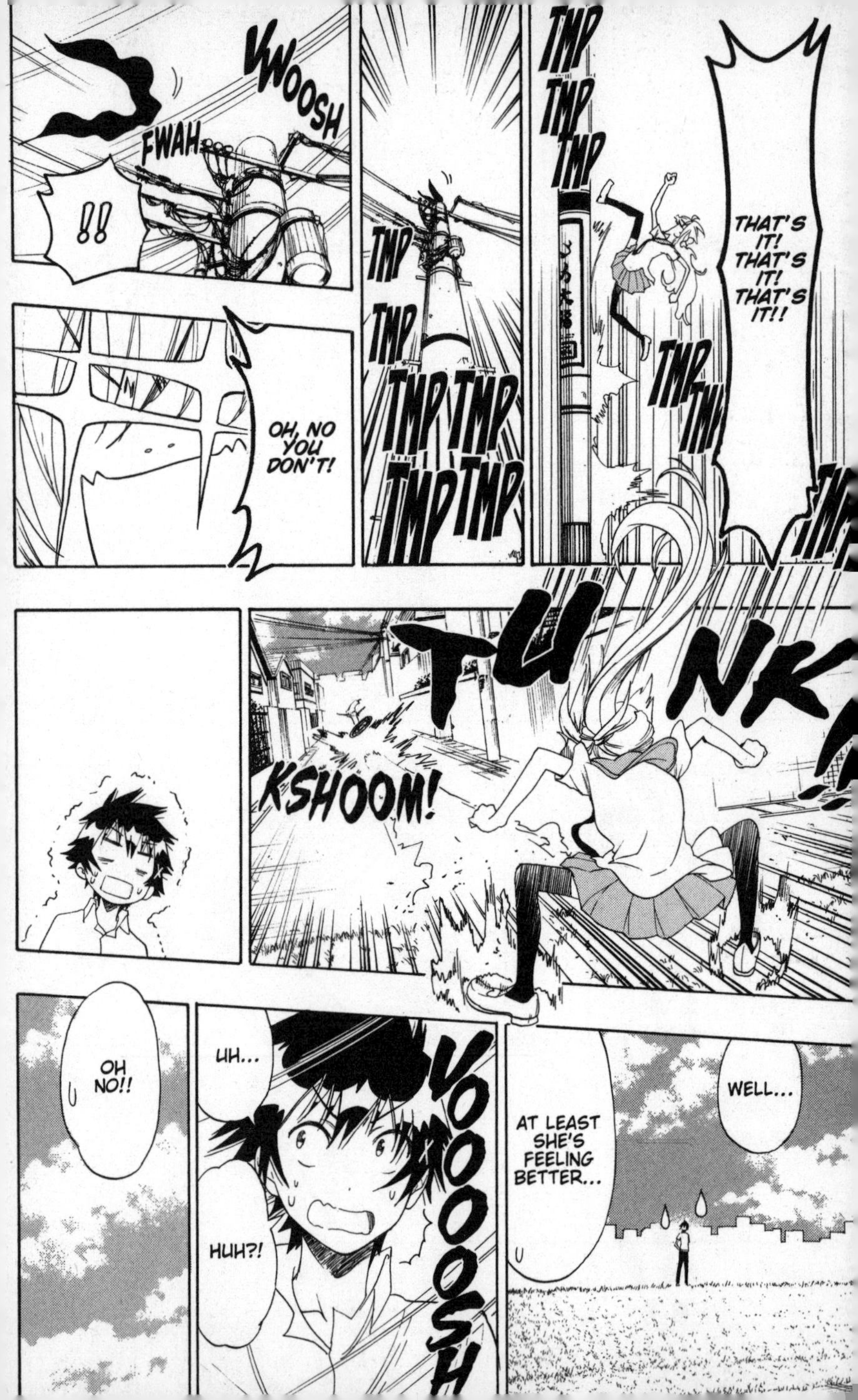

TMP TMP TMP
THAT'S IT! THAT'S IT! THAT'S IT!!
TMP TMP
TMP
TMP TMP TMP TMP TMP TMP
VWOOSH
FWAH
!!
OH, NO YOU DON'T!
TUNK!
KSHOOM!
WELL...
AT LEAST SHE'S FEELING BETTER...
UH...
HUH?!
VOOOOOSH
OH NO!!

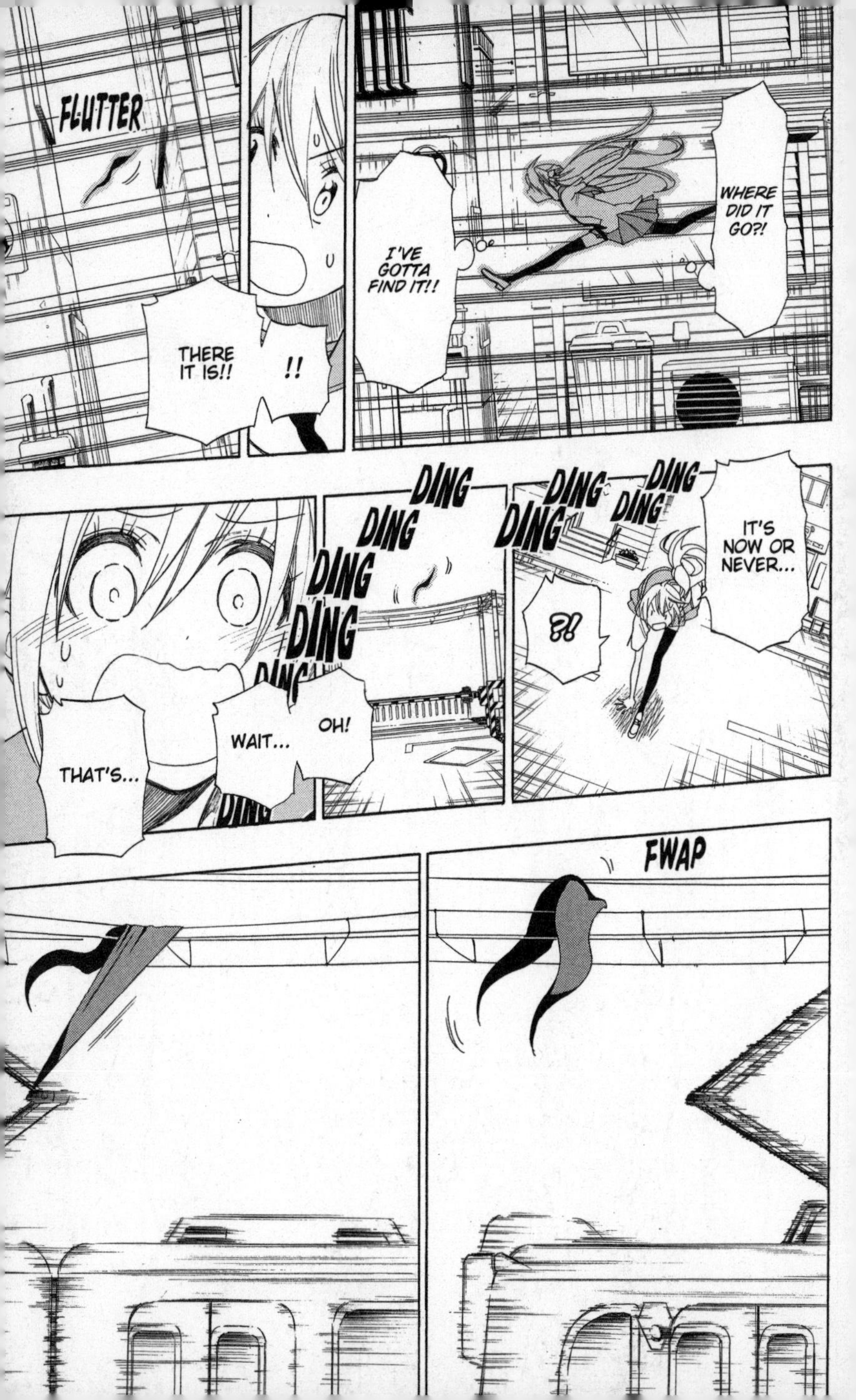
WHERE DID IT GO?!
I'VE GOTTA FIND IT!!
!!
THERE IT IS!!
FLUTTER
DING DING
DING DING
IT'S NOW OR NEVER...
?!
DING
DING
DING
DING
OH!
WAIT...
THAT'S...
FWAP

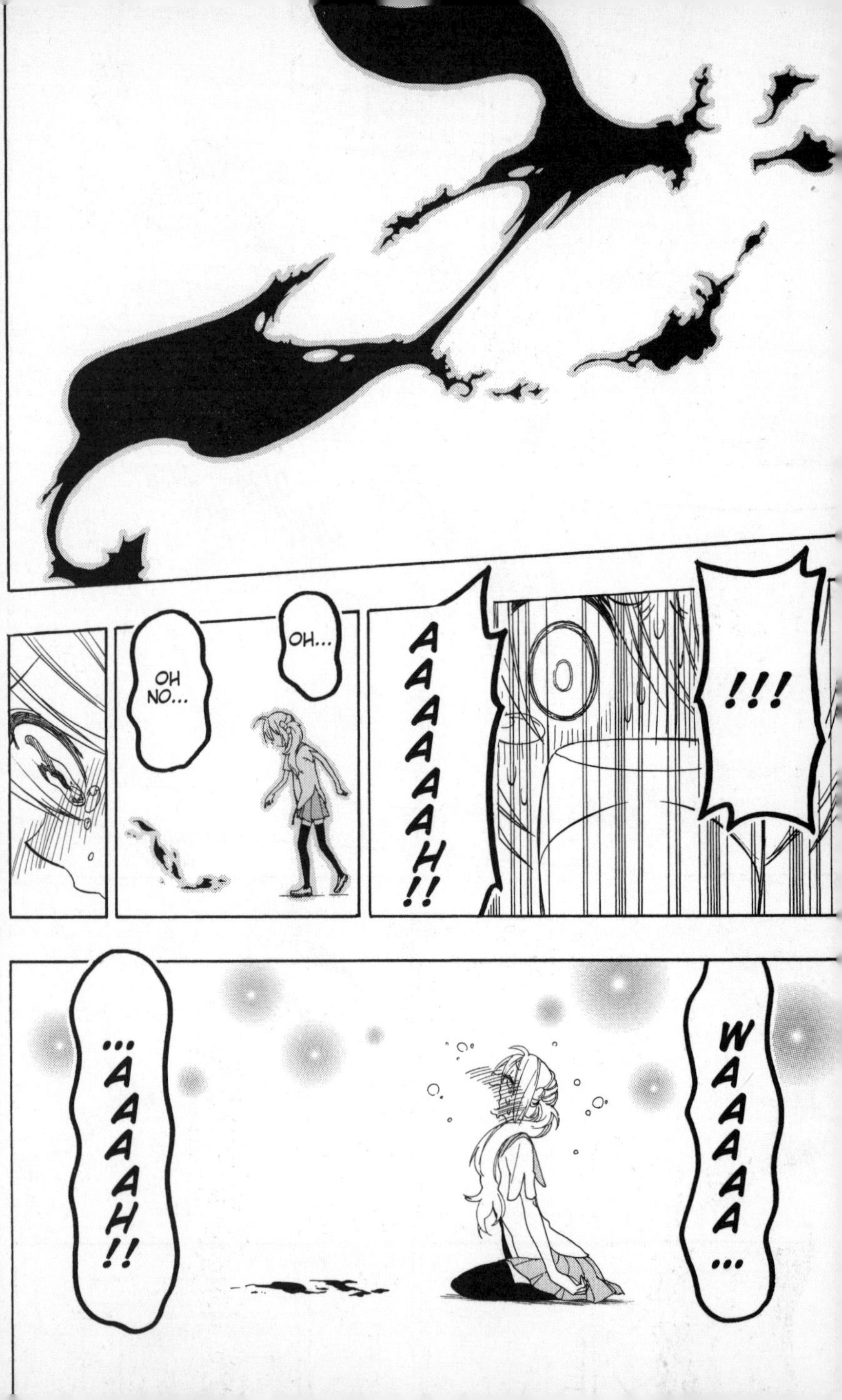
!!!
AAAAAAAH!!
OH...
OH NO...
WAAAAAA...
...AAAAAH!!

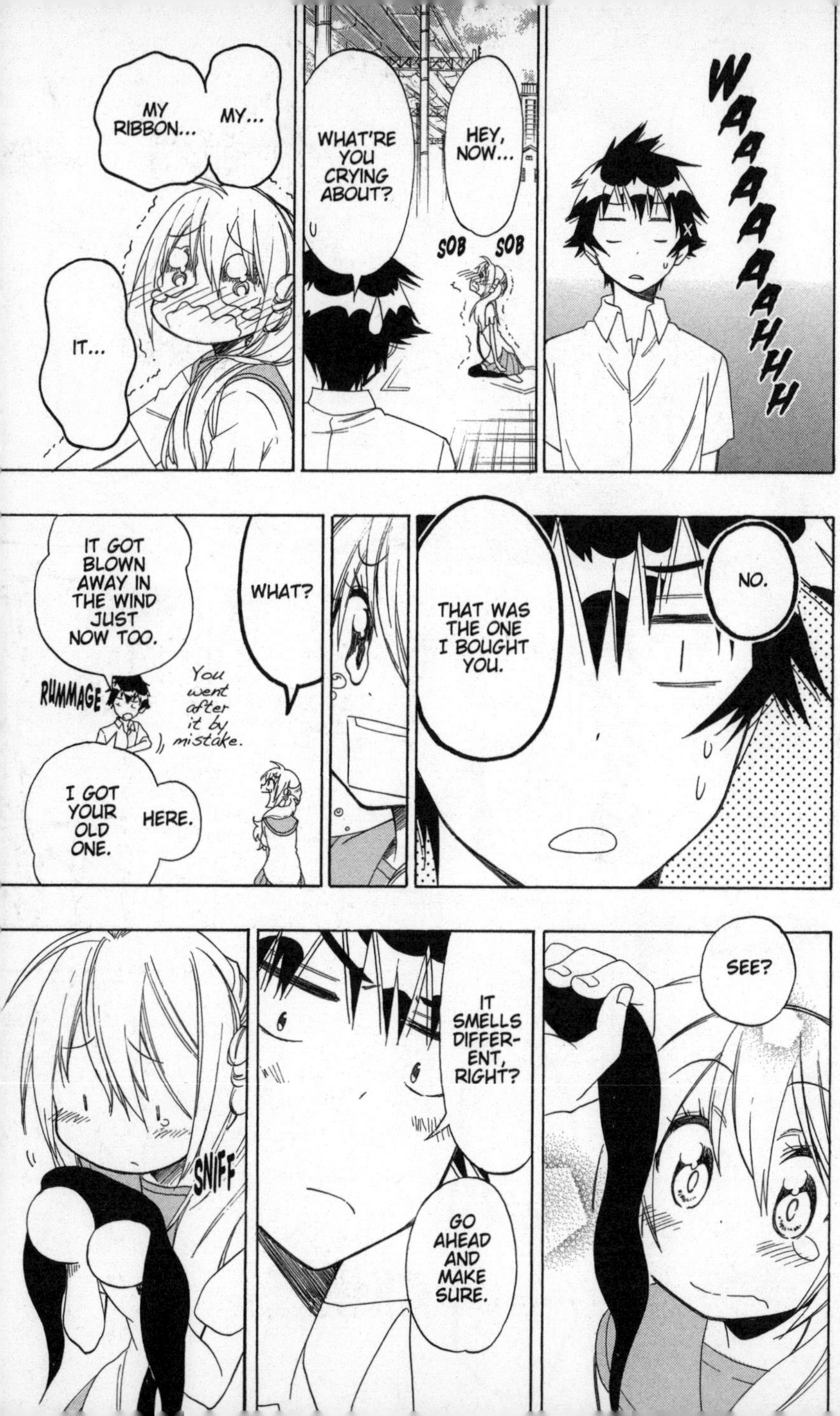
WAAAAAAHHH
HEY, NOW...
WHAT'RE YOU CRYING ABOUT?
SOB SOB
MY...
MY RIBBON...
IT...
NO.
THAT WAS THE ONE I BOUGHT YOU.
WHAT?
IT GOT BLOWN AWAY IN THE WIND JUST NOW TOO.
RUMMAGE
You went after it by mistake.
I GOT YOUR OLD ONE. HERE.
SEE?
IT SMELLS DIFFER-ENT, RIGHT?
GO AHEAD AND MAKE SURE.
SNIFF

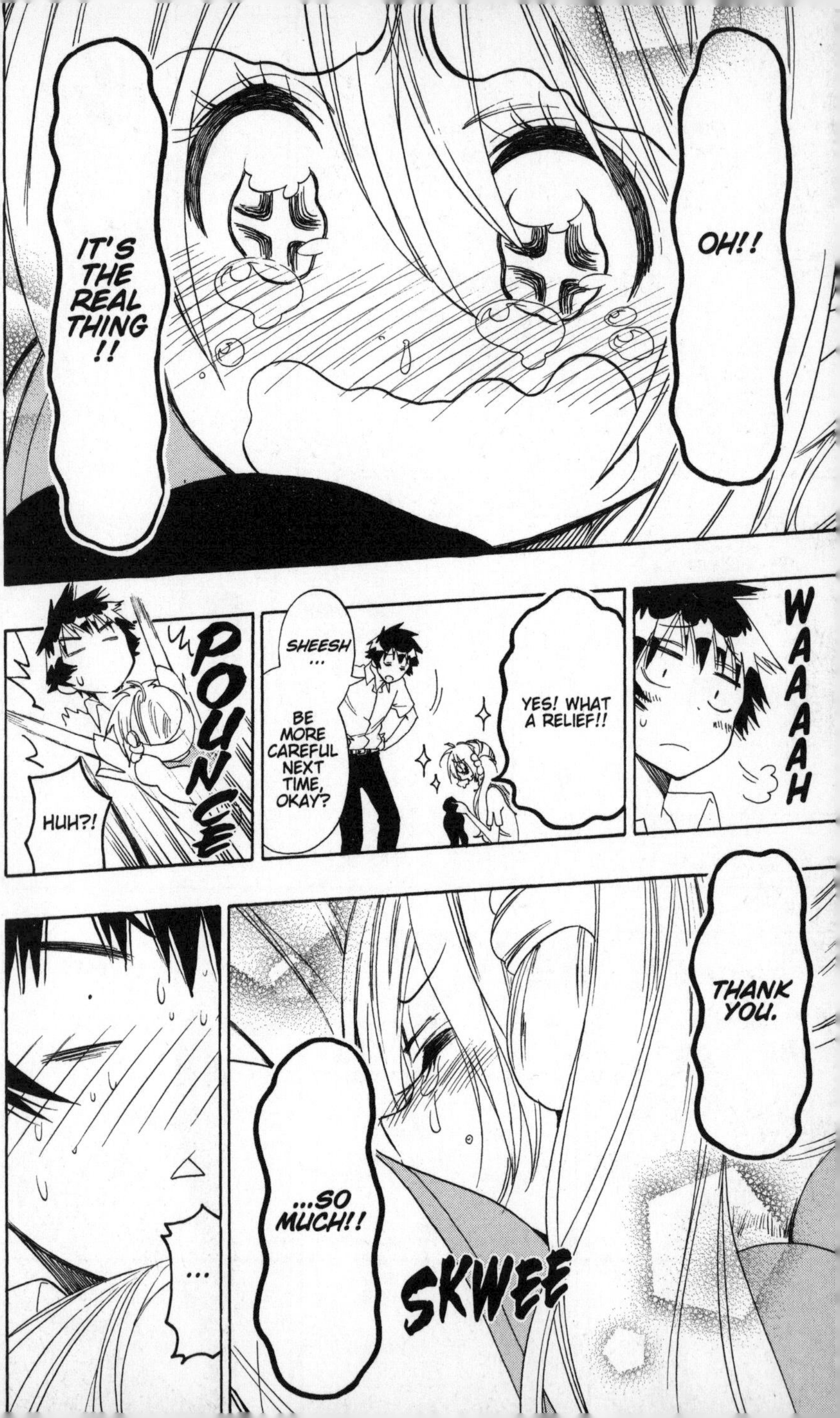
OH!!
IT'S THE REAL THING!!
WAAAAH
YES! WHAT A RELIEF!!
SHEESH...
BE MORE CAREFUL NEXT TIME, OKAY?
POUNCE
HUH?!
THANK YOU.
...SO MUCH!!
SKWEE
...

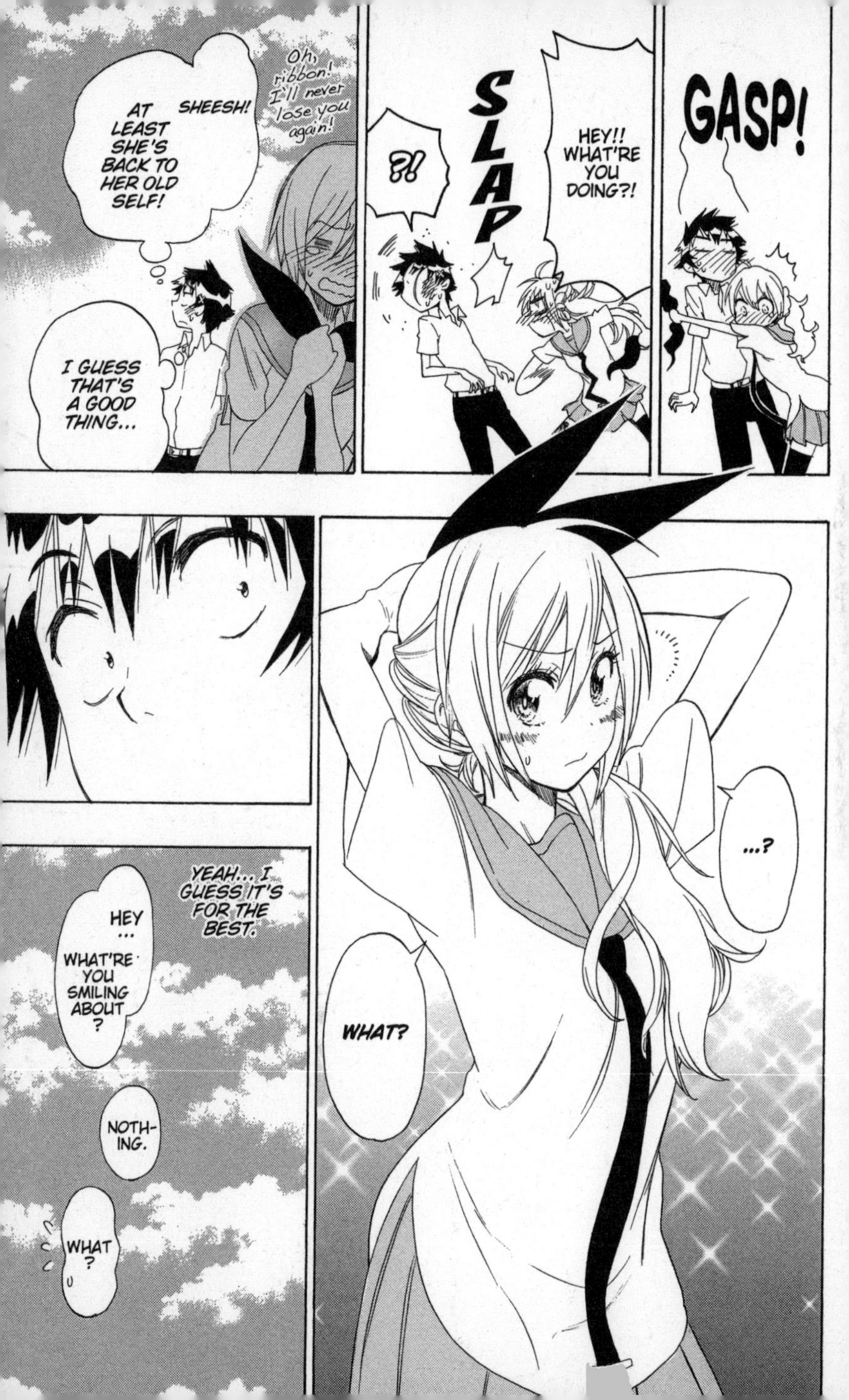
GASP!
HEY!! WHAT'RE YOU DOING?!
SLAP
?!
Oh, ribbon! I'll never lose you again!
SHEESH! AT LEAST SHE'S BACK TO HER OLD SELF!
I GUESS THAT'S A GOOD THING...
...?
WHAT?
YEAH... I GUESS IT'S FOR THE BEST.
HEY... WHAT'RE YOU SMILING ABOUT?
NOTHING.
WHAT?

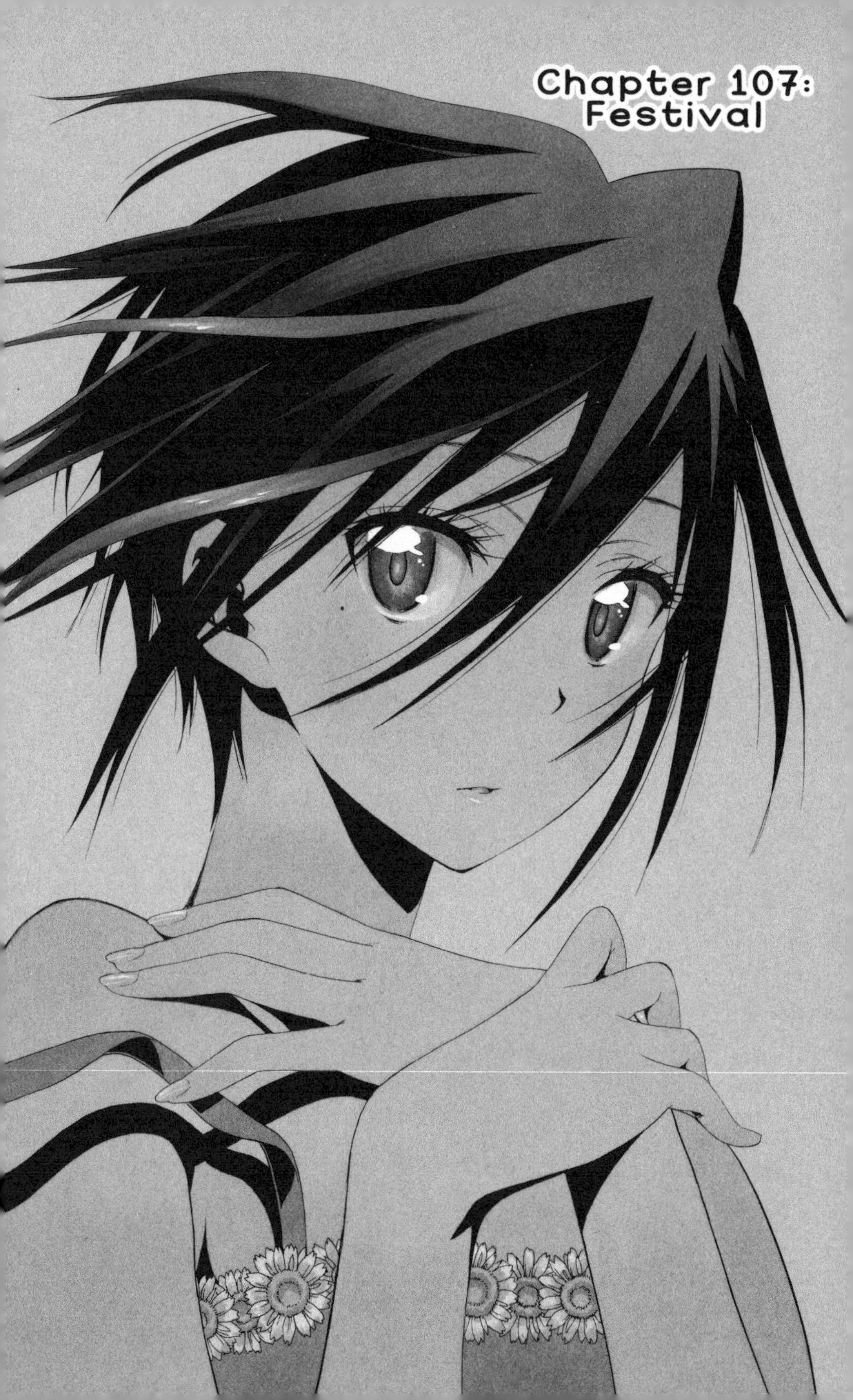
Chapter 107:
Festival

NISEKOI
False Love

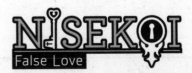

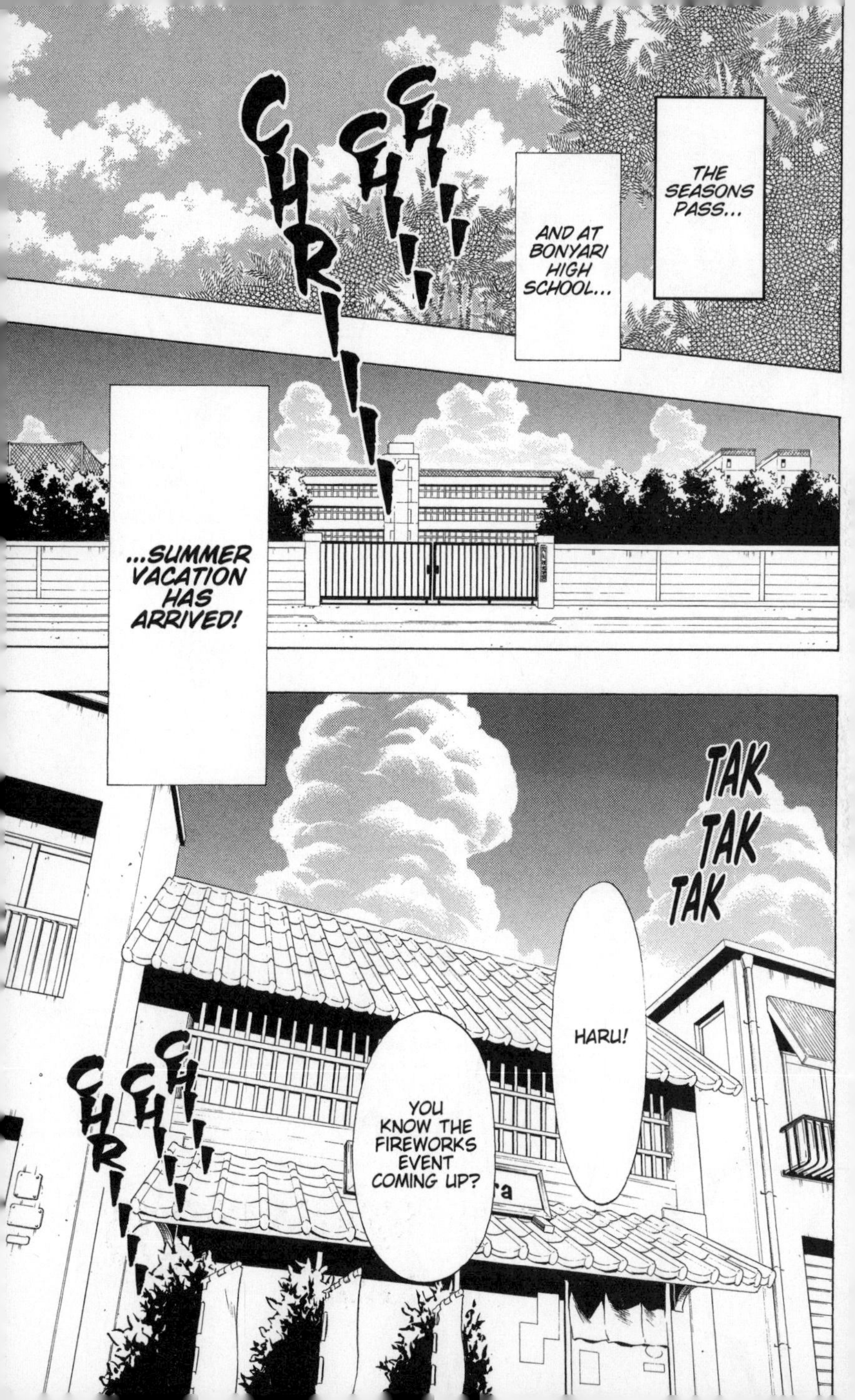

THE SEASONS PASS...
AND AT BONYARI HIGH SCHOOL...
CHIIII
CHRIIIIII
...SUMMER VACATION HAS ARRIVED!
TAK TAK TAK
HARU!
YOU KNOW THE FIREWORKS EVENT COMING UP?
CHIII
CHRIII

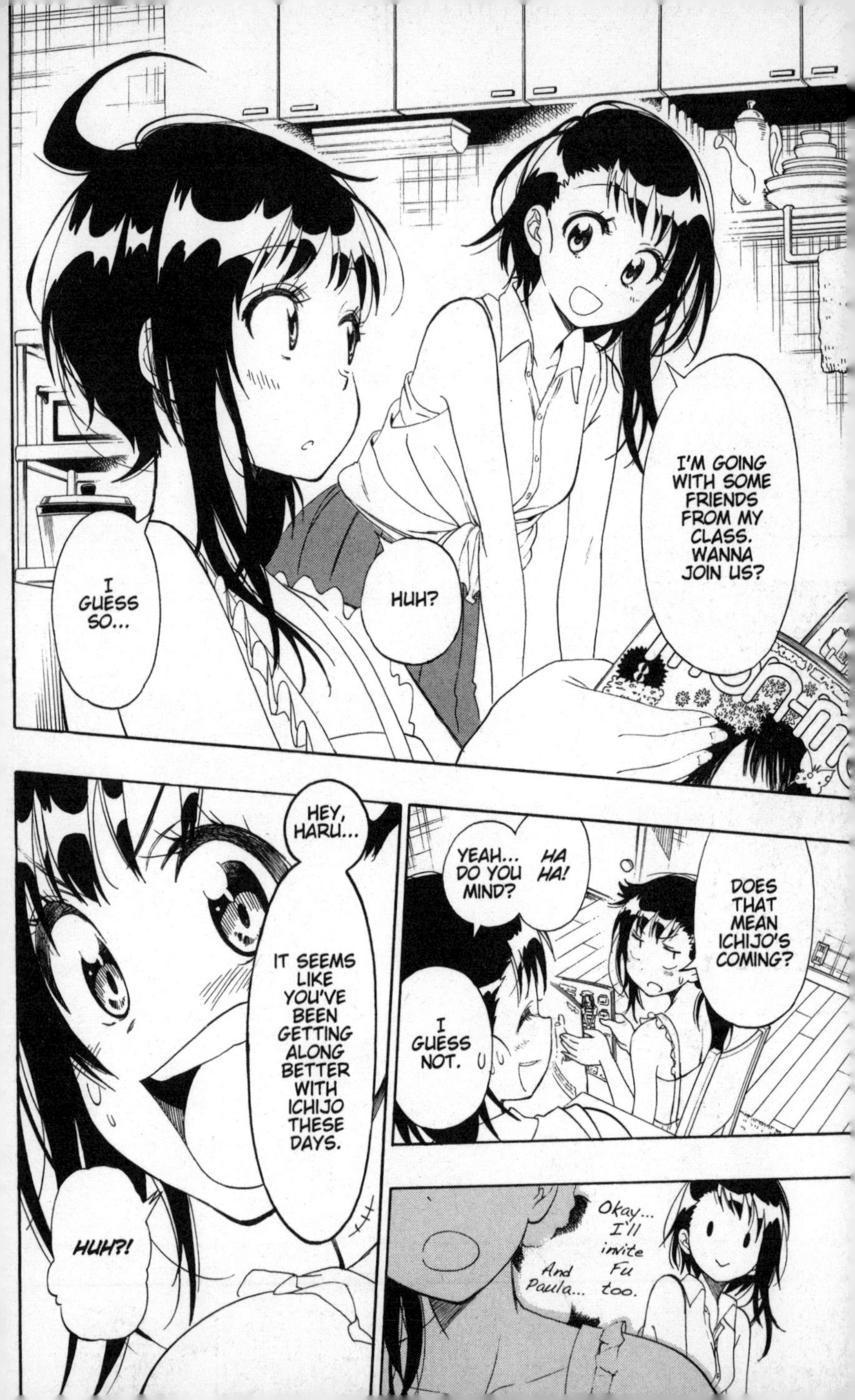
I'M GOING WITH SOME FRIENDS FROM MY CLASS. WANNA JOIN US?
HUH?
I GUESS SO...
DOES THAT MEAN ICHIJO'S COMING?
YEAH... DO YOU MIND?
HA HA!
I GUESS NOT.
Okay... I'll invite Fu too.
And Paula...
HEY, HARU...
IT SEEMS LIKE YOU'VE BEEN GETTING ALONG BETTER WITH ICHIJO THESE DAYS.
HUH?!

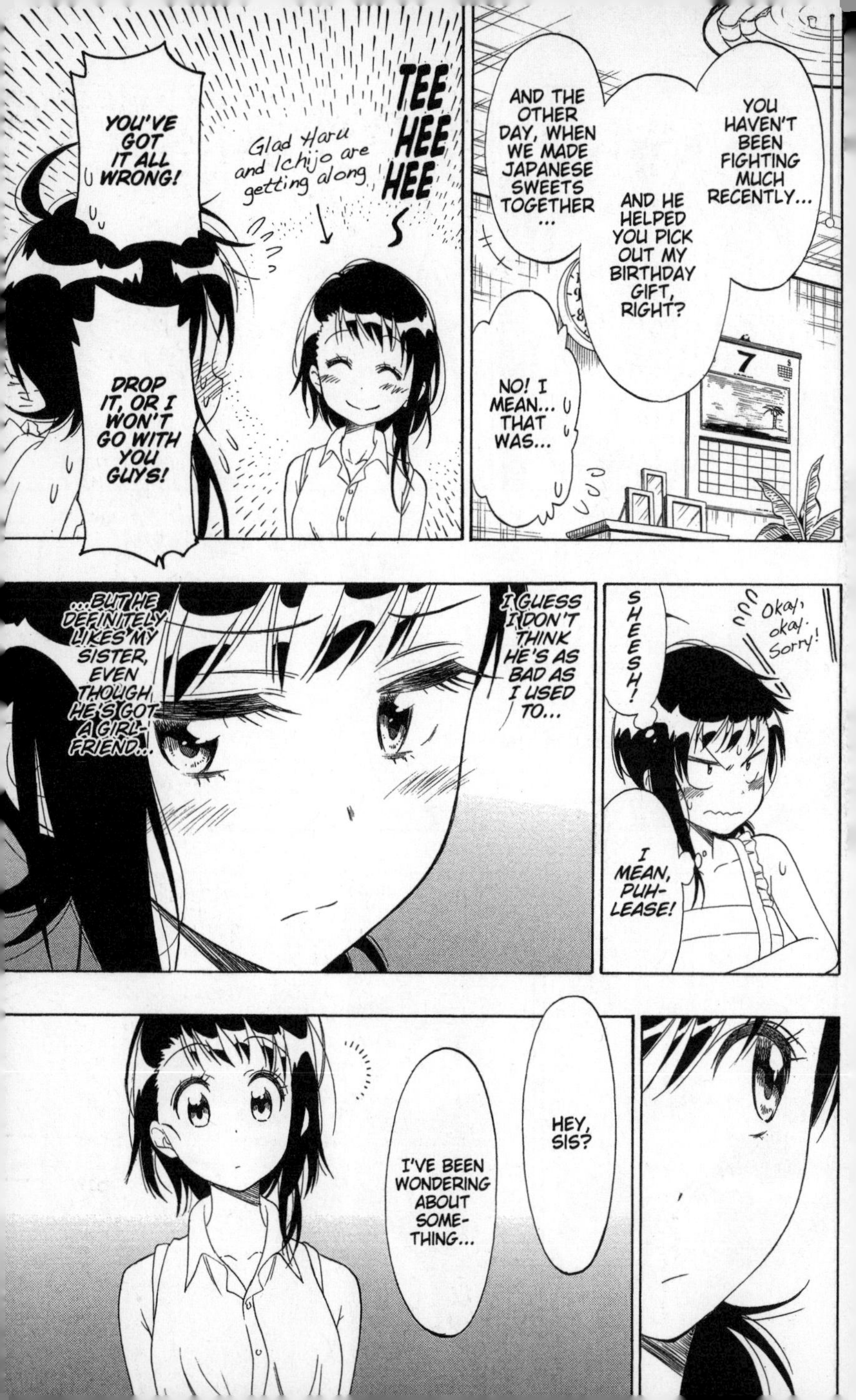
YOU HAVEN'T BEEN FIGHTING MUCH RECENTLY...
AND THE OTHER DAY, WHEN WE MADE JAPANESE SWEETS TOGETHER...
AND HE HELPED YOU PICK OUT MY BIRTHDAY GIFT, RIGHT?
NO! I MEAN... THAT WAS...
TEE HEE HEE
YOU'VE GOT IT ALL WRONG!
Glad Haru and Ichijo are getting along
DROP IT, OR I WON'T GO WITH YOU GUYS!
SHEESH!
Okay, okay. Sorry!
I MEAN, PUH-LEASE!
I GUESS I DON'T THINK HE'S AS BAD AS I USED TO...
...BUT HE DEFINITELY LIKES MY SISTER, EVEN THOUGH HE'S GOT A GIRLFRIEND...
HEY, SIS?
I'VE BEEN WONDERING ABOUT SOMETHING...

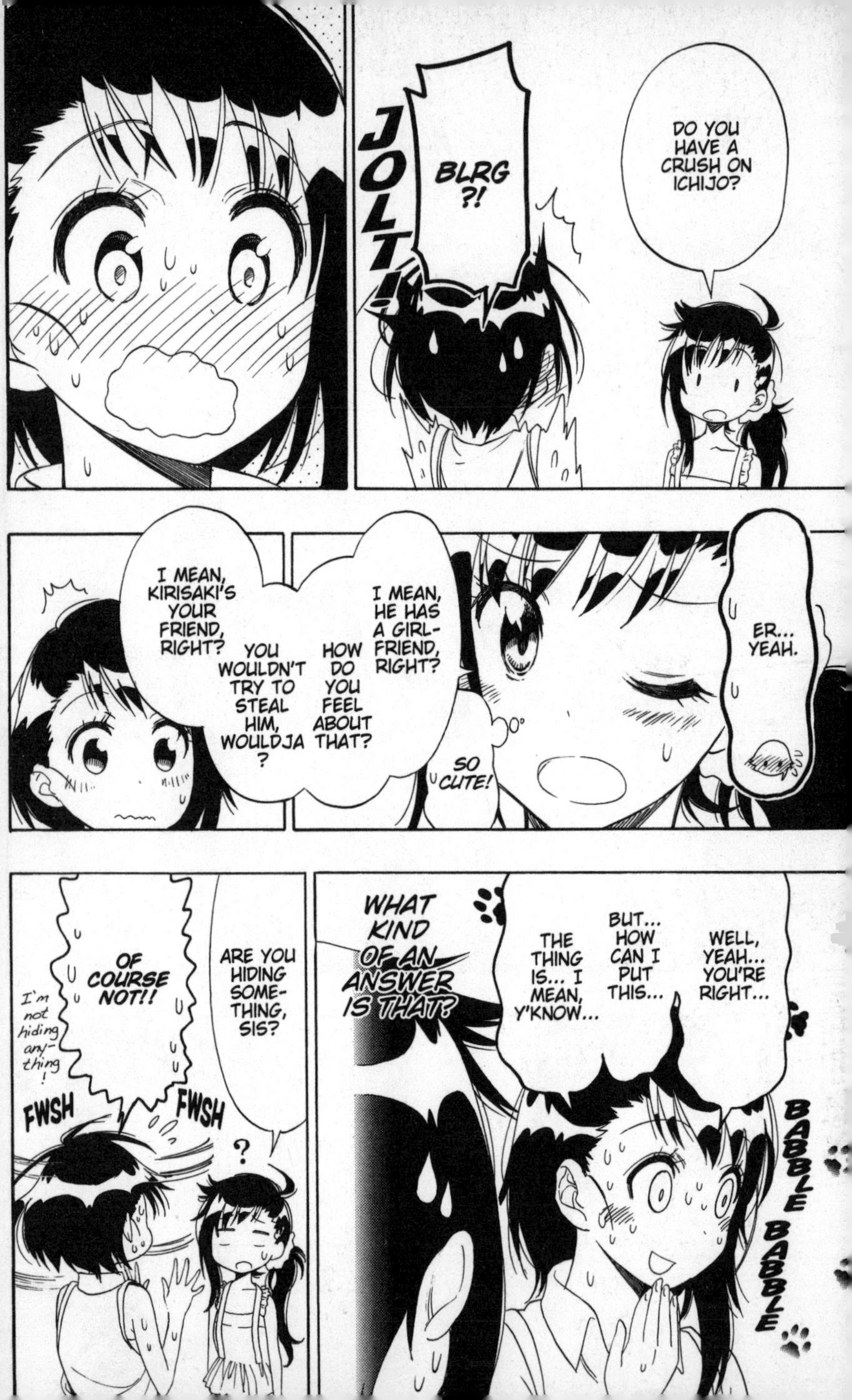
DO YOU HAVE A CRUSH ON ICHIJO?
JOLT!!
BLRG ?!
ER... YEAH.
I MEAN, HE HAS A GIRL-FRIEND, RIGHT?
HOW DO YOU FEEL ABOUT THAT?
YOU WOULDN'T TRY TO STEAL HIM, WOULDJA?
I MEAN, KIRISAKI'S YOUR FRIEND, RIGHT?
SO CUTE!
WELL, YEAH... YOU'RE RIGHT...
BUT... HOW CAN I PUT THIS...
THE THING IS... I MEAN, Y'KNOW...
WHAT KIND OF AN ANSWER IS THAT?
BABBLE BABBLE
ARE YOU HIDING SOME-THING, SIS?
OF COURSE NOT!!
I'm not hiding any-thing!
FWSH FWSH

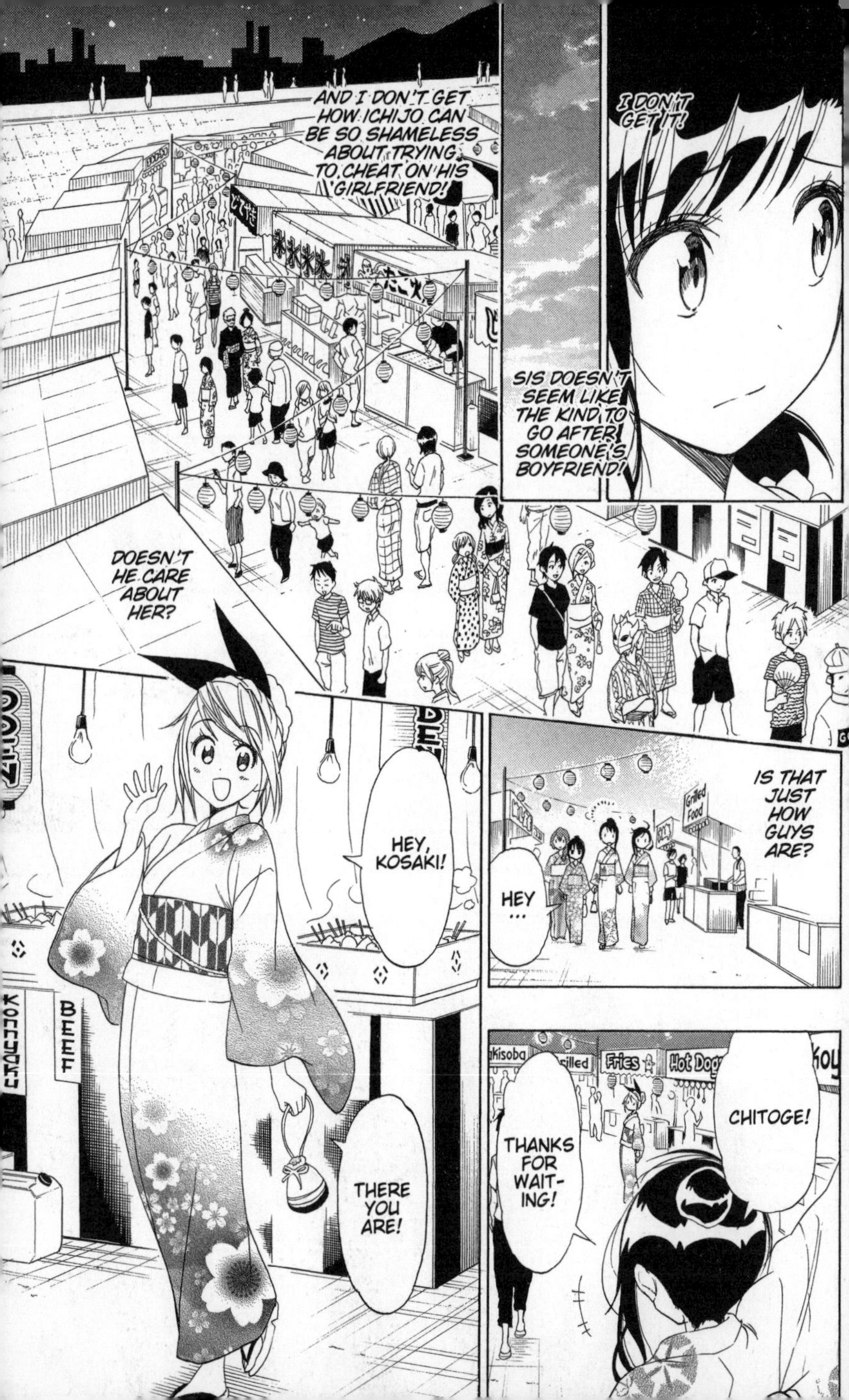
I DON'T GET IT!
SIS DOESN'T SEEM LIKE THE KIND TO GO AFTER SOMEONE'S BOYFRIEND!
AND I DON'T GET HOW ICHIJO CAN BE SO SHAMELESS ABOUT TRYING TO CHEAT ON HIS GIRLFRIEND!
DOESN'T HE CARE ABOUT HER?
IS THAT JUST HOW GUYS ARE?
Grilled Food
HEY...
Fries
Hot Dogs
CHITOGE!
THANKS FOR WAIT-ING!
HEY, KOSAKI!
BEEF
THERE YOU ARE!

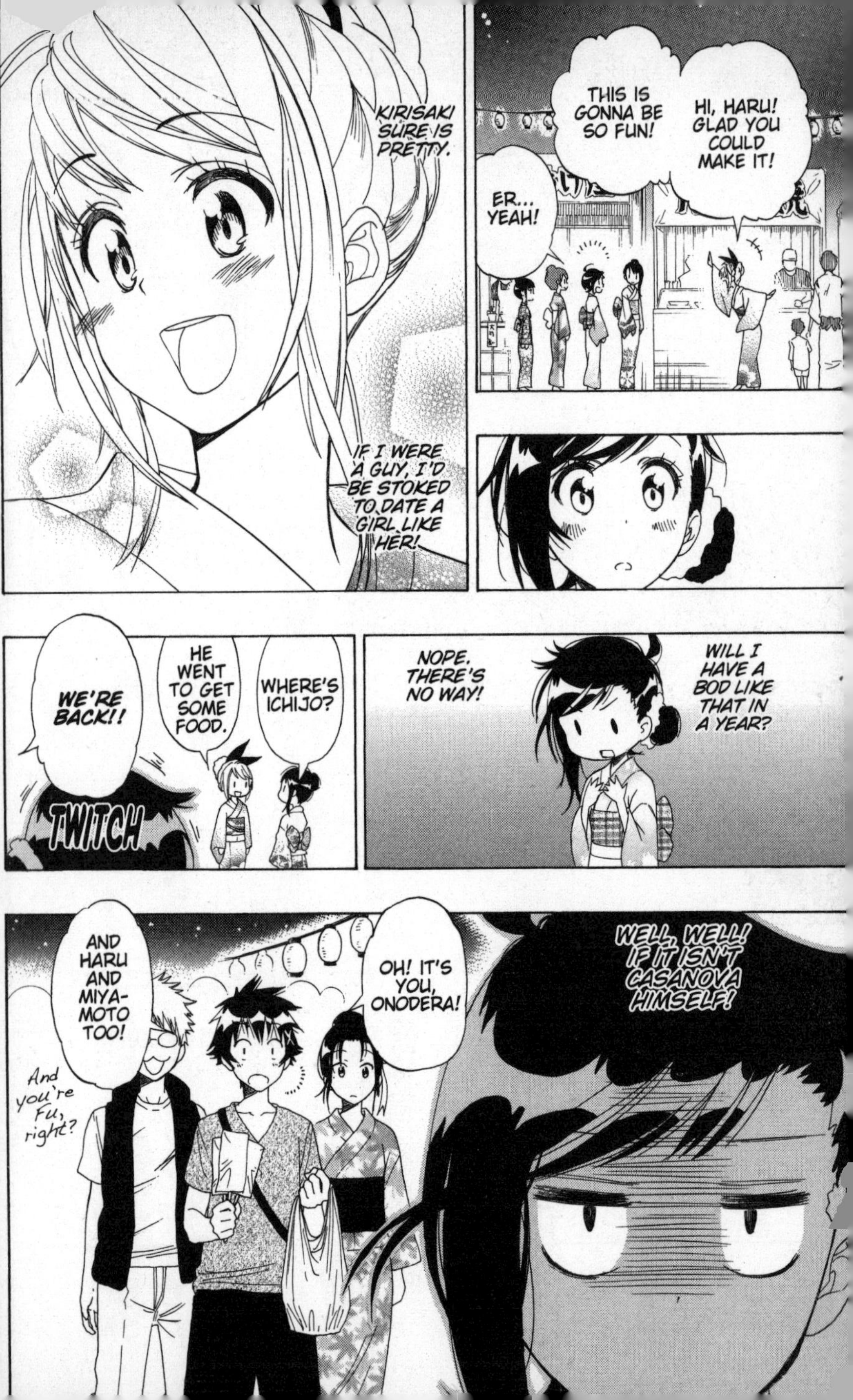
HI, HARU! GLAD YOU COULD MAKE IT!
THIS IS GONNA BE SO FUN!
ER... YEAH!
KIRISAKI SURE IS PRETTY.
IF I WERE A GUY, I'D BE STOKED TO DATE A GIRL LIKE HER!
WILL I HAVE A BOD LIKE THAT IN A YEAR?
NOPE. THERE'S NO WAY!
WHERE'S ICHIJO?
HE WENT TO GET SOME FOOD.
WE'RE BACK!!
TWITCH
WELL, WELL! IF IT ISN'T CASANOVA HIMSELF!
OH! IT'S YOU, ONODERA!
AND HARU AND MIYAMOTO TOO!
And you're Fu, right?

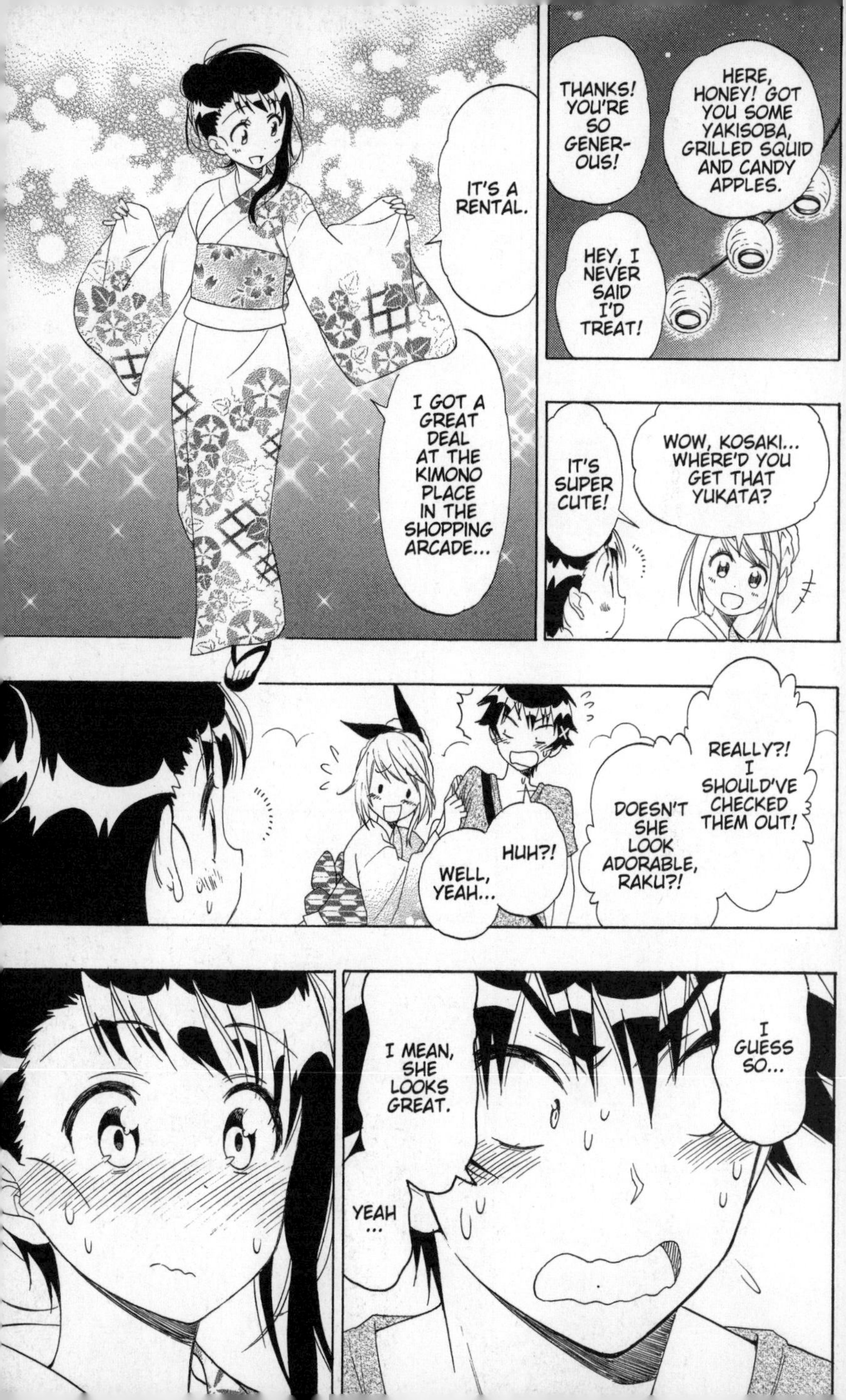
HERE, HONEY! GOT YOU SOME YAKISOBA, GRILLED SQUID AND CANDY APPLES.
THANKS! YOU'RE SO GENER-OUS!
HEY, I NEVER SAID I'D TREAT!
WOW, KOSAKI... WHERE'D YOU GET THAT YUKATA?
IT'S SUPER CUTE!
IT'S A RENTAL.
I GOT A GREAT DEAL AT THE KIMONO PLACE IN THE SHOPPING ARCADE...
REALLY?! I SHOULD'VE CHECKED THEM OUT!
DOESN'T SHE LOOK ADORABLE, RAKU?!
HUH?!
WELL, YEAH...
I GUESS SO...
I MEAN, SHE LOOKS GREAT.
YEAH ...

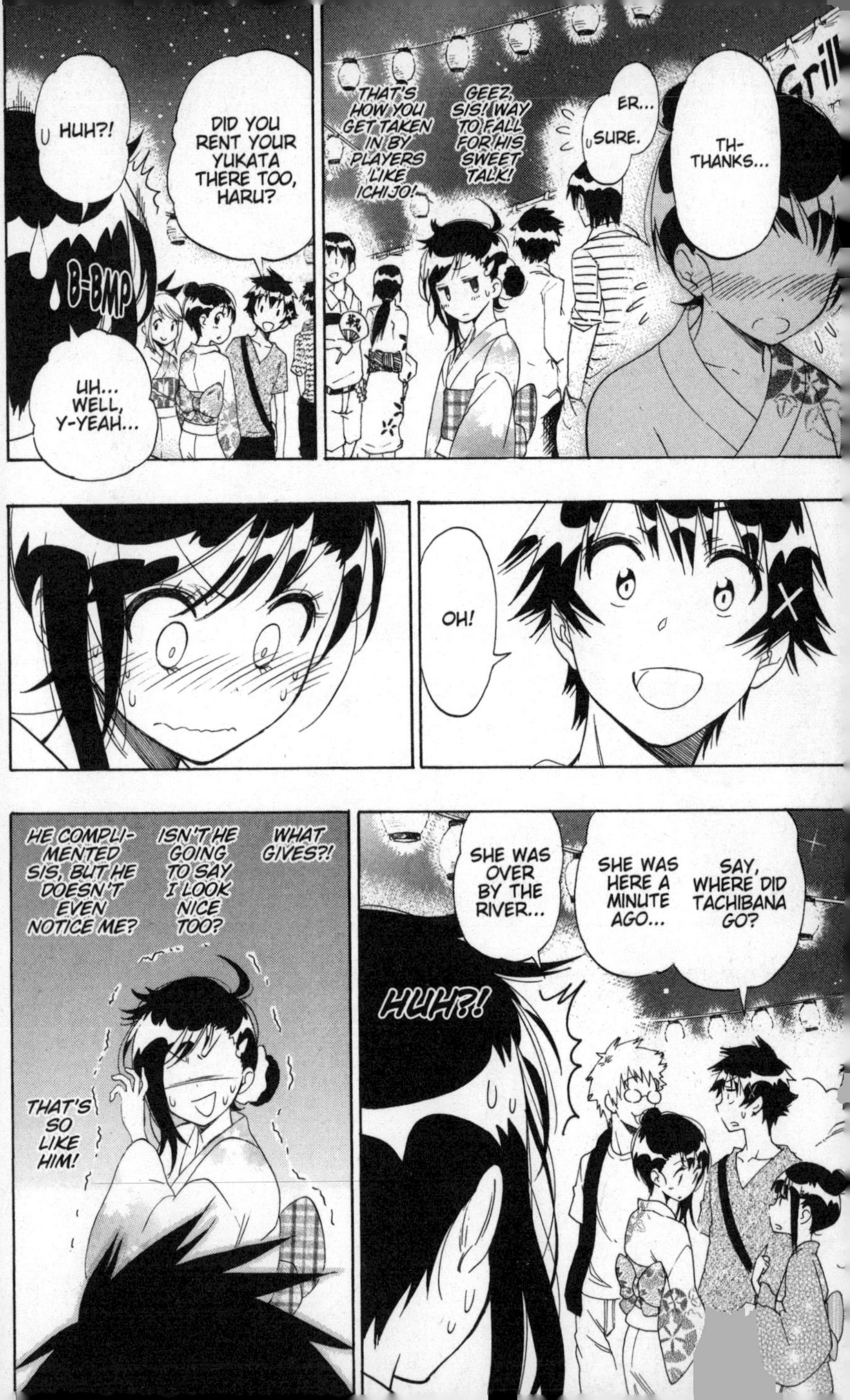
TH-THANKS...
ER... SURE.
GEEZ, SIS! WAY TO FALL FOR HIS SWEET TALK!
THAT'S HOW YOU GET TAKEN IN BY PLAYERS LIKE ICHIJO!
DID YOU RENT YOUR YUKATA THERE TOO, HARU?
HUH?!
B-BMP
UH... WELL, Y-YEAH...
OH!
SAY, WHERE DID TACHIBANA GO?
SHE WAS HERE A MINUTE AGO...
SHE WAS OVER BY THE RIVER...
HUH?!
WHAT GIVES?!
ISN'T HE GOING TO SAY I LOOK NICE TOO?
HE COMPLI-MENTED SIS, BUT HE DOESN'T EVEN NOTICE ME?
THAT'S SO LIKE HIM!

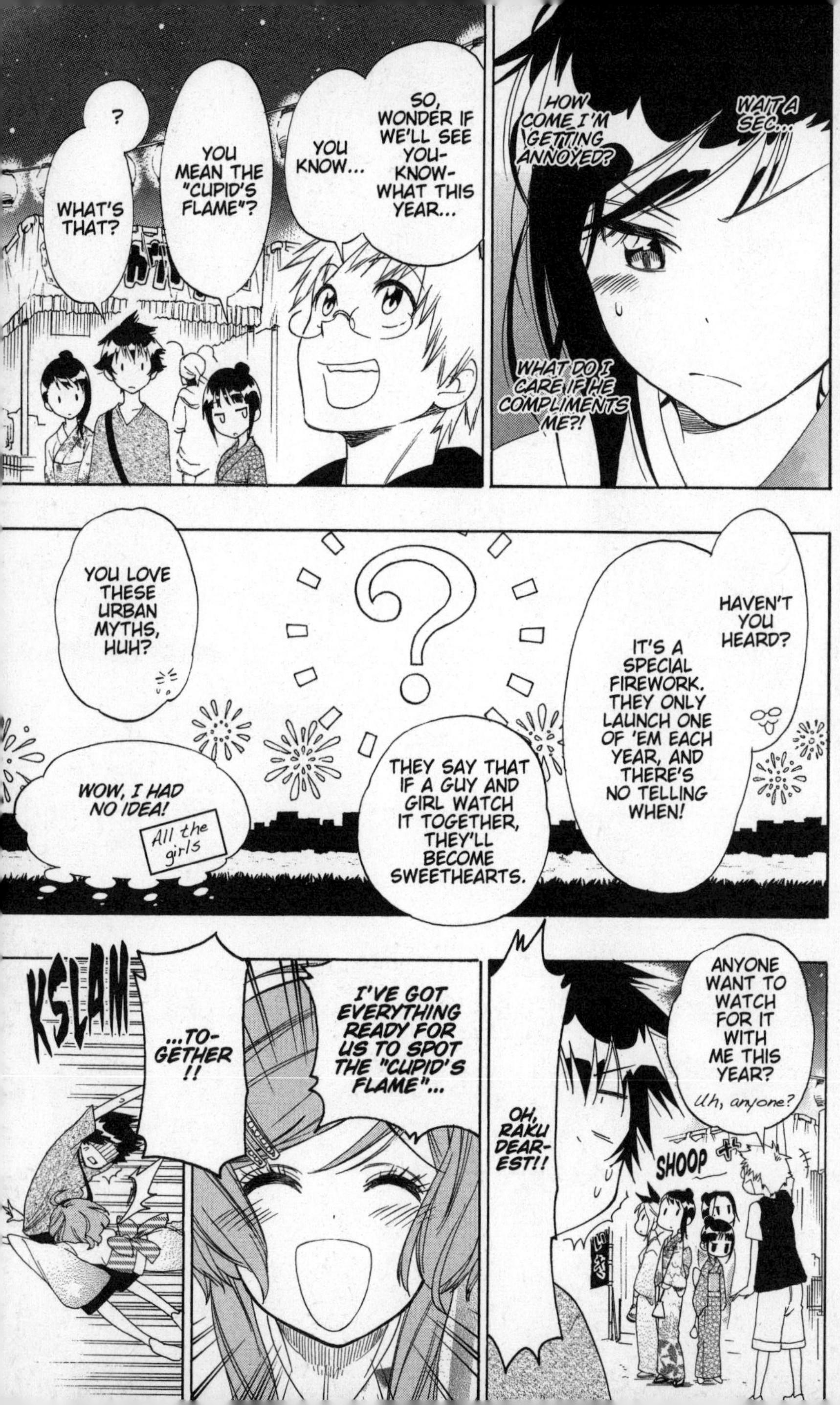
WAIT A SEC...
HOW COME I'M GETTING ANNOYED?
WHAT DO I CARE IF HE COMPLIMENTS ME?!
SO, WONDER IF WE'LL SEE YOU-KNOW-WHAT THIS YEAR...
YOU KNOW...
YOU MEAN THE "CUPID'S FLAME"?
?
WHAT'S THAT?
HAVEN'T YOU HEARD?
IT'S A SPECIAL FIREWORK. THEY ONLY LAUNCH ONE OF 'EM EACH YEAR, AND THERE'S NO TELLING WHEN!
THEY SAY THAT IF A GUY AND GIRL WATCH IT TOGETHER, THEY'LL BECOME SWEETHEARTS.
YOU LOVE THESE URBAN MYTHS, HUH?
WOW, I HAD NO IDEA!
All the girls
ANYONE WANT TO WATCH FOR IT WITH ME THIS YEAR?
Uh, anyone?
SHOOP
OH, RAKU DEAREST!!
I'VE GOT EVERYTHING READY FOR US TO SPOT THE "CUPID'S FLAME"...
...TO-GETHER!!
KSLAM

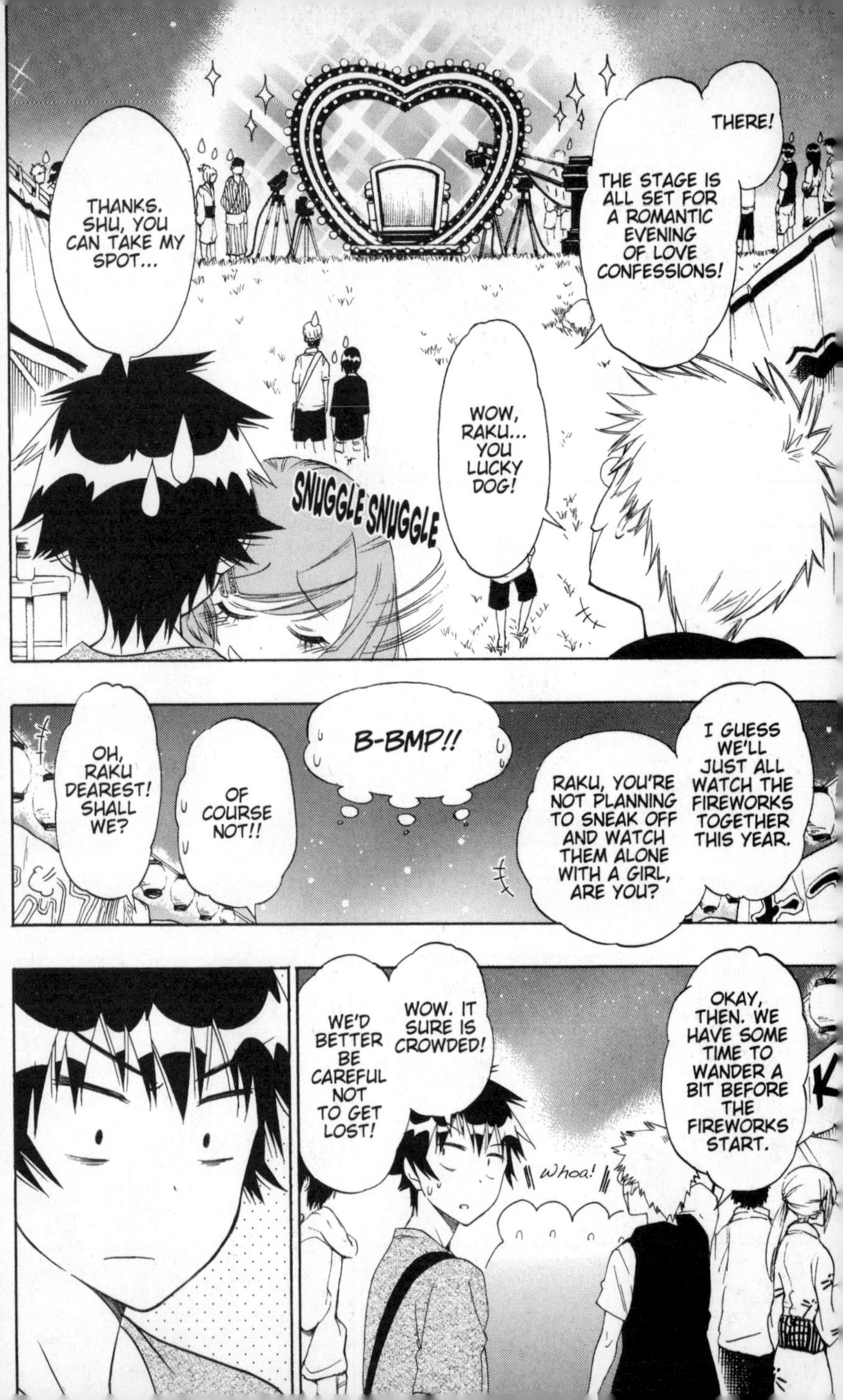
THERE!
THE STAGE IS ALL SET FOR A ROMANTIC EVENING OF LOVE CONFESSIONS!
WOW, RAKU... YOU LUCKY DOG!
SNUGGLE SNUGGLE
THANKS. SHU, YOU CAN TAKE MY SPOT...
I GUESS WE'LL JUST ALL WATCH THE FIREWORKS TOGETHER THIS YEAR.
RAKU, YOU'RE NOT PLANNING TO SNEAK OFF AND WATCH THEM ALONE WITH A GIRL, ARE YOU?
B-BMP!!
OF COURSE NOT!!
OH, RAKU DEAREST! SHALL WE?
OKAY, THEN. WE HAVE SOME TIME TO WANDER A BIT BEFORE THE FIREWORKS START.
WOW. IT SURE IS CROWDED!
WE'D BETTER BE CAREFUL NOT TO GET LOST!
Whoa!

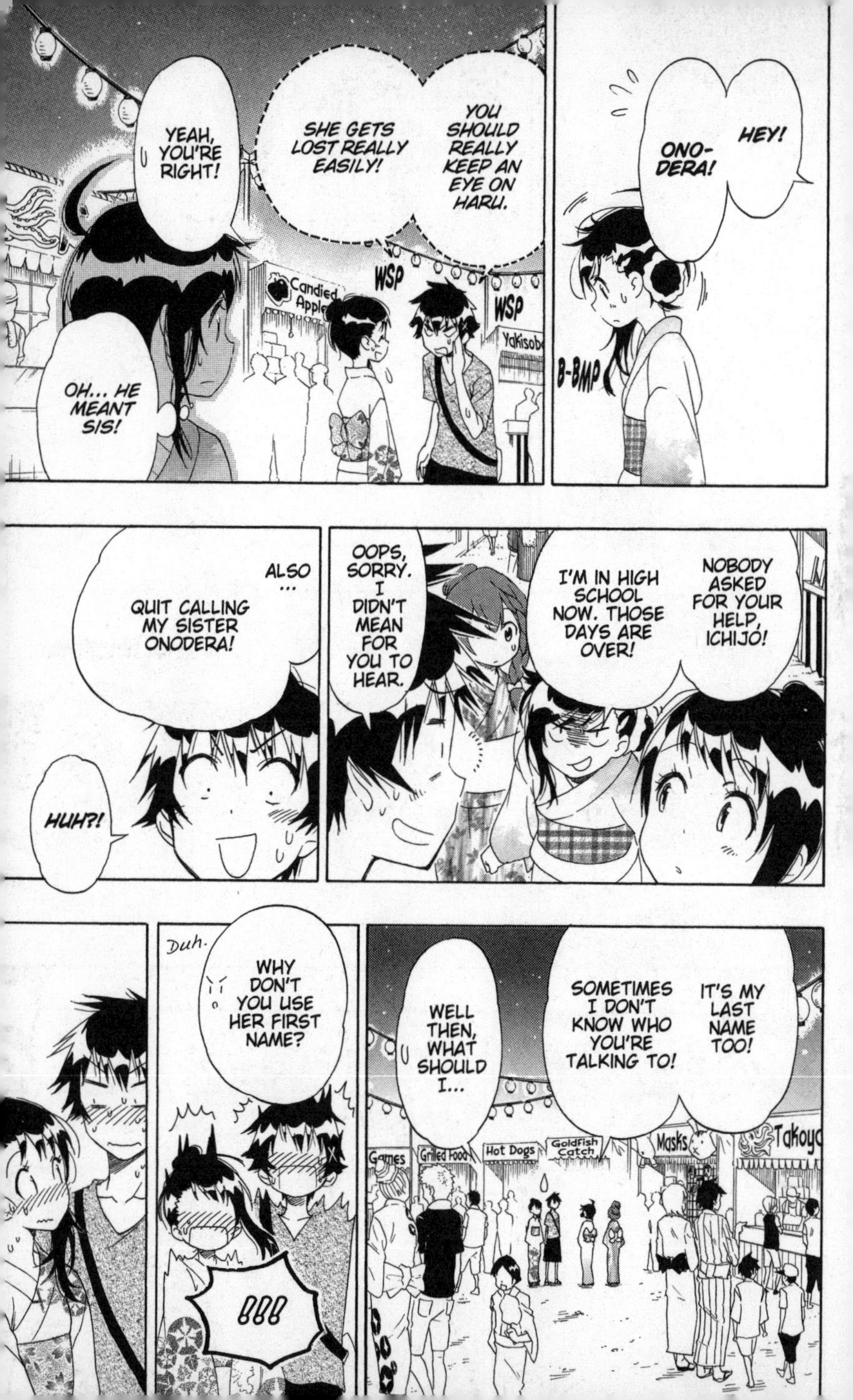
HEY! ONO-DERA!
B-BMP
YOU SHOULD REALLY KEEP AN EYE ON HARU.
SHE GETS LOST REALLY EASILY!
WSP
WSP
Yakisob
Candied Apple
YEAH, YOU'RE RIGHT!
OH... HE MEANT SIS!
NOBODY ASKED FOR YOUR HELP, ICHIJO!
I'M IN HIGH SCHOOL NOW. THOSE DAYS ARE OVER!
OOPS, SORRY. I DIDN'T MEAN FOR YOU TO HEAR.
ALSO...
QUIT CALLING MY SISTER ONODERA!
HUH?!
IT'S MY LAST NAME TOO!
SOMETIMES I DON'T KNOW WHO YOU'RE TALKING TO!
WELL THEN, WHAT SHOULD I...
Takoy
Masks
Goldfish Catch
Hot Dogs
Grilled Food
Games
Duh.
WHY DON'T YOU USE HER FIRST NAME?

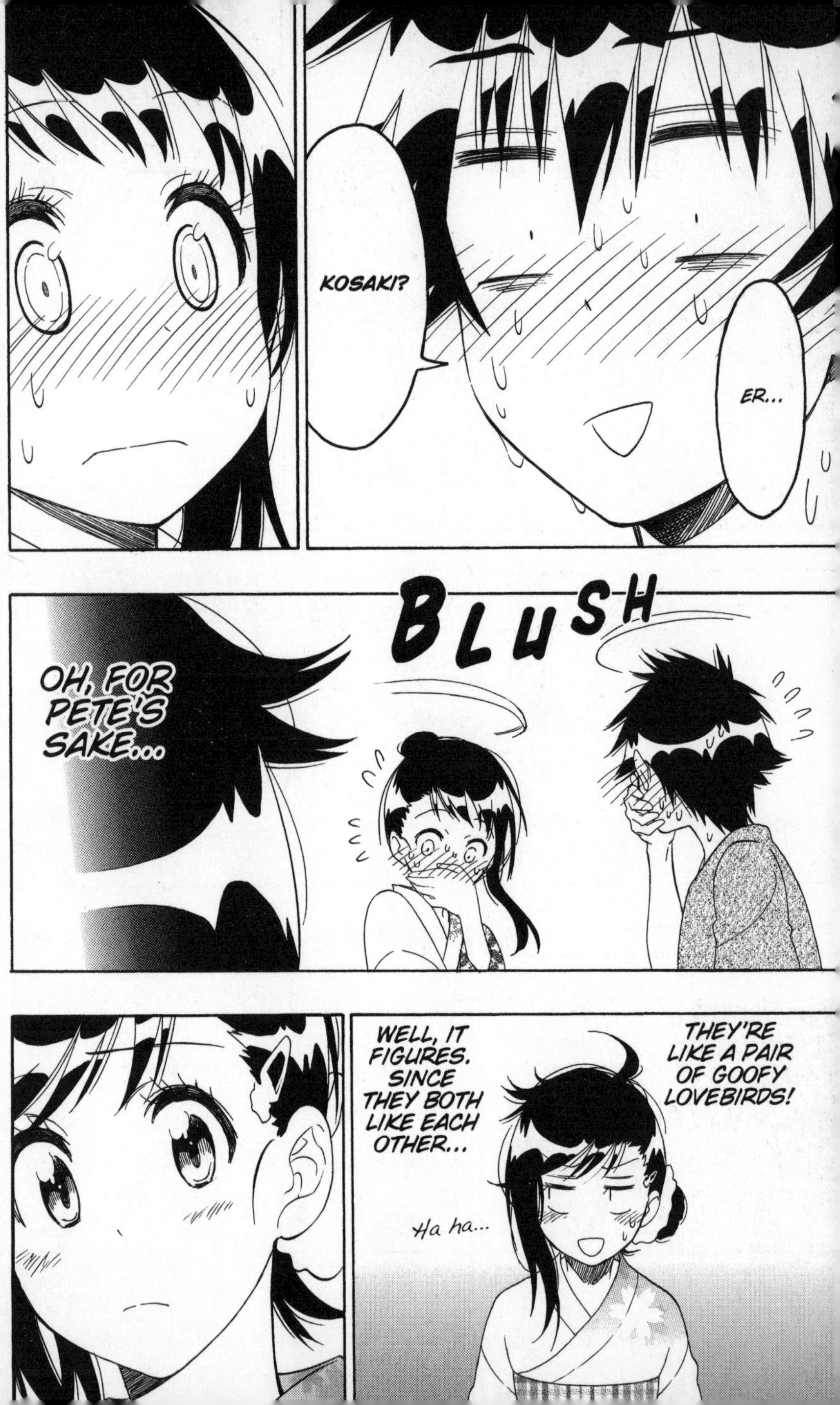
KOSAKI?
ER...
BLUSH
OH, FOR PETE'S SAKE...
THEY'RE LIKE A PAIR OF GOOFY LOVEBIRDS!
WELL, IT FIGURES. SINCE THEY BOTH LIKE EACH OTHER...
Ha ha...

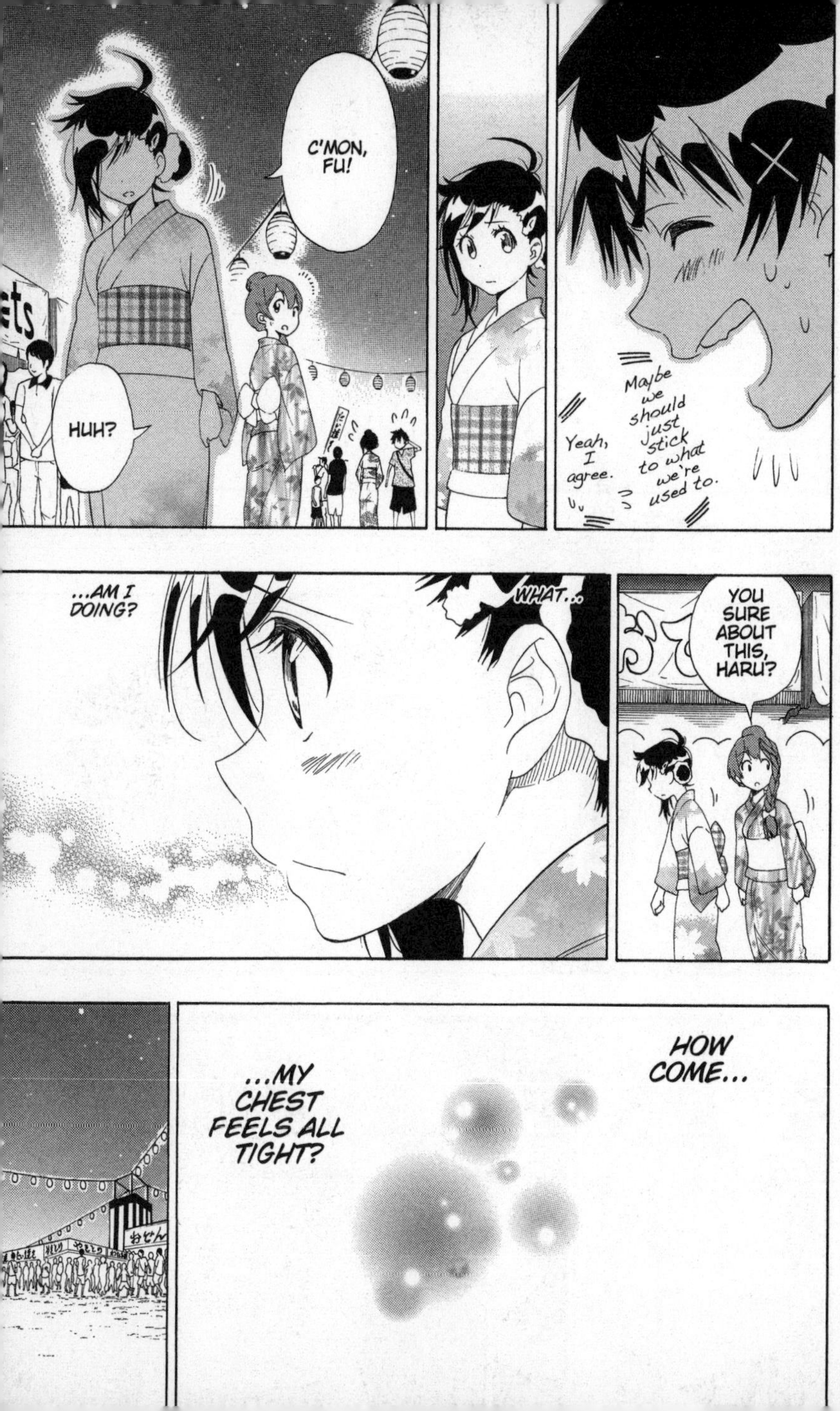

Maybe we should just stick to what we're used to.
Yeah, I agree.
C'MON, FU!
HUH?
YOU SURE ABOUT THIS, HARU?
WHAT...
...AM I DOING?
HOW COME...
...MY CHEST FEELS ALL TIGHT?

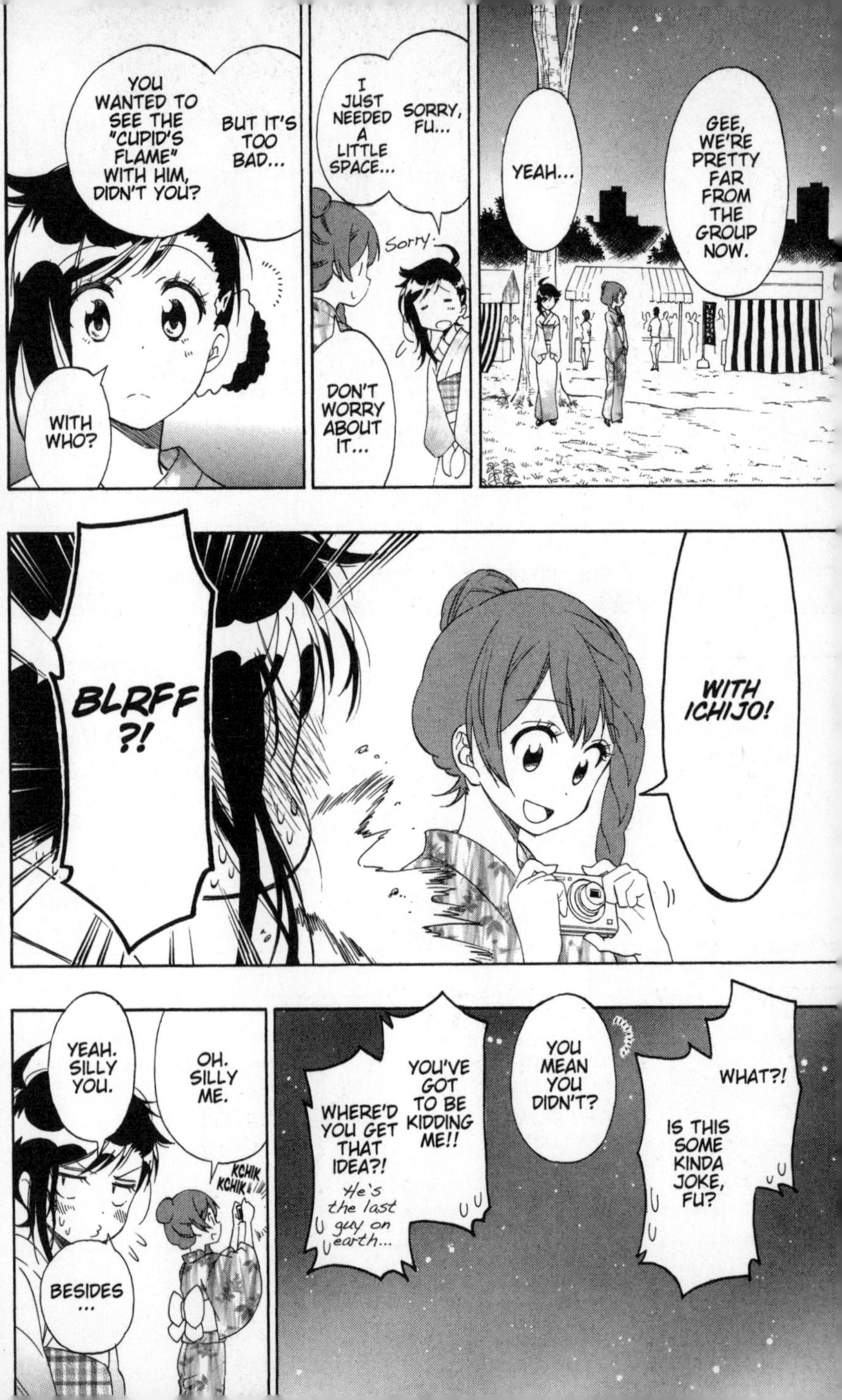
GEE, WE'RE PRETTY FAR FROM THE GROUP NOW.
YEAH...
SORRY, FU...
I JUST NEEDED A LITTLE SPACE...
Sorry
DON'T WORRY ABOUT IT...
BUT IT'S TOO BAD...
YOU WANTED TO SEE THE "CUPID'S FLAME" WITH HIM, DIDN'T YOU?
WITH WHO?
WITH ICHIJO!
BLRFF ?!
WHAT?!
IS THIS SOME KINDA JOKE, FU?
YOU MEAN YOU DIDN'T?
YOU'VE GOT TO BE KIDDING ME!!
WHERE'D YOU GET THAT IDEA?!
He's the last guy on earth...
OH. SILLY ME.
YEAH. SILLY YOU.
KCHIK KCHIK
BESIDES...

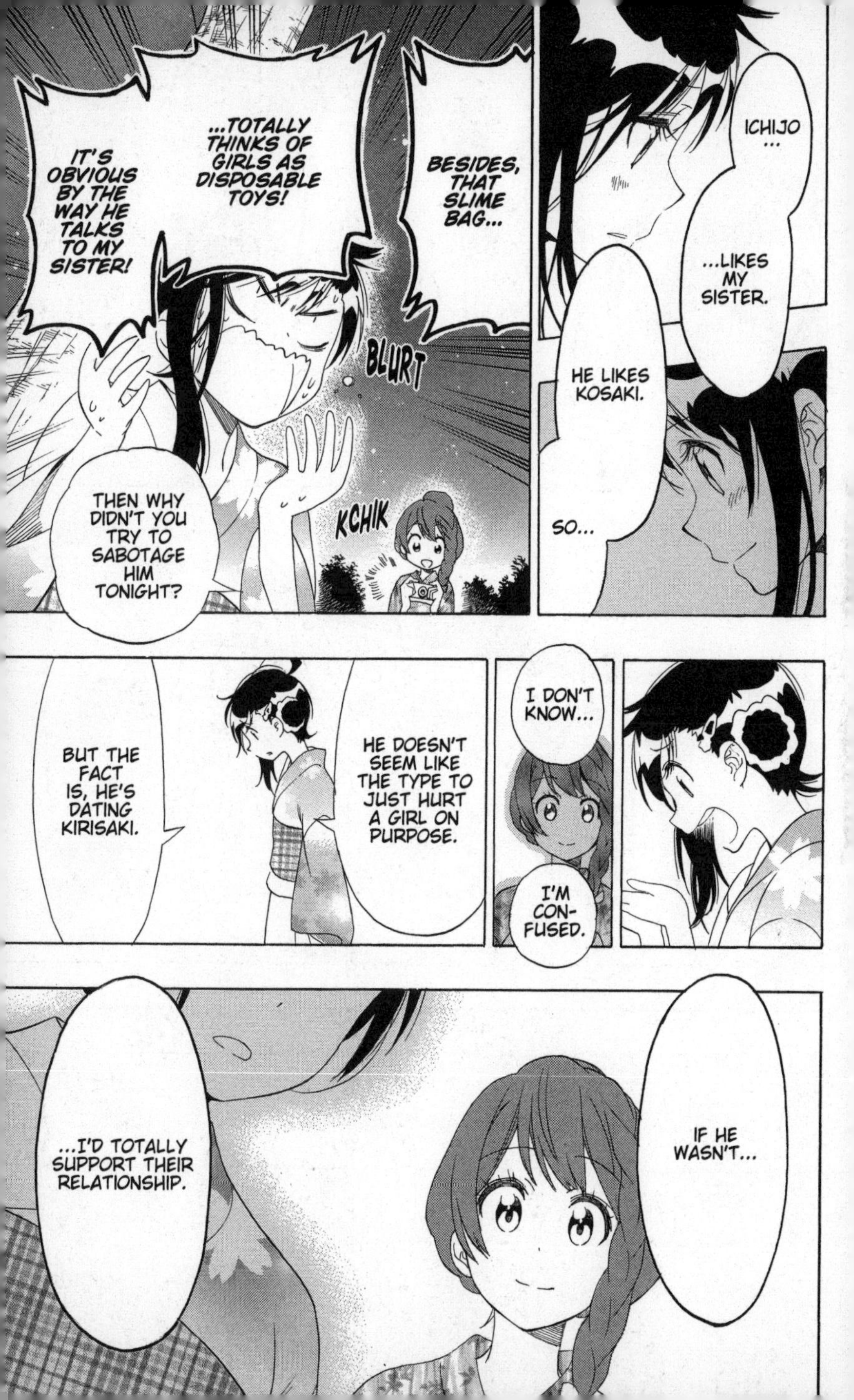
ICHIJO...
...LIKES MY SISTER.
HE LIKES KOSAKI.
SO...
BESIDES, THAT SLIME BAG...
...TOTALLY THINKS OF GIRLS AS DISPOSABLE TOYS!
IT'S OBVIOUS BY THE WAY HE TALKS TO MY SISTER!
BLURT
KCHIK
THEN WHY DIDN'T YOU TRY TO SABOTAGE HIM TONIGHT?
I DON'T KNOW...
I'M CON-FUSED.
HE DOESN'T SEEM LIKE THE TYPE TO JUST HURT A GIRL ON PURPOSE.
BUT THE FACT IS, HE'S DATING KIRISAKI.
IF HE WASN'T...
...I'D TOTALLY SUPPORT THEIR RELATIONSHIP.

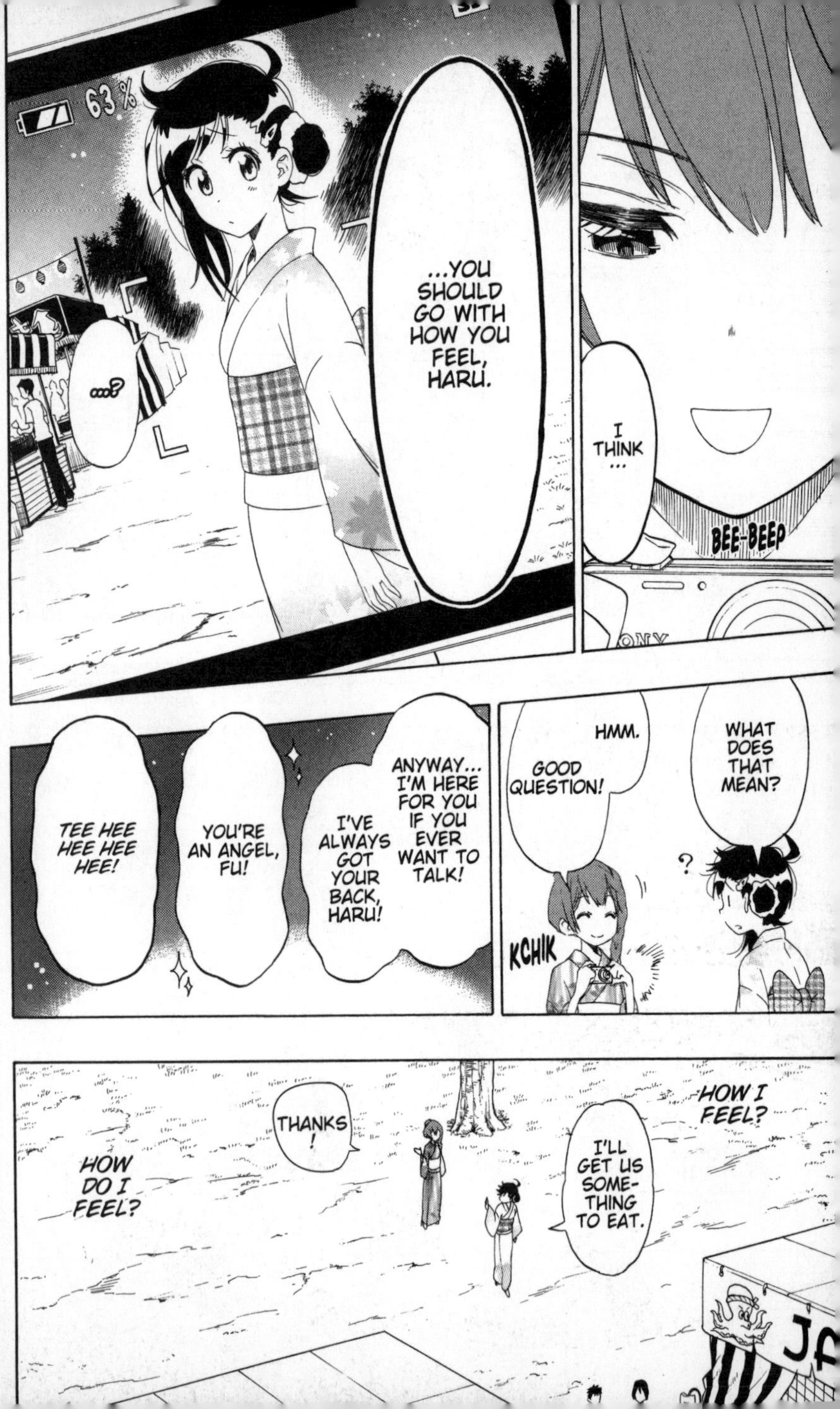
I THINK...
BEE-BEEP
...YOU SHOULD GO WITH HOW YOU FEEL, HARU.
...?
63%
WHAT DOES THAT MEAN?
HMM.
GOOD QUESTION!
KCHIK
ANYWAY... I'M HERE FOR YOU IF YOU EVER WANT TO TALK!
I'VE ALWAYS GOT YOUR BACK, HARU!
YOU'RE AN ANGEL, FU!
TEE HEE HEE HEE HEE!
HOW I FEEL?
I'LL GET US SOMETHING TO EAT.
THANKS!
HOW DO I FEEL?

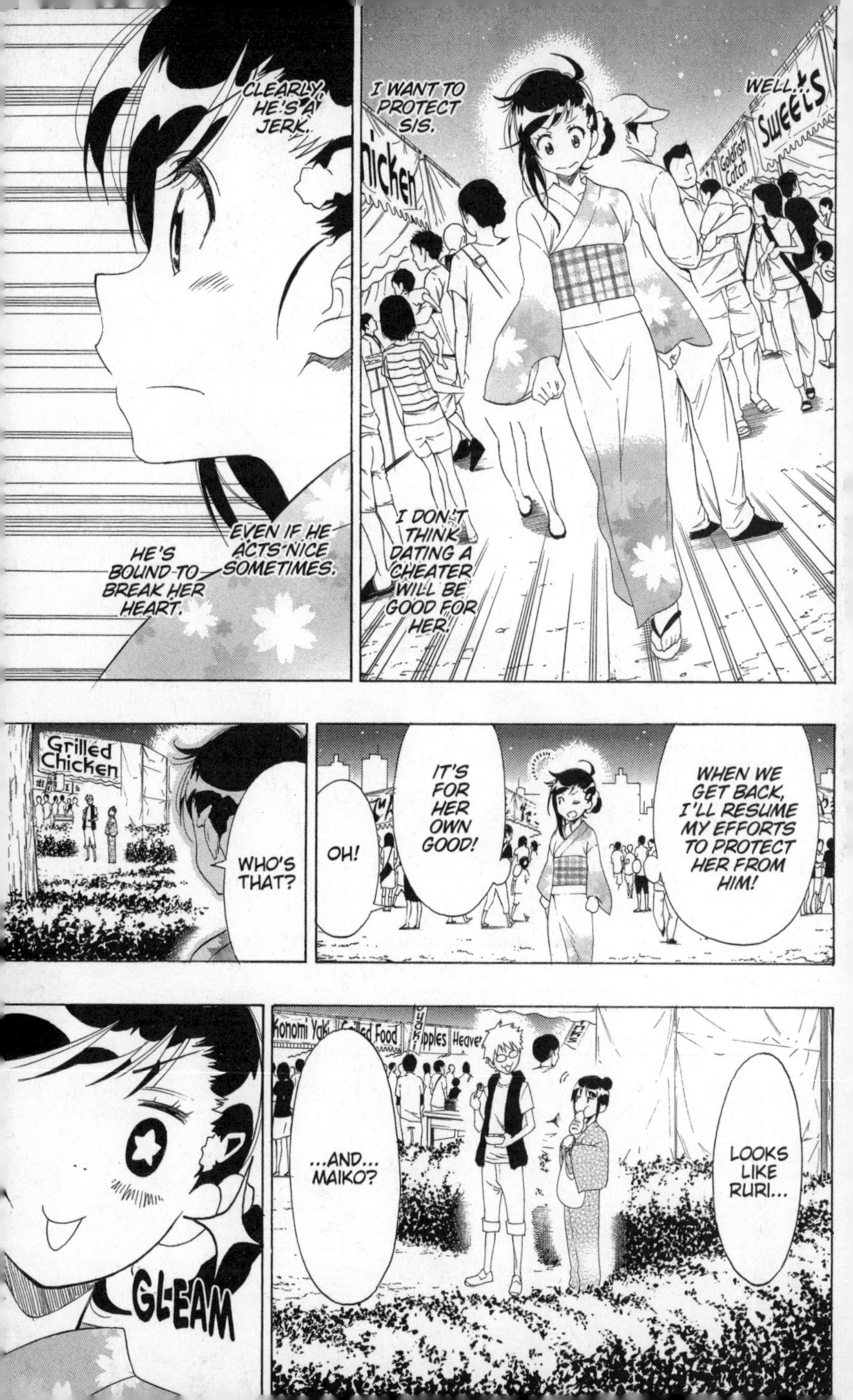

Sweets
Goldfish Catch
WELL...
I WANT TO PROTECT SIS.
I DON'T THINK DATING A CHEATER WILL BE GOOD FOR HER!
CLEARLY, HE'S A JERK.
EVEN IF HE ACTS NICE SOMETIMES.
HE'S BOUND TO BREAK HER HEART.
WHEN WE GET BACK, I'LL RESUME MY EFFORTS TO PROTECT HER FROM HIM!
IT'S FOR HER OWN GOOD!
OH!
Grilled Chicken
WHO'S THAT?
Grilled Food
LOOKS LIKE RURI...
...AND... MAIKO?
GLEAM

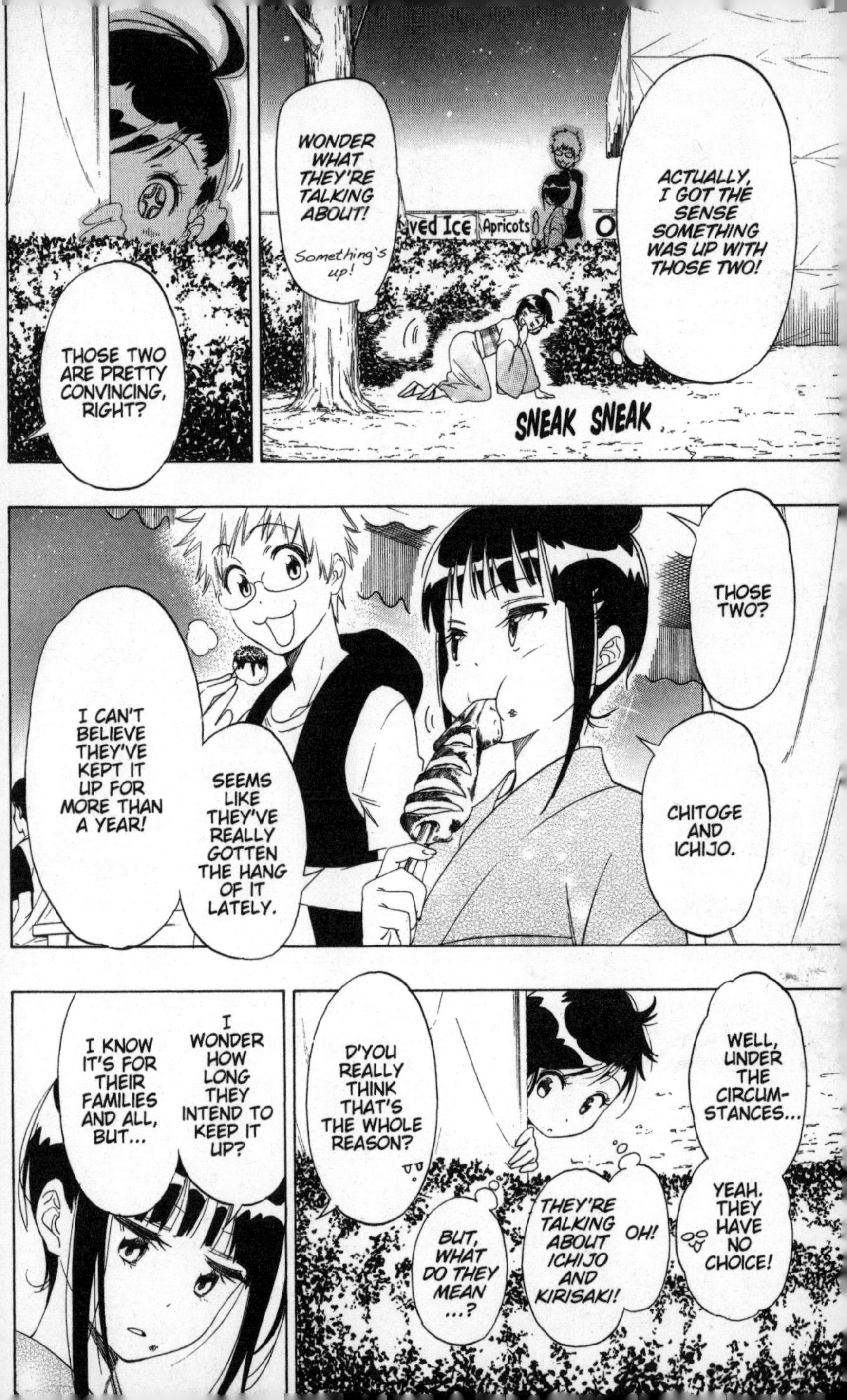
ACTUALLY, I GOT THE SENSE SOMETHING WAS UP WITH THOSE TWO!
WONDER WHAT THEY'RE TALKING ABOUT!
Something's up!
ved Ice
Apricots
SNEAK SNEAK
THOSE TWO ARE PRETTY CONVINCING, RIGHT?
THOSE TWO?
CHITOGE AND ICHIJO.
SEEMS LIKE THEY'VE REALLY GOTTEN THE HANG OF IT LATELY.
I CAN'T BELIEVE THEY'VE KEPT IT UP FOR MORE THAN A YEAR!
WELL, UNDER THE CIRCUM-STANCES...
YEAH. THEY HAVE NO CHOICE!
OH!
THEY'RE TALKING ABOUT ICHIJO AND KIRISAKI!
BUT, WHAT DO THEY MEAN ...?
D'YOU REALLY THINK THAT'S THE WHOLE REASON?
I WONDER HOW LONG THEY INTEND TO KEEP IT UP?
I KNOW IT'S FOR THEIR FAMILIES AND ALL, BUT...

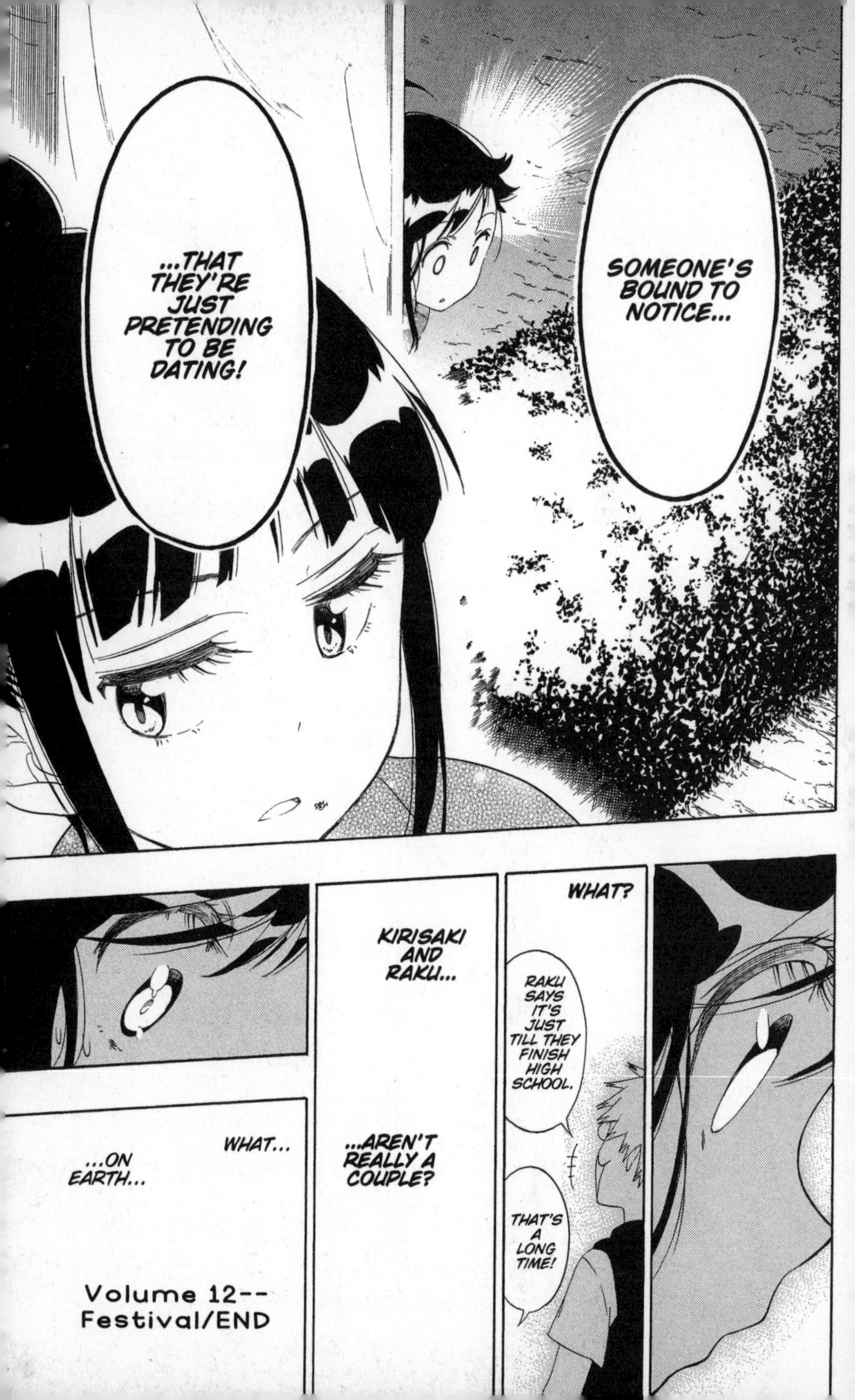
SOMEONE'S BOUND TO NOTICE...
...THAT THEY'RE JUST PRETENDING TO BE DATING!
WHAT?
RAKU SAYS IT'S JUST TILL THEY FINISH HIGH SCHOOL.
THAT'S A LONG TIME!
KIRISAKI AND RAKU...
...AREN'T REALLY A COUPLE?
WHAT...
...ON EARTH...
Volume 12--Festival/END

Bonus Comic!!

For once, all of the magical girls are in one place...
I suppose you're all wondering why I've gathered you here today.
I'd like you all to work as a team from now on.
Apples
Oranges
Magical Confectioner Kosaki!!
You'll need to collaborate to combat the forces of evil that threaten our world.
Leave it to us!
SHOOP
The more the merrier!
Wow...
Oh...
I didn't realize there were other magical girls...
Hope we can be friends...
To start with, you'll need to choose a leader.
Leader?
In that case... In terms of both skill and experience, I believe I am the obvious choice!
Hey, no fair! I want to be the leader too!

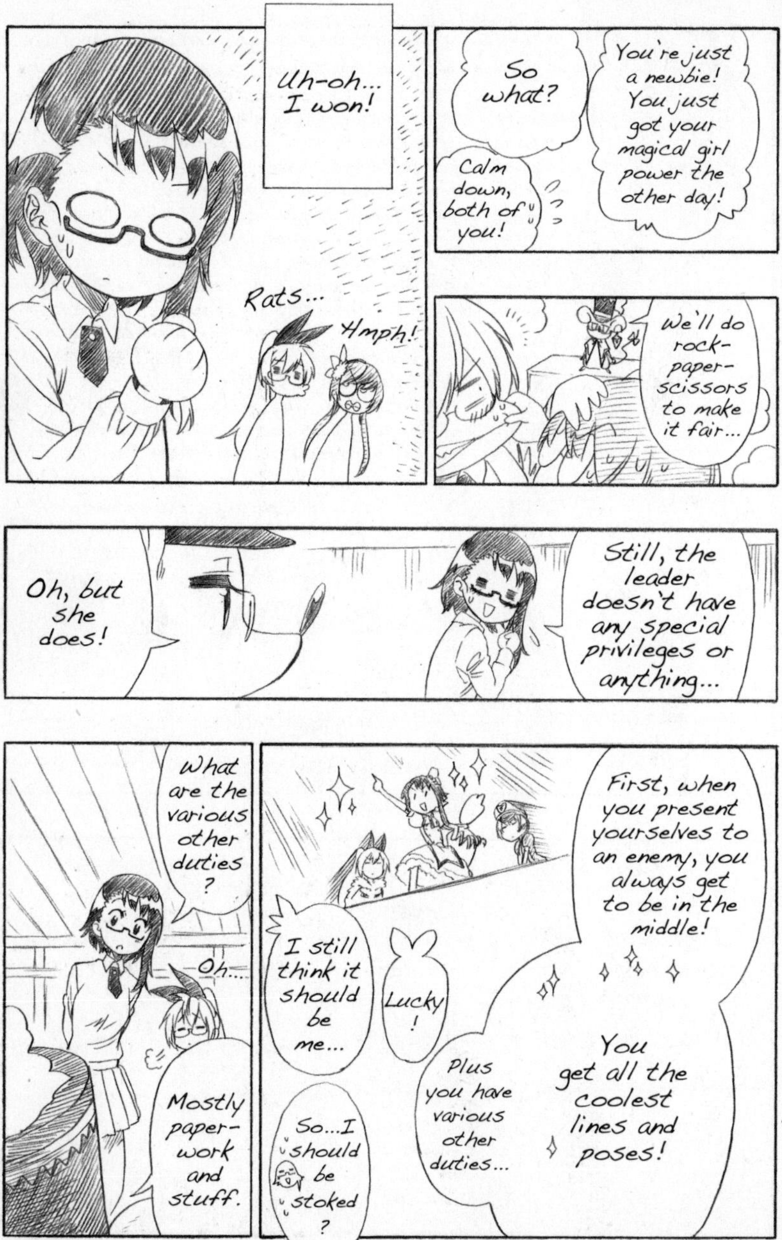

You're just a newbie! You just got your magical girl power the other day!
So what?
Calm down, both of you!
We'll do rock-paper-scissors to make it fair...
Uh-oh... I won!
Rats...
Hmph!
Still, the leader doesn't have any special privileges or anything...
Oh, but she does!
First, when you present yourselves to an enemy, you always get to be in the middle!
You get all the coolest lines and poses!
Plus you have various other duties...
Lucky!
I still think it should be me...
So...I should be stoked?
What are the various other duties?
Oh...
Mostly paper-work and stuff.

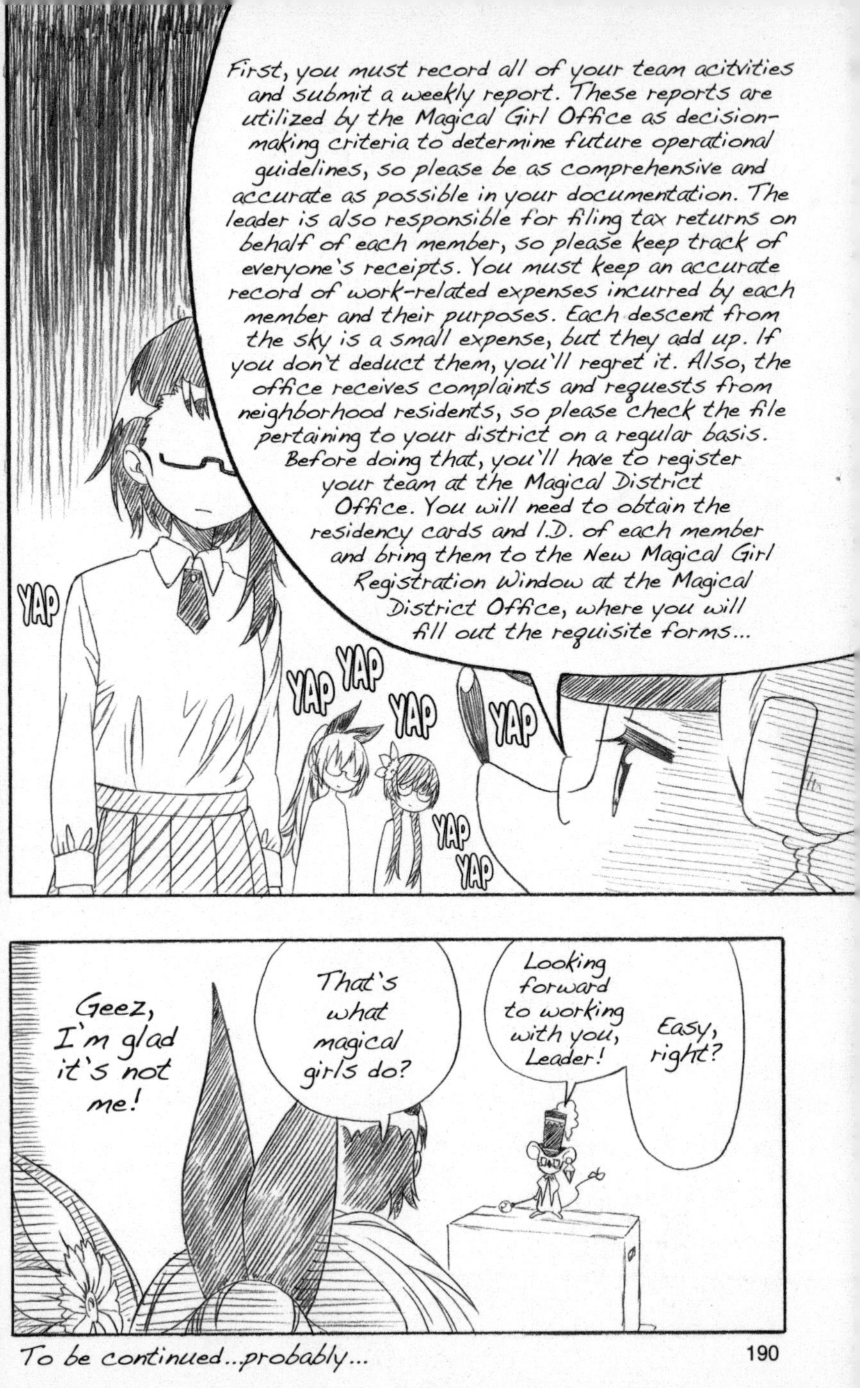
First, you must record all of your team acitvities and submit a weekly report. These reports are utilized by the Magical Girl Office as decision-making criteria to determine future operational guidelines, so please be as comprehensive and accurate as possible in your documentation. The leader is also responsible for filing tax returns on behalf of each member, so please keep track of everyone's receipts. You must keep an accurate record of work-related expenses incurred by each member and their purposes. Each descent from the sky is a small expense, but they add up. If you don't deduct them, you'll regret it. Also, the office receives complaints and requests from neighborhood residents, so please check the file pertaining to your district on a regular basis. Before doing that, you'll have to register your team at the Magical District Office. You will need to obtain the residency cards and I.D. of each member and bring them to the New Magical Girl Registration Window at the Magical District Office, where you will fill out the requisite forms...
YAP
YAP
YAP
YAP
YAP
YAP
YAP
Easy, right?
Looking forward to working with you, Leader!
That's what magical girls do?
Geez, I'm glad it's not me!

To be continued...probably...